The
Dancing Goddesses

Also by Elizabeth Wayland Barber

The Mummies of Ürümchi

Women's Work: The First 20,000 Years:
Women, Cloth, and Society in Early Times

FRONTISPIECE: See fig. 2.1.

The
Dancing
Goddesses

Folklore, Archaeology, and
the Origins of European Dance

Elizabeth Wayland Barber

W. W. Norton & Company
New York | London

For information about permission to reproduce selections from this book,
write to Permissions, W. W. Norton & Company, Inc.,
500 Fifth Avenue, New York, NY 10110

For information about special discounts for bulk purchases, please contact
W. W. Norton Special Sales at specialsales@wwnorton.com or 800-233-4830

Manufacturing by Courier Westford
Book design by Fearn Cutler de Vicq
Production manager: Julia Druskin

Library of Congress Cataloging-in-Publication Data

Barber, E. J. W., 1940–
The dancing goddesses : folklore, archaeology, and the origins of European dance /
Elizabeth Wayland Barber. — First edition.
pages cm
Includes bibliographical references and index.
ISBN 978-0-393-06536-7 (hardcover)
1. Folklore—Europe, Eastern. 2. Folklore—Balkan Peninsula. 3. Goddesses—
Folklore. 4. Agriculture—Folklore. 5. Folk dancing—Europe, Eastern—History—
To 1500. 6. Folk dancing—Balkan Peninsula—History—To 1500. 7. Europe,
Eastern—Social life and customs. 8. Balkan Peninsula—Social life and customs.
9. Ethnoarchaeology—Europe, Eastern. 10. Ethnoarchaeology—Balkan Peninsula.
I. Title.
GR139.5.B37 2013
398.209496—dc23
2012038940

W. W. Norton & Company, Inc.
500 Fifth Avenue, New York, N.Y. 10110
www.wwnorton.com

W. W. Norton & Company Ltd.
Castle House, 75/76 Wells Street, London W1T 3QT

1 2 3 4 5 6 7 8 9 0

To

Ann

beloved sister and colleague,
who taught me to read when I was five,
taught me a *czardas* when I was six,
supported my far-flung endeavors,
and watched over me
all my life

Although such enactments [of dance rituals] . . . cannot now be regarded as sacred there still clings to them a compulsion to perform them on their due date (and no other): a conviction that to omit their performance would be "unlucky", a belief that their performance will bring "luck": that is, that the "representation" of an effect will produce the effect desired.

—Margaret Dean-Smith
(quoted by Violet Alford 1978:xix)

Contents

Acknowledgments

I wish to thank Ann Wayland Peters for drawing all the things I couldn't; Paul Barber for patiently driving me to libraries, constantly egging me on with my writing skills, and putting up with my twenty-year obsession; the Summer Research Laboratory of the Russian, East European, and Eurasian Center, University of Illinois at Urbana-Champaign, for the concentrated use of their extensive Slavic library three different summers—and Mary Zirin for encouraging me to go there; David Fuller for turning my hand-drawn maps into works of art; John Younger, Clara Gresham, Gail Kligman, Ann Peters, and the British Museum for photos; Melanie Tortoroli and Edwin Barber for their help in getting a difficult manuscript into print; and Shawn Longino for helping me design the associated website (http://elizabethwaylandbarber.com) as an ongoing repository for additional information.

All translations from cited books and articles in other languages are my own (and any errors, too). I wish to thank Yuliyana Gencheva and Ivelina Georgieva for extensive help with key Bulgarian texts, Diana Stojanović for help with a Serbian text, Olga Soffer for help with a Belarusian text, and Nastya Snider for poring over Russian wedding songs with me back at the beginning when nothing seemed clear. I must also thank—though they are no longer here to know it—Boris Rybakov, Vladimir Propp, and Dimitŭr Marinov, on whose able shoulders I have so often stood, amazed at the view.

Finally, I must thank the dancers of Oxy's Folk and Historical Dance

Troupe, who enthusiastically brought to life on stage my choreographies of *The Frog Princess* (1993, 1994) and *Stoyan and the Swan Maiden* (1999), inspiring me to dig ever deeper into the history of European folkdance.

TECHNICAL NOTE

In Russian, to preserve ready pronounceability for English speakers without causing phonemic ambiguity, I have used the spelling *y* for й and adopted *ï* for ы—there is no good solution. I have generally marked the accents in transcribed Greek at first citation, in captions, and in linguistic discussions. For those who wish help with pronunciation, the Greek and Russian accents appear in the index. In discussing linguistic material, I have followed standard linguistic practice, citing the form in italics and the meaning in quotation marks (e.g., Greek *koúkla* "doll"), and indicating reconstructed forms with *.

Dancing as Life

*A*s I perused a nineteenth–century Russian folktale one day, a Dancing Goddess caught my eye. She was new to me, yet I instantly saw that I already knew her from medieval Slavic artifacts, and indeed from Classical and preclassical Greek ones, though scholars scratched their heads as to who she might be. Startled, I took up the chase, searching for her and her sisters throughout the ethnographic lore and archaeological reports from eastern and southeastern Europe. For fifteen years I knew not where the paths led; I could only collect each twig of information along the way, until eventually (as the Thracian firedancers would say) "my road was opened" to the ancient patterns. Why was I so smitten? Because as a folkdancer I had danced beside the Dancing Goddesses all my life without knowing it.

"Folkdancing" swept the United States as a cheap, popular pastime during the great Depression and World War II. Unfortunately, the war made it increasingly hard for women to find the male partners required by our Anglo-German dance tradition, so recreational folkdancers began exploring the vast pool of partnerless line dances of the immigrants from eastern and central Europe. Now one could go alone to a dance and not be a wallflower.

I grew up in those "international" folkdance groups (and in ethnically specific ones, too); the mysteriously addicting dances have colored my entire life. Training as an archaeologist and linguist, I centered my career at first on Greece, which at that time meant studying only Mediterranean

1

cultures and languages. But my folkdancing drew me always northward, where I stumbled over many ancient archaeological connections to Greece and to the long development of the folk costumes that we lovingly collected and wore as dancers. Fascinated by the time depth, I began to enlist every science and language at my disposal to illuminate their collective history. Gradually I sensed that the dances, too—though sheared from their cultural moorings and even more evanescent than the textiles and costumes—could perhaps be traced. Then I encountered the Dancing Goddesses.

This, then, is a book about dancing, and about an ancient European tradition of beliefs that *sought to influence the flow of life by means of dance.* Human dance paid honor to, entreated, and even "channeled for" the female spirits thought somehow to dance life into existence. Many relics of this tradition have come down to us—not just as dance but also as symbols, words, superstitions, and calendar customs from New Year through Easter, Midsummer, and Christmas. Unable quite to part with them, we continue to share them with our children.

The tradition seems to have begun with the first farmers of Europe, nestled in the heart of the Balkans and the arms of the Danube, long before writing was invented; and it continued for millennia among people who knew little or nothing of literacy. What knowledge they thought important they passed down through visual apprenticeship and oral tradition. Among the visual were crafts, dances, and rituals; among the oral: myths, songs, stories, and language itself. Some of this worldview spread across Europe with agriculture, six or eight millennia ago. Two millennia ago, Christianity began, soon challenging the old beliefs. Four hundred years later, as we shall see, Catholic versus Orthodox Christianity began to split the tradition in two, with far more surviving in the East than in the West; but the original unity can still be glimpsed in remote rural pockets.

In that conservative, nonurban, and often precarious way of life, dance formed and still forms a sort of glue holding people and life together, bonding communities. It mediated life's joy, pain, hopes and fears, love, hate, tedium, and tingling expectation. Dance also marked off ritual time and space, served to anesthetize fatigue and heal sickness, and even sought to produce life. Dance was not an "art form" but the essence of life itself.

Among rural farmers, struggling to lay in enough plant and animal food to make it through another year, the encouragement of life—the process of germinating or hatching, then growing and bearing issue—was essential to survival. The reasoning, as we shall see, is roughly as follows.

Life causes motion, and motion can give evidence of life. This becomes: "Life causes motion, *hence* motion is evidence of life."* Humans can see that the motions of work have a direct purpose, but *motion for motion's sake* is something else—"dance" broadly taken. (In the languages of eastern Europe, the same word often means both "dance" and "play," and other nondirected motions like swinging, tickling, and laughing may fall in this basket. Medieval western Europeans, too, called the nocturnal dancing and feasting of the spirits *the game*, its goal being an abundance of crops called *luck*.) Supernatural powers, of course, need not work to survive; hence divine life simply "dances" and in this very act of dancing is thought to create life.

Enter the Dancing Goddesses, the repositories and creators of the fertility and healing powers so desperately needed for families, fields, and flocks to prosper. Their dancing created life, their wrath could destroy it.

The spirits that villagers sought to influence were the spirits of the dead. But different categories of dead existed, with different powers and different connections to the living.

First, one's dead ancestors. Since they had begotten the living, one could reasonably appeal to them to help their offspring survive. And because these ancestors had been buried in the ground (where their spirits were assumed to pass much of their time), presumably they could help the seeds down there—the newly sown crops—to germinate and grow. Basic to this belief is the notion of resurrection: the seed seems dead, it is buried, it rises to produce new seed. The eternal cycle of life.

Second were the spirits of the dead of other villages. These were particularly dangerous because they would be busy sequestering all the existing abundance for *their* offspring. So ritual dancers, from the Balkans to Britain, marked out territories and fought intruding bands, to the death if necessary.

---

*This restatement, however, involves a common mistake in reasoning, the Fallacy of Affirming the Consequent: see chapter 3.

Finally, there existed a very special group: young women born into the clan who had died before having any children—hence not ancestors of the living but still belonging to the community. Most important, they *had not used their natural store of fertility.* So, people reasoned, if we're especially nice to them, they might bestow that unused fertility on us. Because unmarried girls in the living community spent much of their time singing and dancing together, people inferred by analogy that the spirits of dead girls would likewise band together and spend their time singing, dancing, swimming, laughing, and so on. These Dancing Goddesses inhabited the wilds, controlling the rain and other waters, creating the fertility and healing powers people needed. The challenge was to lead, cajole, trap, or entice them into the cultivated areas to shed their fertility *here*, and one way to do this was to do what *they* did: dance.

Gradually we shall get to know the spirit maidens, starting with evidence from relatively recent stories about them, for deep into the twentieth century they were still thought to inhabit remote parts of southern and eastern Europe. Following them through the agricultural year, we will come to understand people's terror of them, as season by season the farmers attempted, through both bribery and dance, to influence them to be kind and helpful (Part I). But another sort of Dancing Goddess also was felt to exist right in the village. A fertile bride could potentially become a magical spirit as she danced, channeling coveted strength, beauty, and fertility not just onto herself but onto those around her as well (Part II).

Where and how did this set of beliefs about Dancing Goddesses arise? To find out, we can assemble our "modern" data and begin to puzzle our way back through increasingly ancient evidence, some of which is remarkably beautiful, until we find our answers or lose the trail (Part III). For this is also, along the way, a book about new approaches to understanding the lifeless stuff that archaeologists dig up.

And why should this long agrarian tradition center precisely on *dance*? Why do humans dance anyway? It's a question I've asked myself my whole life, even as I danced. Why can't we stop tapping our feet? And didn't early people, struggling at the subsistence level just to stay alive, have enough to do without spending their time and energy *dancing*? With new tools at hand, we'll ask this question once more at the end of our journey (Part IV). But let us begin meeting the Dancing Goddesses themselves, through the depictions and words of those who knew them best.

Geographical Maps

MAP A: **Eurasia**

MAP B: Eastern Europe—East Slavs (See Map 13 for dialects, medieval sites, and Mongol invasion.)

MAP C: South-Central Europe and Balkan Peninsula, with part of Greece (See Map 19 for southern Greece and Crete.)

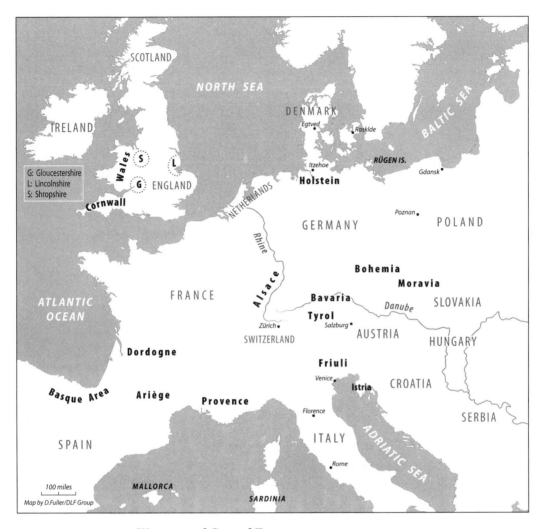

MAP D: Western and Central Europe

Part One

Dancing the Year: The Ritual Cycle of Fertility

CHAPTER 1

Swan Maidens, Mermaids, and Tree Spirits

The *rusalki* live in the depths of the rivers,
but in the month of May, in the morning at sunrise,
they come out from there, naked,
and dance in the rye-fields with their pestles, and sing.
—Pinsk area, 1887[1]

Throughout much of central and eastern Europe, including the Balkan Peninsula, there has long existed a belief in female spirits, bringers of fertility, who spend their nights and days dancing in the forests and fields. A century ago, inhabitants of the province of Smolensk, southwest of Moscow (see map B), described their dancing spirit maidens thus:

The *rusalki* are young, beautiful women, with long braids down to their heels; they live in the woods and marshes, but primarily in the river, in some deep eddy. They seldom walk about on the banks, but if they do climb out, they do not go far from the water; they lure to themselves the men passing by, whom above all they attract with their beauty, and they try to tickle them. Out of having nothing to do, the rusalki play tricks on the fishermen, twist their nets, drag the floats out onto the shore, and wrench the meshes of the sweep-nets. Up until Dukhov Day [Whit Monday, several weeks after Easter] they live in the water; but on Dukhov Day the rusalki leave their homes and splash around on top of the water. After that the rusalki may wander far from their dwelling places, into the groves and forests.[2]

From then until harvest time (according to yet others),

in the fields, glades and copses, the rusalki pull together the leafy willows that hang over the water and the weeping birches, and there they live. At night, under the moon, which shines brighter than usual for them, they swing in the branches, call to each other, and lead line-dances [*khorovodï*], with singing, games, and other dances [*plyaski*]. Where they have run and romped, there the grass grows thicker and greener, there the grain grows more abundantly.[3]

Their presence, their movement, promotes fertility.

The woods and waters in Bulgaria and Macedonia, nearly a thousand miles south, are fraught with similar magical dancing spirits, as we see from the following Bulgarian folktale:

Many years ago, Stoyan the Shepherd was walking through the forest near a remote mountain lake when his ears caught the faint sounds of girls' laughter and of dancing feet, then suddenly—splash!

He froze in fear. He had been told since he was a child that the wild woods, lakes, and streams were the haunts of the beautiful but often malicious willies. He knew, on peril of his life, that he should quietly sneak away, for if they caught him spying on their games they would likely entice him to his death. But he had always wanted to see these lovely spirit maidens and their magical dances, and he was young and daring. So after a few moments, hearing nothing more, Stoyan moved slowly and silently forward till he could see the edge of the lake.

There he saw no one; nothing moved. But to his surprise, along the grassy bank lay three shimmering heaps of clothing. He crept up to them. Each little pile consisted of a soft feather-white chemise, a leafy green sash, and a pair of wings.

"These can only belong to willies!" he thought. "Even the finest cloth in my village is no match for this." Just then, as he fingered the garments in amazement, he heard laughter and splashing once again. The willies were returning and he knew he must hide before they saw him. On a sudden inspiration he snatched up all three heaps and darted with them behind the nearest tree.

No sooner had he hidden himself than three willies swam up and jumped out of the water onto the shore. Seeing their clothes were gone, they wailed in distress, for they feared that without their magic garments they would turn into ordinary maidens and lose their freedom to dance through the woods, swing in the trees, and dive in the lakes and waterfalls.

Up and down they ran, looking for their clothes and crying piteously. Overcome by curiosity, Stoyan peered cautiously around the great oak that sheltered him, and there he saw the three most beautiful maidens he had ever encountered, their long pale hair swirling in eddies around their slim bodies. One, he thought, was even more beautiful than the other two. As he stared, this splendid creature turned and saw him, her flashing green eyes piercing him and capturing him with desire.

Radka let out a shrill cry (for Radka—"Joy"—was her name), and all three maidens ran toward him, beseeching him for their belongings. To the other two willies Stoyan tossed their glistening green and white bundles, and in moments they dressed and flew away. But the chemise, sash, and wings of Radka, the most beautiful, he quickly stuffed into his shepherd's bag and he would not return them to her, for all her pleading. Without them Radka was powerless. And so Stoyan led her back through the forest to his village, where he made her his wife.

Summer became fall, and fall became winter. Another season passed, and in the bright spring, Radka gave birth to a son—a baby as beautiful as herself, with pale skin and green eyes, and Stoyan's dark hair. When the prescribed days had passed, Stoyan joyfully chose a godfather for the baby and invited many guests to the baptism. After the baptism came the traditional feast and merry-making. Stoyan and his guests drank much wine, and the energetic line dances became ever louder and faster.

"Stoyan!" cried the shepherd's friends merrily. "We too have always wanted to see the famous dance of the willies! Make your wife dance it for us!" But when Stoyan ordered her to dance, Radka refused.

"I cannot dance that way," she said, "without my white chemise, leafy green sash, and wings. If you will give them to me, *then* will I dance!"

Now, Stoyan did not dare give her these things, for he feared that if she had them she would fly away and leave him.

"Come now," said his friends, "not only is she wedded to you, but she is now a mother! No mother can bear to leave her child! It's safe enough—make her dance!" Radka agreed this was so.

Thus they persuaded Stoyan, and he went to fetch her belongings, which he had kept carefully hidden all this time. He handed them to her and she went into the side room to change. When she returned, she no longer looked like Radka the bride but like a willy of the lakes and forests. In sudden doubt, Stoyan hastily closed the door to the house and stood guarding it.

Radka began to dance. She whirled once, she whirled twice around the room, and all were enchanted. Never had they seen a girl or a dance so lovely. It was as if a white cloud of butterflies fluttered and swirled in the breeze. A third time she whirled around the room, then she flew up and out through the chimney.

Aghast, Stoyan rushed outside, calling to her and beseeching her not to leave their child. And thus she answered him:

> *Surely you know, Stoyan,*
> *that a willy cannot keep house,*
> *a willy cannot nurture children.*
> *Seek me, Stoyan, there in the forest,*
> *On the peaks of the Rila Mountains,*
> *On the willies' playground,*
> *Beside the willies' lake.*

Then she flew away.[4]

The beautiful and desirable spirit maiden is fertile indeed, but unretainable. To be herself and foster abundant life, she must revert to dancing and romping with her sister spirits in the wild.

The dancing spirit maidens have several names. In English one might call such a creature *fairy* or *nixie* or sometimes *mermaid*. *Willy*, an archaic word lurking in expressions such as "Dark corners give me the willies!" and possibly in *will-o'-the-wisp*, is probably originally the same as the widely used Slavic *vila*. The various Slavic groups call her *vila, wiła, samovila, samodiva, rusalka, rusavka, mavka*, and other names besides. Among the Greeks of today, she is a *neráïda*.

This last term comes directly from the ancient Greek *Nērēíd-*, which meant specifically a sea nymph or mermaid. *Nýmphē*, borrowed into English as *nymph* (where it has accrued its own connotations), was the general ancient Greek term for a spirit maiden. But it was also the word for "bride"— a usage that underscores the ancient view of the "divine nymphs" (Homer's *theaì nýmphai*) as females on the verge of producing new life, just like human brides. For these creatures epitomize female fertility. Other types of ancient Greek nymphs included those inhabiting mountains (oreads), trees (dryads), springs (naiads), and meadows (leimoniads), as well as nymphs in charge of rain (hyades) and the nine art-loving Muses that served Apollo. Most of these terms have been lost in Modern Greek, nymphs of all sorts being called *neráïdes* or euphemistically *Kyrádes* "Ladies," while the word *nýmphē* or *nýphē* now means simply "bride."[5]

Of the Slavic words, *vila* (plural *vily*) and its variants find wide use in southern and central Europe, including western Ukraine, whereas in central Russia and farther north, people prefer *rusalka* (plural *rusalki*), though the areas overlap. *Vila* is already attested a millennium ago in Old Bulgarian, the oldest written form of Slavic.[6] The vindictive white *wilis* in the ballet *Giselle*, who attempt to dance Giselle's beloved to death in the woods, have borrowed their name and their habits from Slavic tales (recounted by the German poet Heinrich Heine), as has the hauntingly lovely nymph Vilia in a ballad in the popular operetta *The Merry Widow*. German itself has a version of the bewitching but deadly water maiden in its *Lorelei*, made famous by Heine's ballad of that name based on a local Rhineland legend, while Dvořák wrote an entire Czech opera named *Rusalka*.

Since all these names carry much cultural baggage in each little region of Europe, however, I will use the relatively uncluttered (because forgotten) word *willy* as a general designation, although in translating local descriptions I will sometimes use the local term. Radka, to be precise, was a *samovila*.

Willies, in Slavic lore especially, are the spirits of girls who died "before their time" and returned to live as spirit beings in our world, near where they had once lived and died.[7]

Dying "before their time" meant specifically that, although these girls were daughters of the ancestral line, they had not yet become mothers. Hence they had no descendants, had not become ancestors *of* anyone, and thus had no stake in the problems of those who still lived. So people could not count on these spirits, unlike those of dead mothers, fathers, and grand-parents, to help their living offspring in a crisis. They represented loose ends on the family tree, and—worse yet—if they had died disappointed or abused, they surely carried a grudge and might behave spitefully.

But the farm folk also saw these dead maidens as possessing a precious commodity that was very much needed and (in this worldview) thought to be transferable: the ability to reproduce that all females have by nature but that these particular girls had not "used up" yet. Perhaps, by understanding their ways, one could persuade them to bestow that unused fertility on one's family, flocks, and fields?

Our Bulgarian folktale contains many traits typical of eastern European willies. Like Radka and her friends, willies generally live in little groups in the wild, particularly around water, where they love to swim, dive, splash, and play together in lakes, pools, rivers, and millraces. Unmarried girls from a particular neighborhood, while alive, went around in little bands, socializing together at working bees and singing and dancing together at important festivals. The willies, also mostly young girls, were assumed to do likewise. And just as Russian girls often swore eternal friendship with each other at the spring festival called Semik, calling each other *kum* after that (see chapter 3), similarly the willies could be heard calling, "*Kum! Kum!*" to each other as they swung in the trees.[8]

According to numerous stories recounted by the East Slavs, the willies live in the water until sometime in the spring (earlier in the South, later in the North), when they move into the wild woods and cultivated fields. In the provinces of Voronezh and Khar'kov, south of Moscow, people said the willies (a.k.a. rusalki) left the water and invaded the fields and forests on the Thursday before Trinity Sunday (the seventh Sunday after Easter in the

Orthodox Church*), where they then stayed, dancing in the grain fields and swinging in the trees, until the summer festival of St. Peter or even into the fall.[9] The populace viewed that particular Thursday or even the whole week as sacred to the willies and knew it variously as Green Holy-Days or Rusalia Week. Farther south, among the Bulgarians, the willies were also most active in spring and summer, ruling over and playing in the lakes and springs, although more inclined actually to dwell in the woods and mountain glens.[10]

To the west, in Croatia, Dalmatia, and Slovenia, the willies have taken to living in trees as tree spirits, although many taboos still relate them to water; there they appear in the folk literature chiefly as supernatural protectors of heroes rather than as bringers of fertility.[11] These are all regions where the rainwater disappears mysteriously into karst limestone without having a chance to form the lakes and rivers associated with willies elsewhere. Apparently this rather different relationship of the local people to water has caused a reinterpretation of the willies' role, but not their complete disappearance.

Around 1900 in Greece, yet farther south, an observer stated that "water is throughout Greece dreaded as the most dangerous haunt of the Nereids," but "their presence is suspected everywhere." People in the south, at least, considered them "half-divine yet not immortal"—young, beautiful, capricious, vindictive, and addicted to dancing, singing, and reveling.[12] The Romanians and Moldavians thought them so dangerous that they usually referred to them obliquely as *Iele* or *Dînsele*, "They" in the polite feminine plural.[13]

Willies also can change shape. Sometimes they look like human girls, sometimes more like large silvery fish, green frogs, or birds—especially white birds of passage such as swans and geese.[14] The windows and eaves of many eastern European farmhouses still bear images of creatures that are half girl and half bird or fish, their smiling faces and ample breasts those of women, while the torso ends in an appropriate tail and the arms may appear as wings or fins (fig. 1.1). When in human shape, the willies (if not naked) usually wear green leaves and/or the basic garment of women's traditional rural dress across most of eastern Europe, a white chemise.[15] But these white

---

*Trinity Sunday is the *eighth* Sunday after Easter in Western Christianity, but in Eastern Orthodoxy it falls on the *seventh* Sunday, hence coinciding with Pentecost (literally "fiftieth day" in Greek: 7×7=49). It is also called *Whitsunday* in English.

FIG. 1.1. 19th-century wood carvings of willies, from faceboards and casements of Russian houses, Upper Volga and Nizhniy Novgorod (Gor'kiy) areas. Mermaid whose hair becomes foliage; mermaid; bird girl; bird girl with both arms and wings.

dresses are special. Often, as with Radka, the garment acts as a second skin that transforms the girl into a bird or other creature when she dons it. In other cases, the pale little rusalka wears at most a rag and begs for a chemise,[16] as in the following song from Smolensk:

> *By the curling birch tree*
> *A rusalka sat,*
> *Begging for a little tunic:*
> *"Dear young maiden,*
> *Stop and give me a shirt,*
> *Even if it's a thin one,*
> *A little white one."*[17]

In fact, in this same province people advised that if you met a rusalka, "it was necessary without fail to toss her a kerchief or at least some sort of rag. And if one had nothing at all of this sort, one must rip a sleeve off one's dress and throw it to the rusalka—otherwise unavoidable death threatened."[18] In some areas, rusalki reportedly sneaked into the bathhouses where women often worked their flax fibers into linen in the helpfully damp air. There the waifs would clumsily try to spin thread and make clothes for themselves but in fact would only tangle everything hopelessly and leave a terrible mess for the poor villager—who left herself vulnerable to such marauding if she went to bed without saying her prayers![19] Greek *neráïdes*, however, dressed nicely in white and had reputations as excellent spinners and weavers.[20]

In addition to appeasing the northern willies with clothing, one could ward them off by carrying certain herbs or wielding a (Christian) cross. Thus we are told by many Russian sources that if you venture into the woods around Trinity Sunday, you must be sure to carry sprigs of curly-leaved wormwood with you (fig. 6.1). For "a rusalka will without fail run up and demand: 'What have you in your hand: wormwood or parsley?'" If you say, "wormwood," she will scream in anger and run on past. "At this moment you must try to throw the herb directly into the rusalka's eyes." But if you say, "parsley," she will say, "Oh, my darling!"—then tickle you till you collapse.[21]* Additionally, objects of iron served throughout much of Europe

---

*"Parsley" in Russian is *petrushka*, while "darling" is *dushka*. Ralston, in 1872 (146), commented that the willies seem partial to rhymes!

to turn away all manner of evil spirits, willies included,[22] and Greek peasants would bribe the willies in advance to refrain from mischief by setting out offerings of honey.[23]

The willies are famous for their singing and dancing.[24] In some regions one can tell where they have danced because the grass grows thick and green there—much as in Britain one can tell where the fairies have danced by a sprouting circle of toadstools. On the other hand, in Belarus they trod the ground quite bare as they danced around their favorite pine trees,[25] and Bulgarian peasants would point out little unexpected clearings in the forest as the sites where willies danced,[26] scorching the grass with their feet.

So much do willies love dancing that one band of Greek *neráïdes* started carrying off a young shepherd who played his pipes especially beautifully. Night after night they made him play nonstop at the threshing floor where they danced, until they disappeared at dawn. But the young man, falling in love with the most beautiful of them, asked a wise old woman how to catch this apparition. Following her advice, just before dawn he jumped up and grabbed the handkerchief that—like all women—his beloved used in the dance. Then he hung on for dear life. "And straightway the cock crew, and the other Nereids fled; but she whose kerchief he had seized could not go, but at once began to transform herself into horrible shapes in hope to frighten the shepherd and make him loose his hold." First she became a lion, then a snake, then fire, but he held on bravely. "Then at last she returned to her proper form and went home with him and was his wife and bore him a son; but the kerchief he kept hidden from her, lest she should become a Nereid again."[27] (Three thousand years earlier, Homer told how the divine Nereid Thetis, who became the mother of Achilles, changed into these same shapes while the Greek hero Peleus clung tightly to her till he won her. Some of these stories began millennia ago.)

But woe to him whom the willies catch spying on them uninvited during their revels. For they normally either drown their captive, as the ancient Greek water nymphs did to Narcissus, or they tickle or dance him to death. Willies love young men and detest girls, both of whom they do in (but from elderly people they simply hide).[28] They entice their victims chiefly through their marvelous beauty, but also by calling out the person's name. Belarusian peasants, in the 1860s, even accused the rusalki of calling out common men's names at random in hopes of hitting upon the name of whatever man happened to be passing nearby.[29]

So widespread was the belief in these picturesque spirit maidens that Romantic poets and writers of the nineteenth century became quite enamored of them. Nikolay Gogol summarizes common notions of his time in the following dramatic passage from *May Night*:

> At the hour when dark fades, . . . from the waves of the Dnepr the maidens who destroyed their own lives [i.e., committed suicide] come forth in flocks; hair cascades from their green heads onto their shoulders, and water, plashing noisily, runs from their long hair to the ground, while the girls shine through the water as though a glass shirt; their mouths smile wonderfully, their cheeks blaze, their eyes bewitch the soul. . . . *She* would burn with love, *she* would kiss passionately. . . . Flee, Christian man! Her lips are poison, her couch cold water; she will tickle you mercilessly and drag you off into the river.[30]

But the willies were not always described as beautiful. The farther north one goes, the more horrid they become—ugly, mean, large and stout, often shaggy, with pendulous breasts so long they could toss the ends over their shoulders.[31] These monsters were quite unlike their southern sisters, who were slim, young, pale, and ravishingly beautiful. Both have large breasts, but in the south these are voluptuous and seductive. They resemble each other, however, in both having tremendously long hair that they often wore loose—unlike proper village girls and women, who carefully braided their hair. This difference between the normal and the spirit world even gave rise to widespread sayings: in Russian, "She let her hair down like a rusalka"; in Serbo-Croatian, "She's as tousled as a witch!"[32] So strong were the taboos on women's hair, in fact, that a female with loose hair was no better than—or might even *be*—a willy or a witch. Or possibly a sickness demon, generally viewed as female.[33] The taboos remain to this day in the traditions of married peasant women of eastern Europe keeping their hair covered with a scarf, and of the Amish of Pennsylvania insisting that *every* proper human female, from birth onward, keep her hair covered.

The willies differed in other interesting ways between North and South. In frigid northern Russia, the female spirits were considered loners, and not only ugly but also downright cruel and malicious—if people knew of spirit women at all[34]—whereas in the more temperate zones (from which came most of our stories so far), the willies merely made mischief and wanted the company of a man, even if their attentions led ultimately to his death. In the South, the willies might even let their captive go, though he would stagger home deathly ill.[35] Furthermore, if you set out the right gifts and did not break their taboos (such as working on their special holidays), the willies might even shed some of their fertility on you and yours or help you in some task. Thus, if your cow wandered off and could not be found, you could leave gifts for the willy at the forest's edge and ask her to take those in exchange for returning your cow.[36] And if you did something nice for them, they would often show their gratefulness, as in the following Belarusian story:

> While gathering mushrooms in the forest, a woman saw hanging from a tree a huge piece of birch bark and on it a little boy sleeping. Pitying the child, she took off her apron, covered the sleeper with it, and moved on. Soon a rusalka—a naked woman with tousled hair— overtook her and touched her on her hand with these words: "Fight in your hands, for you!" From that time on, the woman began to work so strongly that everyone wondered where her strength came from.[37]*

Strength seems indeed to be their typical gift, as we see also in this story from farther south, in Slovenia:

> A small, half-blind shepherd found a vila in a hazel-thicket who was stuck there hanging helplessly by her hair. He pitied her, helped her out, so that she lost not so much as a single hair, and received from the vila as recompense for this service handsomeness and prodigious strength, so that from then on he was superior to all his comrades and could beat them up to his heart's content.[38]

---

*The grateful rusalka's incantation, "*Spor tabe u ruki!*" (literally, "Dispute to you in the hands"), puzzled me and others I asked until I found a statement by a nonliterate Bulgarian storyteller criticizing (to her educated daughter) a modern author's attempt at writing a "folktale." In this tale, a boy hiding from his master the tailor because he had broken the sewing-machine needle, helps a fox's cubs; as a magical reward, the vixen gives him her claw. Said the traditional storyteller: "It is a lie! Tales are ancient; they date from the time men talked with animals, a time when there were no houses, only dugouts. Who ever heard of a sewing machine in a dugout? And that bit about the vixen giving away one of her claws. . . . Do you realize what would happen to a vixen without her claws? Claws are *her hands and her strength*!" (Nicoloff 1983, 224; emphasis mine)

Every wimp should be so lucky.

Surely it is no accident that this geographical gradient of "mean and ugly" in the far North and "beautiful and sometimes kindly" in the South corresponds to how hard or easy it is to grow crops and keep livestock healthy in a given region, for fertility is what the willies purveyed.

✦

Although the spirit maidens form a general class of young women who died before their time—whether by accident, disease, murder, or suicide—the rusalki of Russia, Belarus, and Ukraine often have very particular personal histories, as we see in the following tale from an area east of Moscow:

> In the city of Simbirsk, a young and beautiful widow named Marina fell desperately in love with the handsome Ivan Kurchavïy, and, on the day of his wedding with another bride, she threw herself into the Volga. They searched for her with dragnets and tackle, but could not find her. Later, rumors were heard that Marina had turned into a rusalka and walked in the evenings along the bank. She would sit down on a heap of stones or on the end of a raft and keep washing her head and combing out her long tresses, and she would look at the hut where Ivan Kurchavïy lived with his young wife; then suddenly she would groan and sigh plaintively, piteously, and hurl herself into the water with all her might. Many saw her and also heard her as she wept bitterly and sang mournfully, quietly—so that it grabbed one's heart: "Ah Vanya, my darling! You stopped loving me, you destroyed me! My gorgeous one! You are my beloved!"
>
> And Ivan Kurchavïy heard that out of love for him Marina had drowned herself in the Volga, had become a rusalka, and was living in the terrible great pool where, in both storm and calm weather, the water boils up as if in a cauldron and a white wave billows. Now, it seemed as if Marina-Rusalka along with a grey-haired old man even appeared on this wave and capsized boats. The fishermen said they sometimes saw Marina-Rusalka on the sands opposite Simbirsk: it seems as if a swan is swimming, very quietly; she climbs out on the sand, waves and beats her wings, and turns into a beautiful woman who flings herself down on the sand like a corpse. In the evenings she frightened many. Ivan Kurchavïy began to pine away and got in

the habit of rowing to the great pool at midnight alone, all alone, in a little dugout, carrying a dulcimer [*gusli*], and he would play various songs. He too wept, and now he whistled, now laughed like a wood-spirit, now sang at great length some melancholy song. But hark now: Marina-Rusalka emerges from the water, throws herself into the boat with Ivan Kurchavïy, and they caress and embrace and laugh like crazy! Over and over Ivan Kurchavïy rode to the great pool at midnight, and then the traces of him disappeared: they found neither him nor the lute [*bandura*], only the oars of the boat on the bank. Once at night he came to his wife and said, "Do not grieve over me, little wife! I live happily with Marina on the bottom of Mother Volga: Volnok the Water Spirit took a fancy to me. I play, he dances with his rusalka-wives. He promised to reward me in this world: to allow me to be together with Marina, my adored."[39]

A classic willy, lovelorn and unwed, Marina was readily assumed to have cast herself into the river, then bewitched her beloved and dragged him in too.

Occasionally, instead of joining the willies in their watery realm, clever young men like Stoyan the Shepherd might manage to capture and marry one of these ravishing creatures, but the girl will most likely prove fickle, as Radka did. We see this also in the following tale told by a peasant of Smolensk:

My great-grandfather went one time during Rusalia Week to strip lime-bark; and there some rusalki attacked him, but he quickly drew a cross [on the ground] and stood on this cross. After that, all the rusalki left, and only one still stayed there. My great-grandfather grabbed the rusalka by the arm and dragged her into the [magic] circle, quickly throwing a cross on her, hanging it around her neck. Then the rusalka submitted to him; after that he led her home.

The rusalka lived with my great-grandfather for a whole year, willingly carrying out all the wifely tasks, but when the next Rusalia Week came round again, the rusalka ran off again into the woods. Captured rusalki, they say, eat little—rather they feed on vapor and soon they disappear without a trace from the human dwelling.[40]

This man was lucky, for Rusalia Week figured among the most dangerous times to encounter a rusalka, when she had just emerged from the waters, at her most potent and magically strongest. For she embodied—carried within herself—the growing-power of the fresh green vegetation, bursting into flower in the spring, when both warmth and moisture came together. The waxing sun provided the warmth, while the willies brought the necessary water. Indeed, one of their favorite occupations everywhere was to sit combing the water from their long, heavy green or blond hair, glad (we are told) to be relieved temporarily of its weight. One Belarusian author, tongue in cheek, even wrote: "How great the weight of this water is one can deduce from the fact, for example, that in combing her wet hair in the current, she could squeeze out enough water to drown an entire village."[41] But rusalki were so closely tied to water that they could not survive without it. Like salamanders, if they stayed away from water too long they would dry up and die.

Because of the spirit maidens' close connection to the water necessary for the peasants' crops to grow, farming communities invoked the vily and rusalki regularly by means of festivals and rites held as the seasons requiring moisture came around—celebrations that involved many ritual actions, including dance, to assure their cooperation and turn aside their wrath. We turn now to these seasonal festivals—but first we need to consider the notion of seasons and the calendar into which they fit.

CHAPTER 2

Marking Time

We take our calendar for granted: numbered squares marching in rows and columns across twelve paper grids, where we scribble our daily appointments and reminders among small, preprinted labels like EASTER, or SUMMER BEGINS, or GROUNDHOG DAY OBSERVED.

But why *twelve* months, with their strangely varying numbers of days? Where did all that variation come from, and is it necessary? Was the farmer's calendar like ours? Does the calendar have to be constructed the way we do it?

No. And for just that reason, the history of calendars is full of enlightening surprises.

Keeping to one solar cycle for a "year" makes sense where obtaining food is concerned, so we find this measure worldwide. But the other divisions differ enormously. For one thing, the precise number of 365.2424 days per year doesn't compute tidily, and it certainly doesn't mesh well with the other obvious time-marker besides the sun—namely, the cycle of the moon, which at 29.53 days leaves a messy residue beyond twelve "moon-ths" per year.

But the peasant farmer had worse troubles than messiness. What if you have no paper on which to put your calendar, or even a writing system? What constitutes a calendar then, and how do you keep it? For keep it you must, if you depend on farming for food, like those who courted the Dancing Goddesses.

At a minimum, you need to know when to plant your crops, and weather alone will not serve as a fail-safe guide. On April 20, 2002, New England

and much of the Midwest sweltered in ninety-degree heat, but it was hardly the time for summer planting: four days later, the thermometer plummeted to below freezing again. For crops, one must at least know when the typical seasons come around.

Yet even "seasons" don't stay put. The English-speaking culture takes four seasons for granted: spring, summer, fall, and winter. But in southern California, a long, sere fall slides slowly into a long, balmy spring with only a couple of monsoons between—nothing a northerner would recognize as winter. In Siberia and parts of New England, however, a long winter abruptly leaps to summer without pausing for spring.[1] Different areas have their distinct rhythms, affecting the way people map out their lives.

In Greece, branches might begin budding in February, but not till May in Britain and central Russia, or even June in Scandinavia and northern Russia; so the equivalent ritual has radically varying dates. English speakers think of "fall" and "harvest" as practically synonymous—*harvest* and German *Herbst* ("fall") come from the same root as Latin *carp-* "grab, pluck" and Greek *karpós* "fruit, what's plucked"—and we view spring as the season for planting. But in southern Greece, summer becomes so hot so early that farmers must plant their wheat around November, just *before* winter, so they can harvest it by June to save it from scorching.[2] No "Fall Harvest Home" there.

Farther north, in Thrace, Macedonia, and the Dinaric Alps, the shepherds think in terms of but two seasons. In winter, their sheep must graze in the warm lowlands; come summer, the shepherds and their families move the flocks to the cooler high pastures; then everyone treks down again for winter. (This flip-flop existence is considered transhumant, not nomadic; remote from city life, it has preserved many traditions.)

The farmers of the central Balkan Peninsula and Ukraine—prime habitats of the willies—seem to have thought traditionally in terms of three seasons: a cold, dark winter of largely indoor activities; a warming and revivifying spring; and a hot summer for maturing and harvesting the crops. The Rusalii festivals provided a focus for each of these three seasons: around the spring equinox, and at the summer and winter solstices (English Midsummer and Midwinter). Medieval Christian diatribes against the festivities show clearly that these Rusalii were once dedicated to fertility and to the dancing spirit maidens who brought it, the rusalki.* The *Stoglav*, a church

---

* See chapter 6 for etymologies of Slavic *rusalki*, *Rusalii*, and Latin *Rosalia*.

FIG. 2.1. Woman with extended sleeves dancing at the Midsummer *Rusalii* festival. After miniature in Radziwill (Königsberg) Chronicle, 15th-century copy of 1206 manuscript from Kiev.

document originating in 1551 during the reign of Ivan the Terrible, defines and describes the Rusalii thus:

> on St. John's Day [Midsummer, June 24] and on the eve of Christ's birth and Epiphany, men and women and [unwed] girls come together for excitement at night and for immoral talk and demonical songs and for dancing and for jumping [over fire: see fig. 7.1] and for deeds against God.[3]

Another manuscript passed along a thirteenth century drawing of a woman and child performing a rusalka dance to the accompaniment of a drummer and horn players (fig. 2.1), and an early preacher railed: "A woman dancing is called Satan's bride and the devil's lover, spouse of the demon. . . ."[4] The very idea of women doing fertility dances at the oft-recurring seasonal rituals gave the early church headaches.

Rural calendrical devices, constructed with considerable ingenuity, have occasionally survived, offering windows into agrarian European thinking. Nonliterate women in the Kargopol' district of northern Russia used to embroider

FIG. 2.2. Calendars embroidered in chain stitch on apron; Kargopol' area, North Russia, late 19th century. Months are counted clockwise around central rosette (January is top center petal). From 73 encircling "caterpillar" segments protrude symbols (30 from outer rim and ends, 4 from inner edge) marking agrarian and church holidays; detailed significance is now lost. Calendar at left is slightly different, suggesting these are records, not predictions.

calendars onto linen towels and their red linen aprons, passing them down to their daughters (fig. 2.2).[5] The basic design consists of a circle looking like a fat, segmented caterpillar curled lazily around a central rosette of six petals and six tendrils that indicate the twelve months, clockwise. January is at the top (by the caterpillar's extremities), June at the bottom. Small symbols stick out or cling like parasites at various spots to mark dates for the crucial agricultural work (which only sometimes coincided with church holidays). What was important to farm folk was not the day of the month but how long till the next agrarian landmark. The little "parasite dates" differ slightly from one caterpillar to the next, but unfortunately the Kargopol' women passed the old cloths down so long, and life changed so much, that by the 1970s (when ethnographers arrived) they no longer recalled what many of these details signified.

In prehistoric times, clay pots sometimes served as calendars, at least to designate the months. The prolific Russian scholar Boris Rybakov has nosed out several of these vessels: large tureens with a dozen panels incised on their wide, flat rims (fig. 2.3), and some bowls and jugs with similar (but never identical) strips around the shoulder.[6] Rybakov gradually deduced

FIG. 2.3. Bowls with incised calendars on rims. Left: 18th century BC, from Almásfüzitő, Hungary. December and January at top, marked by Xs; Midsummer at bottom, marked XX; apparently reads clockwise. Right: Profile and rim of tureen from Lepesovka, Ukraine, 4th century AD. X marks winter and spring festivals, XX Midsummer.

that the X symbols represented the key stations of the sun, the solstices and equinoxes—precisely the times sacred to the willies—with the summer solstice distinguished by XX. One of the earliest of these calendars, on a Bronze Age tureen found in Hungary, is divided in four by these Xs (though the distribution of "months" is a puzzle). Perhaps the clearest such calendar is on one of two tureens from the fourth century AD found near Kiev, carrying twelve incised panels (plus three blank patches where the handles attach). Counting from the XX of the June solstice, we could set one of our month names to each panel—if we knew which way to proceed around the vase. Since only three boxes contain Xs, however, Rybakov assumed that these marked the sun stations *culturally important* in eastern Europe: the three seasonal Rusalii festivals. This allowed Rybakov to lay out the month names—in the not-unexpected clockwise or "sunwise" direction.*

Although the other symbols (resembling leafy branches, waves, nets, zigzags, and possibly a schematic scene or two) remain uncertain, we see a structure corresponding to something known. The single X for the spring equinox/Rusalii, falls in March; the double X for the summer solstice/Rusalii, falls in June. No X marks the fall equinox—but there is also no fertility festival honoring the rusalki/willies at that time. After all, as Vladimir Propp points out in his study of Russian agrarian festivals, the crops have finished growing by then and are already being diligently stored away while the willies rest.[7] No need to bother the spirits then.

The third X, oddly to us, is marked in January, rather than in December where the solstice technically falls these days. This may be explained, however, by the fact that traditionally in Europe the winter solstice begins a special holiday period that runs well into January, known in Russian as *Svyatki* ("sacred" days), in English as the Twelve Days of Christmas. This overlap into January makes even more sense if the Xs had come to mark the Rusalii rather than the solar stations. (These Xs will keep turning up.)

I always wondered where the *twelve* days of Christmas came from. If you divide 365 days of the year by 12 months of 30 days, you come out with *five* extra days (which we, in our calendar, hand out one by one to various months). But the lunar cycle is easy to count, and people have known for millennia that alternating months of 29 and 30 days keeps track of the moon fairly well. Now, if you mark off the 12 lunar cycles of 29 1/2 days within a year of 365(1/4) days, you come out with 11 to 12 days left over, which get chucked in as a lump somewhere to make the lunar year fill out the solar.

---

*Both English and Russian use the month labels originated by the Romans (named after their deities, emperors, and numerals). But the Slavs also had non-Roman names, generally reflecting the appropriate work or weather. Rybakov tried setting these folk names, too, around the segments on the bowls but did not find further insights.

Their insertion close to the winter solstice suggests that the start of the New Year once landed on that date.

Or somewhere nearby. Where *does* the year begin, anyhow?

Even just in Europe and within historic times, New Year's Day has fallen at half a dozen different points. The winter solstice, sometimes taken as New Year's Day, currently lands around December 21. Another favorite candidate has been the spring equinox, which falls three months later, around March 21; or the summer solstice, about June 21.

The Romans, who originally set their New Year as March 15, moved the celebration to January 1 in 153 BC and then gradually spread this custom across Europe along with the Roman calendar and alphabet.

The Christian church waffled for a long time. By selecting December 25 to celebrate the birth of Jesus, the church coopted both the solstice and the New Year festivities, since this birth could be taken as a natural starting point. But this gave the spring-equinox partisans new leverage: March 25, nine months earlier, might better count as Jesus's inception. Known as Annunciation New Year, it persisted in Britain till the adoption of the Gregorian calendar there in 1752. The Byzantine church in Constantinople, however, selected a New Year in September, while the citizens continued with a civil New Year in March. Chaos. Of course, if we go outside Europe, we find yet other dates, such as Chinese New Year, celebrated on a date calculated (like Easter) from lunar cycles and falling anywhere from late January to mid-February.

The fact that the sun stations, not the moon, had long formed the backbone of the European calendar shows up in another group of dates that most of us no longer recognize as part of the system. The solstices and equinoxes divide the year into quarters of roughly 91 days, but these quarters can be halved again, producing what are known as the *cross-quarter days* at 45- or 46-day intervals (table 2).

These days fall, therefore, early in February, May, August, and November and correspond to the great Celtic festivals of Imbolc, Beltane, Lughnasad, and Samhain. Beltane and Samhain correspond respectively to the traditions in Britain of May Day eve (with its ancient sexual license) and Halloween (when spirits rampage). As with other ancient celebrations, the

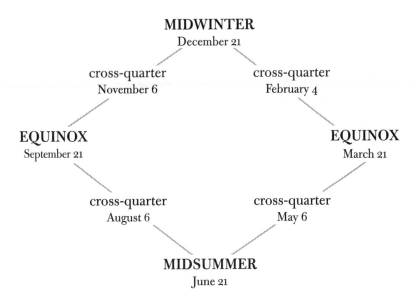

MIDWINTER
December 21

cross-quarter
November 6

cross-quarter
February 4

EQUINOX
September 21

EQUINOX
March 21

cross-quarter
August 6

cross-quarter
May 6

MIDSUMMER
June 21

TABLE 2: **CROSS-QUARTER DAYS**
(solstice dates normalized, leap year ignored)

Christian church did its best to remold the cross-quarter-day rites into more demure and acceptable church festivals.

In fact, the clergy attempted to take over, revise, and rename every traditional festival that they couldn't stamp out entirely—a problem that will haunt us throughout this book. The farmers, for their part, clung ferociously to the periodic rituals they viewed as ensuring fertility and the food supply—but if *renaming* things would get the church off their backs, that could work. For example, the old celebrations around the beginning of November hosting communal feasts for the family's dead ancestors—so as to secure their good will in propagating next year's crops and livestock—became All Saints' Day and All Souls' Day on November 1 and 2, while the eve of All Saints'—a.k.a. All Hallows' Eve—retained some of its ancient riotous character as Hallow-een.*

Further obfuscation of the old agrarian rites stems from inaccuracies

---

*Dressing children as goblins and witches to demand "trick or treat" at every door reflects an old Celtic belief that hordes of spirits of the dead roamed the earth during the night of Samhain. Food was left out for them in hopes the rowdy spirits would be pleased and

in the classical Roman or "Julian" calendar, named after Julius Caesar and spread across Europe by Roman armies in the early centuries AD. A slight surfeit of leap days, intended to correct once every four years for that extra almost-but-not-quite-a-quarter day beyond 365, slowly accumulated over many centuries and shifted the calendar out of whack. By 1582, when Pope Gregory decreed the adoption of an adjusted system, the solstices and equinoxes fell eleven days after the calendar said they did. Gregory ordered the omission of eleven days, so the date jumped from October 4 to 15 overnight. Voilà—the "Gregorian calendar" was born. (Autocrats have their uses!) His advisers devised and built into it a clever system that *omits* the leap day at each century mark, unless the century number divides evenly by 400. (So we *had* a leap day in 2000, but not in 1900.) Different countries switched from the Julian calendar to the Gregorian at different times, the American colonies doing so with Britain in 1752 and the Eastern Orthodox countries still later: Russia in 1918 and Greece, the last holdout, in 1923. By then the gap was fourteen days, not eleven, since the Gregorian calendar had already abstained from three leap years (1700, 1800, and 1900). In the process of conversion, some of the agrarian rituals got shuffled away from their intended times, further obscuring their original purposes, as we shall see. Knowing the problem is there, however, will help us in untangling those purposes, so tightly bound up with the Dancing Goddesses.

So when did the Dancing Goddesses start *their* year? When did they start their cycle of supernatural duties? Although the willies were called upon to divine future marriages and the like during the Twelve Days, they began their main duties around the spring equinox. And since, for traditional rural farmers, the Twelve Days sometimes came to represent the twelve months in miniature for purposes of magic and divination, we need to know what events typically occurred in those months before looking at their counterparts. So we'll begin our tour of the goddesses' year with the spring Rusalii, when the willies began to dance their way out of the wild into the world of farmer and shepherd.

---

not do too much damage to the premises. (Of course, local boys in disguise also used that night to settle grudges against neighbors.) See chapter 9.

CHAPTER 3

To Bring the Spring

A branch of May I've brought you here
And at your door I stand:
It's nothing but a sprout
But it's well budded out
By the work of Our Lord's hand.
—traditional English May Day verse

Russian village girls, dressed in their gracefully flowing *sarafans* (gowns) (fig. 3.1), used to set forth in the spring, on the day they called Semik, to capture some much-needed life force for the community by "curling the birches." Birches and willows were the first to bud out and turn green in the northern forests, welcome signs of spring returning at last, as this song suggests:

Curly little birch tree,
Curly and vigorously sprouting,
Beneath you, dear little birch, . . .
That is not fire that glows,
Nor poppies that bloom—
Those are beautiful maidens
Who lead the round-dance:
For you, dear little birch,
They sing all their songs.[1]

Seeking out a handsome birch sapling with space around it, the girls "curled" it by decorating it with brightly colored ribbons and binding some

FIG. 3.1. Young Russians dancing a *khorovod* in the forest while others swing or feast. Each girl wears long gown (*sarafan*) and cylindrical or tiara-shaped headdress (*kokoshnik*). Painting by Konstantin Makovskiy (late 19th century).

of its branches into circlets, symbols of infinity. After kissing through these leafy rings and swearing lifelong friendship (*kum*), the girls picnicked on omelets and crepelike pancakes, because eggs, like greenery, symbolized life. They also led *khorovod* (follow-the-leader) line dances around the birch, singing songs like:

> *Jump, dance, beautiful maidens,*
> *and you, young men, admire us.*[2]

If the tree stood at the edge of the forest beside the cultivated fields, they bent its crown till it touched the field. There they tied the tip down to divert the life energy of the green tree out of the wild (where it seemed wasted) and directly into the village crops, already sown there and waiting to grow. Otherwise, they cut or even uprooted the tree and carried it with joyful song and dance back to the village like a maypole. Then everyone hauled the festive tree out into the fields, ripped it to shreds, and strewed the pieces about to impart the growth-energy of the wild birch to the nascent crops.[3] Just as the birch had thickened with growth, they hoped to induce the grain to do likewise. A song from Vladimir province, published in 1914, says:

> *Where the maidens have walked,*
> *Trailing their sarafans*
> *There the rye becomes thick,*
> *Fat-eared, a joy to thresh.*
> *From just one ear*
> *You fill three sacks![4]*

Villagers clearly perceived the girls, who were of marriageable age but not yet married, as having the same sort of as-yet-unused fertility that the willies had. Although one couldn't control the willies directly, one could delegate the village maidens to behave *like* the Dancing Goddesses, in hopes of either jump-starting the goddesses' activities (reminding them of what was needed) or even creating the same effects directly.

As the girls dance, so may the goddesses; and as the goddesses create life by dancing, so may the girls. Magic through analogy.

Analogy, in fact, forms the backbone of most mythical and magical thinking. Pins in the voodoo doll bring pain to the intended person; rice and coins showered onto the bride bring her fertility and riches—all by analogy.

It's hard to overestimate the importance of analogy in human thinking. Everything we see we analyze by matching patterns: this resembles that, or this is partly like that and partly like something else. Later, even partial likenesses will trigger memories of what we saw. In language, every sentence we concoct or figure out is based on analogical processes—utterances that are partly like and partly different in form and meaning from previous data. Our template is something like AX is to AY as BX is to BY:

AX : AY ::
BX : BY

So we match such snippets as

Eat berries is to *Eat plums* as
Pick berries is to *Pick plums*

or

work-s is to *work-ing* as
jump-s is to *jump-ing*

Proof of this ubiquitous brain process pops up when babies say *foots* (which they never heard from adults), forming it from *foot* by analogy to plurals they *have* heard, like *book-s* and *cup-s*. We've been honing these linguistic skills for many tens of thousands of years; indeed, we've reshaped our brains to become whiz-bang good at analogical thinking (while committing many a fallacy of logic).

If *this* is at least partly like *that*, the thinking goes, then if I perform an act or produce an object similar to what I want, maybe I can cause the desired thing or event to appear: so-called sympathetic magic. So I throw coins and grain on the bride to produce a *semblance* of wealth and abundance, hence *real* wealth and abundance in the future. I can pipe water onto the garden through a hose; why not pipe growth-energy onto the field through a burgeoning tree?

Desperately dependent on the oft-capricious weather for their crops, the villagers turned to sympathetic magic to ward off hail and drought and to bring rain, fecundity, and protection from illness and other evils.

But analogical thinking did not stop there. If I "will" something to happen, I take actions to make it happen. By analogy, if something happens, it must have been willed.* So if my pig dies, or the house falls down, some

---

*This statement unfortunately partakes of our human brain's favorite logical goof, the Fallacy of Affirming the Consequent (mentioned also in the Introduction). It goes as follows:

Willful Creature must have caused the misfortune. But if I can't *see* the culprit, then some Willers must be invisible. Enter the spirits: invisible, insubstantial Willers of events.[5]

Even before the leaves bud out, as the snow begins to thaw, one must invite—indeed coax—the spring to arrive. If one simply waited, Spring (being willful) might not *choose* to come, and then, with last year's food bins already almost empty, one could not survive. To bring the spring proactively, Russian mothers baked bird-shaped pastries in early March, and their children clambered about, setting these little larks and snipes out like duck decoys on the rooftops, fence posts, and snowless patches of ground, hanging them from trees and bushes or even tossing them into the air,[6] meanwhile singing such songs as:

> *Larks, Larks,*
> *Give us Summer,*
> *We'll give you Winter—*
> *There's no food left for us![7]*

Birds and spring, after all, return at about the same time, so people reasoned that the birds—being animate, hence willful—must *cause* the spring to arrive. This follows another basic tenet of how people thought before the use of writing let them stockpile enough evidence to figure out actual causes of things. The reasoning is: because Event Y *followed* Event X, X must have *caused* Y to happen. There may or may not, however, be a causal connection between X and Y: mere temporal proximity doesn't prove causality. (Consider this statement: "I ate pizza; now I have a headache; therefore pizzas cause headaches." No proof there.) Logicians call this form of reasoning by its Latin formulation, *post hoc, ergo propter hoc*—"after this, therefore

---

Premise: "Having A entails having B (its consequent)."

I happen to have B, so I *assume* A is present/true.

But that's bad reasoning, as we can see from a concrete example. If I caught a cobra (A), then I know I have a snake (B). But if what I caught is just some snake (B), it's fallacious to assume it's a cobra (A). See Barber and Barber 2005, 37–38, for evidence of the ubiquity of this error, especially in myth and folklore.

because of it"—and it turns up regularly in both law cases (to the distress of careful lawyers) and mythology.*

So one sets out flocks of pastry birds in hopes of causing Nature to do what we want it to do: when the landscape teems with birds, spring will arrive. The pastries also provide proper forms or templates for the desired bird souls to come and inhabit: analogy again. Similarly, the ancient Egyptians placed statues and paintings of the deceased in that person's tomb to provide his or her soul with a handsome choice of templates—"houses"—of familiar shape to live in. This kindness not only makes the dead soul happy but keeps it from wandering disconsolate among the living, making trouble like a willy.

In Bulgaria, farmers view the birds as a sort of animate calendar and allow the swallows and storks, harbingers of spring, to nest anywhere they choose.[8] From Greece and Turkey north to Hungary, Alsace, and beyond, storks nesting on one's chimney still "bring luck" and/or protect the house from evil spirits. In Crete we watched a pair of swallows feed their young in the kitchen rafters while the farmwife complained mildly that to accommodate these feathery good-luck charms she had to leave her house door open all the time! The regular departures of the storks in late July and the swallows in mid-September also indicate that the birds cleverly hold keys to calendrical knowledge.

Birds with keys? A Russian ditty sung in early spring proclaims:

> *The sandpiper has brought*
> *All its nine keys:*
> *"Sandpiper, sandpiper,*
> *Lock up winter,*
> *Lock up winter,*
> *And unlock the spring—*
> *Warm summer!"*[9]

Just as one locks a watchdog into a cage and unlocks the door to let it out, so some animate force must possess keys that lock up or unlock the weather,

---

* See Barber and Barber 2005, 121–23, for *post hoc* reasoning in myth and folklore; 34–40 for more on how analogy works; and 160–75 for more on spirit templates. These principles will keep recurring as we explore the spirit maidens.

be that animus a bird, an archangel, or the king of the winds. Spirits that warehouse the weather turn up repeatedly in eastern European lore and also in Homer, but a yet older image persists too—that of *waking up* spring and, for good measure, killing winter. Actions quite different from making pastry birds follow analogically from this image.

The celebration we know as Carnival in the West corresponds to Russian *Maslenitsa*, or Butter Week (from Russian *maslo* "butter"), when everyone indulges in eating and merrymaking just before the austerities of Lent. On the Thursday before Lent, young villagers would construct an effigy from straw or from a small tree, dressing it as a woman (occasionally as a man) and propping it up in a sleigh with food and drink in its hands. Dragging the sleigh through the village with much singing and dancing, they installed the doll in a very visible place, such as the top of the local sledding slope. For days people gorged themselves—the "Christian" reason being to eat up the remaining stores of food that the church would not allow during Lenten fasting, but the pre-Christian reason being that much food on the table at the end of winter would by analogical magic produce copious food in the next agricultural cycle. (Remember the rice thrown over the bride.) On Sunday evening, as Maslenitsa ended, the villagers staged a mock funeral, carting the effigy to the fields just beyond the village. There they tore it apart, strewing the shreds all over the plowland: or they burnt it, grabbing the embers and flinging them about the field; or they simply buried it there with loud wailing—and louder laughter.[10] If no effigy was at hand, the villagers hauled away in a cart "a drunken man . . . dressed in rags with his face blackened," whom they had provided with a cask of beer, a tumbler of brandy, and "a large box filled with cake, fish, eggs, and pancakes." According to Angelo Rappoport, a Western observer writing in 1913:

> After his departure old people invite one another to their respective houses: "Ah! little brother, come and keep us company; we are going to drink and finish up our provisions; we cannot keep them for Lent, it would be a sin. During Lent I never drink a drop of anything, and I only eat the tail of a radish. Come then, little brother, come."

This "finishing up" could last yet another two days among old people, says Rappoport, causing Maslenitsa to end on Tuesday as Carnival does in the West (*Mardi Gras* being literally "Fat Tuesday"). The younger ones, who must go back to work, end Carnival on Sunday night by setting afire piles of straw outside the village.[11]

Over the millennia, the meaning of these rituals has become somewhat scrambled, or perhaps multivalent, as so often occurs with analogical thinking: the more analogies that fit, the stronger the magic will be.[12] The Butter Week effigy carrying food represents the butter-filled bounties of the last agricultural cycle, now running out with the end of winter and the end of last year's food. It also stands for winter and its hardships, which the crowd kills with glee. Hence the loud laughter: some deaths promote life.

The Russians were not alone in analogically slaying Winter. In parts of Germany, two men arrayed as Summer and Winter would fight, with Summer invariably trouncing Winter. In other areas in Germany, Poland, France, and the Basque country, people burned, stoned, clubbed, shredded, or drowned a straw doll representing Winter or Death, while the Swiss of Zurich incinerated a huge cotton "snowman."[13] As in Russia, the residual magical energies were often buried or strewn about the fields where the seeds of the new crops awaited the returning warmth to rise again.

Unfortunately for us, the Christian church has "shredded and strewn" the traditional spring festivals like so many Carnival effigies, a scrap surviving here, a shred there, at different places and dates running from January to June, depending on how far north one is and when Easter and New Year fall.* Reconstituting these rites takes some doing. Spring customs and particularly the spring Rusalii (the March equinoctial X on the calendar bowls) sustained the worst damage because blatant celebration of fertility (and hence sex) offended church principles. But to the farmers, fertility meant

---

*For New Year, see chapter 9. Easter falls the Sunday after the first full moon after March 21, the day taken by Christianity as the vernal equinox; so it can land anytime from March 22 through April 25. But since Orthodoxy calculates by the Julian calendar and Catholicism by the Gregorian, Orthodox Easter may occur from April 4 through May 8 in the international Gregorian calendar (since Julian March 22 = Gregorian April 4 by now). The establishment of Easter also owes much to the Jewish festival of renewed life, *Pesach* (Passover)—Jesus happened to be crucified at Passover—including its name in Greek, Πάσχα *Paskha* (the Semitic word being remodeled to resemble Greek *paskh-* "suffer"), which most non-Germanic languages adopted. (*Easter* is a West Germanic word of debated origin.)

food, and they struggled to keep what the church was trying to suppress. After all, if the church promoted having many offspring as good, then how could the act that *produced* children be so despicable?[14] The populace's chief ally consisted of yet another analogy that was fortunately central to Christianity—resurrection.

Just as Christ was buried and rose from the dead, so the crop seeds, buried in the dead-looking soil, must rise again.

Easter was so sacred to Christianity, however, that the Balkan farmers fastened their precious spring growth rituals onto a different resurrection within church lore—Jesus's raising of Lazarus from the dead a few days before his own death. In Bulgaria on Lazarus Day, the day before Palm Sunday, groups of young girls called *Lazarki* still dress up in special costumes and visit each village house to bring "good luck"—life force for crops, animals, and occupants—for the coming year, through their songs and dances.*

Spring comes early in the South, and although the Bulgarian *Lazarouvanè* falls a week *before* Easter, whereas the Russian "curling the birches" falls seven weeks *after*, considerable sameness of purpose in these two "girls' festivals" appears in the following Bulgarian Lazarka song, so close in thought to the Russian one quoted above:

> *Wherever we have passed,*
> *the wheat has grown, and grown so rich*
> *that it weighed down on the Earth;*
> *from two ears it bore a bushel,*
> *from two grapes—a cask of wine!*[15]

Again we glimpse Dancing Goddesses behind the activities of the unmarried village girls, whose initiation into and participation in Lazarouvane traditionally marked them as ready and available for marriage.[16] Let us watch them.

Weeks before Lazarus Day, as the world around them bursts into bloom, the girls begin meeting together, beginning, in some areas, with dancing all night

---

* Similar customs occur also in Greek Macedonia and Thessaly, among both Vlachs and Greeks, who call the girls *Lazaríne* (Hunt 1996, 59–62). The ways in which the custom has been simplified in some of these southerly areas shows that the original agricultural purposes are getting attenuated and lost, Lazarus weekend becoming either purely biblical or purely a "coming out" of the maturing girls.

FIG. 3.2. Bulgarian girls richly dressed as *Lazarki*, wearing gold wedding jewelry and flowery headdresses topped with feather grass, dancing with handkerchiefs "for abundance" on Lazarus Day.

around a bonfire on a mountaintop, where they are closest to the sacred world above, on the first Sunday of Lent.[17] Over the next weeks, they must learn the requisite songs and dance (the *bouenek*) of Lazarus Day, older teaching younger. For each household they need appropriate verses for the master and mistress, for married and unmarried offspring of either sex, for the beehives and lambs, barns, fields, and woodlands. The tunes are few, the words many. Two girls, called *Shetalitsi*, do most of the dancing, while the rest sing. On Lazarus weekend, the girls dress in their best holiday costumes (fig. 3.2), loading themselves with bridal jewelry, fancy metal belts, antique coin necklaces, and special headdresses covered with bright paper flowers (which they call "tulips") and topped with long feathers, tall feather grass (*Stipa pennata*), and boxwood sprigs, called *koylò*.[18] The coins and other metal trappings jingle as the girls walk and dance, so that "all evil is chased away by the ringing of metal."[19]

Setting out in bands of six or more, they go round the village. People open their doors, awaiting them eagerly. On the shoulder of a person to be addressed, one Lazarka places a white towel as a symbol or marker for the good forces the song will send him or her. The songs direct health, prosperity, and a good harvest to the farmer and his wife, love and betrothal to unmarried young men and girls in the household, happiness and many children to newlyweds, and so on. For example:

> *Dance for this young bride,*
> *This year's bride,*
> *And for next year's cradle.*

During the antiphonal song, the two dancers perform their steps, changing places back and forth as they dance to the 7/8 or 5/8 rhythm, hands raised, often waving white handkerchiefs. "Be sure to wave them high," an old lady told her granddaughter, "for they chase away the evil." When the song ends, the recipient of the wishes returns the towel, with coins, eggs, or a bag of flour wrapped in it for the collection basket of the Lazarki. The girls will later use these gifts to make a ritual meal of pancakes, omelets, and the like, which they will eat together.

If the woman keeps bees, all the Lazarki surround her like bees around their queen, holding hands and dancing to the right in a closed circle so the bees will swarm at the woman's hive and not fly away. "The 'Lazarki' stamp from foot to foot, they swing their bodies, jingle with their trimmings, and hold their hands in order to close the ring and 'shut in' fertility."[20] The hive owner often spins white wool as they sing, with her spindle resting in a bowl of water (a spirit medium); she may also "harvest" stalks of *koylò* from the girls' headdresses like a bee collecting pollen, placing them in the water to gather some of the girls' magical force. According to one ethnographer:

> The housewife afterwards sprinkled this water over the bees and surrounded their hives with the yarn she had spun. It was believed that as the dance and the spindle whirled about, so would the swarms of bees whirl around the hives, i.e. they would not escape.[21]

The woolen yarn tied around the hive in a magic circle also serves the analogical purpose of sequestering "the good"—the valuable bees.* If "luck" for the sheep is wanted as well, the Lazarki might sing:

> *Jump, jump, Lazarke,*
> *So that a lamb would jump*
> *In the landlord's yard.*
> *Whirl, whirl, Lazarke,*
> *So that the bees would whirl*
> *In the garden of the landlord.*[22]

---

*One of the oldest known texts in German, the 10th-century *Lorscher Bienensegen*, is a charm to make a wayward swarm of bees return to the hive (Echtermeyer 1962, 26–27). In our era of refined sugar, we forget how important bees were.

For many of the girls, this festival marks their "coming out" as newly matured young women, so tension mounts at the house of an eligible bachelor. When the time comes to return the towel, he may refuse to give it up. The girls must then approach him one by one, reaching for the towel, which he withholds until the girl he wishes to marry tries it.[23] Handing it to her signifies a proposal to become engaged; the way she receives it indicates her reply. For in the easy-living South, young people often had more freedom to choose their partners than in the barren North.

Again, as with the Russian birch ceremonies, we see the entire community looking to the unmarried girls of marriageable age—those with as-yet-unused fertility—as "conduits" of sacred fertility, magically passed along by dancing as they sing blessings.[24] The dances, although energetic and life-affirming, are not lascivious or even suggestive, yet the church has expended far more effort to keep women from participating in such events than men. The men, on the other hand, in effect openly acknowledge the paganness of the Rusalii festivals by rigidly separating their fertility rites from church practices, swearing not to enter a church, pray, or cross themselves during the period of *their* ritual contributions to communal abundance. They also swear not to have sex during this time—quite the opposite of the church's expressed fears of promiscuity. Among both the male Rusalii dancers and the Lazarki we see, in fact, a pattern of celibacy as prerequisite for ritual potency: only those not participating in sex can summon up the magic power to bring fertility to all.[25] As church pressure increased, however, the rituals thought to be key to survival often got handed over to children, who because of their youth and innocence (a type of celibacy) could fly below the radar of the church. Thus children set out the pastry birds, and children color Easter eggs.

People today still generally recognize that Easter bunnies and colored eggs once represented fertility. But fertility has less immediacy to city dwellers with steady supplies of groceries from a store than it does to remote farmers whose storage cellars are nearly empty. Spring, in fact, is the hardest time of year: flowers may bloom and crops sprout, but nothing edible has yet come ripe. In Greek Macedonia, the Lenten fare we received consisted of the last onions from the garden stewed with the last beans and cabbages stored the previous year, while in some places the Lenten diet is little more than bread and water, progressively sapping both energy and spirits. John Lawson, the assiduous collector of Greek folklore a century ago, told of the "general air of gloom and despondency" hanging over villagers by the final days of Lent. Questioned about this, an old woman replied, "Of course I am anxious; for if Christ does not rise to-morrow, we shall have no corn [grain] this year."[26] Analogy and reality had merged.

Lowest ebb comes at the funereal drama of the Good Friday service, centering on a shrouded effigy of Christ on a bier in the nave, a service "in lamentation for the dead God lying there in state," as Lawson put it.[27] A restless Saturday follows. At midnight as Lent ends and Easter Sunday begins, Orthodox Christians crowd the churches and spill into the courtyard. Inside in the dark, a curtain opens, light blazes, and the priest announces, "Christ has risen!" as his taper sets aflame the candles of the nearest bystanders, who light the tapers of those behind them in an ever-widening glow. "Christ is risen!" one cries to one's neighbor, who replies, "He is risen indeed!" Bells ring, fires are kindled, the fast is over, feasting begins. And everyone carries eggs, colored red and/or patterned with traditional designs (fig. 3.3).

In the Anglo culture, we hide the eggs for children to hunt; in Orthodox countries, eggs are presented to one's friends or tapped against their eggs— a person whose egg breaks will be outlived by the other person and/or the broken egg is forfeit. (The custom of giving eggs as gifts led the last Russian tsars to commission the court jeweler, Fabergé, to design his now-famous eggs of gold, enamel, and jewels as Easter presents for their queens.) The egg as fertility symbol goes so far back that we cannot find its origins, but we

FIG. 3.3. Left: Romanian Easter eggs painted with fertility motifs such as birds and fish. Right: Bulgarian Easter bread shaped like basket with a whole red egg baked into it.

see it repeatedly as a sign of both life and the cosmos: the asymmetrical little ball has the power to grow into a living entity. Seeds, grain, have a similar power within the plant world. No wonder everyone at the spring festivals eats pancakes, confected of eggs and grain.[28] In parts of Greece, the Easter bread has whole, uncracked eggs baked into its top.

Aside from the renewed life implicit in eggs and resurrection, the Easter activities themselves seem remarkably barren of the life-bringing goddesses who apparently once danced their fill at the spring equinox, the ancient spring Rusalii, the March X on the old calendars. The Balkan Lazarki and the Russian girls "curling the birches" clearly represent them, however, dancing and singing to bestow fecundity on fields, animals, and households. The farther north one goes, the later the date of budding and blossoming, so similar rituals occur in the Balkans in March, in Britain on May Day, in Russia on Semik (the seventh Thursday after Easter, hence mid-May to June), and in Scandinavia at the summer solstice.

Willies/vily/rusalki were not the only Dancing Goddesses. The sun, whose increasing warmth causes the budding, was believed to be a goddess in many parts of northern Europe, not a male god (a Mediterranean notion). She too danced. From Britain to Ukraine, people went out very early on Easter hoping to see the sun leap three times for joy as she rose that morning. One can guess she originally danced at the equinox, when the balance of day and night began tipping to her side, toward more daylight than dark. But those northerners who reckoned the event by warmth rather than light looked for the divine sundance at Pentecost, several weeks later.[29]

Farther south, in Hungary, the Balkans, and Greece, enough grass had sprouted by a month after the equinox that St. George's Day, April 23, could become the festival of shepherds, the day when the hungry animals first left the barns for the pastures, the beginning of real spring. As the animals departed, shepherds and farmwives performed many little rituals to keep the sheep safe and boost their fertility. After the ritual sacrifice or slaughter of a lamb (whose blood they smeared on doors and children for yearlong protection), the family prepared a feast, roasting the lamb and baking special festive bread (*kravai*) decorated with pastry figures representing sheep huddled in the sheepfold (fig. 3.4 left, cf. fig. 3.5).[30]

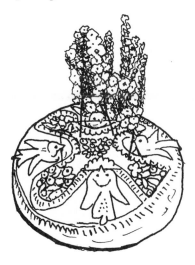

FIG. 3.4. Decorated festive bread (*kravai, karavay, korovay*). Left: St. George's Day loaf with dough figures of sheep in fold guarded by shepherd. Elkhovo, Bulgaria. Right: Wedding loaf with birds holding straws; flowery twigs inserted. Gabrovo, Bulgaria.

FIG. 3.5. Minoan bowl with clay flock of sheep guarded by shepherd (bottom center). Early 2nd millennium BC. Palaikastro, Crete.

FIG. 3.6. Swinging for health and tall crops on St. George's Day in Bulgaria. (Note long fringes on back-aprons.)

In Bulgaria the young men also scouted out sturdy trees from which to hang swings made from hempen ropes they had just twisted. Each marriageable girl, dressed in her best clothes so as to make a good impression on the bachelors and their mothers, and each bride in her full regalia sat down in turn on the wooden seat to be swung three times by the boys, while the other girls sang wishes for health and a good marriage (fig. 3.6). In some areas everyone, young and old, got to swing, so as not to be left out of the fun. The higher the swing went, the taller the hemp would grow.[31] Like dancing, swinging is an activity that accomplishes no "work" and thus belongs among the life-promoting activities of the willies, who, as we saw, loved swinging on branches in the forest after leaving the water in the spring.

St. George's Day celebrations clearly revolved around animal fertility, but whereas the older folk concentrated on the sheep, the young focused on water. Hungarians swam or splashed each other,[32] whereas Bulgarian girls went out long before dawn to gather dew and springwater and to pick curative and magical herbs, believing that the potency of all these depended on collection before sunrise.[33] They placed the fresh herbs in water, along with other plants saved from rituals on specially potent holidays like Easter, then washed their long hair in the mixture, "so that their hair might grow long and thick." They even added ears of wheat or rye to the water, saying, "As the rye grows, so may the hair grow."[34]

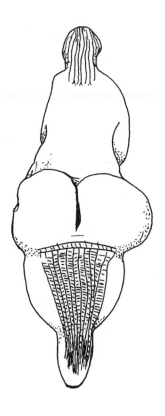

FIG. 3.7. Venus of Lespugue. Palaeolithic carving of woman wearing string skirt in back. Lespugue, France, 20,000 BC.

This attention to hair runs far deeper than mere vanity. Europeans had believed for millennia that women's fertility resided in their hair. Whence this belief? One of the first signs of a girl's sexual maturation is the arrival of pubic hair, so people associated her new fertility with her new hair—then postulated that the hair *caused* the fertility (*post hoc, ergo propter hoc*, again). In Europe twenty thousand years ago, we already see portrayals of women of childbearing age wearing a string skirt that echoes both pubic hair and head hair (fig. 3.7). Women's use of string skirts and other long fringes as symbols of their childbearing ability continued through the Neolithic and Bronze Ages, through the Classical period, and into modern times (see figs. 17.1–3, 23.2). These fringes, which may occur on head, shoulders, sleeves, and/or sash as well as apron (figs. 3.6, 3.8), may not be donned till puberty. "Fertility resides in hair" presently extended to female *head* hair, too, which is why married women in Europe were supposed to cover their hair. (Remember all those caps on married women in Jane Austen movies?) In most of Europe, however, unmarried girls' hair remained uncovered, and in eastern Europe girls wore it in a single long braid symbolizing maidenhood. The most important moment in the agrarian wedding (as opposed to the Christian one) was when the girl's single braid was combed out, divided, and rebraided into two braids that were wrapped around her head and covered forevermore with a cap. (Hence our expression of a girl

FIG. 3.8. Girls dancing *lesnoto*, wearing traditional rural dresses heavy with long red woolen strings or fringes from head, shoulders, sash, and apron. Drenok and Mariovo, Yugoslav Macedonia.

"setting her cap for" a man.) Her hair and fertility now belonged to her husband alone. The symbolism here is that on the wedding bed her pubic hair also will be divided—by the sexual act that will produce babies.[35]

So the longer and thicker the girl's hair, the more suitable a bride she will be—and the more like the ultrafertile willies combing the water out of their thick tresses to make the crops grow.

⬥

Water has two signal properties in the traditional agrarian culture: it is a major source of "fertility," since without it the crops don't grow, and it is a primary abode of the spirits. You can often catch glimpses of the normally invisible spirits in water (although people versed in modern physics and optics would consider these images reflections of light rays). Without the laws of optics, water *looks* haunted. When early humans saw their reflections in a pool, they noticed they could neither touch nor hear these evanescent creatures: here indeed lived spirits. These spirits, moreover, were very contrarian: if I move my right hand, that image or spirit moves its left! (Shadows, equally insubstantial, do likewise.) People concluded that spirit people looking much like humans lived down below, but inverted and reversed. Beliefs and behavior based on this conclusion occur all around the world. For instance:

> The people of North Asia conceive the otherworld as an inverted image of this world. Everything takes place as it does here, but in reverse. When it is day on earth, it is night in the beyond . . . ; a scarcity of game or fish on earth means that it is plentiful in the otherworld; . . . the left hand corresponds to the right hand on earth. In the underworld rivers flow backwards to their sources. And everything that is inverted on earth is in its normal position among the dead; this is why objects offered . . . for the use of the dead are turned upside down, unless, that is, they are broken, for what is broken here below is whole in the otherworld and vice versa.[36]

The reversed nature of the spirit world explains many details of the ways people have perceived and treated spirits, including the Dancing Goddesses. It explains why fortune-tellers consult mirrors and crystal balls (both reflective surfaces that reverse the image), why breaking a mirror is bad luck, and why left-handers once seemed so dangerous. After all, if normal humans are right-handed, left-handers must be spirits walking abroad in our world.[37]

Conclusion: If you need information from the spirits, seek them in the mirroring substances where they live, such as water, and do so on days when spirits are likely to be active, such as their festival days.

~∞~

On St. George's Day, we find fortune-telling that probably once belonged to the spring Rusalii, since it's also a central activity at the summer and winter Rusalii. Each girl tries to learn what the future holds for her: whom she will marry and when, how many children she'll have, or whether she'll die first—precisely the concerns of the willies. This custom is known in various forms throughout the Slavic world (fig. 3.9), but also in Greece, Italy, and other parts of Europe. The Bulgarians call their version "singing the rings," because each girl drops her ring (or bracelet or earring) into a pail of water that is made special in various ways. Thus, the water may have to be drawn and/or held by an auspicious child (usually a particularly beautiful

FIG. 3.9. Russian girls divining their marital futures at New Year. Top left: "Singing the rings." Right: Using mirror. Bottom: Using birds and water. From 19th-century Russian broadside.

one, both of whose parents are still alive) or a newlywed bride. It may also be decorated with particular magical herbs or flowers, or with nosegays of such plants dropped into it by each girl with her ring. The pail-holder then draws the tokens out of the water one by one while the girls sing riddles. Whatever they are singing about when the water spirits send forth a ring (that is, when a ring is drawn out) tells the token's owner what her fate will be. For example, a line about "blue pants, wet bottom" means marrying a fisherman, "multibranched pear tree" means marrying into a big family.[38]

The major festival called Semik (from Slavic for "seven") falls on the seventh Thursday after Easter: young women conduct it, and it clearly has strong ties to the Dancing Goddesses. We started this chapter observing some of it, but now more will become clear.

First, the peculiar scheduling of this feast invites inquiry. Church holidays, if not fixed to a calendrical date (like December 25), usually fall on Sunday (Laetare Sunday, Trinity Sunday, etc.) or replicate the chronology of events in Jesus's life. Semik does none of these. Why is it on a Thursday? And why the *seventh* Thursday after Easter?

Let's count: 6 full weeks plus 4 more days puts it 46 days later. If, as we have already suspected, the church attempted to preempt with Easter the very un-Christian resurrection and fertility rites of the spring Rusalii, and if the spring Rusalii originally fell on the equinox, as Rybakov reconstructed, then Semik makes perfect sense: 45.6 days after the vernal equinox comes the spring cross-quarter day (see table 2), halfway between the spring equinox and the summer solstice and a key marker in the old agricultural calendar.

The following Sunday is Trinity Sunday (Troitsen) or, in English, Whitsunday. In some places, the rituals elsewhere associated with Dukhov Day or Whit Monday (which lands on various dates because it is calculated from Easter) occur on May 10.[39] Now, Semik falls four days before Dukhov Day, and the actual cross-quarter day is four days before May 10. This congruence confirms that Semik must indeed represent the old cross-quarter day.

Next, let's review Russian Semik, adding more details.

The girls and newly married women began by going to the forest and "curling" a selected birch tree that was leafing out, either twisting its branches into wreaths ("crowns") or hanging upon it wreaths made of birch shoots and flowers, to capture and contain in these circlets the life force visible in the sprouting birches. Then the young women made pacts of eternal friendship as each other's *kum*:

> The girls attached their crosses [worn on necklaces] to these crowns, then, taking position two by two on either side of a crown, they exchanged kisses and crosses, while singing songs the contents of which called for friendship. The girls thus linked were considered friends for life. . . .[40]

After this exchange, "any dispute or quarrel is viewed among them as the worst of sins."[41] (The traditional Russian epic poems similarly describe heroes swearing on their little golden crosses to become adoptive brothers: to fail to aid each other would then be the worst of sins.) In some places, the girls swore *kum* with *all* their girlfriends, wishing each other such things as "May you fill out!" (as in pregnancy) or, to a girl who had just reached puberty, "May your braid be divided in two!"[42]

The women also offered eggs to the decorated trees and their spirits and then danced solemnly around them. Soon the young men joined the girls for a picnic of omelets and pancakes, adding flasks of liquor to the supplies, and singing:

> *Near you, little birch,*
> *Girls who are beauties*
> *And dashing youths*
> *Speak in sweet words,*
> *Drink hops-beer, home-brew,*
> *And sing mellifluous songs.*[43]

Eventually—at least originally—the young people wandered off two by two into the woods for the night. This, of course, horrified the Russian clergy quite as much as similar spring rambles upset an English reformer, Phillip Stubbes, in 1583:

> Against May 1, Whitsunday, or other times, all the young men and maides, olde men and wives, run gadding over night to the woods . . . where they spend all the night in pleasant games, pastimes; & in the morning they return, bringing with them birch & branches of trees, to deck their assemblies withal . . . But the cheifest [sic] jewel they bring from thence is their May-pole, which they bring home with great veneration. . . . I have heard it credibly reported . . . by men of great gravitie and reputation, that of fortie, threescore, or a hundred maides going to the wood over night, there have scarcely the third part of them returned home againe undefiled.[44]

A week later, the Russian girls retrieved their wreaths from the forest, throwing them into a nearby stream to divine their futures. She whose wreath floated away fastest would marry first—they believed it had pleased a willy, who was swimming off with it. She whose wreath sank would die.*

Vladimir Propp integrates the *kum* ritual (*kumlenie*) and all the various happenings at Russian Semik into one cohesive theory, pointing out that

---

* But "die" could also mean "marry" (Dobrovol'skiy 1908, 14; Alexander 1975, 27), since a newly married girl left her natal family as completely as if she had died, especially if the groom lived in another village. In Macedonia and elsewhere, in fact, a woman's bridal dress served as her funeral dress, "so her family would recognize her" upon meeting in the next world (Robinson and Canavarro 2009, 58).

kumlenie concerns not individual pairs of girls so much as all the young women together . . . [whereas] the men know neither the rite of *kumlenie* nor predictions about their matrimonial future. The precise significance of the rite is the creation of a union of the women among themselves . . . female solidarity. The second salient feature of this festival is that the kiss is not given simply as such, but through the living branches of the birch or under birches whose tips have been tied to each other.[45] [See fig. 3.10.]

FIG. 3.10. Panels from 12th-century Kievan silver bracelets A and M (see appendix). Top: Gilded panels showing arches "ticked" to resemble birch arbors; under them, woman dancing with extended sleeves, bagpiper, hare and cup, bird; beneath these, "interlace" scroll (water symbol), hopslike foliage. Bottom: Niello panels showing birchlike arbors containing birds with paws instead of claws; beneath these, winged dragon with tail forming "interlace," and bird with wing and tail becoming foliage.

That is, the vegetal generating-force of the earth transmits itself to the women, who then engage in sexual intercourse, many for the first time. Thus, "the rite of *kumlenie* prepares the women for future maternity,"[46] providing bonds of female solidarity for the coming dangers and ordeals of childbirth, just as the men's ancient swearing of brotherhood prepared them for the dangers and ordeals of battle.

In the Balkan Peninsula, we saw solidarity among girls of the same age group forged during the Lazarus festival, although the sort of archaic initiation seen in Russian Semik does not seem to occur (or survive) in the South. (Bulgarian Semik maintains different archaisms, which will become clearer when we investigate Rusalia Week.) Both areas, however, associated the young women with willies, and willies in turn with both fertility and water.

Water, of course, occurs in streams and lakes, just where the willies were thought to live. But since European farmers had not developed irrigation, they depended on the spirits to *bring* water directly to the fields at certain key points in the growing cycle. The villagers needed rain—not drought, not killer hailstorms, but sweet spring rains to foster the crops. Tradition said that those in charge were the willies, or maybe some leader of theirs, such as a Mother Rain; the church said it was God, or maybe St. Peter, since he held the keys to heaven where the clouds were kept. So, into the well-stirred pool of rain customs we will now wade, looking not only for our Dancing Goddesses but also for deeper familiarity with the peasants' analogical approach to solving life's problems.

CHAPTER 4

Dancing Up a Storm

Then the Tsar thought to assemble 5000 little children and
make them beg the Tanner—maybe he would pity *their* tears!
The children came to Nikita and, weeping, began begging
him to go fight the dragon. Nikita the Tanner shed a few tears
himself, just watching them cry.

—Russian folktale[1]

Farmers throughout the Balkan Peninsula have traditionally
depended on rain, in the right quantity and at the right times in the
spring, to mature their crops. If it failed to come, they assembled
the children to beg the spirit world for rain. But they did the tsar of the Russian folktale one better—they headed their delegation with that most pitiable child of all: an orphan. Causing the Chief Spirit's tears to flow would
make rain.

Only children—virgins—could succeed in questing for rain, according
to popular belief.[2] Whether organized by older women or by the children
themselves, a group assembled and formed a tightly knit band for the dura-
tion of the ritual, choosing one child—a needy orphan if possible—for the
unfortunate post of dancer. Old accounts mention both boys and girls participating, but especially girls. (In these dancing girls we see a nod to the
willies, despite the Christian veil.) The chosen one was stripped (unless her
clothes were already in rags) and then covered head to toe with whatever
greenery the group could gather, till only her feet were visible and no one
could recognize her (fig. 4.1). As they began dressing her, they might pray
thus: "Pity us, Little Lord and Little Mother of God. Give rain, dear God,

61

FIG. 4.1. Young girl dressed entirely in leaves, for rain ritual. Chakalarovo, Bulgaria.

so the earth will be drenched, . . . so that we poor ones not die."[3] In one village they even hung dead frogs from the girl's ears.[4] Everyone went barefoot (more pitiable, but also in more direct contact with the suffering earth), as they walked around the village boundaries and then from one farmhouse to the next. At each stop, the leaf-clad orphan danced while the children sang a doleful plea for rain, like these Bulgarian verses:

> *Vaj, dudule! May God give rain!*
> *That it may grow—the millet-grain,*
> *So that they may eat—the orphan-girl, the orphan-girl,*
> *Poor ones.[5]*

> *Oj vaj dozhdole,*
> *We are burnt, naked, barefoot,*
> *Naked, barefoot like wasps,*
> *Oj vaj dozhdole,*
> *May you sprinkle a little dew. . . .[6]*

Or this Romanian one:

> *Paparuda-ruda,*
> *Come and wet us,*

For the rains to fall
With the water pails
That the ears may grow
As high as the hedges. . . .[7]

Moving "by dancing steps and small capers," the orphan would wave her hands over her head in motions imitating showers: "palms turned up as if to take something and then with a jerky movement thr[o]w it over her head" or "arms are raised high and she waves her wrists with palms turned to herself." During the refrain she would swing them down with a sweep crossing in front of her face—no longer showers but a deluge.[8] When the song ended, as the farmwife cried something like "Let the rain fall for us this way!"[9] either the farmwife or one of the children sloshed a pail of water over the dancing shrub, demonstrating to the obtuse spirits what was needed: *water on plants!* The mistress of the house gave the children fruit, vegetables, butter, cheese, flour, coins—whatever she had, with extra for the dancer who had to suffer the drenchings. And so they proceeded around the village. A century ago, people welcomed them, offering refreshments and refilling their buckets. Drought was serious business. Everyone concentrated on getting the message through to the spirits. Occasionally several girls at once danced for rain, but they moved their dance line to the left. Normally, Christians danced to the right;[10] left was therefore the (reversed) direction belonging to the spirit world.

By sundown, the green-clad dancer in particular could stand no more: cold and sopping wet, exhausted from dancing, her feet cut and bruised. The others removed her leafy wrappings (and her rags, and her frogs), discarding them in an inaccessible place,[11] while each member of the troupe chipped in some fresh clothing for her—chemise from one, sash from another, and so on. Then they all feasted on the food they had received, divided the remaining food and money evenly (except for a much larger share to the dancer) as "pay" for serving the community with the long ritual, and repaired homeward, confident that rain would arrive in a day or two.*

---

*Pop and Eretescu 1967 (170) report similarly that in Romania several naked little girls clothed in greenery dance the rounds of the village, and that anyone seeing them must drench them—here interpreted as "watering" the fertility of the future. Eckert 1951 (100–101) describes a remarkably similar ritual occurring in Daghestan (northeast Caucasus) and mentions another in India, ascribing the source to some unknown prehistoric substrate culture. It could also, of course, have moved with population migrations.

If rain failed to come, another "sisterhood" of older girls and women tried something else. (Grown men played no part in these rituals, though they had as much interest as anyone in the outcome.[12] This was female magic.) The women would model a small male figure out of clay, which they treated as the dear departed, calling it variously Gherman or Caloian (fig. 4.2). (The name *Caloian* evidently derives from the late-twelfth-century folk hero and Vlacho-Bulgarian emperor John Assan, known as *Ionitză* "Little John" and *Calo-Ian-* "Handsome John," and remembered as a savior of his people.)[13] They laid the doll on a little bier decked with flowers, lit candles and incense, recited the funeral service, wailed and

FIG. 4.2. Clay figures of Caloian (Gherman), laid out as though dead, with candles and flowers, for Romanian rain ritual.

wept (real tears had to flow: sniffing raw onion helped), then carried the effigy out and buried it, preferably near the well or in the wheat fields,[14] singing verses like this:

> *Caloyene, yene,*
> *Go to heaven and demand*
> *That they open the gates,*
> *That they set free the rain,*
> *So that the streams pour forth*
> *Day and night,*
> *So the grain may grow.*
> *Caloyene, yene,*
> *Just as our tears flow,*
> *So should the rain flow,*
> *Day and night. . . .*[15]

If rain still didn't fall, they exhumed the figure three days later and either shredded it in the fields or tossed it into the river (much as Russian girls shredded their Maslenitsa effigy in the fields for fertility). This second theme of vegetal resurrection becomes explicit, in fact, in the following song:

> *Brother, brother Caloian,*
> *We bury you not so you will decay,*
> *But so you will turn green!*[16]

Analogy piles on analogy, for greater efficacy.

In the mountains, the Romanian farmers sometimes got too *much* rain. In that case they made a clay figure of Mother Rain (*muma-* or *baba-ploii*), which they either buried on a mountaintop (always the rainiest spot) or threw over a cliff.[17] In other areas, where sometimes too little, sometimes too much rain fell, people prepared on a specific date *two* clay effigies, one male ("Father Sun"), one female ("Mother Rain"), to be ready for either contingency.[18]

Far to the northeast, in South Great Russia, sending the message took fewer steps. The men simply ambushed passing women and pushed them into the water while shouting, "Rain, rain, come to us!" It had to be unexpected and the woman had to end up soaking wet as if drenched by heavy rain.[19]

As we see, these rituals differed somewhat from one place to the next, but the preceding descriptions constitute a fair sample of what Croatians, Serbians, Romanians, Bulgarians, Slavic Macedonians, Greek Macedonians, Albanians, and Vlachs* did to mitigate drought. The names for the rain dance also vary, falling into two groups. As in the songs quoted, some use words similar to *dudule* or *dodole*, others words related to *paparuda* or *peperuda*. Where do these expressions come from? Linguists agree that the first group goes back to an old Slavic song refrain, something like *oj-dodo-le*—like our *tra-la-la* only less cheery—but they have struggled to trace the second group.[20] Two archaeologists, A. J. B. Wace and M. S. Thompson, who spent much time recording the dying archaisms around them, put it quite perceptively in 1914:

> The Roumanians and Vlachs point out that *Pāparună* and *Pirpirună* are words that occur in their language, and mean "poppy" and "butterfly," but they fail to explain what poppies and butterflies have to do with rain-charms. Those who claim a Hellenic origin overlook the point that it only occurs in Northern Greece, where there is so much mixed blood, and not in Crete and the south, and they provide a Greek derivation for *Perperia* and *Porpatira* and say it means merely procession, but it is hard to see why any procession should be a rain-charm. In Bulgarian too the word *Peperuda* means butterfly. . . .[21]

In short, we have a fistful of folk etymologies for terms which, like the rituals themselves, are thoroughly pre-Christian. The suggestion that the form *peperuna* points toward the ancient Slavic god of thunder and lightning, Perun,[22] at least involves rain! The name of St. *Gherman*, in the second ritual, was apparently chosen because, charadelike, it "sounds like" the Slavic word for thunder, *gr(o)m*. (It appears to have replaced the old Slavic—non-Christian—name Yarilo, belonging to a buried-then-resurrected deity

---

*The Vlachs speak eastern Romance dialects closely related to Romanian. Until very recently, they lived—indeed, hid out—mostly as shepherds in the high mountains of the Balkan Peninsula, from Istria in the northwest to Thessaly and Thrace in the south.

whose traces in Serbia, Ukraine, and Russia bear a marked resemblance to Gherman/Caloian.)

Reworking a saint's name by means of folk etymology was common practice. Thus, for example, Serbs must not climb trees on St. Bartholomew's Day because the Serbian version of his name, Vratolom, sounds to them like "neck-breaker."[23] Our brain has a problem when it encounters something that matches nothing in its data bank—there is nowhere to file it, no convenient way to remember it. It's easy to learn words like *anti-Herculean*; we already know the parts, though we've probably never heard this combination. It's much harder to learn *Bartholomew*, or *culottes*, or *asparagus*. Instinctively people crush a strange-sounding word into a shape they know at least in part: *Vrato-lom*, or *cool-outs*, or *sparrow-grass*. This is the source of "folk etymologies." Thus the unfamiliar *dodole* spawned the Bulgarian *dozhdole*, because *dozhd-* means "rain" in Slavic.

Note the role of analogy throughout. Water sloshed on dancing greenery *resembles* rain on growing crops; this name *sounds like* that one (so it should mean something akin); this spirit should *act like* that champion; pastry birds all over fences and bushes *look like* spring. The efficacy of these analogies depends, of course, on the existence of spirits capable of acting like whatever the ritual implies. But first one must get their attention. We see the children trading on pity and tears (we heard that tears affected even belligerent Nikita the Tanner—*likewise* they might affect God); we also see the adults launching messengers—asking the spirit of Caloian to travel to heaven and *demand* rain.

Here too is analogy. When people die, their souls go to the Other World, so if we fashion a creature and give it proper burial, its little soul, too, will go off to the Other World—carrying our message. An old hope: archaeologists excavating ancient Athenian graveyards often find little lead tablets with messages, usually vengeful, that the living clearly hoped the dead would carry to the Other World for them.[24] Throwing messages (texts, dolls, wreaths, etc.) into water has the same intent, since water is where so many spirits live.

The willies once thought to bring rain by combing their long, waterlogged hair have clearly been to some extent supplanted—or at least supplemented—

by notions from Christianity, however distorted we and the clergy might view their version of that religion. Church strategy was to demote, to the status of demons, all pre-Christian spirits and the evil attributed to them, while the good these spirits were thought to bring was transferred to the saints. So rain came from God or St. Peter, but hail came from the willies—obviously, *angry* willies, for central and southern European hailstorms inflict severe damage. These are not the pea-size hailstones I grew up seeing. Summer hail I experienced in Hungary and Yugoslavia was more like large marbles, falling so thickly and so loudly on the car roof that one could only pull over and wait, fingers in ears against the deafening sound, hoping the larger stones wouldn't break the windshield and that one wouldn't be hit by the accompanying lightning. This hail beats down the grain and destroys the crops—disastrous to the farmer. Worse yet, hailstones from such storms occasionally reach the size of oranges and even grapefruit, killing the sheep and cows and even people.*

No wonder the farmers feared the willies' wrath, thought to be visible not only in hailstorms but in any strange atmospheric turbulence, including high winds and dust devils, and also in any strange turbulence of the mind and body. For madness and certain other human maladies were thought to come from the willies. We have seen the rain rituals; it is to the rituals for curing people of willy sickness that we turn next, for these dances, too, took place specifically in the spring, during Rusalia Week.

---

* Hail forms when water droplets are carried so high in a turbulent thundercloud that the droplets freeze into little pellets, which gravity then pulls earthward. If the strong winds in the thunderhead catch these and carry them upward again, another layer freezes onto each, or they may freeze onto each other. The more times this happens, the larger the hailstones become, until they get too heavy for the wind to keep them airborne. Then down they come. (If you quickly slice into one, you can see the layering.)

CHAPTER 5

Crazy Week—Rusalia Week

When *he* began to pipe the Rusalia tune *Florichika*,
even the stones began to dance!
—Uncle Opro, aged Bulgarian dancer[1]

For all that the customs varied from place to place, and even the dates shifted somewhat, one thing is certain: Rusalia Week was crazy—topsy-turvy. Spirits walked abroad in daylight, the incessant farmwork stopped cold, and, though the society was heavily patriarchal, women ruled, while men—most men—did what they were told. The consequences of misstepping were undesirable at best and fatal at worst. To honor, address, and placate the spirits, dancing was ritually employed.

Rusalia Week, also known as Rusalnaya Week or Green Holy-Days (*Zelyonïe Svyatki*), occurred around Pentecost, fifty days after Easter (table 5). (*Pentecost* comes from the Greek for "fifty.") Because of the shifting of Easter, it could fall anywhere from May to mid-June.

That Sunday, Pentecost, is called Trinity Sunday (Troitsen) by the Eastern Orthodox (Whitsunday in English). Monday is Dukhov Day, Day of Souls, a major occasion for honoring one's dead kin who, the belief goes, get let out of the Other World briefly at that time. The preceding Thursday in eastern Europe is Semik, apparently the old cross-quarter day (see table 2) and a focus of Rusalia Week.

In the central Balkans—Bulgaria, Romania, Serbia—spring sowing began one week before Semik, on Ascension (Spasov) Thursday, the fortieth day after Easter.[2] As Christ ascended to heaven, so might the sprouts ascend heav-

6th Thursday: *Spasov* (Ascension) Day (sowing begins)

7th Wednesday: Mad Wednesday

7th Thursday: *Semik*

7th Sunday: Pentecost/ Whitsunday/*Troitsen* (Trinity)

8th Monday: Whit Monday/*Dukhov* (Souls') Day

Rusalia Week

TABLE 5: KEY DATES AFTER EASTER

enward. The willies appeared happy during this week of sowing; then they got cranky.

On Semik, as we saw, the rusalki in South Great Russia left the water to invade forest and field, and that week was sacred to them.[3] Rusalia Week, in fact, was sacred to the willies everywhere and always included Semik and Troitsen, though its starting point might differ slightly. During it, Balkan women and girls avoided going out of doors for fear the willies would harm them. Churches, too, closed their portals extra tight so the willies couldn't sneak in and trash the sanctuary. Wormwood decked the houses. If women had to go out—households always needed water—they went with a companion and carried wormwood, which willies detest. Work was taboo during Rusalia Week—in some villages, to work on *any* day, in others to work on that Monday, Wednesday, Friday. Women dared not spin, weave, or do laundry in the river, and men dared not labor in the fields and vineyards, lest the furious rusalki destroy the work and send terrible rusalka sicknesses.

In Bulgaria, for example, when neighbors noticed a man named Purvan preparing to go to his fields on Friday of Rusalia Week, they said, "Aren't you afraid of the rusalki, Be Purvanè?" He retorted, "I'm not afraid of women," and left. In the evening, some people from another village who had passed his fields came to his house and told the residents they had better go get Purvan, for he lay paralyzed, in no condition to get home on his own. He remained ill for three months—no medicine could help him—and finally he died.[4]

Then there was Baba (Grannie/Auntie) Pechovitsa, who once worked on Wednesday of Rusalia Week, and by evening

she went crazy, and the madness lasted three years, until she died. They went to the churches and monasteries, to the *Rusaltsi* [see below] and the sorceresses, but nothing helped. They even tried [the herb] dittany—again, nothing worked. "They [the rusalki] hit her hard—they were very angry!" concluded [her friend] Baba Marija.[5]

Mostly the willies caused craziness, paralysis, or injury to the limbs.

The *rusaltsi* consisted of tightly organized brotherhoods of men who went from village to village at this season, using dance to bring abundance generally as well as to heal individuals of illnesses caused by the various willies—rusalki, samovili, samodivi. Identical bands of dancers called themselves *rusaltsi* or *kalushari* in western Bulgaria, *căluşari* in Romania (fig. 5.1). Where the dancers pass, it was said, crops and fruit ripen and no one gets rusalka sickness, for "the rusalki are content";[6] everywhere the men were met with joy and invited to every farmyard to dance. So strongly did each group feel about its responsibility for a particular territory that if two bands met on the road—although they tried to avoid each other's routes—they fought it out, sometimes to the death.[7] A century ago, the Bulgarian ethnographer Marinov collected detailed accounts of this ritual cycle, including interviews with both patients and dancers. Let us follow his account.[8]

Well before the start of Rusalia Week, the group's captain, the *vatafin*, chose whatever new members were needed, for the number of band members had to be odd (and prime?): 3, 5, 7, 11, or 13, but typically 7. Theoretically, any male could become a rusalets/kalushar (these are the singular forms), but he had to be a skilled dancer and nimble jumper; neither womanizer nor thief; neither drunkard nor glutton; known as a good and honorable villager; strong and healthy of body, who could withstand privation; tenacious of character, who would guard secrets and follow orders; and it helped if he were suggestible. The crucial post of vatafin, however, stayed within a single family, which guarded the ritual flag and the staves carried by the dancers and passed down in secrecy the magical incantations and other lore needed for successful healing. The vatafin was the absolute ruler: upon him and his decisions depended both the efficacy and the safety of the proceedings, for only he could communicate directly with the willies.

Newly chosen dancers dedicated themselves to the brotherhood for life in a solemn oath-taking ceremony, then were assigned to older members for

FIG. 5.1. Romanian *călușari* dancing with ritual staves, May 1997. Ribbons on costumes may perpetuate details of Roman military garb.

training and mentoring. They had to learn both the dances and the rules that applied once Rusalia Week began. All orders of the vatafin had to be carried out immediately without question; only the vatafin could converse with people outside the group (dancers could not even say hello to friends); each had to defer to any member older than himself; members could not have sex, get drunk, steal, speak shameful things, quarrel with anyone, cross

FIG. 5.2. Typical leather sandals/moccasins from various parts of southeastern Europe. Characteristic turned-up tips, which help prevent stubbed toes, were depicted already in Bronze Age Greece and Anatolia.

themselves, sleep away from the group, or go home during the ritual week. They could not dance in a village where another brotherhood had danced, and if they needed to cross a stream, they must not wade—they had to use a bridge or conveyance. (This stemmed originally from beliefs about water as the chief habitat of spirits, as we saw in chapter 3, rather than—as people later rationalized—from worries about the dancers' leather sandals [fig. 5.2], which they were not allowed to remove.)

As Rusalia Week began, the troupe assembled. In Bulgaria they wore ordinary clothes, a wreath or nosegay twined from magical rusalka herbs on their hats, and iron spurs, bells, and other jingly bits attached to their leggings and *opintsi* (sandals), to clink and jingle as they danced or walked. Each received from the vatafin a three-to-four-foot staff of special wood, tapering to an iron-shod tip to support the dancer's full weight and decorated at the top with more "jinglies" to make noise when waved. The staff had a stoppered hollow freshly filled with magical rusalka herbs. Without this staff, the rusalets/kalushar could not function, like a magician without his wand. Although kept by the vatafin during the year, each staff "belonged" to a particular dancer until he became too old to participate,

FIG. 5.3. Bulgarian musicians Samir Kurtov and his uncle Lubcho Fetov, playing on double-reeded wooden zurna (or zurla). Nigrita, Greek Macedonia, March 2008.

which might be after thirty years. Then it was ceremonially transferred to a new dancer, perhaps his son.

Fresh rusalka herbs also decorated the troupe's linen banner or flag, an emblem deemed so potent in its magic that dancers were forbidden to touch it or even stand in its shadow. Only the vatafin could handle it or its pole. While the leader sewed herbs onto its four edges, the rusaltsi would dance to a rusalka melody played by the musician who served the group. This man, the most famous and skilled they could obtain, knew the ritual melodies. By preference he played the *kaval*, an eight-holed end-blown flute; or the *gaida*, a goatskin bagpipe (see fig. 9.1); or—last choice—the *zurna*, a double-reeded shawm, fig. 5.3. Finally the vatafin fastened to the top of the pole some magical herbs, including wormwood, garlic, dittany, and iris (named *perunika* after the ancient Slavic storm god Perun).* If a new flag was needed, every-

---

* Iris was the Greek rainbow goddess, hence also associated with rainstorms. The rainbow "bridge" connecting earth and sky, humans and deities, seems as appropriate to this ritual

one knelt to it while the vatafin made it, dedicated it, and kissed it; then the others kissed the pole.

From the vatafin's house the group set out to perform two types of dances. One kind was "for pleasure, for the curiosity of the onlookers, and for *bereket*"—that is, the welfare and "good luck" of the community.[9] These dances consisted of particularly fast, virtuoso steps with lots of twists, jumps, and foot slaps.

The other kind was for private patrons, who paid for a dance cure for illnesses sent by willies in revenge for broken taboos (such as working on the willies' sacred days, or pissing under the eaves at night*), or for unfulfilled vows (perhaps made by an ancestor), or for encroaching on some watery place secret to the willies. The vatafin seriously considered each case, and if he felt the illness was not willy-sent, he refused; otherwise he worked out a price in money and goods for the ceremony.

⌘

In preparation for a dance cure, the vatafin fills a new clay pot with magical herbs and water, covers it with cloth, and sets it out on the floor; then he fills a bowl with vinegar and garlic. The sick man or woman, fully clothed, is laid on a rug near the pot. Ordered by age, the oldest dancer leads the line around the invalid and closes circle with the youngest at the other end. At a sign from the vatafin, who stands outside the ring holding the flag and bowl, the piper and dancers begin a gentle, lulling dance. Speeding up, slowing down, the dancers follow the piper's pace, eventually dancing several minutes in place while leaning back onto their staves. Suddenly they grab the edges of the patient's rug, fling him up in the air and lay him down. They back off while the vatafin anoints the invalid with vinegar, blows to the four sides, and administers a sip of the vinegar—all this under the flag. As the vatafin withdraws, the men begin to dance vigorously, three times alternately circling the invalid and leaping over him with great shouts. Then they circle the pot instead of the patient, still shouting, dancing ever faster,

---

as storm clouds, but why that particular flower receives the association (it is not the only multicolored flower!) I know not.

*The Basques, whose conservative customs frequently parallel Balkan ones, buried their dead under the eaves before (or outside) Christianity and still observe many taboos concerning this space (Barandiarán 2007, 81–82, 121–23). Since willies are dead souls, possibly the Balkan taboo has similar origins: Do not befoul the abode of the family dead.

while the vatafin administers sips of vinegar and sprinkles them with magical herb water, holding the flag over them as he says incantations. At a signal from him, the piper launches into the fastest and most sacred melody, *Florichika*, while "the rusaltsi simply fly in their dance, as if not stepping on the ground."[10] At a signal, the eldest rusalets strikes the pot with his staff. The pot shatters, spraying everyone, just as one to three of the rusaltsi fall down in a dead faint and the patient jumps up and starts to run around, healed.

They explained that if the illness was easy to dislodge, only one dancer fainted, but if the illness was bad, two or three had to fall. If no one faints, healing has failed.

The invalid cured, the vatafin must now attend to his fallen dancers, for if he leaves them unconscious too long, they will die. To revive them, he directs his remaining rusaltsi to dance the same dance *in the reverse direction* (the most efficient way to retrieve souls from the spirit realm*). As with the invalid, they use a rug to fling the unconscious men up, then they move them around while the vatafin administers water containing *different* herbs. The fallen come to, and all is finished.

❧

Curious and thorough, Marinov asked some of the healed patients and fallen dancers what they had felt. One patient said he felt limp and increasingly drowsy lying on the rug, until suddenly they flung him up. Awakened, he already felt better, and better still when the vatafin splashed him with vinegar and water. As the dancers jumped over him, his pain seemed to be lifted bit by bit. "And when the pot breaks, it's like someone tells me, 'Stand up and run!' and I jump up and run and feel as though I'm completely healthy. And I get well, and that's that."[11]

Some dancers got dizzy from the dance, others from being hypnotized by the vatafin. One kalushar Marinov interviewed, a villager named Opro, was the member of his band who fainted most often. Marinov describes him

---

*See chapter 3. Marinov (1914, 484) specifies that "reverse direction" was "from left to right," that is, counterclockwise or *widdershins*—against the sun, hence appropriate to the reversed spirit world (see Barber and Barber 2005, 164–75). The "normal" Rusalia dance was therefore clockwise, *sunwise*, traditionally the good, healthful direction—that is, moving to one's *left*. But to Christians, the *left* is the direction of the devil, so most European folkdances now move to the right (but see chapter 23). The Rusalia dances were viewed as pagan; the dancers were not to cross themselves during that week, nor enter a church.

as big and sturdy but very suggestible. The vatafin, it seems, chose sturdy members for fainting because they recovered better, and the weaker ones didn't stay hypnotized long enough. During the dance, he selected who was to fall with his eyes and actions. Opro described his sensations thus:

> When we go round the invalid, I feel like I'm becoming mesmerized bit by bit. When I approach the vatafin and sip from the vinegar and he stares me in the eyes, I get dizzy; when he hangs the flag over my eyes, I feel that everything gets dim . . . like when there's a mist. When we begin to go round the pot—already I remember nothing, not even what the vatafin does—as though someone were carrying me. When they hit and break the pot and it shatters and the water sprays out—then I go limp, my legs fail me, and I fall. After that I remember nothing.[12]

Why must someone faint? And why was this swoon so dangerous? The answer becomes clearer in another description of rusalii dancing, from a Vlach area in nearby eastern Serbia:

> at Whitsuntide male dancers with knives and yatagans [short sabers] used to perform a dance known as the *rusalj* over women who had previously fallen into a deep trance. The object of the dance was to bring the women back from their trance, in which, according to the local lore, they had been in contact with the departed.[13]

Loss of consciousness (whether in swoon, trance, sleep, or death) has been interpreted, worldwide, as the soul leaving the body for the intangible spirit world. After all, in dreams (and hallucinations, another form of "seeing") we can see and converse with people who may have died years ago. But recall that the rusalki were considered to be souls of girls dead before their time. To get these spirit maidens to undo the malady they had sent, someone must enter their world. If the rusalki aren't *very* angry—the illness isn't too bad— one messenger may suffice; otherwise, more must go.

Whatever their reasons for going, if the Serbian women and the rusaltsi have gone among the dead, they must receive immediate help to get back before being swallowed up forever. The life-giving dance, reversed to reach the spirit world more directly, retrieves them. The details follow quite logically from the initial premises about sickness and spirits.

Marinov published his compendium of Bulgarian customs in 1914, men-
tioning that fewer and fewer villages carried them out. By 1928, when
Marcu Beza briefly described the Romanian căluşari,[14] clearly the people
he observed were forgetting yet more of the original reasons for the details,
although preserving other antique traits.

These căluşari still had a leader, who, however, carried a sword; a different member carried the flag (with wormwood and garlic tied to it); another
wore a skin mask and bells and kept ritual silence; and a fourth carried a
sort of hobbyhorse (fig. 5.4): "a wooden horse's head borne by a dancer and
entirely or partly hidden under a kind of framework."[15] Beza remarks that by
his day the hobbyhorse was rare, although the name *căluşari* is usually taken
to come from Romanian *căl-uş* "little horse."* He adds:

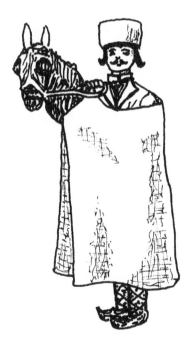

at a certain point the dancing turns into
acting. The leader touches with his sword
one of the dancers, who at once feigns
dizziness and falls down. All then gather
round and exchange remarks to show
that the dancer is dead. Accordingly they
take him away a short distance, . . . and
the dancing resumes when the supposed
dead man comes to life again.[16]

FIG. 5.4. Romanian *căluşar* with
hobbyhorse, 1920s.

---

*Beza (1928, 50) mentions that in "Macedonian Romanian"—i.e., Vlach—the hob-
byhorses are called *aluguciar*, the first part being borrowed from Modern Greek *álogo*
"horse" plus the Romanian diminutive suffix *-uciu*.

Here the earnest healing ritual and actual fainting of the Bulgarians have been lost; instead, we find it metamorphosed into the winter Resurrection play belonging to the cycle of Twelve Days. Also diluted, the rusalki have become the disgruntled ghosts of "three damsels at the court of Alexander the Great" who, when alive, "were not paid sufficient attention"![17] Yet the villagers still protected themselves with bunches of wormwood, lovage, and hedge hyssop, fearing that during Rusalia Week dangerous female spirits would "wander about, chiefly round the fountains and crossways, raise whirlwinds and sing to lure folk to their doom."[18]

These călușari—7, 9, or 11 in number—danced for nine days, beginning with meeting at a country crossroads or boundary junction.

> The leader then ties garters of bells to the ankles of each dancer. Then in a circle, whilst the leader sprinkles them with the water brought from . . . nine springs, they all pray to a certain Irodeasa, supposed to be their guardian goddess. Afterwards, during the dancing, whenever they are offered drinks, they empty their first glass out as a libation to this Irodeasa.[19]

Though some details have lost meaning, when compared with Bulgaria, different and clearly archaic details crop up in Romania: Irodeasa, and the horsehead or hobbyhorse (see chapters 9, 19). The rituals in the two areas have preserved different pieces of the original picture.

In the 1970s, Gail Kligman, an American researcher, joined Romanian ethnographers observing and recording the călușari rituals still practiced in southern Romania. Much resembled what Marinov saw, but some interesting differences draw our attention. Although the healing ritual occurred when needed, these Romanian călușari spent most of their time dancing in families' courtyards for fecundity, "luck," and good health. Unlike the spectacles reported by Beza, one dancer truly fainted at each of these performances, albeit very briefly—the dancers viewed this as a sort of rehearsal to give them courage for the much harder, longer fall during a curing.[20]

The leader, called by the old Romanian term *vătaf* "ritual speaker; authority" (see chapter 18), received his post from a retiring vătaf, who chose him for his courage, exceptional dance skills, etc.—the line was *not* hereditary—and taught him the secret magic charms for healing and for consecrating the flag, the other implements, and the group itself each year.[21]

Preparations for Rusalia Week began exactly halfway between Easter and Pentecost, on *Strod-ul Rusalii-lor* "half-Rusalii" (*strad-* is from Slavic *sred-* "middle"). On that day, as during Rusalii, work was taboo.[22] The men trained new members and prepared their special outfits—longtailed white shirts and pants (contrasting with the black worn by the villagers, for whom Rusalii involved commemoration of *all* dead family members, not just dead maidens[23]); a woven sash into which they tucked garlic and wormwood; black hats decorated with beads and ribbons; and in some areas ribbons crossing over the chest, with more ribbon ends hanging from the sash all the way around.* Their flat-soled leather sandals (see fig. 5.2) carried spurs and bells.

As Beza observed, at the start of Rusalia Week the călușari and their musicians met not in the leader's courtyard but outside the village—at a crossroads, mound, or edge of a marsh. (Note that all have associations with dead souls. The ancient Greeks already believed that spirits collected at crossroads; and mounds over burials became common in the Bronze Age, being henceforth, like water, a prime abode of spirits.) There they dug up the implements they had buried the year before: the flag and the *cioc*.

The *cioc* "beak" or *iepure* "rabbit" consisted of a rabbit skin on a stick, an object of powerful fertility magic with which a special member of the group, the *mŭt* "mute," chased women and inquisitive children. In some areas, the mute carried a large red phallus instead, stowing it under his shirt or apron until needed; in one case he had a wooden horsehead on a stick. Dressed in very grubby ordinary clothes, with a woman's apron or skirt over them and a fur or skin mask over his whole head, the mute ranked second after the vătaf but behaved like his reverse. The vătaf spoke serious orders; the mute carried on comic pantomimes, mocking the proceedings to the delight of the onlookers. The călușari danced fast and with agility; the mute danced slowly, bumbling, in the wrong direction—or, occasionally, performing the dance upside down (fig. 5.5)! Viewed as responsible for the members' welfare, the mute sequestered food for them and thwacked those who made mistakes dancing.[24]

---

*The strong resemblance of this costume (mostly linen) to the lappeted leather tunics of Roman legionnaires—who settled what is now Romania nearly 2,000 years ago and gave the country its name and language—was noticed and researched by Gary Larson some years ago (for a UCLA course project). The crossed ribbons and belled leggings also resemble those of English Morris dancers, Basque ritual dancers, etc. Marcu Beza's photographs, however, show that in 1928 not all such groups wore the ribbons.

FIG. 5.5. "Mute" *călușar* dancing upside down, hanging from staves of two fellow *călușari*. Mute typically does everything wrong or backward. *Călușari* from Frâncești, Vîlcea, Romania. Photo by Radu Răutu, courtesy of Gail Kligman.

The flag constituted the other most powerful object in the Romanian tradition. As in Bulgaria, its very shadow was viewed as lethally dangerous. One group complained that they had gone to a stadium to watch a match and some man "walked under the flag, and he began to yell. . . ." So they had to take him outside the stadium and dance a cure over him until he recovered and left.[25] Once dedicated, the flag and its pole always had to stand upright. If it tilted even slightly, the dancers would find it harder and harder to dance.[26] If it fell, in that instant the magic power of the călușari would cease and they might all die. Therefore, they designated a special person—*not* a călușar, often a boy— as flagbearer, to devote his entire attention to the welfare of the flag.

The vătaf created the "flag" by placing into a large white cloth a spear of green garlic and a sprig of wormwood for each member of the company, then drawing everything up into a bag and tying it to the top of the pole like a hobo's bindle, along with more garlic and wormwood and sometimes a flask of water.[27] After the vătaf charmed the flag with incantations, the dancers took their oath on it, although the rite's details varied. In one area, the men had to kneel along the shore with their hands in the water, holding garlic in their mouths to protect them from the water spirits[28] while the vătaf "said" the binding oath silently—actually a terrible curse should they break the rules. (Kligman reports that Romanian sorceresses also usually "said" their charms silently.)[29] In another area, each dancer sewed as many stitches into the flag as the number of years he bound himself to dance. (In Romania, they could touch the flag.) The dancers then ran off into the woods or tall grass.

> Meanwhile, the mute and vătaf raised the flag, at which point the musicians began to play. The călușari returned, greeted each other by shaking hands, and danced around the mute who held the flag. Their ritual silence [during the whole ceremony] was broken by their shouts that accompanied the dancing.[30]

The brotherhood now possessed the magic powers of Căluș.[31]

Just as the flag bound the group together initially, so at the end of Rusalii the group disbanded by unbinding the flag and making the flagpole fall. Each supported the pole equally with their staves, dropped them simultaneously so that no individual was responsible for the fall, and ran off into the woods as the pole toppled. Then they returned, greeting each other like long-lost friends—now merely fellow villagers.[32] From their point of view, they had not been normal humans while dancing Rusalii but instead, special messengers between their community and the spirits. Their particular rules of existence, intended to protect them while in limbo, set them apart from both their families and the church.

In the villages, the dancers went from house to house, dancing only in the courtyards (never inside the houses). The mute began by drawing a magic circle in the dirt around their flagpole. No one else could enter this arena; if they did, they had to back out immediately, exactly where they came in, or suffer possession by the spirits. The dancers showed off their virtuoso dances while the mute amused the crowd—bumping the women made them fertile; swatting the children made them healthy. Further interruptions included little skits joshing social, political, and sexual topics.

Eventually the vătaf caused one dancer to go into a trance and faint, using either the *cioc* or the flag. Dancers told Kligman the trance was real—that one of them had even sustained a concussion once when he fell—and that "the fall induced by the flag lasts longer, is stronger, and more painful than that resulting from the *cioc*."[33]

The onlookers joined in dancing a final village-style *hora* with the căluşari, during which the căluşari, if requested, danced over (or while carrying) the young children—so by magical contact they would grow up as robust as a căluşar. As the dancers departed for the next courtyard, the mute sold garlic and wormwood to the women if they wanted it, for healing during the coming year. If these plants were given or stolen, however, they lost their special Căluş powers.

When someone became "crazed by Căluş" (possessed by *Iele,* "Them") and needed healing, the vătaf first visited the patient with the musicians, who played each of the group's dances. Here, we learn, the vătaf paid careful attention to which melody affected the invalid the most, deducing thereby what sort of infraction had precipitated the illness: the melody *Cal* "horse" for working with horses or oxen; *Bîţi* "stick, club" for working with tools in field or vineyard, or for washing (laundry was pounded with pestles); *Chiser* "adze" for carving, splitting, breaking; and *Floricică* "little flower" for projects that grew and flowered (like building, painting, weaving).[34] Trances could be induced only during these four dances. (Apparently a "flowering" infraction precipitated the healing ceremony that Marinov witnessed, for he mentions only *Florichika*. Remember that most kinds of work were taboo on days special to the willies.)

Then the vătaf set out one to three new pots containing vinegar and garlic mixed with "unstarted water" (water drawn before anyone else got to the well/spring that morning) and placed a black chicken in each. ("Why not white ones?" asked the ethnologists. "Because it doesn't work with white," came the usual answer.)[35] The Romanian dance ritual over an invalid closely resembled the Bulgarian one, except that, at the climax, when a dancer passed out, the vătaf both shattered the pot and killed the chicken; if the chicken didn't die, the cure didn't work. At that moment, two căluşari stepped forward and hoisted the patient to his feet, supporting him as they ran him around. (He didn't have to jump up and run on his own, like Marinov's informant.)

In the Romanian view, the dancer who passed out took onto himself the sickness of the patient as he fell,[36] so only one dancer need faint, never more. Some also explained that because the dancers (excluding the lone, omnipotent vătaf) worked in pairs like twins, the moment a dancer fell, the patient immediately had to stand up *and occupy his place* to effect the desired transfer of illness from invalid to călușar.[37] Hence the requirement of an odd number in any călușari band.

Although chosen for his robust constitution and loaded with protective garlic and wormwood, the unconscious călușar had to be revived quickly—dragged back from the land of the dead—before Iele could overpower him completely. If the rite was successful, the illness stayed in the Other World. Sometimes, however, they had to repeat the entire rite three times (hence three pots and three chickens), or even more. Black chickens, as we'll see, have served as sacrifices to placate irritable spirits in many different situations throughout southern and eastern Europe.

Bands of călușari used to fight if they accidentally met. The winners would break the flagpole of the losers, thereby destroying the latter as a band.[38] Yet in the 1930s, groups began meeting on purpose, as dance competitors on stage, showing the world their prowess. By now, although competitive tempers may flare, little remains but the spectacular dancing.*

A dove is cooing, . . .
Sending a message, my sweet lamb,
To the lasses, . . .
At Rusalia, my sweet lamb,
On Wednesday and Friday . . .
Not to work, my sweet lamb,
Not to sew. . . .[39]

---

*The library of the English Folk Dance and Song Society in London contains 45 minutes of silent film of călușari dancing for abundance, taken in a Romanian village in 1935. The vătaf leads, the mute does his antics, the men circle single file counterclockwise, then dance in a line, paired by holding opposite corners of a white handkerchief; a călușar dances back and forth over various babies laid on the ground; plus a clip of making the flag. My warm thanks to Malcolm Taylor and the EFDSS for graciously sharing their resources.

Both the Lazarki and the rusaltsi/călușari formed tightly knit groups that, at least originally, danced through the village for well-being and "luck" in the community. Their very presence, people felt, brought abundance and health. But the rusaltsi/călușari also carried out intense healing rituals, full of magic and incantations, very different from anything the Lazarki do. Was the focused magical rite then the sole purview of men?

No. At times of epidemic it was women who performed the intense magic rituals to drive the sickness away, excluding men not just on principle but on pain of death. In Russia a century ago, widows and young girls gathered secretly in the dead of night, naked or wearing only their chemises, their hair hanging loose, to isolate the village from the infection by plowing a magic circle around it.

> The procession is opened by a young girl bearing an icon, surmounted by a candle; she is followed by another harnessed to a plough, which the other women push behind to help her. A third girl follows, cracking a whip without ceasing—this is to drive away the epidemic, personated by the devil.
>
> All are armed with pokers, brooms, and sticks [i.e., women's weapons]. They chant prayers in loud tones, and lower their voices in passing an *isba* [hut], so as not to be heard. Woe to the curious who would assist at this spectacle; if he is discovered he runs the risk of being torn to pieces.[40]

It was absolutely taboo for males to see the women's hair, the women in undress, and the ritual itself. Apparently the women concentrated their natural reproductive forces, by baring their "potent" bodies and hair, to overwhelm and cast out the sickness demons and to establish a boundary these demons could not cross. Just as the rusaltsi/călușari had to keep ritual silence at times, so the women in many areas maintained ritual silence during their ceremony.

Comparison of these traditional rituals suggests that *everyone* had responsibilities for promoting the well-being of the village and warding off sickness. But different situations were best handled by different classes of villagers. The willies send sickness and withering death; they also heal and bring abundant life. So when the willies have smitten someone with rusalka sickness, perhaps the men—willies love men—are the best emissaries, striving to make the willies content so they release their victim. The women had other powers and obligations. By coming to understand the one group, we learn more about the other.

꼭❈ꝋ

Women had charge of cooking and baking. On Wednesday of Rusalia Week, Mad Wednesday, in some parts of Bulgaria they got together to make new earthenware baking pans (*podnitsi*) for the bread, an act that needed special rituals if the pans—active participants in the act of baking—were going to treat well the bread so important to life.[41]

Each woman lugged her bag of clay to a secluded glade, flinging the clay together in a heap on the ground. Since they could not be seen there—the men knew enough to stay away, on pain of being trampled ruthlessly by the angry women—the women could now take off their shoes and stockings and knead the clay with their feet. For, once women reached puberty—became Lazarki—they could never again let any stranger or even their husbands see their legs bare. (In other regions, poverty overruled: women young and old went barefoot much of the year.)

To knead the wet clay, after hoeing it into a big round patch, they clutched each other to avoid slipping and danced the *rŭchenitsa* on it, singing appropriate songs to mark the beat. The rŭchenitsa is danced to a 7/8 rhythm, counted *short-short-**long*** (1-2, 3-4, 5-6-7), which invites two quick steps followed by a longer, heavier step. Many different rŭchenitsa dances exist. They can be done in long lines, alone, in pairs, or in sets of three, with a wide variety of steps ranging from simple to complex, but always with a feeling of emphasis or resolution on the last, longer beat. Likewise they might dance the *paidushko*—literally, "limping"—a 5/8 rhythm counted *short-**long*** (1-2, 3-4-5), landing heavily on the longer final beat as though the other foot hurt. In either case, how perfect for mashing clay—and a welcome release of pent-up tensions.*

During Rusalia week, women deemed too old for such things got to

---

*Western historians of music and dance such as Kurt Sachs formerly claimed 2/4 (march), 3/4 (waltz), and 4/4 (like the polka) as the only rhythms. But many other wonderful rhythms occur, and the Balkans are full of them, danceable in many ways. The *kalamatianós*, danced endlessly at Greek weddings, for instance, puts a long segment of 7/8 first (1-2-3, 4-5, 6-7), while the Irish slip jigs in *Riverdance* use a form of 9/8. India is full of such rhythms, and Dave Brubeck even used a 5/8 rhythm in *Take Five*. See chapter 23.

dance again "like a bride" while they kneaded the clay. Dance and sing like brides—like crazy rusalki during their special week. The rising frenzy of dancing and singing—many of the songs told of girls raped or betrayed—produced potent enough female magic for each woman to form a lump of the kneaded clay into an effective *podnitsa* for next year's baking, and in so doing protect herself from snakebites and dragons.[42] This was a day when men dared not stop what the women did, even if they killed: Mad Wednesday.*

✤

Women also traditionally maintained the relations with the family's dead. Early in the morning, at Rusalii and other feasts of the dead, women clad in black still visit the cemeteries with food offerings to lament the deceased. They may vocalize these often poetic laments for hours—a short lament would show lack of respect for the departed. The deceased kin provide the household's bridge to the world whence life comes; their good will is essential for protection, advice, and fertility. Farmers also felt that the return of dead spirits in the spring brought or caused the resurrection of the grain and the fruitfulness of animals and humans, and this recycling process reached its peak when the fields were sown, just before Rusalia Week. The unruly spirits often caused havoc, especially if they felt "dissed" or forgotten; undoing that harm required the most virile of men, the rusaltsi/călușari. But *communing* with the dead fell to women. In Serbia and Croatia, this aspect of the Rusalia season sometimes prevailed.

In eastern Serbia, at *Rusalje* on Trinity Sunday, the Vlachs living in a remote pastoral region in the Homolje Mountains "gather in an open space, eat, and listen while the priest prays for health and prosperity."[43] To this extent, the church has wrested the ritual from the pagans. Then, espe-

---

*Aleksieva and Ancheva (n.d., 42–43) tell of Shope women (along the Serbian/Bulgarian border) using this license to punish their own, by stoning village women who had broken the strongest taboos, such as getting pregnant out of wedlock.

Making pottery involved multiple links to the spirit world, since pottery comes from the application of Fire to Earth mixed with Water and produces something unlike any of its ingredients—a miraculous transformation. Toporkov (1987) collected many Russian superstitions about potting. (Anyone who has done hand potting knows that the pieces may come out of the kiln perfect, strangely deformed, or shattered, seemingly at the whim of some gremlin.)

cially in the village of Duboka, as the Sunday afternoon dancing begins, women start to fall into spontaneous trances, communing with the dead. In 1893, a bemused onlooker, a Serbian school teacher named Gligorić, remarks:

> By no sort of sign can you spot the woman who will fall. She might before this be dancing, sitting, standing, or engaged in some errand. When the unknown illness befalls, she merely trembles, and if standing, collapses onto the ground, but if sitting, she tumbles over, and with all her strength begins to knock on the ground with her feet and wave about her with her arms; her head and neck remain quiet, eyes shut as if sleeping, her chest rises unusually and her breathing speeds up. No voice comes out of her.

The women around her hold her down so she won't hurt herself before the healers arrive:

> At once three girls come, who are *kraljitse* [queens], and three strong young men, together with the *karabash* (bagpipe player).
>   The karabash at once begins to play music and the kraljitse lead a *kolo*-dance around the sick woman; the kolo-leader is a young man who holds in his hands a knife; beside him are two girls, and beside these again another young man, beside him a girl, and at the end a young man. [fig. 5.6].

The leader "makes a cross with his knife above the sick woman's chest" and they dance briefly—a sequence repeated three times. Then, as they carry her toward the river, he makes a cross on the ground; they lay her on it and dance around her three more times. Eventually, as they continue to dance, splash water with garlic and wormwood (now familiar as driving away spirits), and finally sing, the woman opens her eyes. They lift her up and dance with her. Although at first she appears groggy, she gradually gets her strength back.[44]

If, however, no kraljitse are available to heal her—as, for example, with a woman who "falls" but has married out of the village—she reportedly remains in a state of confusion and semi-insanity. Native women of this village apparently were liable to trance—sometimes every year—until

FIG. 5.6. Order of dancers who bring aid to women in trance on Trinity Sunday, Duboka, Serbia, according to 1893 source. (Compare figs. 17.4, 17.5.)

they reached menopause.* Our onlooker of 1893 remarks that he might see upwards of forty women "falling" on a given Trinity Sunday, "in good weather or bad."[45]

It is interesting that the mention of these dances in 1966 (by Kulišić, quoted earlier) refers to only male dancers "with knives and yatagans," whereas the 1893 description includes an equal number of women, the kraljitse. As we shall see, the Christian church has worked hard to push women out of the ancient dance rituals.

Elsewhere in the Yugoslav region, *kraljice* refers to groups of eight to ten girls of marriageable age who, also on Trinity Sunday, don their festive costumes plus a man's hat decorated with feathers and gold ducats, ribbons behind, a little mirror in front, and (in some areas) a diademlike crown on top. Then they make the rounds of the village houses, each carrying a beribboned sword (real or wooden) with fruit stuck on its point. A second group of girls, dressed in white with faces veiled, accompanies them to sing good wishes to the household while the first group dances. In Croatia, the Catholic Slavonians perform kraljice rites at Pentecost (or *Duhovi*—"souls'" day).[46]

Note the mirror worn above the kraljica's forehead. It clearly refers to the spirit world (which is why breaking a mirror is widely considered to bring bad luck), as does the tiny undressed doll above the forehead of Slovenian girls from the Croatian-Italian border, who also dressed all in white for this occasion and wore men's hats. The cloth that covered the hat and face carried little bells that jingled as these girls, too, danced for health and fertility. Visiting house after house in foursomes, they would perform three dances, inviting the housewife to join the fourth; then the men would join in. Afterward, the girls left in total silence. This ritual had shifted to Lent, although the white-veiled girls clearly derived from the willies feted during Rusalii.[47]

---

*George Kennan (1870/1903, 352–56) describes women in eastern Siberia spontaneously falling into trances, together with a rather different means to revive them.

As with the Lazarki, these rites constituted a sort of "coming out" of the young women now eligible for marriage, presenting the potential mothers of the next generation for all to see. And as the Lazarki use a pail of water to "sing the rings" and divine their marital prospects, so mirrors were and still are widely used to divine answers to the same key questions during the Rusalii holidays (see fig. 3.9). Reflective surfaces provide little windows on the world of the spirits, and who better to ask about marital prospects than the willies on their special days. Since water was the normal abode of these spirit maidens, it was into the rivers and lakes that Russian maidens cast their wreaths at the end of Rusalia Week to learn marriage-related answers— the very wreaths they had twined of birch and other magical plants on Semik to capture the burgeoning life force of the vegetation. So important was this rite that, around Smolensk, if a man happened upon the girls as they were carrying it out, they would grab him, drag him into the river, and dunk him, like a band of vengeful rusalki,[48] much as the Bulgarian girls had the right, without fear of retribution, to kill with firebrands any male intruders upon their spring mountaintop initiations.[49]*

For a short while, for "crazy week," women ruled indeed.

---

*"One time," a Smolensk woman told Dobrovol'skiy in 1908 (14), "we dunked a clerk and got some papers wet that he had in his breast-pocket. The clerk slapped a lawsuit on us, and after that we gave up dunking the men." Thus do urban habits kill rural ones.

CHAPTER 6

Flowers with Powers

Bitter as wormwood!
—popular expression

Here's rue for you, and some for me. . . .
—Ophelia, *Hamlet*, Act II

Garlic and wormwood we have seen used repeatedly to drive away willies, but dittany, roses, parsley, and birch were thought to attract them. Why? How did rural villagers view plants, to come up with these attributions? And what did the less familiar of these plants look like?

Botanists classify flora by genetic relations, using primarily the shapes and colors of leaves, stalks, flowers, and seeds to help identify species. Traditional observers, however, tend to classify vegetation by known uses and hazards, while identification may extend from shape and color to the smell, taste, or feel of a plant, or to any other noteworthy property. Thus, linguistic evidence shows that during the late Palaeolithic in the far north of Europe, people classified plants by such designations as "sticker-bush" for anything with painful barbs—whether thistle, nettle, or wild rose—and "fiber-plant" for those known to have usable fiber.[1] (We still sometimes lump things by use, referring to household "linens," whether made of linen, cotton, or polyester.) We've seen that birches got their reputation for life force by being the first tree in the cold North to bud out in the spring. Peasants also noticed that ferns, unlike other plants, never bore flowers; so they concluded that the fern must have a *magic* flower that blooms only for an instant.

91

Of all the qualities plants possess, however, the most startling is smell, since a plant can mysteriously announce its presence through invisible, intangible aromas. Now, human beings can make themselves neither invisible nor intangible, but spirits easily assume such attributes. So aromas seem an ideal calling card—or early warning—of willful spirits. And just as angels love sweet smells like roses and incense,* so evil demons will reek of sulfur, brimstone, and the like, and can be repelled by strong, not to say overpowering, smells.

Take garlic, which figures so prominently in keeping the rusalets dancers safe from the willies. Vampires too, as we all know from the movies, can be kept at bay with garlic. This tradition had a practical side. If your terrified comrades make you help dig up a corpse suspected of preying on the living, chewing on garlic will so overwhelm your smeller that you hardly notice the nauseating stench from the grave. But using garlic was more than "practical." It stemmed from a deep-seated folk belief in homeopathy—that like can be fought off with like, that the evil smell will itself combat the evil force. Thus, Bulgarian farmers used to eat most of a plate of garlic "for health" after Christmas dinner and then rub some in their armpits, so that during the upcoming year, should they encounter a sick person, they could ward off the sickness demon by passing one hand through their armpit and smelling it.[2]

The second plant so often used to repel willies is wormwood (fig. 6.1), which, although its scent is rather heavy, is most noticeably

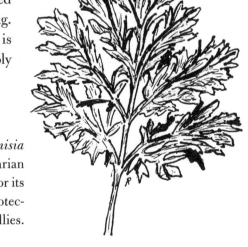

FIG. 6.1. Wormwood (*Artemisia absinthium*; Russian *polïn*, Bulgarian *pelinŭ*, Romanian *pelin*), known for its extreme bitterness and used as protection against willies.

---

*The movie *Michael*, starring John Travolta, tapped into this tradition. The women always recognize the archangel's presence from the delicious aroma of fresh-baked cookies he exudes. And showers of sweet roses serve God to drive the devil away from the dying Faust's soul, in Goethe's epic.

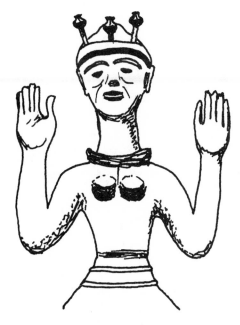

FIG. 6.2. Large Minoan clay statue with crown of poppy heads slit in manner used to extract opium. Gazi, Crete. Late Bronze Age, ca. 1200 BC.

bitter (vilely bitter, as I can attest). Despite their bitterness, plants with strong, bitter alkaloids have long attracted human attention, since they include both hallucinogens and preservatives. That wormwood had been noticed and singled out millennia ago is shown by the fact that its other English name, *absinth*, comes via Greek from the language of the Minoans of Crete, who died out soon after the end of the Bronze Age. (*Mint/ menth-* also carries a Minoan name.) These same Minoans, around 1200 BC, often represented a "goddess" with a crown of opium-poppy pods (fig. 6.2), while residues of marijuana and opium have been found in sacred vessels in the Merv Oasis of western Asia dating from as far back as 2000 BC.[3] Marinov mentions that wormwood grows both wild and domestic. The domestic variety (both green and dried) carried magical properties of protection, while the wild type is synonymous in Bulgarian with desolate places.[4]

Another bitter plant associated with the willies is hops (fig. 6.3), which brewers in central Europe seem to have begun using by the eighth or ninth century to flavor and preserve beer, drunk at the Rusalii festivals. In fact, the early evidence for using hops radiates outward from Bohemia, even today near the center of European beer-brewing districts. (Budweis and Plzeň— whence the names *Budweiser* and *Pilsner*—are Bohemian cities.) The hops vine itself became a symbol of verdant growth—little wonder, since it grows fast and produces little raspberry-shaped "fruits" by the thousands.

Other plants attract and please willies. Who wouldn't prefer parsley to wormwood, as the Ukrainian rusalki did? Or geranium, which the Bulgarians call *zdravets* (from *zdrav* "health") and which girls, dead or alive, liked

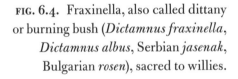

FIG. 6.3. Hops (*Humulus lupulus*), the traditional flavoring of European beer, showing leaves and small conical "fruits."

FIG. 6.4. Fraxinella, also called dittany or burning bush (*Dictamnus fraxinella*, *Dictamnus albus*, Serbian *jasenak*, Bulgarian *rosen*), sacred to willies.

to wear in their hair. Its leaves can have many sweet-smelling flavors, from lemon to rose to chocolate. Willies also love healing herbs, such as the fragrant willows surrounding their springs and streams. People believed willies caused certain illnesses, especially fevers and aching, but also provided means to cure them. Thus, some of the Balkan folk healers whom Phyllis Kemp studied in the 1930s knew to counteract fevers with tea from willow bark. Willow bark in fact contains the ingredient active in aspirin, a modern fever reducer. (In other cases, the information had degraded to "Willow cures fevers," and the practitioner merely rubbed the patient with willow boughs!)[5]

Another plant name associated with willies is dittany—although which plant it refers to depends on the locale. In Bulgaria and Serbia, the dittany in question is *Dictamnus albus* or *Dictamnus fraxinella* (fig. 6.4) of the rue family, which they call *rosen* or *jasenak*. It figured among the herbs we saw vatafins sewing into their flags. A native of southern Europe, growing in warm, damp, out-of-the-way meadows, *rosen* bears spikes of dark to light pink flowers and exudes a lemony scent.* But most mysteriously, it produces a volatile oil, the vapors of which, botanists say, "accumulate all round the plant, especially on hot, windless days. They may reach the point at which a lighted match, skillfully applied in the evening, gives rise to a swift, bright flame that leaves the plant itself quite unharmed."[6] Marinov described the plant thus, in the Bulgaria of 1914:

> *Rosen* is an herb/weed that doesn't grow everywhere, but only in special places in isolated areas. It is medicinal, but also has magical power. *Rosen* is a flower, many-leaved and dear to the rusalki, samovili, and samodivi, who gather it for Spasov [Ascension] Day, gathering bunches and binding wreaths of it, with which they adorn themselves throughout . . . Rusalska [Rusalia] Week.
>
> And formerly the girls, so as not to be harmed by dragons and samovili, gathered *rosen*, twined wreaths and made bouquets, which they wore themselves and gave also to their beloveds, especially to plowmen and shepherds, who go constantly through the fields where they may be attacked by dragons and samovili.[7]

In researching Balkan folk medicine seventy-five years ago, Kemp encountered dittany rituals repeatedly:

> In Bulgaria at the feast of the *Rusalje* or *Samovile, Vile*—the date varies, but Ascension Day will do as an example—on the eve of the feast a person suffering from a *vila* disease went to a field near water where the *Vila's* plant—*Rosen*, dittany—grew, with someone of the opposite sex, who was willing to become a brother or sister. An offering of food and wine was made, and one of the flowers was balanced over a new vessel of unbroken water,† beside which the sick person lay down and slept while the other watched. After one o'clock the flowers were supposed to fade, and the watcher covered the pot with a new cloth. The next morning before dawn the position of the flower was inspected to

---

* It belongs to the family *Rutaceae*, which includes citrus. Rue, also in this family, is remarkably appropriate for Ophelia, who, willylike, drowns herself unwed.

† "Unbroken water" is water collected before anyone else reaches the well in the morning. It is used for many rituals, such as "singing the rings."

see whether it had been visited by the spirit and the sick person drank the water with anything that had fallen into it overnight.[8]

Or the patient ate, baked into bread, any bugs found under the pitcher, on the assumption that vily had put them there as medicine.[9] As to Serbia, Kemp relates:

> In Srem, on Ascension Day, the sick slept in a field where dittany (*jasenak*) grew, bread, water, and wine being placed beside them. The next day, any insect found under the roots of the plant was given to them as a medicine.[10]

The word *dittany* comes from Greek *diktamnos*, an adjective referring to Dikte, a mountain on Crete apparently sacred in Minoan times and home to another dittany, a highly fragrant type of oregano (fig. 6.5) much sought in Venetian times as a miraculous restorer of health. It was even touted in the 1560s as driving off venomous beasts and curing "goats stricken with arrows."[11]

FIG. 6.5. Cretan dittany (*Origanum diktamnus*), a fuzzy-leafed and potent relative of common oregano, here growing on Mt. Ida, Crete.

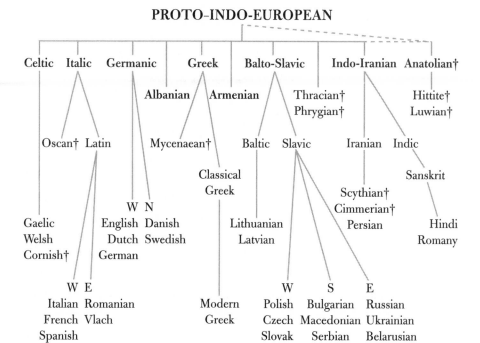

TABLE 6: INDO-EUROPEAN LANGUAGE FAMILY
Simplified version—some languages and one family omitted. Major families
boldface; extinct branches marked †. Modern languages listed in groups
rather than by subbranches. Linguists debate whether Anatolian, though
clearly related, is daughter or sister of Indo-European.

Rosen, however, may come etymologically from the Slavic term for
"dew," like *rusalka* (see below), or from the same word as *rose*, another pink
flower associated with willies.

Our word *rose* we borrowed from the Latin designation, *rosa*, related to
the plant's ancient Greek name, *rhodon* (whence flower names like *rhodo-
dendron*). Greek and Latin, like English, Russian, and many other tongues,
evolved from an earlier language known to linguists, for lack of its original
name, as proto–Indo-European (table 6). But whereas many words (like
English *three*, Russian *tri*, Latin *tria*, Greek *tría*) descend from proto-
Indo-European, *rosa* and *rhodon* do not. They seem instead to have been
borrowed from the local languages when the ancestral speakers of Greek
and Latin first reached the Mediterranean lands during the Bronze Age.

To receive a special name so early, roses must have been culturally important. It seems no accident that Bulgaria still ranks as one of the world's greatest producers of attar of roses, a fragrant liquid simmered down from the rose petals of whole valleys of rosebushes. How could the glorious fragrance of amassed roses *not* herald the presence of divinity, especially of flower-loving spirit girls who had died before their time? The rosebushes themselves, like blackthorns and willows, might receive offerings and prayers from people anxious to influence the associated spirits.[12] In the Homolje Mountains of Serbia, an endangered person could ritually "shift" death to a chosen animal, then kill the animal and bury it under a rosebush for the rampaging vila to take instead.[13] A sick person or sickly child might also shed their illness by creeping between two close-set magical bushes, such as rose, blackberry, or thorn, tied together at the top to form a hoop.[14]*

To the Romans in Italy, roses also became important, especially when tending the dead at a May festival called the *Rosalia*. Many have assumed, in fact, that this Latin *Rosalia* is the origin of Slavic *Rusalii* and *Rusalia*, the spring festival we have examined. But both the details of the Roman festival, utterly different from the Slavic one, and the rules of sound change in Slavic, show this not to be so. The words *Rusalii* and the related *rusalki* must originate in a Slavic word for water, riverbeds, and dew, *rus-/ros-*,[15] probably merely being influenced later by the Latin festival name *Rosalia*.

We must remember that the "fertility" cult of the willies centers on bringing and controlling the divine moisture that will make the crops and other plants grow. If willows flourish around the springs, their unforgettable fragrance, their medicinal value, and their fat early buds that we call pussy-willows signal the presence and powers of the willies. In the far north, the birches that leaf out well ahead of other trees likewise mark the presence and magical life forces of the willies. If the flax and hemp plants require lots of water for women to grow, ret, and spin them, this too connects them to the rusalki with their streaming wet hair. Useless weeds and useful herbs, the willies fostered them all.

---

*Kemp mentions medicinal hoops made of cut and split stalks of rose, willow, or nettle (95). Note also the herbal wreaths described in chapter 7.

CHAPTER 7

Midsummer Rusalii

> Enjovden [(St.) John's Day, June 24] marked the summer
> solstice, with the sun reaching the farthest point on its
> journey. As the sun forgot which way to go, his sister, the
> Morning Star, pointed the right way. Before he started on the
> return journey, the sun took a bath. People were therefore
> urged to bathe on this particular day . . . , a day on which
> even bears are said to bathe.
>
> —Bulgarian tradition[1]

The eve of Midsummer must have seemed spooky. Everywhere in the fields and forests, women, girls, and sorcerers were sneaking about, trying to remain unseen as they collected magical and medicinal plants. People thought these herbs had more potency when collected during that night—in fact, some plants might not just lack curative power but even turn from good to evil if culled at another time.

Likewise the Midsummer dew held magic—water is a spirit medium—especially for rejuvenating skin and healing eyes;[2] so people with rags around their feet shuffled through the long grass to sop up the dew, wringing it out into a vial and shuffling for more.[3]

During that night, too, occasional desperate men would brave the woods in hopes of finding the elusive fern flower. Legend had it that the fern flowered once a year, producing a blindingly beautiful red blossom for an instant at midnight on Midsummer's Eve, and if one could find and pluck this flower during that moment, it would reveal the location of buried treasure. According to some, it would also protect the bearer from demons, but according to others, so many greedy demons surrounded the fern flower as it bloomed that snatching it was virtually impossible. For spirits, too, were out in force all night, and even for those who stayed home in bed, Midsummer Night's dreams were special, as English lore suggested to Shakespeare. Many people even held them as prophetic.[4]*

At dawn, however, one might have the luck to see the sun dance again as it rose, refreshed from bathing in the "living waters" while it rested.[5] (During the solstice, the sun appears to stand still for several days.) The church called the day St. John's Day, after John the Baptist, but Russians called it Ivan Kupalo—John the Bather—and jumped naked into the nearest lake or stream for a ritual bath. In 1914, the tireless Bulgarian ethnographer Marinov ruefully described the Bulgarian attitude thus:

> As I studied the life of the populace, I met with one very sad fact, namely that our villager, and our townsman too, very unwillingly betakes himself to a bath; he bathes unwillingly. His body sees water only when it is little. . . . [But] on Enyovden [(St.) John's Day], he bathes it like a bridegroom.[6]

This dunking, for protection against illness throughout the coming year, took place early in the morning, often at sunrise, either at the river or at springs that flowed only then—with water that the Sun Spirit had made potent and sent specially.[7] Similar ideas occur widely across Europe. Thus, for example, the Portuguese say that "one bath on St. John's Night is worth a month of cure."[8] As the sun rose in Belarus, people sang:

> *Iván and Márya*
> *Bathed on the hill:*
> *Where Iván bathed*
> *The bank shook;*
> *Where Márya bathed,*
> *The grass sprouted.*[9]

---

*The legendary demons of St. John's Night inspired Modest Mussorgsky's famous composition *Night on Bald Mountain*. At the end, the serene tolling of the church bell at dawn sends them packing.

Marya (Maria/Mary) here has the powers of a willy or of Mother Earth, while Ivan (John) those of the ancient god of thunderstorms. The song, like the occasion, is cosmic, and the ancient calendars marked the summer solstice with not one but two Xs.

⟨∞⟩

The women and girls, who did most of the healing all year, brought their baskets of herbs home at dawn, preferably culled untouched by iron and with the magical dew still on them. In the seventeenth century, the Russian tsar Aleksey Mikhaylovich even gave out special instructions for collecting his St. John's Day herbs.[10] In Bulgaria, women made these plants into a bouquet that they hung in the house or under the eaves. They might also make a giant wreath from the plants and ceremonially climb through it "for health."[11] This wreath, too, they hung up for future use. According to a Bulgarian folk theory, seventy-seven and a half illnesses exist, of which seventy-seven correspond to some remedial herb, but the "half" has no cure. If, during the year, man or beast came down with an unknown malady, a healer pinched off a few herbs and either laid them on the patient or infused them into a beverage.[12] Herbs from the wreath especially benefited women in childbirth.[13] The Russians of Siberia, however, searched out a mere twelve herbs, not seventy-seven.[14]

In mountainous parts of southern Bulgaria and eastern Thrace, the girls then commenced another agrarian ritual, called "Enyo's Bride." They had previously selected a beautiful little girl, three to five years old, who had to be *iztrŭsŭk*—defined as "the last born of her parents, and her parents must be living and also in their first marriage."[15] In other words, she had to be ritually propitious and unblemished. Going to her house on Enyo's Day, four chosen girls called "carriers" dressed her in special ritual clothes: first, a grown woman's chemise (a long-sleeved white tunic), often a bride's; then outer garments, bridal ornaments, and always a transparent veil—usually red like a bride's, occasionally white. Girls who had married during that year gladly lent their ornaments, since this would bring them good luck. As they dressed the child, they always sat her on their skirts, since, should her feet touch the ground or even the rug, they would scorch it, as willies' feet sometimes do.[16]

The four girls then took turns carrying her on their shoulders, while all the other village girls followed in pairs. While the rest circled the house three times singing, the girl carrying Enyo's Bride started into the road, followed by the other three carriers and the remaining girls. Dancing the horo and singing, the procession began to tour the village and its environs, starting to the east. All the while, the little Bride, her arms and hands completely enveloped in linen, would "wave the long sleeves of her shirt like a bird with wings."[17] Hearing them approach, women would run out and lay their freshly collected medicinal herbs on the path, in full belief that their efficacy would increase even more if the girls stepped over them as they danced.[18] St. John's Day concerned health.

The procession went around the village, stopping at every spring and well to dance the horo and sing, blessing with their actions the water sources, homes of the willies. At a crossroads, the girl carrying Enyo's Bride could sit and rest, with the little girl carefully placed on her skirts, while the others sang and danced around them. Then another of the four carriers might take up the burden to continue.

At the river, two carriers crossed over, leaving two carriers and Enyo's Bride on the near shore. The girls on the far side then asked, "Will the year be plentiful?" and the little Bride answered softly whatever came into her head, yes or no. If the answer was "plentiful," the girls called out loudly, "Listen! The year will be plentiful!" Now the girls asked in turn, "Will there be wheat? Barley? Wine? Millet? Sesame?" and so on, whatever they grew in the region, and to each question the child would answer yes or no. Marinov adds that people believed implicitly in these random predictions that Enyo's Bride delivered, viewing her as a faithful "channel" directly from God. St. John's Day also concerned abundance.[19]

After circumambulating the village, grain fields, vineyards, and pastures, they returned to the little girl's house, circled it again, then entered. The carriers sat on the bed with the Bride on their skirts, and everyone sang a ballad such as the following, which reveals much about girls' lives in the villages:

> *Smallpox became notorious,*
> *The great ugly-maker.*
> *As we hear, it came to the village,*
> *To Ena's, where it settled in.*
> *It struck down all the maidens,*
> *All fifteen maidens,*
> *Along with slender Ena sixteenth,*
> *Struck them down; then they stopped aching.*

But slender Ena did not stop aching,
Did not stop aching, did not recover:
In her two eyes she got blind,
In her two ears she got deaf.
Ena's mother said to her:
"O Ena, Ena, my daughter,
How you have become ill, bedridden;
It would have been better had you died.
I would have stopped aching for you,
Stopped aching, stopped mourning."
Slender Ena replied,
"Dear Mary, my old mother,
If I am a bother to you,
Am a bother and make you tired,
Get up early on Sunday,
Change my clothes, adorn me,
Tie around me a red scarf,
Throw over me a light veil,
Take me by the hand,
Lead me to the horo.
So I can either die or begin to see,
To look upon my beloved—
With which maiden he chats
And which gives him her nosegay."
Ena's mother listened to Ena,
Got up early on Sunday,
Changed her clothes, adorned her,
Tied around her a red scarf,
Threw over her a light veil,
Took her by the hand,
Led her to the horo,
So that she could die or start seeing.
But slender Ena did not die:
Her two eyes saw again,
And her two ears heard again.
She saw her beloved—
With which maiden he chatted

And which one gave him her nosegay:
Young Rada gave him her nosegay.
Her beloved did not look at it,
But quickly ran to Ena
And with Ena he began to converse.[20]

Songs about smallpox or other serious diseases had, in fact, great relevance to the ritual of Enyo's Bride, through which villagers sought to ward off such diseases from themselves, as well as evils like hail from all those fields and vineyards that the girls—the ritually potent maidens—had visited. As on Lazarus Day, the maidens also brought general "luck" and abundance.[21]

After completing the ritual by re-dressing the little girl in her original clothes, the older girls "sang the rings" as they had at New Year, Lazarus Day, and St. George's Day, to predict their future husbands. The child playing Enyo's Bride pulled their tokens from the water for them.[22] By 1914, however, according to Marinov, this custom had become more a game of clever improvisation of verses than serious divination.[23]

❧

Meanwhile, the men and boys brought loads of brushwood for the Midsummer bonfire, for in most of eastern Europe and the Balkan Peninsula, people made a point of jumping over the St. John's Day fire to ensure health during the coming year (fig. 7.1). A Russian description from 1896 says that people jumped through the fire (another spirit medium) to "protect themselves in advance from illness, malevolent spirits,

FIG. 7.1. Boy jumping over bonfire in Greece on St. John's Night (June 23–24), for health and abundance in the coming year.

and sorcerers."[24] Fire purified. In Bulgaria, the jump could also involve love. If a girl and boy, holding hands, managed to jump through the fire without losing hold of each other, they were viewed as all but married.[25] In general, however, people had two main purposes in fire-jumping. Purification for spiritual and bodily health was first (and if the flames also killed the fleas, so much the better). Second, the higher you jumped the higher the crops would grow, just as with swinging on St. George's Day.[26] In Belarus, women would throw birch boughs into the flames, saying, "May my flax be as tall as this bough!"[27] After the youngsters had leapt the flames, the oldsters hurried through the smoke of the dying embers and handed the babies across. Then they drove the cattle through the smoldering patch for *their* health.[28]

This bonfire, however, like that against epidemics, had to be started with "new" fire, magic fire, fire started by rubbing two sticks of wood together in the ancient way.[29]

Much of Europe knows the Midsummer bonfire—Britain, Denmark, Germany, France, Spain, Portugal, etc. In fact, the word *bonfire* comes from the habit in parts of England of lighting a great heap of dry bones on the occasion—literally, a *bone-fire*. The Basques, living in the remote Pyrenees, traditionally lit two types of fires, separating out the mingled purposes of the eastern European conflagration. To help the sun, they "make a bonfire in front of each house or at a crossroads. The inhabitants form a line and walk single file clockwise [sunwise] around the fire. . . ." They also burn "sheaves of straw in cultivated fields in the hope that such combustion will cause the burning of the enemies of the crops planted there." To help the fire drive out evils, they sing:

> *On our property no thieves,*
> *If there are any, let them be burned,*
> *Let the wild beasts, the toads, the snakes be burned, burned,*
> *And the harmful pests be burned, burned.*[30]

The Basques, too, bathed on Midsummer for yearlong health.[31]

Throughout Russia, Belarus, and Ukraine, water and fire, the basic elements of the spirit world, might be combined variously to the same end. Some burned a special tree, others cut it down and drowned it, still others set up an effigy beneath a chosen tree—usually a huge one—and burned or drowned the effigy. Or the effigy or a small tree was shredded and strewn about the kitchen gardens.[32] These effigies received the name Kupalo, Kostroma (Ukrainian Kostrubonka), or Yarilo—often assumed to be the names of some bygone pagan Slavic deity. Like the effigies of Gherman or Caloian, the villagers destroyed them with as much laughter as mock mourning. Channel the god's life force into the vegetation—then kill so that life may rise renewed.[33]

Shortly before St. John's Day—sooner or later, depending on when Easter fell—the willies' spring holiday ended. Since the week before Pentecost, they had run riot, dancing in the fields and swinging in the forests and scaring everybody, but now they had to settle down. Farewell to the Rusalki occurred either the day before or the day on which St. Peter's Fast began (the second Monday after Pentecost, itself the fiftieth day after Easter), shortly before St. Peter's Day.*

The Russian Farewell to the Rusalki often started with the village girls choosing one of their number—usually a tall beauty—to impersonate a rusalka. In the province of Zaraysk, with her hair loose (a sign of fertility) and wearing a long chemise, she led a procession of women and children out of the village to the rye fields. The women pounded on frying pans (noise to chase spirits) while the kids teased her, daring her to tickle them like a proper rusalka. On reaching the rye fields, the "rusalka" would try to grab and tickle someone while others tried to prevent her. During the scuffle, she would escape into the tall rye and hide there. At this point, people would shout that they had escorted the rusalki home again and now they could go anywhere they wanted without fear. No more did they need wormwood and a companion just to fetch water! After the crowd dispersed, the "rusalka" would sneak back to the village unseen.[34]

In Mogilyov (Belarus), the ritual differed slightly. All the girls wore white, let their hair down, and wore newly made wreaths; the chosen "rusalka" they decorated with ribbons and flowers. With her in the lead,

---

* So if Easter was late, the Farewell to the Rusalki came nearly at Midsummer. Ralston (1872/1970, 142) says, "After St. Peter's Day, June 29, the Rusalkas dance by night beneath the moon, and in Little Russia and nearby Galicia, where Rusalkas . . . have danced, circles of darker, and of richer grass are found in the fields."

they filed through the village two by two, holding hands. As they went, the first couple made an arch while the rest passed through; then the new leading couple made an arch, and so on, over and over, until they reached the fields.[35] The whole way they sang, one verse going thus:

> *I will lead the rusalki*
> *Into the green rye;*
> *There in the green rye*
> *The rusalki were sitting.*
> *Ah, my little grain-spikes,*
> *Like little trees [you are] . . . :*
> *In the oven we'll have pastries,*
> *On the table we'll have loaves.*[36]

Reaching the fields, they made fires and jumped over them, just as on St. John's Day, while the rusalka impersonator tried to catch and tickle the young men as they arrived for the fun.

The continuous arch resembles not only the arches made from birch trees at Semik but also an old game called "bringing the grain-spike" in the Russian province of Vladimir, in which a little girl walks slowly forward on the linked hands of couples while they sing:

> *The grain-spike went to the field,*
> *To the white wheat!*
> *All summer may it grow—*
> *The rye with the oats, the buckwheat,*
> *And the wheat.*[37]

Once she has passed, they run around and relink at the front of the line, so that she progresses without ever touching the ground all the way to a rye field. There she grabs a handful of rye, runs off, and places it at the church.[38]

Other versions involved dolls. The older women of Saratov, Russia, made an effigy from a sheaf of rye, dressed it like a woman, and carried this "rusalka" to the rye fields, where they buried it. In Ryazan', groups of dancers led khorovodï, each group with its own rusalka doll. Others would struggle to snatch the doll. Upon succeeding, they rushed out to the fields, scattered pieces of the effigy all about, then returned loudly "mourning" the rusalki. In some areas, a similar doll called Kostroma (meaning "beard of grain") was buried in or beside a field.[39] One way or another, the willies no longer held danger for humans.

◦◦◦

With a final push to the crops at Midsummer, the willies have now finished their work: the grain and hay have grown and ripened and await harvesting. All that remains is to reap what the Dancing Goddesses have created. Cohorts of young people go out all day to mow the hay, all the while chanting slow, rhythmic, antiphonal songs to time the long swings of the sharp scythes, until the movement becomes almost a dance and the sound dulls the senses of time and fatigue—a scene memorably captured, apparently from direct experience, by Leo Tolstoy in *Anna Karenina*. Then everyone harvests the grain. The reapers carefully cut and bind the first sheaf and give it as an offering of "first fruits" to God or the gods, taking it either to the church or to the mistress of the farm, since the farmhouse was the old religious center (where, to hedge their bets, the farmers added Christian icons to the "sacred corner"). Then the teams cut, bind, and store the remaining grain, until they approach the end of the last field.

But this again requires care, for now the reapers feel they have driven the "spirit of the grain" into a corner, and if they anger her, there will be no harvest next year. What to do? All over Europe, from Russia and the Balkans to Ireland, the last sheaf has traditionally been made into some sort of corn dolly (fig. 7.2), whether by twisting a few stalks into a human shape or dressing the whole sheaf in human clothes. But who will take the responsibility of cutting these last stalks? In Ireland and ancient Greece, people reasoned that it is the *blade*, not the person, who actually kills the deity—especially if no one is touching the blade when it cuts. In the Irish case, therefore,

> the reapers stood back and each one in turn cast his reaping hook at the standing sheaf of corn in an effort to cut it. When, finally, one of the reapers succeeded in cutting the last sheaf—the *Cailleach* or old woman representing the corn [grain] crop just harvested—the sheaf was taken home and placed around the neck of the farmer's wife during the harvest supper. Later it was hung up in the kitchen. In some cases, it was left there until the next harvest, but otherwise the grain was rubbed off and mixed with the seed being sown in the springtime. . . . In this way, the continuous cycle of the death and resurrection

FIG. 7.2. Corn dollies or beards, traditionally fashioned from the last stalks of grain harvested. Left: English. Right: Bulgarian.

of the corn was shown. . . . [An old] photograph shows the reapers throwing their reaping hooks at the *Cailleach*. In this picture they are not blindfolded, as was sometimes the case, as a reaper might feel reluctant to be the one to kill the goddess. But it had to be done, for, "unless a wheat grain falls on the ground and dies, it remains only a single grain; but if it dies it yields a rich harvest" (John 12:24).[40]

Now the willies can rest—no need to bother them while people gather the ripened crops. Thus the notion of "thanksgiving" celebrations for harvest home does not form part of the rituals where the willies live. They have done their job, and throughout the fall there will be no more festivals importuning them for help until time to ready the fields for the next year's crops—unless perhaps to ask them, once again, whom one will marry. But there was always one willylike divine spirit on call, no matter what the season: St. Friday.

CHAPTER 8

Friday, St. Friday

Friday's child is loving and giving;
Saturday's child must work for a living.

—old nursery rhyme

Friday belonged to the willies, who, while addressing women's concerns, enforced strong taboos on their sacred day.

We have seen that willies typically wanted clothes. In northern Russia, they would either steal them or sneak at night into the bathhouses, where the women had left half-worked flax or hemp, and try to spin thread to weave into shirts, making a tangled mess.[1] Or they would beg a passerby for any old cast-off shirt—if you didn't throw them *some* bit of clothing, you risked your life.[2] In other parts of Russia, they enjoyed spinning and washing linen,[3] while in Greece the willies spun and wove marvelously well, arraying themselves in beautiful white gowns with golden trimmings.[4] Because of the willies' connections to spinning and laundering, these activities were taboo on Fridays.

It wasn't all bad: women needed a rest, and divine wrath gave them an unassailable reason to take it.

People who buy their clothes readymade off a rack are mostly unaware of the amounts or even types of labor that go into making garments of fiber. From the Bronze Age until the Industrial Revolution, however, making cloth and clothing required more than half of everyone's labor—more even than providing food. And making cloth was women's work. Of the

FIG. 8.1. Bosnian women in 1980s, spinning or knitting while herding sheep in the high pastures and singing antiphonally with other shepherdesses so that both women and sheep know where everyone is.

hours spent, spinning thread gobbled up the majority, for it took several hours to spin on a hand spindle what one could weave in an hour on even a simple loom. Treadle-operated spinning wheels, which entered Europe in the Middle Ages, sped the process by a factor of four, but spinning still created a bottleneck; and in southern Europe, where women customarily spun while doing other jobs, the spinning wheel never caught on because women couldn't carry it around with them (figs. 8.1, 8.2). Even in 1962, while living in rural Greece, I often saw women and girls spinning while herding sheep or riding a donkey to a neighboring village—a remarkable feat of dexterity. They lengthened their new yarn until the whirling spindle *almost* reached the roadway, then gave an expert flick that made the spindle climb the thread like a yoyo right into their hand. Then they started spinning anew.

Russian farm women also continued to use hand spindles instead of wheels, but probably out of poverty, since a spindle consists merely of a stick equipped with a flywheel (spindle whorl) formed, if need be, from a pierced potsherd or apple. For them, spinning started in the fall when outdoor chores eased off and days became cold and dark, as we see in the Russian fairy tale "Vasilisa the Beautiful":

> Fall came. The stepmother gave out evening work to all three girls: she obliged one to plait lace, another to knit stockings, but Vasilisa to spin—to each their tasks. She extinguished the fires throughout the house, leaving only a single candle where the girls were working, and went to bed.[5]

FIG. 8.2. Village woman who ran bus kiosk in Kalambaka, Greece, while tending daughter and spinning. Here she takes time out to teach author to spin, August 1962.

Although the stepmother has (of course) evil intent, forcing Vasilisa to go to the ferocious witch Baba Yaga to get a light when one of the stepsisters "accidentally" puts out the only candle, the cold, dark picture finds echoes in the 1913 account by a Western traveler:

> It is almost beyond comprehension how a Russian woman can possibly fulfil all her duties.
>
> Besides field-work, she has the care and feeding of the family, all the cleaning and clothing of it. The husband has nothing to do with that. If the work in the summer is hard, in the winter he can do what he likes, but the woman finds no moment's recreation. If there are two or three women in the house, they take the work by turns, but where there is only one, her work is harder than a convict's. She has a piece of ground and sows hemp-seed. She must spin and weave and bleach to clothe the family. She also keeps some sheep at the farm. The wool and skin are used for clothing. What happens if the hemp burns out or the sheep die? That is her affair. She is worried and goes on spinning while the others sleep, by the evil-smelling lamp light; or if her husband allows her no oil, in the dark by touch: it is everything to her to

have enough linen for the family. Any woman buying linen instead of spinning it herself, would be an object of ridicule!

No matter if the woman be well or ill, her work must be done. She lies up for two or three days at most when her children are born. Every one is against her then, not only the men, but the women also. Customs are very cruel. . . .

Fires are frequent, and it is not a rare occurrence for everything to be burnt; or if the husband be a drunkard it sometimes happens that in his fury he tears up the linen. All must be done over again: the husband seldom helps. Indeed it is no exaggeration when we say that one of the worst things in Russian peasant life is the low estimation in which women are held. . . . The woman is certainly not the beloved companion, but the servant of her husband. And when he won her hand, her charms had less to do with it than the certainty that she was a strong and right good worker.[6]

No wonder women looked forward to—and perhaps, long ago, even set up—periodic festivals sacred to the willies that contained strict taboos against working. In this way, at least, the willies did give to the women who honored them some strength to go on.

⟨∞⟩

It is remarkable that in western Europe, too, Friday related historically to women's work. *Friday*, after all, was literally "Freya's day," and Freya (Freyja) was the old northern goddess of love and fertility, of women's crafts (like spinning) and other female concerns. Similarly in southwestern Europe, Friday once belonged to Venus, Roman goddess of love and fertility: Latin *dies Veneris* "day of Venus," giving Italian *venerdì*, French *vendredi*. Venus corresponded to the Greek goddess of love and fertility, Aphrodite, who, like the Three Fates (*Moîrai*), magically created life by spinning:

> Why should the goddess of love and procreation be a spinner? For the same reason, ultimately, that the Moirai who attend the birth are spinning [a thread of destiny]. Something new is coming into being where before there was at most an amorphous mass. Listen to the description of a naïve onlooker; the scene happens to be laid in Africa:

"The woman . . . took a few handfuls of goats' hair and beat them with a whippy stick so that the hairs became separated. Then, taking a stiff piece of dried grass stem in her right hand she twisted some hair round it and continued to twist, while a thread as if by magic grew out of the mass of hair continually fed into it by her left hand."[7]

Such is the creational magic of spinning. The Greeks, however, do not call Friday after Aphrodite but rather *paraskeví* (*paraskeuĕ*) "preparation"—that is, the day for preparing for the Sabbath—a Jewish (and very early Christian) concept. Yet even the eastern European farm folk, from southern Greece to northern Russia, honor Friday as a day related to women's concerns. How did this happen?

The notion of the seven-day week seems to have started in the ancient Near East, when the Assyrians captured the Jews and removed them to Babylon in the sixth century BC. Their temple destroyed, the Children of Israel clung together in exile by making every seventh day one of rest and of meeting, in commemoration of their belief that God rested on the seventh day after creating the world. They called this day *shabbath* "Sabbath," apparently from a verb *sh-b-th* "cease from labor," and called the interval *shavu'a* "week," from the number *sheva* "seven."[8] The practice found reinforcement in an Assyrian custom, documented already from the seventh century BC, of viewing the 7th, 14th, 21st, and 28th days of the 29 1/2-day *lunar* month as inauspicious, hence bad days to do any work.[9] But by resting *every* seventh day, the Jews divorced their "week" from the irregularities of the moon, making it an evenly recurrent cycle.[10]

The next step seems to have come from a confluence of Greek and Egyptian notions with the Mesopotamian fixation on astrological prediction. Very early, the Egyptians had divided the day into twenty-four hours.[11] The Mesopotamians, for their part, reckoned the movable celestial bodies as seven—sun, moon, and five visible planets—and believed that these ruled the events of the world hour by hour in succession.* To examine this influence was thus to make a *horo-scope* (literally, "hour inspection").

---

* The specialness of the number 7 was not, however, purely astronomical. Since at least the fourth millennium BC, the Mesopotamians had considered 6 a magical number because of its flexible mathematical properties (1+2+3=6, 1×2×3=6); but the next number, 7, a prime, was so balky that they called it the number that "doesn't compute"—a divinely obstinate

After Alexander the Great's conquests brought Mesopotamian astronomy to the Greeks, Greek savants habitually arranged the seven movable bodies according to the observable lengths of their cycles. From longest to shortest, these are: *Saturn—Jupiter—Mars—Sun* (*Earth*, actually, but they didn't know that yet)—*Venus—Mercury—Moon*. Horoscope-casters then took to distributing these seven divine bodies *in that order* across all 168 hours of the seven-day week. Thus, the first hour of the first day is Saturn's, the second hour Jupiter's etc., through seven hours; repeating through hours 8 through 14 and again 15 through 21; and finishing with 22=Saturn, 23=Jupiter, and 24=Mars. The next hour—the first hour of the second day—must then belong to the Sun; and so on.

The properties of the numbers 7 and 24 are such, however, that the first hour of each day of the week will always begin with a new "reigning celestial divinity" and will do so in this order: *Saturn, Sun, Moon, Mars, Mercury, Jupiter, Venus*—with no repeats, no omissions. This, then, is the source of the day names in Latin and the derived Romance languages (table 8.1), with the exception of Sun-day, which the Christians changed to the Day of the Lord and treated as both the start of the cycle and a day of rest.

Deity	LATIN	ITALIAN	FRENCH	ENGLISH
sun	*dies Domini*	*domenica*	*dimanche*	Sunday (Sun-day)
moon	*dies lunae*	*lunedi*	*lundi*	Monday (Moon-day)
Mars	*dies Martis*	*martedi*	*mardi*	Tuesday (Tiwas-day)
Mercury	*dies Mercuri*	*mercoledi*	*mercredi*	Wednesday (Woden's-day)
Jupiter	*dies Jovis*	*giovedi*	*jeudi*	Thursday (Thor's-day)
Venus	*dies Veneris*	*venerdi*	*vendredi*	Friday (Freya-day)
Saturn	*dies Saturni*	*(sabato)*	*samedi*	Saturday (Saturn-day)

TABLE 8.1: WESTERN EUROPEAN DAY NAMES

The Germanic speakers had to have picked up the notion of the seven-day week and its day names from the Romans *after* the Romans assigned a planetary deity to each day of the week and *before* the Christians renamed

---

"book-end" or completion to the series of important numbers before it. So 7 came to symbolize totality, the universe. See Barber and Barber 2005, 214–16.

Sunday.[12] Apparently Germanic men returning from mercenary service in the Roman army—hence conversant with Roman culture—brought home the concept of the week, but instead of borrowing the Latin names, they carefully *translated* the names to those of Germanic deities with corresponding attributes. Thus Mars became Tiwas, a god of war; Mercury became Woden/Odin, conductor of the dead to the Other World; Jupiter became Thor the thunderer; and Venus became Freya.

That explains how Venus's Day became Friday, and since Venus/Freya was the goddess of procreation, recurrent female customs naturally gravitated to her—in the West. But how did the Eastern *paraskeví* "preparation" day get this same treatment? Was there some yet older notion of the week and its sacredness to womankind bubbling up in both East and West?

Not that we can prove. Remarkable accidents may have caused this congruence. But let's look at the evidence.

To begin with, the Eastern Orthodox Church named the days not for celestial bodies but mostly by counting (as was the Jewish custom)—although which day counts as "first" differs between Greek and Slavic.

ENGLISH	GREEK (Modern)	RUSSIAN/Slavic
Sunday	*kyriakí* "Lord's (day)"	(Bulg. *nedelen* "do-nothing")
Monday	*deftéra* "second"	*ponedél'nik* "after do-nothing"
Tuesday	*tríti* "third"	*vtórnik* "second"
Wednesday	*tetárti* "fourth"	*sredá* "middle"
Thursday	*pémpti* "fifth"	*chetvérg* "fourth"
Friday	*paraskeví* "preparation"	*pyátnitsa* "fifth"
Saturday	*sávvato* "Sabbath"	*subbóta* "Sabbath"
Sunday		*voskresén'e* "resurrection"

TABLE 8.2: GREEK AND SLAVIC DAY NAMES

Second, the Gospels tell us that Jesus died on the cross on the day before the Jewish Sabbath (hence on Friday) and rose from the dead on Sunday. This Friday became so important in Christian tradition that it received a special name, "Good Friday" or "Holy Friday," which in Greek (the language that spread early Christianity) was *Hagía Paraskeví*. Now, *hagía* means not only "holy" but "saint." As a result, several centuries later, people began to reinterpret such abstractions: the name of the great cathedral in Constantinople. *Hagía Sophía* "Holy Wisdom" got reinterpreted as *Saint* Sophia and *Hagía Paraskeví* "Holy Friday" as *Saint* Paraskeví—just as in the West *Santa Lucia* "Holy Light" got reinterpreted as *Saint* Lucia (or St. Lucy). Now, if there was a saint with a name, she must have lived a holy life and been suitably martyred. Saints' histories had come into vogue as pious readings after Constantine stopped Roman persecution of the Christians upon converting in AD 312, so the hagiographers (writers of saints' biographies) obligingly created cookie-cutter "lives" for these ladies, complete with titillating details of their martyrdoms.[13] Enter St. Paraskevi.

Our earliest attestation of this saint comes in the mid-eighth century from a Greek priest, John of Euboia, who wrote about both Paraskevi and St. Anastasia,[14] with whom Paraskevi remains linked to this day.* The Greek text rambles so badly that one modern scholar condemned it as having "neither literary qualities nor historical value,"[15] and an irate twelfth-century prelate consigned it to the flames as "unworthy"—while asking his deacon to write a better one![16] Thus runs a summary:

> Paraskeve is the only child of a rich, noble and pious family. Her parents die when Paraskeve is twelve years old. She then distributes her fortune to the poor and leads an ascetic life. Due to her Christian way of life, she is brought before the governor who tortures her. The torture-machines do not affect her body and her torturer, witnessing such a miracle, converts. Then Paraskeve goes to another city in order to teach God's word. She is arrested a second time and brought before the governor. She undergoes new tortures and is finally killed by the sword.[17]

This sketch gives a good sense of the "once upon a time" quality of the original, which gives no places, dates, or names except for an unknown Roman tyrant Tarasios and a Christian transparently named Timotheos ("honoring God") who piously buries Paraskevi at night after her martyrdom.[18] We

---

*In Greek, *hagía anastasía* means "holy resurrection," which occurred two days after Holy Friday.

should add that, in another version, her torturer converted to Christianity because she miraculously cured his blindness.[19]

Somehow—our evidence is scanty—from there she became one of the most popular saints among Greeks, Slavs, and Romanians, and even among non-Orthodox Sicilians (living among many Greeks), who translated her name into the local word for Friday: St. Venera or Veneranda.[20] In Russia, she became known as Paraskeva-Pyatnitsa, which adds the Russian name for Friday to the Greek one! Christianity made little headway among the East Slavs until the late tenth century, but by that time people had embroidered John of Euboia's legend with the explanation that, after her parents prayed to God for a child, their daughter was born on a Friday, hence her name.[21] Eventually the church assigned October 28 (birth!) and July 26 as days sacred to Paraskevi.*

With no true history, the saint could morph into anything necessary for those who needed a patroness. Certainly the early Christian church gave no aid or comfort to women, any more than the heavily patriarchal Greek and Slavic cultures did. If vengeful willies could no longer help them relax occasionally, perhaps a female saint could. Paraskevi became the women's saint par excellence—patroness of water, spinning, healing, and midwifery.[22] In time, Paraskevi's cult even came to compete with that of the Virgin Mary, to the dismay of the clergy. In Russia,

> Paraskeva was envisaged as a young woman with long unbraided hair who traveled the countryside making sure that women observed the interdictions against certain kinds of work on Friday. Her image was confused with that of the "Twelve Fridays," unofficial days of special fasting and devotion. . . .[23]

The Friday taboos included both textile work and washing either children or clothes.[24] In Greece, too, these taboos held. One peasant woman stated, "Don't ever work on Friday, because St. Paraskevi doesn't want it." Another added that a woman who broke this taboo saw St. Paraskevi standing in front of her, threatening her.[25] Every Russian house contained her icon,[26]

---

*Actual saints of this name also came to exist, further confusing matters. A Bulgarian hermitess took the holy name of Paraskevi, becoming St. Paraskevi of Tŭrnovo (celebrated October 14), and a Lithuanian noblewoman, later Protectress of Lithuania, did likewise (October 20).

and "in Red Square, in Moscow, there stood a chapel dedicated to Paraskeva [Russian *Praskov'ya*] that was open only to women, who came there to worship on Fridays."[27] Because Paraskevi's two feast days didn't always fall on Friday, women viewed the tenth Friday after Easter as her main festival and carried out their rituals beside water.[28]

Note that Paraskevi wears her hair long and loose like a willy (fig. 8.3). Furthermore, breaking taboos against spinning and washing are sins against the willies, as we have seen. Paraskevi's chapels and shrines sprang up beside springs and crossroads,[29] springs being the natural homes of willies and crossroads the places where spirits of the dead in general hung out. The correspondences between Paraskevi and the willies are close, and Ukrainians in Khar'kov actually considered Paraskeva-Pyatnitsa to *be* a rusalka.[30]

The association with spinning also gave her the sobriquet *Paraskeva L'nyanitsa* "Linen Paraskeva."[31] On her October 28 feast day, Russian women began to prepare their flax for winter spinning,[32] taking the first stalks to be processed and hanging them on her icon like a corn dolly,[33] along with the embroidered towels, flowers, and fragrant herbs that they constantly lavished on her image.[34] Yarn, cloth, and clothing, after all, were the main things that women had to offer a divine protectress—those were what they spent most of their time

FIG. 8.3. Early 17th-century icon of St. Paraskeva (St. Friday) with long, loose hair. Halïch, Ukraine.

making. Quantities of rags, clothing, and yarn still festoon the trees around the icon-filled shrines beside her springs (figs. 8.4, 8.5), for Paraskevi became the patron saint of water,[35] the ancient abode of the willies. These cloths are gifts dedicated in thanks for, or to request, healing, since people also sought cures from Paraskevi. On Paraskevi's icons in Greece, one often finds silver votive offerings of eyes, since she was known especially for curing eye diseases[36]—although in Russia she *gave* eye diseases to spinners who ignored her Friday taboos, by throwing tow* in their eyes.[37] The willies, too, traditionally cured as well as caused illness. Phyllis Kemp, studying Balkan folk medicine in the 1930s, explains:

> objects brought to healing streams and wells are typically sacrificial things. In Bosnia a handful of wheat, bread, and salt is thrown into the Bosna river while the sacrificer says: "This I give to the fish and the sea animals that kind God may give me health." . . . I have heard it said that, should these [rags, etc.] be taken away, the spring will be angered

---

*Tow consists of short slivers of fiber that fall from flax during processing—hence our term *tow-headed* for someone with short blond hair. These slivers are fine and sharp.

FIG. 8.5. Votive cloth and clothing hung on trees. Left: Around shrine of Agia Paraskevi near Nigrita, Greece, March 2008. Right: Beside spring sacred to willies. Serbian Banat, 1930s.

and either disappear or cease to heal. . . . Some say simply that it is a "sin" to do so; others speak as though these rags, etc., were the disease itself, which it is therefore dangerous even to touch. . . . Those who keep these customs are used to making substantial offerings of food, money, flowers, often with the addition of some personal fragment in the case of illness.[38]

The personal item serves to transfer the disease from the affected person elsewhere, as in magical rituals on other continents.

Among Paraskevi's "healing arts" was midwifery. One night, according to people in Vladimir province, a fellow came to the saint's cottage, asking her help as midwife. When she took the infant to a servant girl at the bathhouse for washing, however, some demons grabbed it. With the help of a cross and prayers, she rescued the baby, but the disappointed demons got

FIG. 8.6. 19th-century North Russian bathhouse on stilts. Kostroma.

their "devil tsar" to demand she give up her Christian faith. When she refused, he condemned her to be beheaded—on a Friday, which, according to *this* legend, is how she got her name.[39]

Midwifery, healing, washing, and spinning all came together in Russia in the bathhouse. The Russian bathhouse was a small, dark wooden hut, often set on stilts a bit away from the village, with nearby supplies of water for washing and wood for heating the stones one splashed with water to make steam—a sort of sauna (fig. 8.6). Obviously people went to the bathhouse to bathe, but men and women also went in hopes of washing away sickness, often viewed as a nasty demon that had attached itself to the invalid. Collars, cuffs, and hems—the openings in the clothing—were embroidered with protective red designs to keep sickness demons from climbing inside (fig. 8.7); protective herbs and amulets like Christian crosses hung about one's person for the same reason. But clothes and amulets (fig. 8.8) had to be removed for bathing, leaving one vulnerable to the malicious bathhouse demons that spooked around in dark corners like the spiders. Home to two spirit elements, fire *and* water, the bathhouse was an inherently dangerous place.

Women visited the bathhouse for several other reasons: for childbirth (a practical arrangement for cleaning up the mess), for preparing bast fibers like flax and hemp (which work up much more easily when damp), and sometimes for divining their future married life. All these matters related to both Paraskeva and the willies. Since these events excluded men, the bathhouse came to be viewed as the hideout of witches in particular, although wizards who didn't turn up at church on Sunday were suspected of being off trucking with spirits in the empty bathhouse.[40]*

---

* In parts of Austria where flax is grown—Styria, Carinthia—the place where flax was prepared for spinning was also off limits to men, and if a girl spied a boy lurking nearby, she

FIG. 8.7. Russian men's homespun hempen shirts, embroidered especially around openings with red and with rose patterns, for protection against malevolent spirits (ca. 1915).

All in all, one deduces not only that St. Paraskevi/Paraskeva attracted to herself the old beliefs about willies and women's affairs but also that this system already contained a mechanism for periodic resting that "blamed" the work taboo on female spirits. After the arrival of the new calendar reckoned in seven-day cycles, women apparently shifted the system—which may also have existed in western Europe—to (St.) Friday, dressing old customs in saintly Christian trappings.* The church fathers, however, were not favorably impressed. In particular, they railed against women's scandalous behavior on the Twelve Fridays set apart by the church for particularly rig-

---

would "pull him in with all her strength, compel him to dance with her, and blacken his face for him." (Alford 1978, 131–32)

* Levin (139) suggests that all these traits came to Paraskevi from a Bible passage about the "ideal woman" (Proverbs 31), but the parallels to the willies are more extensive. Parallelism of the willies to something biblical could have helped, however.

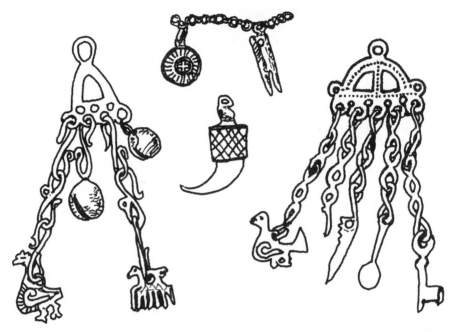

FIG. 8.8. 11th-century Russian amulets of cast brass. Smolensk, Moscow, and Vladimir provinces. Note birds, bells, and horse (atop comblike element), and cross inside circle. Set on right, with key, spoon, and tiny saw, is reminiscent of medieval western European lady's chatelaine.

orous devotion;* for "on these days, men and women, both young and old, would strip naked and jump and shake, saying that they had seen Saints Paraskeva and Anastasia and had been ordered to honor them with their lascivious dances."[41] The Dancing Goddesses, purveyors of fertility, were still causing people to dance in their honor, and it is reported that "the cult continued, especially in Ukraine, where Friday was considered the Sabbath over Sunday until well into the eighteenth century."[42]

---

*These Fridays preceded key Sunday feasts such as Easter, Michaelmas, Christmas.

CHAPTER 9

The Twelve Days of Christmas

> The kallikantzaroi . . . are a species of goblins, or spirits,
> who appear only once a year, at Christmas time. . . . All the
> year round, equipped with axes, they strive to cut away the
> tree which supports the earth; but by the time they have near-
> ly done, Christ is born, the tree grows anew, and the spirits
> leap to the surface of the earth in a rage.
>
> —Greek tradition[1]

W e come now to the final season of our farmers' year—the dark,
cold winter.

The dark of night belongs to the spirits, as we have seen,
especially the stretch from midnight till cock crow when it was dangerous
even to venture outdoors for fear of abduction by Dancing Goddesses and
their ilk. The darkest part of the year occurs around the winter solstice, and
the twelve-day span from Christmas to Epiphany (January 6) was viewed
as especially dark across much of Europe. It too belonged to the spirits,
whether these were seen as escapees (like the Greek *kallikántzaroi*), always
nearby (like the willies), or let loose for an annual visit (like the ancestors).
Whichever, it was a time of extreme danger, when the waters were "unchris-
tened, unhallowed";[2] these were the winter Rusalii.

Now, the roaming spirits were viewed as predominantly the souls of the
dead. But some of them were direct ancestors, even parents, of the living
and should want to protect their offspring. From the pool of spirits, moreover, came the souls of the newborn. So how could all spirits be evil? On the
other hand, how could one tell a benevolent from a malevolent spirit?

Clearly the spirit world was ambivalent and had to be treated as such. The army of the dead, loose on earth during the Twelve Days, could bring either more dark or the return of sunlight, could bring disease or abundance, famine or feast. Trick or treat.

Propitiating the dead by setting food out for them might quell any anger and start things right, especially if done as the Twelve Days began, on Christmas Eve. ("Days" used to be reckoned as beginning at the onset of evening rather than midnight or dawn, a custom preserved in terms like *Twelfth Night* and *fortnight*.) Since the souls will come to the door, or down the chimney like Santa, the food and drink should be set on the doorstep or hearth that evening. On Christmas Eve some of us still help our children place milk and cookies—our version of the ancient propitiatory milk and honey cakes*—beside the fireplace in hopes that Santa will bring nice presents. Santa Claus, derived from *Saint Nicholas* (the resuscitator of three murdered boys, hence a bringer of souls), developed as part of a Christian takeover of the leader of dead souls (still called Perchta, Berthe, Berchtolda, or Holda across the Alps and parts of Germany), for whom food was laid out[3] and who brought gifts to the good and punishment to the wicked at this time of year. Naughty or nice—trick or treat.[4] Householders "welcomed" the returning spirits to their old hearth and home by leaving them the wherewithal to warm and feed themselves; then they hid safely out of the way. (Our children, too, must go to bed and not encounter Santa—an ancient tradition convenient for modern parents.) On New Year's Day, halfway through the Twelve Days, Greek women and children brought propitiatory offerings to the *neráïdes* in the local well or fountain, as they began drawing water to replace all water in the house with "new" water. Throwing treats such as figs, currants, nuts, and grain into the spring, they would say, "May riches flow as water flows."[5]

Throughout much of eastern and western Europe, masked men and boys roved in bands during the Twelve Nights, impersonating the unruly dead. These impersonations involved extensive use of reversals, since, as we've seen, the spirit world is conceived as the reverse of ours. Thus men painted their faces black (or occasionally white), cross-dressed as women or as animals, and did things upside down or backward, including suspending

---

*The cakes were called *libum* in Latin, whence the Christmas *Leb-kuchen*, a favorite Christmas cookie in Germany and now America (Russ 1983, 21).

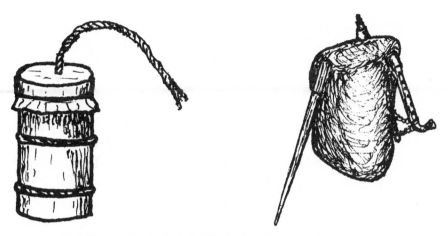

FIG. 9.1. Left: Romanian *buhai* "bull": hollow drum with bundle of horsehair (or stick) fixed through drumhead. Stroking or pulling on hair/stick produces deep roaring sound. Right: Goatskin bagpipe (Romanian *cimpoi*, South Slavic *gaida*), a favorite Balkan instrument.

work and/or electing as leader a Lord of Misrule, who broke all the normal rules (except for those that the *real* spirits might not forgive!).

In Germany, men wearing masks and furry costumes—Midwinter spirits usually seem to be hairy—went around making lots of noise, especially with bells and a homemade friction drum that groans and bellows (fig. 9.1).* Noise imitated the spirits—but also drove them back.

In Austria, on the three Thursday evenings before Christmas, masked youngsters went house to house making great noise with whips and cowbells, knocking on doors and windows to scare away the evil spirits, and crying out, "In with good luck, out with bad luck!" For this service they expected a reward of sweets or nuts.[6] In Salzburg, according to an account around 1800,

> masked youths, decorated with bells, leapt with the help of their staves over ditches and walls during their progress through the valleys at night. When their troop arrives noisily, the lights in the houses must be doused, "to keep the windows intact, and no one dares let himself be seen by them on the way who doesn't want to subject himself to

---

*This drum-shaped instrument is called *buhai* in Romanian (Beza 1928, 11) and *rommelpot* in Dutch. Vermeer, Brueghel, and others depicted it ca. 1600.

disagreeable encounters. . . . Many of the disguised lads use their long staves for all kinds of jumping with a strength and agility seldom seen among the greatest acrobats. One of the boys even touched the ceiling of the room with the soles of his feet."[7]

Tyrolean farmers viewed this prodigious jumping as crucial: if the "Perchten-runners" didn't leap about enough in the fields, the crops would fail.[8] One is reminded both of the young Lazarki dancers—"Jump, Lazarke, so lambs will jump in the master's yard!"—and of the staves and fancy jumping of the rusaltsi and călușari dancers. Jumping, like dancing, promotes life. A gloss from a millennium ago already mentions Perchten Night, often held on Twelfth Night, the eve of Epiphany.[9]

In Ireland, although the cosmic cracks-in-the-year that let the spirits loose occurred on the eves of November first and May first, the idea was the same. On the eve of May Day, the start of the "light half" of the year, happy fertility spirits abounded—but watch out, they might steal your child. On Halloween, the start of the "dark half," the spirits (and their human impersonators) played vicious and destructive tricks, especially if you didn't leave food out for them—the source of *our* "trick or treat."

In Wales and other heavily Celtic areas, a horseheaded demon called the *Mari Lwyd* "Grey Mare" (fig. 9.2) thumped high windows and clacked its jaw threateningly at passersby on one or more of the Twelve Nights. This huge, terrifying apparition consisted of a horse's skull (or life-size wooden imitation) fixed on the end of a pole like a hobbyhorse, while a white sheet or horsehide concealed the person carrying it. A rope attached to the movable lower jaw allowed the carrier to snap it loudly and menacingly as the creature and its disguised companions roved about.[10] Its less scary cousin, the wooden hobbyhorse, ridden astride with or without a clacking jawbone, also made the rounds in rural England during this season, sometimes accompanied by Morris dancers or bands of mummers disguised as old men and women.[11] In fact, our expression *old geezers* comes from these decrepit-looking dis-*guisers*. In England and America, the wooden hobbyhorse, like Halloween and many other ancient customs, ended up in the hands of children, although in Romania the călușari still use it (see fig. 5.4).

The kallikantzaroi of Greece are big, hairy, black, quarrelsome demons with enormous male sex organs and often animal limbs and claws, who are thought to spend most of the year trying to cut or gnaw through the tree sup-

FIG. 9.2. Horseheaded "demon" with jaws arranged to clack. Left: Welsh *Mari Lwyd* "Grey Mare," from Glamorganshire, 1932. Center: *Mari Lwyd* with young "handler." Right: Rather similar *Schnappvieh* "snatching critter," from Austrian Tyrol.

porting the world.* Emerging on each of the Twelve Nights, they leave trails of chaos and destruction, disappearing into caves and other dark lairs at the third cock crow—the one provided by black roosters (more "potent" than white or red roosters). Kallikantzaroi are so stupid, fortunately, that their victims can often outwit them, keeping them amused (they love to dance) or arguing over some enigma till sunup.[12] In some villages, people would "hang a tuft of tangled flax over the door; by the time the Kallikantzaroi have finished disentangling the flax and counting the threads, the cock crows and the sun scatters the spirits of darkness."[13] These monsters were thought to be the souls of people who died in some "wrong" or untimely way (like willies), died unbaptized (like some willies), or had the misfortune to be born

---

* This tree or pillar originally denoted the pole around which the earth turns. This axis currently points to the North Star, Polaris, but every year it shifts a little. See Barber and Barber 2005, chapter 16, for its trajectory and mythology.

during the Twelve Days, which belonged to the dead, not the living.[14] To prevent this fate, the mother of such a baby "must bind it in garlic tresses or straw . . . [or] singe the child's toe-nails, for it cannot become a Kallikant-zaros without toe-nails."[15] The *karakondzuli, kalakantseri*, etc., of Bulgaria arise from similar sources.*

But where are the willies in all this?

Probably perching in the rafters, overseeing taboos against spinning, weaving, washing, and grinding.[16] But the relative unimportance of things female in the Midwinter antics shows us, in fact, the other side of the coin. This is the time of the male principle; and from that opposition, the notion of the female fertility embodied in the Dancing Goddesses comes into sharper focus.

For the crops (or babies) to grow, the earth (or female) must be insemi-nated by the male; and after insemination, one must wait awhile before seeing evidence of new life. Normally that new life appears in the fields in spring, therefore the insemination must be ritually encouraged earlier—in the winter and/or at the time of plowing and sowing.

The vagaries of local climate, Christian meddling, and other incidents, however, have tended to drag the "masculine magic" here and there through the winter calendar, where we must hunt it down. Note that all these mask-ers and mummers are traditionally men. When female personae are needed for enacting little dramas, men play the parts cross-dressed. This, of course, only adds to the general hilarity, and laughter, like dancing and jumping, was felt to promote life. Evidently male magical power, in the European agrarian tradition, is expressed through *masking* the men, whereas female magical power comes from *baring* the women's bodies—as in the midnight nakedness of women driving away plague and in the undress of the willies.[17] Churchmen never saw the latter because such rites were done in secret, but

---

*The Greek and South Slavic terms (listed at length by Pócs 1989, 70 n.61, with copious references) sound so similar that they must be related, yet their origins are disputed. One possibility is Turkish *kara* "black" + *koncolos* "ghoul, demon" (Turkish *c* = English *j* in "jump"), with Greek turning *kara-* into Greek *kalo-/kalli-* "beautiful, good" by folk ety-mology, in a euphemistic attempt to turn the curse. See chapter 20 for another possibility.

they objected to masks on the ground that, since Man was made in the image of God, masking the face was blasphemous.

Like the willies, most of the Midwinter demons derived from dead souls, and these were widely thought to revisit the living during the "extra" days in the calendar as the old year ended, since intercalary days were a sort of temporal no-man's-land. Prudent people visited the cemeteries at that time to pay respect to their deceased family members.

But when did the year actually end—or begin? As we have seen, even just within Europe, New Year has fallen at several different times, the reasoning being varied.[18] The Romans—who, like other Mediterranean peoples, reckoned by solstices and equinoxes—began their year around the March equinox, until they moved it to January 1, close to the winter solstice. Traces of the intercalary Twelve Days persist in early March in much of the Balkan Peninsula.[19]

Dedicated Christians, however, had by AD 400 chosen to celebrate their "beginning" with the birth of Jesus,[20] for which they selected December 25 (so as to preempt the celebrations of both the Roman New Year and the "pagan" agrarian solstice) . . . except for those Christians reasoning that Jesus really "began" with conception nine months earlier, hence March 25—just about the spring equinox.[21]

The Celts, who functioned with two half-year seasons (like the Balkan shepherds) and started their "day" with the dark part, started their year with the dark season, at Samhain, November 1. The Germanic peoples, who also did not go by solstices and equinoxes, apparently divided the year into six two-month sections.[22] One of these double months ran from mid-November (Martinmas) to mid-January and was called *Yule* (Gothic *Jiuleis*), preserved in such terms as *Yuletide* and *Yule log*, which refer to Christmas festivities.[23] Its start may have functioned as New Year's Day, since Martinmas (November 11, Gregorian) corresponds to the Julian November 1 (Celtic Samhain) and also carries many pre-Christian "beginning" customs.[24] On this day, families brought their animals in from summer pasture and held great feasts, slaughtering the animals they wouldn't be able to feed through the winter.

For our purposes, the date of New Year matters far less than the observation that residual New Year's customs now lie scattered across the entire period from November through March. New Year's customs seek, like New Year's resolutions, to end or drive out the old, death-ridden and tired, while ushering in (or even driving in) the new, vigorous, and hopeful. We can recognize these customs, then, by the pairing of these two aspects—starting with our own New Year's cartoon images of the tired old man with long beard and scythe chatting with a plump baby boy wearing a banner bearing the date of the coming year.

Another cue: Europeans have traditionally treated each new year as not so much a returning cycle but rather a new lease on life.[25] Three types of actions flow from this attitude: (1) analogically showing the spirits the sort of health and abundance wanted under the new lease; (2) determining what one can about the future year; and (3) wresting abundance from the hostile spirits while keeping them from following us into the New Year (new time space), where they could bollix everything up again.*

Analogical actions to promote a bountiful new year include bringing greenery into the house ("Deck the halls with boughs of holly"), wearing new clothing (still observed even recently at the old March date by donning new "Easter bonnets"), and laying the Yuletide dinner table with the greatest possible abundance—deliberately overeating and even spilling food to show how plentiful it is.[26] Across Europe, the mummers and maskers,† who visit each house in the village to work abundance magic, expect a generous reward of food and drink, known to English ethnographers by the French term *quête* "quest, search; collection." No milk and cookies here. Especially in the North, alcoholic punch often flowed till the visitors, after making the rounds of many houses, barely made it home. (Our word for Christmas liquor, *wassail*, derives from the Old English toast appropriate to the occasion, *Waes hāl!* "Be healthy!") It's not just a matter of recompense. Manifest abundance during these rituals, like the rice showered on brides, analogically induces abundance in the year to come. If the householders do *not*

---

*I'm aware of the highly explanatory schema developed by Gaster (1955), building on Frazer, whereby such initiatory customs consist of four phases: *mortification* (abstention from normal food and work), *purgation* (cleansing from all evils), *invigoration* (positive actions to renew life and vigor), and *jubilation* (renewal of bonding and solidarity through festivity). I have deliberately used instead a schema that emerged from my own range of data, to see what light that sheds. The two analyses do not necessarily exclude each other.
† I will (somewhat arbitrarily, but conveniently) distinguish *mummers* as those who play out little dramas, and *maskers* as those who do not.

show largesse to the visitors, they may incur the displeasure and retaliation of more than the human mummers. It's treat, or trick.

By the same token, one must do and say nothing resembling what is *not* wanted. So nothing may be removed or lent from the house; debts and trespasses are forgiven; nothing may sit empty, broken, or dirty; unfinished tasks such as spinning are hastily completed.[27]

The abundance magic delivered by mummers may include dancing, jumping, laughter, songs and ritual statements full of propitious wishes, and dramas enacting key elements of what's needed. These little plays have been observed with remarkably similar contents across Europe from central Greece through the Balkans and the Alps to the Pyrenees and all the way to England as well as Russia, best preserved where the long arm of the pope did not quite reach. For they are at base fertility rituals. Some depict plowing and insemination directly; others, only slightly veiled, center on resurrection. All of them celebrate the male contribution.

Some of the best preserved of these rituals were recorded in rural England a century or more ago and continue today as a partly revived, partly continuous tradition.* In one type, the first member of the band of mummers enters the parlor reciting doggerel and, like Romania's călușari, drawing a large magic circle that the spectators may not cross during the performance. He introduces each mummer, who enters reciting more doggerel and possibly dancing. The hero, styled as anyone from Bridegroom to St. George, begins to woo a young woman (played, like all parts, by a man) but is interrupted by a well-upholstered older woman (named Dame Jane or the like) who announces that the swaddled bundle she carries is his child, whom he must care for. He fobs her off to resume his courting, only to find a Foreign Knight (perhaps a Turk, or Napoleon) wooing or abducting the Bride. The two men fight, and one is killed—which one dies doesn't seem to matter, although each troupe has its tradition. As the Bride loudly laments the fallen suitor, in comes an absurd Doctor, who applies all manner of hilarious remedies and eventually revives the dead man. The mummers perform a final vigorous dance (usually akin to Morris dancing), wish their hosts abundance, and depart after the quête.

Compare with that the rituals performed in northern Greece, also

---

* Interested readers can consult the extensive English literature, starting with Sharpe and MacIlwaine 1907–13, Tiddy 1923, and Chambers 1933.

recorded a century ago. In Thessaly in 1912, the archaeologist Alan Wace wrote that mummers called *karkantsaroi* and the like (local variants of the word *kallikántzaroi*, but referring to the impersonators) went about from New Year's Day till Epiphany. Near Karditsa, for example,

> young men and boys dress up in goat and sheep skins and put on gipsy costumes, masks and beards, old arms of any kind, and innumerable bells. One is a bride, another a bridegroom, and yet another an Arab loaded with bells and weapons. They go round the houses and the neighboring villages singing suitable songs to each person from whom they solicit contributions. They say that in olden days when two bands met one another, while touring the other villages, each band wanted the other to submit . . . which sometimes ended in bloodshed.[28]

Here, though the play has been lost, the good wishes, the quête, and some of the cast of characters remain (as in fig. 9.3). We also see a rusalets/căluşar–like rivalry over the control of abundance.

Elsewhere, the drama survived. Near Halmyros the cast included eight singers plus

> (1) the bride (νύφη), a boy dressed in a bride's costume, (2) the bride-groom (γαμβρός), wearing a fustanella [men's traditional tightly gathered skirt] and a red fez, carrying a rusty sword, and with bells slung about his waist and tied on his elbows, (3) the Arab ('Αράπης), wearing a black mask of sheep or goat skin, a sheepskin cloak, and sometimes a tail as well, (4) the doctor (γιατρός), dressed in a black coat . . . to resemble a graduate of Athens University.

Arranging itself in a semicircle around the actors, the chorus sings good wishes to each householder, much as the Lazarki do. Meanwhile, the Arab accosts the bride, stealing kisses or some such. The bridegroom takes offense, and

> a lively quarrel ensues, which ends in the Arab killing the bridegroom. The bride in despair flings herself on the body and gives way to violent weeping. Then, remembering the doctor, she . . . fetches him to cure her husband. The doctor assumes a professional air, feels the

FIG. 9.3. Pre-Lenten Carnival maskers: "Bride" and "Beast." Vamvakophyto, Greek Macedonia, March 2008.

pulse, etc., of the bridegroom, thumps him, and thrusts some drug such as a piece of soap into his mouth, or indulges in other horseplay at his expense. This has a miraculous effect, the bridegroom comes to life again, jumps up, and dances with the other actors. The play usually ends with an obscene pantomime between the bride and groom. When the song and play are over [,] the band is treated by the householder with a gift either of money or of food and wine for them to make merry with on the morrow. But if there are any chickens about they do not hesitate to steal one. . . . If, however, the householder does not open the door to the band, they, besides stealing chickens, will do any other damage they can. . . . In addition they sing songs of bad omen wishing him ill and not good for the year. . . .[29]

Trick or treat yet again.

Noteworthy variations exist across northern Greece, where around 1900 these rituals were performed by Greeks, Bulgarians, Vlachs, and Albanians.[30] On the island of Skyros, for instance, each company of maskers consisted of a "girl," an "old man" (*g[h]éros*, as in English *geriatrics*), and a "Frank" (instead of an Arab), the two latter wearing masks and numerous sheep bells.[31] In Macedonia, near Kastoria, besides a bride, doctor, Arab, and several bridegrooms, the company included an old woman who carried a doll like a baby and helped bewail the death of the bridegroom.[32] In Macedonia and Thrace, the maskers are often called *baboúgheroi*, a name apparently compounded from Turkish *baba* "father; venerable man" and Greek *ghéros* "old man."[33]

From these examples, corroborated by many others, we can begin to piece together the basic elements of this drama for the new agricultural year, parts of which are lost and parts preserved at each end of Europe.

There are actually two pairs of opposing characters. First we have two females. They differ in age and the older one has a child. The bridegroom rejects the dame who has already, as it were, borne a crop; he wants the virgin girl, who, like the willies, has not yet used up her store of fertility. One could even say that the young woman represents the New Year and its crops, whereas the older one is the Old Year, already used up.

Then we have two males, rivals for the fertile bride. One is "ours," the other "alien"—where any otherness will do. Indeed, in Bulgaria, where similar dramas are enacted by groups called *kukeri* or *startsi*,* the alien rival often dresses as a beast—an "other" in species (fig. 9.4, cf. fig. 9.3) instead of nationality. The males fight; one dies. The notion that the male must die so as to be resurrected in the new crop is traceable all the way back to the death of the young god Dumuzi, lover of the fertility goddess, as a New Year drama in ancient Mesopotamia, where agriculture originated. In those regions in which the alien is a beast, however—and that includes not only Bulgaria but Catalan and Basque areas of the Pyrenees[34]—it is always the beast, often a bear, that dies.† In Bulgaria, where the kukeri come forth at Lent, the priest-doctor in the troupe (fig. 9.4) uses comically obscene means to revive the corpse; then everyone dances.

---

* *Startsi* is Slavic for "old men"—equivalent to the Greek—while *kukeri* apparently came from Greek *koúkla* "doll" back when it meant a conjurer or masker, itself from Latin *cucullus* "hood" (Liungman 1938, 773; Vasmer: *sv.* кукла). See chapter 17.

† Surely we are seeing reinterpretation here, perhaps a mixing of agrarian and hunter traditions. Originally, some hostile outside force kills the agrarian male—but war is more edifying when *we* kill the *outsider*.

FIG. 9.4. Bulgarian *kukeri* from Burgas region (1985): "Girl" (young man in girl's dress, never masked), "beast" (with blackened face, fur suit, bells, carrying moplike pole), "priest" (with mask, priest's hat and robe).

In Belarus, it is a "goat" that dies—although in describing the getup of this character over a century ago, the Russian ethnographer Pavel Vasil'evich Sheyn remarked that it looked more like a bear. Wrapped in sheepskins, his face blackened or masked, horns tied upon his head, the "goat" went about in the company of "Grandpa" and some singers and musicians. "Grandpa" would clown with the house owner, then start beating the goat, which would fall down dead. When the singers came to a line about the goat reviving, it would jump up.[35] The song ended:

> *Where the goat treads,*
> *There the wheat grows. . . .*[36]

Furry beasts abound in Macedonia, Thrace, and Bulgaria. Without a play they need not always die, but their ties to fertility are clear. Some of the most magnificent are the babougheroi that still congregate in the village of Anthi, in Greek Macedonia, near the beginning of Lent. They go around with straps capturing girls and women of childbearing age—dragging them off their porches, if necessary, to a patch of grass or soil (never pavement) and laying them flat on Mother Earth (fig. 9.5). If the girl is pretty, these days a young monster may require a long kiss; then he politely helps her up, restoring any shoes she lost in the scuffle.

In the nearby village of Phlambouro, equally magnificent babougheroi accumulate in the central square during the afternoon (fig. 9.6), performing a slow, mesmerizing dance as the zurnas wail and the drums pound. Step, cross, step, a quick brush behind; then reverse—back and forth, back and forth. Every few measures the dancer leans over to brush the tip of his tall, conical headdress across the ground—"for fertility"—then up again. This headdress is constructed on a sturdy six-foot wooden pole strapped to the dancer's waist and shoulders over his suit of fur; its tall cone of black cloth, with holes for seeing and breathing and a colorful tuft at the tip, glitters with cheap jewelry. The whole contraption weighs many tens of pounds, so to dance with it for hours, especially to make its top brush the ground and come back up repeatedly, requires great strength and endurance. As with the rusaltsi/călușari, this ritual was for only the most virile of men. It celebrates the masculine, the Venerable Elders of the patriline.

Is the conical shape originally phallic? Probably. Is the dance intended to represent impregnating the earth? Probably. But these farmers are no prudes, as we see from a second type of little drama.

In Thrace a century ago—and even today among refugees in neighboring Macedonia—mummers called *kalógheroi* (literally, "good/beautiful old men," also "monks") enact a ritual drama closely akin to those we have seen. As described in 1906 by Richard Dawkins,[37] the participants consisted of: (a) two kalogheroi (always married men), with tall headdresses of hide (goat, fox, or wolf) covering their faces and sheep bells around their waists, one carrying (with blackened hands) a wooden phallus, the other a mock crossbow that shoots ashes; (b) two unmarried men dressed as girls; (c) the Babo—an old woman cradling a swaddled wooden baby in a basket (*liknítes*—an unusual word, used of the god Dionysos in his winnowing-basket cradle twenty-five hundred years ago: see fig. 19.4); (d) a ragged old

FIG. 9.5. *Baboúgheros* pressing young woman to ground "for fertility" during pre-Lenten Carnival. Anthi, Greek Macedonia. (Videographer J. Aydın on ground; Greek dance expert Y. Hunt behind.)

FIG. 9.6. *Baboúgheroi* dancing in central square. Phlambouro, Greek Macedonia, March 2008.

couple called *katsivéloi* (roughly, gypsy smiths), hands and faces ritually blackened; (e) young men called Policemen, with swords and chains for capturing people; (f) a bagpiper. The company visits each house during the day, wishing abundance and collecting food (a quête), while the katsiveloi swipe chickens and carry out "an obscene pantomime . . . on the straw heaps in front of the houses." Ending up in the village square amid a crowd of spectators, the group performs a line dance, the Policemen waving their swords like the healing dancers of Serbian Duboka. Then the katsiveloi pretend to forge a plowshare as the "woman" waves her skirts like bellows. Meanwhile, the Babo's baby (now enacted by the first kalogheros) pretends to grow up and demand a wife, so his companion, as best man, mock-marries him to one of the two "girls." The bridegroom saunters about with his phallus until the second kalogheros shoots him "dead" with his bow and pretends to bury him. The "wife" laments loudly, joined by all—until the dead man suddenly comes alive and gets up. Finally, several unmarried men pull a real plow around the village square, while the kalogheroi guide the plow, another man sprinkles seed, and everyone chants wishes for an abundant harvest.

Refugees from Thracian Kosti, now living at Agia Eleni in Greek Macedonia, continue similar customs, on the Tuesday before Lent, with household visits, a kalogheros death-and-resurrection drama, and a ritual procession around the plaza at sundown with unmarried men pulling the plow while married ones scatter grain and clack big red wooden phalli (fig. 9.7). For good measure, everyone enacting the ritual gets ambushed and dunked in the nearest pool—the kalogheros last of all—to ensure rain for the crops.*

Similar plow plays occur in Britain, too, just before plowing begins. For example, in nineteenth-century Lincolnshire, on Plough Monday (the day before fieldwork resumed after the Twelve Days), men called "plough jacks" dressed themselves like Morris dancers (looking remarkably like the călușari) and went the rounds performing a wooing-type play.† The characters included "two rival suitors and two transvestite characters, the maiden and the witch," as well as a "fool" and one or more hobbyhorses. Other groups called "plough bullocks," who did not perform plays but pulled a plow with them and exchanged good wishes for "alms," concluded their day by "running with the plough round the cross in the market-place." True to form, these bands fought with rival parties from the opposite side of the river.[38]

Since plowing to sow the new crop marks the functional start of the agricultural year, such rituals occur sometimes at New Year (the current one or

---

* Photos and videos of the kalogheros and babougheroi are available on the website http://elizabethwaylandbarber.com. The "pool" was created by opening the village fire hydrant an hour before needed!

† Researchers found that English "mumming" falls into three basic types: Hero Combat, Wooing (Bridal), and Sword Dance (Cawte et al. 1967, 14). As in the Balkans, troupes run the gamut from using all three ingredients (possibly the original form) to keeping the characters with no play or dance left.

FIG. 9.7. *Kalógheros* ritual, Agia Eleni, Greek Macedonia. Top: Unmarried men pulling plow around village square, guided by older man and followed by *kalógheros* (with mop-pole and large mustache). Bottom: Grain to be sown and wooden phalli to be clacked during ritual plowing.

some older one), sometimes at plow time. Thus the rusaltsi and călușari may also dance and enact fertility plays (but do not "cure") during the Twelve Days, the old *winter* Rusalii.[39]

But whatever date these fertility rites occurred, authorities tried to suppress them. In Russia in 1648, Tsar Aleksey decreed that, on New Year's Eve, Moscow police should stop people from singing *kolyadï* (now simply Christmas carols wishing abundance)* and from "charming the plow"—

———

*Slavic *kolyada* (Romanian *colinda*) for New Year's carols, like *calendar*, was borrowed from Latin *calendae*.

apparently a ritual that, like spells used on spindles, swords, and other weapons, strove magically to make the tool function to the owner's benefit.[40] (American culture still uses expressions like "This bullet has your name on it!") The Orthodox Church, for its part, has attempted to Christianize any winter or spring rite involving masks by attaching it to the "Christian" Carnival.

After all this pot-stirring, the calendar may not be clear, but the effort given to the male principle is.

Besides conjuring analogically what they wanted for the next year, people wanted to know the year's course in advance. So they tried to divine certain events and took many actual occurrences during the Twelve Days as presaging the year to come. Thus the first person to enter the house on a New Year's Day must say and/or carry propitious things:[41]

> In Scottish tradition, the "First-Footer" is the person who first comes into the house early on New Year's Day. . . . The "Luck of the Year" was dependent on the "First-Footer" and so householders were anxious that a fine, handsome, wealthy person would present himself at dawn of day rather than some beggarman. The First-Footer had a present for the family . . . often symbolic of health and prosperity for the New Year—gifts such as fuel, money, food, and salt, and a branch of evergreen to denote the continuity of life. . . . The [Irish] Brídeog Procession, in which Brigid is believed to visit each house at the beginning of the agricultural year, may be considered as an ancient and elaborate form of First-Footing which Brigid undertakes to bring her people the "Luck of the Year."[42]

(This Brigid fuses a Christian saint with the pre-Christian fertility goddess of the same name.)

At the other end of Europe, a Bulgarian villager told of receiving an unexpected invitation to go hunting with an acquaintance early on St. Ignatius's Day in December. When he arrived, gun in hand, it turned out that this was merely a ruse to make him the First-Footer, since the previous year, when he just happened to be the First-Footer, the poultry had done exceptionally well![43]

Coins, nuts, and other tokens hidden in Christmas food told the finders something of their fortunes or tasks in the coming year,[44] while ancient Roman farmers presaged what was to come by performing a tiny bit of every kind of agricultural work on New Year's Day.[45] From the Balkans to Scandinavia, St. Lucy's Eve in particular was oracular.[46]* And, as with our Groundhog Day, the weather during the Twelve Days foretold good or bad weather for farming; in Romania and elsewhere, in fact, each of the Twelve Days presaged the weather during the corresponding month of the next year.[47]

In addition to presaging, there was divination. If the souls of the dead roamed the world during the Twelve Days, then people had a handy pipeline to the spirit world to learn about the future. As usual, the young women, having the least power, were the most anxious to learn their fates. Whom would they marry, when, with how many children—or would they die first? These questions were the province of the willies (themselves dead souls), so girls especially in Russia spent many of the Twelve Nights consulting the willies. In fact, prediction constituted the main duty of these spirits during the winter, when they rested. Half a dozen basic methods existed (fig. 9.8; see also fig. 3.9): inspecting reflective surfaces like mirrors and plates of water (typical spirit abodes); interpreting sounds, or the movements of birds (which can fly messages to and from the spirits), or the shapes taken by molten wax or lead poured into water (a method known also in Italy); interpreting prophetic dreams (induced by putting special objects under one's pillow); or "singing the rings."[48]

The Russian version of "singing the rings" works much like the Bulgarian one, and also like the Greek *klédonas* "lots," but early researchers preserved Russian "divination" songs that hint of great antiquity. Divination ditties appear in the first collection of Russian folk songs ever published, that of Ivan Prach in 1790, followed soon by enlarged editions in collaboration with Nikolay Lvov. Mussorgsky borrowed the melody and first line of one of these, finding the refrain *Slava!* "Glory!" suitable to the coronation opening his opera *Boris Godunov*, although ripped completely out of its original context:

---

* *Santa Lucia* originally meant "Holy Light" (compare Holy/Saint Friday), and St. Lucy's Day celebrated the return of more sunlight. It is December 13, but when the maladjusted Julian calendar was abandoned, that was where the solstice had been falling. Note that *Perchta* (English *Bertha*) also means "bright" (Russ 1983, 17).

FIG. 9.8. Girls using chickens to divine their marital fates at New Year. From 19th-century Russian broadside (*lubok*). Compare fig. 3.9 for ritual; note large oven for baking, heating.

Like the glory of the beautiful sun in the sky, Glory!
So also glory to Tsar Boris of Rus', Glory!

The notion of a special sunlike radiance called "glory"—which the celestial deities bestow on a king and which he can lose through wrongdoing—pervades the ancient mythology of the Slavs' longtime neighbors, the Iranians, who called it *xvarəna*. And the ancient propensity of the Persians to divine the future at every step suggests some interesting cultural influences here.

Ultimately, as the Twelve Days close, one must obtain the new lease for living, even by fighting if necessary. Then, it's time to drive the spirits back to the Other World!

In western Europe, people claimed to spend many of the Twelve Nights waging fierce battles against the spirits of the dead, to wrest from them next year's crops, which some of the spirits, presumably *other* people's ancestors, were loath to hand over. In some areas, these battles took place analogically as rituals, with a "beautiful" group, clothed in bright, handsome outfits (often white, but among the Basques red), ranged against an "ugly" band, often wielding brooms, in ragged clothes with their hands so sooty that they shared their blackness with every girl they grabbed (for abundance magic).[49] The Perchten, spreading from Austria and Slovenia through Bavaria and Switzerland, also came in "beautiful/ugly" pairs, the beautiful with handsome, pale face masks and tall headdresses, the ugly dressed in dark rags, fur, and horrible horned masks.[50] In Romania, too, masked "uglies" indulged in folk dramas, countered by undisguised "beautiful" characters.[51]

In other places, the battles took place in spirit. The body of the participant, usually a woman, remained in bed at night while its animating spirit flew off to the "games" of the Good Lady (who led the army of the dead) to eat, dance, do the lady honor, and fight for the crops. Although these night riders considered themselves devout Christians and benefactors of their communities (Italian *benandante*), the Christian clergy eleven hundred years ago took an increasingly dim view of such notions. As Carlo Ginzburg has shown so brilliantly,[52] from these accounts arose the medieval notion of the witches' Sabbath and of witches themselves. The clergy, with a modicum of classical education, associated the Good Lady (a clear euphemism) with the goddess Diana, who in Greco-Roman mythology led the hunt.

In late Roman times, Diana had become associated with the Greek goddess Hera, appearing in inscriptions as Herodiana—but the Christian inquisitors interpreted that name as biblical: the wanton daughter of Herod (Herodias), who caused the beheading of John the Baptist. In western Europe, those who confessed to following the Good Lady were burned at the stake as witches. But in eastern Europe "witchcraft" did not become a polarizing force, and there were no witch hunts. Evils that befell humans came straight from the devils without need of a devil-worshipping human intermediary (the witch). So, to this day the călușari pray to Irodeasa as they begin their "games," dancing in this world and sending one of their number to the Other World to carry away the illness of the patient. Despite the term *game*, the battle is serious: someone might die.

Another way to rout evils is via a scapegoat—originally a goat, slave, or other expendable creature on whom the sins and evils of the community were ritually heaped before the unfortunate being was driven out of town with its accursed load. Both Jews and Babylonians recorded chasing out scapegoats in ancient times.[53] One could also beat the willful spirits directly—show 'em who's boss—for instance, by thrashing fruit trees or threatening them with an axe or gun so they would bear copiously.[54]

If the evils are perceived as willful, then a good way to roust them is with noise—a belief mentioned already by the Hittites around 1450 BC (see chapter 20) and a ritual still carried out worldwide by mere tradition at midnight on New Year's Eve as people set off firecrackers and ring bells. In much of Europe, people believed that the tolling of consecrated church bells drove demons out[55]—Mussorgsky portrays the peaceful dawn church bell routing the demons at the end of his *Night on Bald Mountain*.* But bells on one's person helped, too. The babougheroi, kukeri, Alpine Perchten, and other maskers often wear fifty pounds or more of enormous sheep- and cowbells, creating a deafening racket (fig. 9.9).[56] Those expected to do fancy jumping, however, like the rusaltsi/căluşari, Morris dancers, and Basque dancers, traditionally wore shin pads studded with lots of small bells like sleighbells. In fact, any metallic clinking drove away evil spirits. We saw the Lazarki donning coin necklaces for the purpose, while brides throughout the Balkans wore masses of clinking coins until the birth of their first child, since brides were thought to be particularly vulnerable to the wiles of envious spirits.

The last refuge of the spirits, however, was apparently thought to be water—that reflective substance in which one can actually see them. So on Epiphany, the day on which John the Baptist baptized Jesus, the church fathers deliberately ended the spirits' holiday and set the human world back in order by blessing the waters, on the premise that demons can't inhabit *blessed* water.

Up north in Russia and Ukraine, the solemn company must break a hole in the ice to get at the water to throw a cross in. From Greece down south comes a softer picture:

In many villages, from Christmas to Epiphany . . . , people never go out into the street without a candle or torch [to ward off spirits]. But

---

* Living in Scandinavia in 1937, my parents watched on Sunday mornings as poor people waited by the churchyard to bury their dead when the bells tolled for service—they were too poor to pay for special ringing.

FIG. 9.9. Heavy bells worn by *baboúgheroi* and other pre-Lenten mummers to scare away demons. Phlambouro, Greek Macedonia, March 2008.

the only truly effective means of dispersing the Kallikantzaroi is the blessing of the waters at the Epiphany. Then all the evil spirits scuttle away in a hurry, pursued by the priest's sprinkler (a cluster of sweet basil dipped in holy water). As they leave the world of the living, they whisper to each other: "Let us go, let us go—for here comes the blasted priest—with his sprinkler and holy water."[57]

Part Two

Bride-Dancing For Fertility: The Frog Princess

CHAPTER 10

The Cosmic Arrow

The Dancing Goddesses we encountered throughout the agrarian year were mostly willies, the spirits of dead girls esteemed for their presumed fertility. In fact, most of the agrarian calendar rituals involved appealing to the world of the dead—as much to the ancestors for protection, intercession, and resurrection as to the willies for the moisture crucial to germinating and raising the crops.

But another sort of Dancing Goddess existed who was very much not a dead girl. This divine creature shared with the willies her skill at dancing, her youth, femaleness, beauty and fertility, even the tendency to metamorphose into egg-layers such as swans and frogs. Unlike willies, however, she was the picture of health, gorgeously arrayed, exceedingly clever rather than malicious, and faithful to her mate. She had no particular name and also every woman's name: we could call her the Cosmic Bride, for the world she inhabits is that of the wedding. In the particular tale where we'll make her acquaintance, she is the Frog Princess.

To us, a woman is called a bride for the most part only at the time she gets married. Not so in most of eastern and central Europe. There she enters the special status of "bride" when she gets engaged and does not leave it till the birth of her first baby. During this period she must prove her worth to the family line; if she dies, she becomes a willy. In Lithuania the equivalent term starts even earlier:

> First of all, a girl is called *marti* when she is of marriageable age, a future bride. *Marti* is also a woman who is already married, spending her first days at her husband's house, still as a guest. *Marti* continues to be used for a married woman up to the time she delivers her first child: "She was a *marti* for a long time; married for eight years without children."[1]

We would never refer to a woman eight years married as a bride. But we like to think of marriage in terms of romance rather than as a contract for baby-making. In the subsistence-level agrarian world, marriage occurs to provide workers and heirs. The wedding, however, is not without poetry. Where we emphasize romance, the agrarian culture emphasizes the cosmic attributes of the union of Male and Female: each man becomes momentarily the Cosmic Hero, each girl the Cosmic Bride. But whereas the man can repeat his role, the girl is virgin only once. Only *she*, however, can bear children. So the wedding is much more her story than his, and the Cosmic Bride proves to be a Dancing Goddess.

∞

One of the clearest portrayals of the eastern European Cosmic Bride occurs in the Russian fairy tale "The Frog Princess." It first saw print under the direction of a young Russian lawyer named Aleksandr Nikolaevich Afanasiev, in the mid-nineteenth century, a time of new interest in old stories. Jacob and Wilhelm Grimm had begun to popularize folktales in 1812–15, when they published the first edition of *Kinder- und Hausmärchen* (Children's and Household Fairy Tales)—the book still famous as *Grimms' Fairy Tales*. The Grimms' tales, in fact, are so much better known in the West than Afanasiev's that English speakers assume "The Frog Princess" will resemble the Grimms' "The Frog Prince"—a vastly different story.

The Grimms had collected their narratives from old peasant women and other tellers of traditional lore all over the German-speaking area. From both the linguistic and the folkloric content of their collection, the Brothers Grimm extracted consistent evidence for the antiquity and common origin of certain story motifs (such as the use of the number three: three sons, three witches, three wishes, etc.) and of the forms of the Germanic languages and dialects involved. That is, they all descended from a common cultural ancestor (cf. table 6). Similarly, Afanasiev's collection of nearly six hundred tales, published in eight parts between 1855 and 1864, assembled data for reconstructing earlier forms of Slavic dialects and stories. It includes three versions of "The Frog Princess" (*Tsarévna-Lyagúshka*: #267–69). Internal details suggest the story originated before the Mongols invaded in 1240–41 and decimated the population of medieval Rus'—roughly modern Ukraine—while its patently non-Christian character places it in a yet earlier stratum. It thus provides us with a valuable window deep into the history of these belief systems.

Despite its fairy-tale trappings, the essence of the story consists of finding a potential bride for a potential groom, then testing each in turn, so that when both have been proved adequate (by whatever real or fairy-tale methods) the wedding can take place and the life cycle will revolve properly one more turn. It reflects, in fact, the basic progression of a pagan Slavic wedding, traces of which remain in rural wedding customs, in medieval documents, and in the material relics from bygone times.

We shall now explore "The Frog Princess" one segment at a time.*

The Frog Princess (1)

In days of old, there was a tsar who had three sons, all of them grown up. The tsar said, "Children! Take your bows and shoot, each in a different direction—she who brings back your arrow is to be your bride." The eldest son shot, and the arrow was fetched back by a nobleman's daughter. The middle son shot, and his arrow was returned by a merchant's daughter. As for the youngest prince, Ivan Tsarevich, his arrow was brought back from the swamp by a frog carrying it in her teeth. The two elder brothers were merry and happy, but Ivan Tsar-

---

*For readability, I have translated a rather simple version of the story, pasted together from Afanasiev's two longest (#267, 269), with discussion of variants from all three as warranted. Although Afanasiev edited his texts—they are not verbatim copies of his informants' narratives—he apparently did not edit these particular tales in major ways.

FIG. 10.1. Frog Princess claims Prince Ivan's arrow. After Russian lacquer box.

evich became melancholy and cried, "How can I live with a frog?" He wept and wept, but there was no help for it—he had to take the frog for a bride. And so they began living together.

This first little episode involves finding brides for three eligible bachelors. What's curious is the means for finding them; shooting arrows seems rather like hurling darts at balloons to win a carnival prize (fig. 10.1). But traditional Russian wedding songs and customs provide a key.

Slavic farming society has long been heavily patriarchal and patrilineal—the elder males of the household had control (usually life-and-death control) over everyone else, and inheritance went through the sons. Women, upon marrying, left their natal families and went to live lifelong with their husbands' kin, coming under the absolute control of the husband—and also of the mother-in-law, since the patriarch's wife ruled the younger women of the household and directed much of their endless hard work. (Mothers-in-law from hell are nothing new.) Because marriage and its fertility carried such central significance to this agrarian society, the entire wedding, from locating partners to the final consummation, became a sacred drama, a play with stock characters and traditional songs to accompany each little scene and act. Rather similar wedding rituals continued almost to the present in rural Bulgaria, Russia, and other Slavic areas.

The "play" formally began with the man's matchmakers going to the prospective bride's house to bargain for her hand. Negotiations would begin nicely veiled: "You have a little flower, and we have a gardener. So, might we perhaps transplant this little flower . . . ?"[2] If the maiden's family rejected the suit, the girls of the young man's village might make fun of him, including playing pranks like slipping a log into his bed that night.[3] But if they accepted, elaborate preparations began on all sides, attended at each important step by ancient rote-memorized songs that suggest the original nature of that part of the marriage drama. One cycle sung during the premarriage week typically extols the bridegroom, calling him a brave falcon, wondering why he has stayed so long unmarried—no such brave youths have been seen hereabouts before. The young hero (so they chanted in Archangel in 1927) strides through the countryside and pulls his strong bow to shoot an arrow, saying to it,

> *Fly thou, my red-hot arrow,*
> *Higher than the forest and through the sky;*
> *Fall thou, my red-hot arrow,*
> *Neither into water nor onto land:*
> *Fall thou, my red-hot arrow,*
> *To the girl in the lofty tower.*[4]

This same imagery, patently sexual, occurs sometimes on traditional wedding chests containing the linens and woolens the bride has made up ahead for her married life. For example, a symbol of the female vulva on the front edge of the lid would fit down over an arrow painted on the chest.[5] Storeroom door locks also often took a vulvalike lozenge shape; inserting the key gave access to the goods. Little fell to the imagination. Arrows, too, were placed in each corner of the room in which the nuptial bed had been laid—laid, in fact, on sheaves of grain, to augment the fertility of the marriage act.[6]

Another wedding song carries a similar theme with a slightly different twist:

> *Break open, thunder-arrow,*
> *[Break open] also the mother, the damp Mother Earth.*[7]

The thunder-arrow refers to the pagan Slavic belief that Perun, the ancient storm god, by means of his thunderbolt and its accompanying rain, impregnated Moist Mother Earth (*Mat' Sïra Zemlyá*)—herself a central deity, the giver of grain, never quite hidden by the thin veil of Christianity.

So the young man of the first wedding song went right to the heart of the matter: he desired intercourse with this particular young woman. And in ordering the three princes to shoot their arrows and marry the recipient, the fairy-tale tsar is metaphorically suggesting that it's time his sons marry whomever they like sleeping with: far more practical than darts lobbed at balloons.

∞

The linking of a prince bearing the commonest of Russian names, Ivan (John), with the magical Frog Princess, who, moreover, receives in one version the name Vasilisa (Greek for "princess, queen"—hence she is "Princess Princess"), warns us again that the story is cosmic and universal. In Slavic weddings, calling the actual bride and groom "Princess" (Russian *knyaginya*) and "Prince" (*knyaz'*), no matter how low they might stand in society, constitutes a traditional form of analogical magic by association (or contagion, as anthropologist Sir James Frazer labeled it), representing them as the richest of the rich. The other wedding participants are named accordingly: the bride's friends are "noblewomen" (*boyarki*), the groom's "noblemen" (*boyare*). Although many Russians assume this custom comes from the silver wedding crowns worn by the bride and groom during Eastern Orthodox wedding ceremonies, the magic principle involved is much older and basically pagan.

Weddings taken as cosmic go back to the beginning of recorded history. In the ancient Near East, the high priestess typically "wedded" the king in a sacred ceremony held at regular intervals. Their intercourse symbolized and magically ensured the fertility of the entire land—its crops, animals, and people—for another year or cycle. Samuel Noah Kramer describes thus the situation in Mesopotamia for the third millennium BC:

> The most significant rite of the New Year [festival] was the *hieros-gamos*, or holy marriage, between the king, who represented the god [of youthful male prowess] Dumuzi, and one of the priestesses, who represented the [love] goddess Inanna, to ensure effectively the fecundity and prosperity of Sumer and its people.[8]

But in the cold, inhospitable North, where life was hard and growing seasons short and uncertain, everything and everybody needed all the help they could get. In Slavdom, *every* marriage had to partake analogically of the cosmic magic of fertility. It did so, moreover, as often as possible and in as many ways as could be thought up, from bedding the new couple on sheaves of grain in the barn the first night, thereby sharing the fertility magic with the crops and livestock, down to surrounding the bride with every outward manifestation of prosperity, such as gold, furs, and precious fabrics (often borrowed for the occasion), boy-children set on her knee, and showers of coins, grain, hops, and (nowadays) candy. Frequent reference in the wedding songs to uncommon sexual prowess on the part of the bridegroom (e.g., a red-hot arrow, a great upstanding tree) didn't hurt the cause either.[9]

Viewed the other way around, the cosmic tale tells the felicitous story of *every* good couple, every new prince and princess, bride and groom. They will live happily and prosperously ever after—once their mettle has been tested enough that they have earned their happy fate. Every bride will become by analogy as clever, skillful, and breathtakingly beautiful as the princess, every groom as handsome, heroic, and resourceful as the prince.

❦

Understanding the source from which the hyperbole of marriage rhetoric flows so copiously allows us to understand many other details. For example, in the first wedding song above, the bridegroom-hero wishes his arrow to fall into the "lofty tower" (*vïsokiy terem*) of the young maiden. In folk poetry the tower denotes an inaccessible room where the unmarried girl sleeps. Adam Olearius, an extremely observant ambassador to the Russian tsar from the Duke of Holstein in the 1630s, remarks in his memoirs that "even the lesser notables raise their daughters in closed-off rooms, hidden from other people."[10] No actual tower existed in the Russian peasant house, which was built of earth or of squared logs, like early American log cabins. The humble sleeping room becomes a castle turret by the same stroke that makes the ordinary girl a beautiful and desirable princess, walled up by her royal father to guard her from evil would-be seducers and abductors.* After all, if the princess isn't hard to get, then the groom counts as no hero for

---

*In some areas, marriage followed from simply abducting the girl, whether by force or with her connivance. No matchmakers were required.

getting her. In the story of "Vasilisa Golden-Tress" (another "Princess Princess"), the tsar has locked his beautiful daughter into a lofty chamber of his palace for the first twenty years of her life, and the minute he finally lets her out to play in the garden, she is whisked away by a mighty whirlwind, the traveling-disguise of the evil Savage Serpent—and the whole family has to spend the rest of the tale fetching her back.[11]

The image of the young man shooting his arrow *before* the wedding, as a prelude to marrying, leads to another important observation. Throughout northern Europe, east and west, into the twentieth century and despite the Christian church, conception, not intercourse, defined the consummation of the marriage. A woman who grew up in the 1930s and 1940s on the border between Devon and Somerset in southwestern England comments:

> I never saw a farm hand marry until his girlfriend was pregnant. . . . A girl had to prove herself fertile before marriage. Because country people needed children during those days (country children work very hard), a man and a girl needed to assure themselves of a family before they married.[12]

The same held true in parts of Scandinavia. Marriage existed to ensure the stable care of the children, so if no children appeared—if the couple proved infertile—both could return home without penalty, the marriage annulled. Fertility, not virginity, was the issue.[13] To find out who was fertile, therefore, young men and women were allowed, even encouraged, to sleep around, and fertility festivals such as the Rusalii and May Day originally provided special opportunities for such encounters.

Thus, in the coldest North, in Russian provinces such as Archangel and Olonets, where life was the hardest and most uncertain, everything moved toward the greatest economic gain and ensuring the propagation of more workers to keep the farming going. Neither Social Security nor Medicare existed, so the elderly, in addition to working at whatever tasks they could till they died, relied on their offspring for food and care. So neither bride nor groom had anything to say about whom they would marry—the parents chose as they saw fit, and they chose not according to beauty but rather for fertility and the ability to work hard (as we'll continually see). In 1860, a Russian ethnographer published the following "typical" dialogue from a village in Archangel:

"Van'ka, we're going to get you married."

"No, Papa, I don't want to. . . ."

"What do you mean, you blockhead, you don't want to—who'll do the work around here? Your mother works alone, and she's gotten old. . . . Not a word; we're going to have a marriage!"[14]

Farther south, in central Russia and parts of Ukraine, the parents would suggest suitable girls to the young man but had to have his consent before the matchmakers could visit the girl's parents. The girl, however, had no real say. If her parents liked the match and the girl didn't, she was simply overruled. Many a sad Russian song tells of a young girl about to be married off against her will to some fat old tyrant from the next town.

Yet farther south, in the clement climate of Bulgaria, not only would the boy generally choose the girl but having her consent as well was preferred. They had ample chance to meet others of the opposite sex and sort things out on their own—at spinning bees, at the well, or at the dance. In Thrace, for example,

at the round dances a lad would try to snatch something from the girl he had chosen and that was most often the handkerchief stuck in her belt. . . . If she did not grow angry and demand it back, this was already an answer in the affirmative. Then, in her turn, the girl took the liberty of snatching either by force or with his compliance some minor possession of the young man—a looking glass, a comb, a handkerchief or a pocket knife.[15]

Marriage proceedings here were thus initiated at least sometimes from mutual desire. On the other hand, in the warm South in general, the girl must at all costs be found a virgin on her wedding night—as in Bulgaria:

If it was proved that the bride had not been a virgin, then the wedding [celebration] was stopped. Everyone was shocked, the bridegroom was angry and bristling and the bride was beaten.

Where the shame could not be concealed [guests expected to view the bloody chemise], everyone was scowling, her mother-in-law wept and addressed ugly curses to the bride, while some of the relatives among the wedding guests left the feast as a sign of protest. Such an

attitude . . . was based on the widespread belief that she would bring
ill luck to the family she was joining[,] . . . that there would be an epidemic and plague. . . . When it became known that the bride was no
good, her mother-in-law gave pieces of bread to the dogs and shouted:
"May it be for you!" Thereby she transferred the menace threatening
the farm animals onto the dogs.[16]

The girl remained wed, after her family paid heavy reparations for the ill
luck, but she was taunted, often cruelly, for the rest of her life.[17]

We can thus deduce that in ordering his sons to shoot their arrows to
find their own brides, then live with them before the wedding, the tsar of
our story places himself geographically somewhere between the extremes
of North and South, perhaps around the latitude of Ukraine or South Great
Russia. (Christianity, an urban Mediterranean religion, shared and spread
the tradition of virgin brides.) We will see other evidence pointing in the
same direction.

CHAPTER 11

Bride Testing

The Frog Princess (2)

The tsar wished to discover which of the brides was the most skilled in making things. He summoned the princes and commanded, "Have each of your brides make me a shirt in a single night!" Ivan Tsarevich became very sad again and wept, "What can my frog do! They will all laugh at me." The frog only crept about the floor and croaked. But when Ivan fell asleep, she slipped outside, threw off her frogskin, turned into a beautiful maiden, and called out, "Nurses! Servants! Come make something!" Her serving maids instantly brought her a shirt of the most beautiful work. She took it, folded it, and laid it beside Ivan Tsarevich, and then turned herself back into a frog as if nothing had ever happened.

When Ivan Tsarevich woke up, he was overjoyed. He took the shirt and carried it to the tsar. The tsar took it and looked at it, exclaiming, "Now *there's* a shirt worthy of wearing on a feast day!" The middle brother brought a shirt, and the tsar said, "Only for wearing to the bath!" And when the eldest brother brought a shirt, he said, "For wearing only to a sooty hovel!" As the princes went away, the two elder brothers agreed together, "It's clear that we were wrong to laugh at the bride of Ivan Tsarevich—she isn't a frog at all but some kind of cunning magician!"

The first new worker provided by an agrarian marriage was actually the bride herself. We saw this with the Archangel family in the far North—the mother had grown too old to do it all, so the son had to bring in a new factotum through marriage. We see it again in Bulgaria in the South, in an experience related a century ago by the Bulgarian ethnographer Marinov, himself a city man, when he had to lodge unexpectedly at a stranger's house in a village:

> Next door in the courtyard belonging to my host's brother, I saw a 20–25-year-old bride: she was tall and beautiful; she went to the hay-stack, took a sleeping boy in her arms and carried him to the couch. All this could be seen very clearly and it attracted my attention. This could not possibly have been her child, because she was a young woman, in fact [her clothes showed her to be still] a bride; it might have been a brother of hers—I did not know what; I mustered courage and asked the villager: "When was that bride married and who is her husband?" "This is my brother's daughter in law; we had the wedding during the winter, and her husband is the boy she carried to his bed!" "Well, he is too young!" I mumbled. "You see, he is not young, he only looks young." In the morning, led by curiosity and accompanied by the mayor, I went to that house; I called the boy and saw him—he was not older than 12 or 13. He still showed no signs of virility. "Why have you married him off so young?" I asked his father, and he answered me composedly: "So that there might be someone to work instead of him!"[1]

So the young man's family needed to know first off whether the prospective bride possessed the skills for doing the work. Making all the cloth and clothing for her family would consume a huge share of her time, for clothes did not come from a shop, nor did cloth, thread, or yarn. She would have to raise the sheep, flax, and hemp; harvest, clean, and process the fibers; spin all the thread; then weave it, sew it; and finally embroider the results with the traditional magical designs that would keep the householders safe from sickness demons. So for starters, could she make a shirt?

Farmgirls spent much of their adolescence readying for marriage: learning to spin, weave, and embroider, then making the bridal outfit and the trousseau, which included workday and festive clothes, towels, and sheets for herself and her future husband, plus all the textiles that tradition required she give people during her engagement and wedding. Principal among these, besides shirts and belts, were the ritual towels, or *rushniki* (as Russians call them): swatches of linen a couple of feet to a couple of yards/meters in length, the ends covered with age-old magic symbols for fertility and protection.

Stylized goddesses dance singly or in long chorus lines across these tow-

FIG. 11.1. Figures of "Maiden" (arms raised, often holding birds or flowers) and "Mother" (arms lowered to breasts). From 18th- and 19th-century Russian ritual towels (*rushniki*) and women's chemises. Top left: Typical embroidered Maiden (cf. fig. 11.3), alternating with less typical Mother (winged?). Top right: Stylized Maiden satin-stitched onto net (Kostroma). Second row: Cross-stitched row of Mothers (Archangel; cf. fig. 19.10). Third row: Three woven patterns (typically repeated across a fabric): left, two Mothers in 180° rotation (Archangel); center and right, four Maidens in 90-degree rotation (Olonets). Bottom: 7th-century BC "proto-Slavic" bracelet found near Poznan, Poland: Maidens between swans, under sun disk.

els. The motifs strike one at first as geometric, but that effect comes from weaving or embroidering on the square grid of the woven cloth (fig. 11.1). On closer look at both the rushniki and women's sleeves and aprons, one can discern birds, plants (including protective roses, fig. 11.2, see fig. 8.7), pairs of facing animals, ornate lozenges (female fertility symbols already noted on the wedding chests), and the silhouette of a bell-skirted woman known as *Berehinia* or *Bereghinya* "Protectress"—the protectress of women in child-bearing. The Bereghinya figure, faceless (for who knows what divinity looks like?), usually stands between two birds that rest on her outstretched hands, while a pair of animals faces her (fig. 11.3). To her the women prayed in childbirth, illness, and other times of distress. Some rushniki bear domed churches surmounted by crosses—churches that often look remarkably like a bell-skirted woman with arms outstretched, a tidy Christianization that avoids shutting out and offending the goddess altogether (fig. 11.4).

Slavic women generally executed these patterns in red and black on a white ground, a three-way color scheme inherited from at least the Bronze Age, whereas Romanian and Greek embroidresses used lots of bright blue.*

---

* Among the early Indo-Europeans, white signified rulers, whether kings or priests, as well as the purity of young women; red represented the blood of life, associated especially with virility and the warrior class; while black seems to have denoted the fertility of the black earth, as well as the lowest class that produced food and other necessities from it. As late as the 1870s, this color scheme still marked a tripartite social structure, as the Swiss adventurer Henri Moser found upon reaching a remote city in Kazakhstan on his way to Tashkent. There, among an isolated group of originally Iranian—that is, Indo-European—inhabitants (but not among the Turkic Uzbeks, Kirghiz, and Kazakhs living there), he noted that the mullahs or priests wore white turbans, the warriors red ones, and the merchants blue ones (Moser 1885, 69). (Dark blue dye was often the closest one could get to black.)

In Russia and Ukraine, men traditionally donned a red sash as a sign of their virility; in Bulgaria, wearing the red sash specifically denoted that the young man was now old enough to marry (Ivanova 1987, 9). Although the women of many Slavic regions enriched their embroideries and weavings with other colors, too, the red-black-white color scheme dominated. In Belarus, Macedonia, and Croatia, the white chemises, aprons, and head-dresses were decorated principally in fiery red, while in Ukraine and parts of South Great Russia, married women of childbearing age wore a special back-apron, woven principally in black and red (fig. 17.8, right). Weaving this square-patterned back-apron, in that area, was one of the tests of a girl's readiness to enter the bride pool. (See Barber 1999b for full discussion and illustrations.)

Placed on clothing, the magical red designs promoted prosperity and fertility and protected the wearer from evil, following the belief that sickness came from demons that crawled into one's clothes and thence into the body (see fig. 8.7).

FIG. 11.2. Protective rose pattern embroidered on Russian woman's chemise and on Polish ritual towel. (Compare man's shirt, fig. 8.7.)

FIG. 11.3. Embroideries of faceless *Bereghinya* "Protectress" with raised arms (Maiden), flanked by birds and animals (shapes completely filled with small geometric designs on originals). Left: Towel end: Tver', 1880s. Right: Woman's sleeve; Archangel, early 19th century. (See also figs. 11.1, 19.10.)

FIG. 11.4. Ritual towels (*rushniki*) with "evolved" patterns. Top: Maiden-shaped plant flanked by birds, with flower head between spread "legs" (Russian, modern). Bottom: Christian church, with side towers in particular presented in shape of skirted Maidens (Polish, ca. 1900). (Cf. figs. 11.1, 11.3.)

Rushniki marked all critical events, such as weddings and births. They also stood guard in time of sickness, wrapped the loaf of bread sacred to hospitality, decorated the icons propped in the "sacred" corner of the house, and hung as votives on rails around the saints' coffins (where we saw them—new ones—in the just-reopened cathedral in Kiev in 1993). The sick still hang linen cloths as ritual gifts on the trees and shrubs around healing springs sacred to the willies, such as those beside a rural chapel of Agia Paraskevi in Greek Macedonia (see fig. 8.5).

Villagers viewed the rushniki as protective to the point of magic. Old women would wipe their faces with the ritual towels sent to the groom's family by the bride, so as "to become younger," and at the critical moment in more than one Russian fairy tale a magic towel saves the day. For example, in Afanasiev's tale of Prince Danila-Govorila (#114), when the prince's embattled sister and her girlfriend, the horrid witch's beautiful daughter, finish embroidering a splendid towel together, they trick the witch into the oven where she normally bakes people for dinner, lock her there, and run away carrying a brush, a comb, and the towel. The witch, of course, escapes and begins to pursue them:

> They ran and ran, and took a glance back—the wicked witch had got free, spied them, and was hissing, "Hey, hey, hey! You're there somewhere!" What to do? They threw down the brush, and thick-thick sprang up a stand of reeds, impossible to crawl through. The witch spread her claws, plucked a path, and was catching up to them again. Where to take refuge? They threw down the comb, and dark-dark sprang up a dense forest—not even a fly could fly through it. The witch sharpened her teeth and set to work: whenever she bit, a tree fell by the roots! She hurled them to all sides, cleared a path, and again was catching up. How close she was! They ran and ran, but there was nowhere to run and they were at the end of their strength. They threw down the towel of gold and silk, and a sea spread forth, vast, deep, and fiery. The witch soared high, wanting to fly across it, but she fell into the fire and was burnt up.

And so they were saved. The prince got back his sister and found in her friend a beautiful wife as well, thanks to the magic towel the girls had embroidered. Moral: skillful embroidery could serve as a ticket to a good marriage.

In the millennium-old town of Usvyat on the border between Belarus and Russia, the matchmakers traditionally

> take gifts from the bride-to-be: shirts for the men, lengths of cloth for the women. . . . The fabric is thrown over the shoulder, crossed over the chest, and the ends tied behind the back: "the groom's kin is bound." Upon rising from the [bargaining] table, the "bound" matchmakers dance and go home with their "bindings," "so everyone will see."[2]

Dancing and singing, as we have seen, also marked ritual space and time.

In northern Russia, when the matchmakers returned from a successful negotiation, signaled by bells on the horses and fancy rushniki on the envoys, the women of the groom's neighborhood ran to inspect and touch the textiles sent as betrothal gifts by the bride. Although her abode might be only three miles away, she was most likely a stranger to them (the word for a bride in many regions was *nevesta* "unknown one"). They wanted to see what kind of worker would come into their midst and to absorb magically something of the bride's youth and vigor by touching her creations.[3] In the magic power of her as-yet-unused fertility, the bride exactly resembles the Dancing Goddesses—and the young Lazarki, their representatives.

Although friends might scramble to help her finish the rest of her trousseau, the prenuptial gifts were

> exclusively the work of the bride's own hands—shirts, handkerchiefs, and towels, woven and embroidered by her, with which, frequently, the whole cottage is ornamented at the time of the wedding feast, while the groomsmen are covered with them, and the shafts of the horses' harness in the wedding procession are adorned with them. All this is, as it were, an exhibition, for general inspection, of the proof that the bride is a good worker, one who can weave, spin, and embroider.[4]

How could the peasant girl be expected to make and embroider ahead of time the shirts for the various future male relatives when she couldn't possibly know their sizes? One solution consisted of making each piece—sleeves, collar, front, etc.—with plenty of extra material and without sewing anything together. The traditional square cut of the pieces facilitated the process. The young woman could embroider the collar, cuffs, and front opening to her heart's content and lay them away as kits, like sections of a prefab house, to be made up into shirts of the requisite sizes whenever needed—even in a single night, as the tsar required of the Frog Princess. Forty years ago, tourists in Moscow could still buy the lavishly embroidered makings of Russian shirts in this one-size-fits-all form.

The new family and neighbors, then, got their first impression of the bride's worth from her ability to provide quantities of well-crafted textiles, just as the fairy-tale tsar intends to do. But families expected other skills as well.

The Frog Princess (3)

Then the tsar gave another command, that the brides should each bake a loaf of bread and bring it to him, so that he could judge which was the best cook. The two brides at first had laughed at the frog, but this time they sent an old woman to spy on how she would do her cooking. But the frog realized this. She stomped flour in the kneading trough, rolled it up, then dug out the top of the oven and dumped the mix straight in. The old woman watched and ran to tell her mistresses, the royal brides, exactly what had been done. But the clever frog no sooner saw that the woman had gone than she pulled the dough out of the oven, tidied up as if nothing had ever happened, hopped outside and slipped out of her frogskin, and cried, "Nurses! Servants! Bake for me just such a loaf as my father ate on feast days!" Her serving maids instantly brought the bread. She took it, laid it beside the sleeping Ivan Tsarevich, and turned herself back into a frog.

In the morning Ivan Tsarevich woke up and took the bread—and what heavenly bread it was, all decorated with artful figures! He carried it to his father. At that moment the father was receiving the loaves of the elder brothers, whose brides had dropped their bread into the oven exactly the way the frog had—and come out with dumpy lumps. The tsar took the loaf of the eldest brother, looked at it, and sent it off to the servants' kitchen; he took the middle brother's loaf and sent it off to the kitchen too. It came the turn of Ivan Tsarevich and he presented his loaf. His father took it, looked at it, and exclaimed, "Now *this* loaf—*this* is worthy of eating on a feast day!"

The second test (Indo-European fairy tales of course require three): Can she also prepare food? The English rhyme, too, asks, "Can she bake a cherry pie, Billy Boy?"

In all Slavic wedding rituals, despite their variations, bread and its preparation formed a central element (see fig. 3.4). The making and baking in fact took place in both houses, the bride's and the groom's, for much feasting of guests on both sides would occur during the course of the wedding.

But the bread was not just for eating—it served as the central focus of the entire ritual, being the most sacred of all foods, the main sustenance of life itself. Even ordinary hospitality required that the host offer guests bread and salt: for ritual presentation, the saltcellar perched in a hollow atop the loaf and the loaf nestled in a rushnik well embroidered with magic symbols. Children were never to wander about holding a piece of bread but should sit and eat it quietly, reverently.

For the wedding, both families created specially decorated ritual loaves. During the marriage ceremonies at both houses and sometimes also at the church, a ritual loaf occupied the centermost spot at the table around which the central participants sat or moved. Bride and groom bowed to the ground in front of it, as before a holy object on an altar, while key participants carried specially decorated loaves. In some regions, the bride tucked a small loaf into the front of her dress when she left for the church; in others, a chosen participant of the wedding threw a hunk of bread into the oven as an offering to the spirit that guarded the house.[5] In Belarus even now, anyone with the traditional bread and salt may block the wedding party's route and demand vodka and sweets to clear the way. (One enterprising bus driver regularly equipped himself for such rewarding roadblocks on his intercity runs during wedding season.)[6]

The Slavs shared their preoccupation with the act of making bread with their Germanic cousins, from whom they borrowed their ordinary word for bread, *khlebŭ*, from the same source as English *loaf*, German *Laib*. So central was bread that in English the word *lady* came from the Anglo-Saxon word *hlāf-dīge*—literally, "loaf-kneader"*—while *lord* came from *hlāf-weard*, or "loaf warden, loaf guardian"—two of the most important jobs in early agrarian society, elevated to the highest titles in the land.

---

* Cognates of the second element, -*dīge*, survive in the modern English *dough* (that which is kneaded) and German *Teig* "dough."

In Bulgaria, sieving and mixing the dough in the bread trough consti-tuted the first important ritual of the wedding. The unmarried younger sis-ters and girl cousins of the groom went through the village inviting people to the "sieving." Each woman contributed a bag of flour laced with good-ies such as fruit, nuts, and coins that would remain in the sieve for the loaf-makers to keep. Both the flour and the "treasures" analogically boosted the fertility and prosperity of the new couple, of course, as well as spreading the expense a bit. Only a girl with both parents still alive could lead this bread-making party—all ritual acts moved toward creating a "complete" new family.[7] The songs sung during mixing and baking carried veiled and not-so-veiled allusions to insemination and childbearing, such as one from Belarus that exhorted the wedding loaf to grow and grow in the oven till it burst out the door.[8]

The kneading trough itself figured prominently in Slavic marriages. The Bulgarian mother-in-law gave to the bride as a gift the kneading trough used in the groom's house for the wedding bread—the better to make bread with for the household. In some areas of Russia, the young couple had to pass under an arch made by the parents holding up the lid of the bread trough. As the parents had "mixed" successfully to produce the child now marry-ing, so might the new couple succeed.[9] Bride, bread trough, bread; fertility, procreation, prosperity—we see them linked over and over. The bride had to sit on the kneading trough itself at various points during the wedding,[10] sometimes with a fur pelt—a common Russian symbol for riches. Here the bride seems analogous to the mixing bin itself: as bread comes from the one, so children will come from the other, and both remind participants of the grain issuing from Mother Earth.

⌘

The finished loaves themselves were extremely varied in shape and deco-ration. Around Usvyat, for a wedding the *karavay* or festive loaf* is "a round white loaf, 30 to 35 centimeters [roughly a foot] in diameter, deco-

---

*In other dialects, the form is *korovay*, *kravai*, etc. The term, which occurs in all major branches of Slavic, appears to have come from the word for "cow" (Russian *korova*) and to refer to the fecundity of the bride; the groom is often called the bull. We have seen that families baked appropriately decorated loaves for important calendrical holidays, too, such as Easter and St. George's Day (see figs. 3.3, 3.4): loaves "worthy of eating on a feast day!" as the tsar exclaims. In many regions, these loaves contained a wide variety of grains, like

rated with pine cones and figures of animals and birds, and it has flowers, leaves, and twigs baked into it."[11] In Bulgaria (see fig. 3.4, right), wedding bread carried "figures of birds molded out of dough, their eyes made out of red corn. Other loaves were decorated with winding strips of dough resembling snakes."[12] Birds we have seen as a prime fertility symbol among the Slavs, while snakes (as among other peoples who notice that the snake looks younger after shedding its skin) referred to the cycle of renewed life. One of the decorated loaves served as the stand for a branch heavily ornamented with fruit, flowers, and ribbons, known as "the godfather's tree"—the godfather being a central participant in the wedding. The future mother-in-law presented another loaf, shaped like a large doughnut, to the bride, who then wore it like an oversize bracelet as she led the women in a ritual line dance.[13]

While helping the bride bake her loaf, the older women sing traditional songs about such things as the tall young pine tree growing in the forest— the pine being an old symbol for a young man, as the birch is for a young woman. When the moment comes for the bride and her party to visit the groom's house for the first time, in some areas,

> the bride is conducted from the house along with the *karavai*, and as this occurs, people say to her: "Cake, cross the threshold!" . . . It is as though the *karavai* opens the road to the groom's house to the procession, if they are not immediately admitted:
> "You came to the wrong place. There is no wedding here: it is farther on."
> "But with such a loaf, will you let us in?"
> "Well, with such a loaf we can—how can one not?"

Thus the bride's loaf of bread, piled with fertility symbols, constitutes her entry ticket into the family. Everyone then eats of the bread "for the sake of a well-fed life."[14] The preliminary denial of there even being a wedding belongs to a large class of wedding customs designed to confuse and discourage any evil spirits that might be lurking about. Once the demons have gone on down the road, the presentation of the sacred bread may proceed without ill luck.

---

the ancient *panspérmia* "all seed" (see chapters 19, 21), representative of all that is edible and hence of abundance (Liungman 1938, 619).

The Frog Princess clearly provides "such a loaf," the sort that will let the bride in. One of Afanasiev's storytellers (#269) specifies her bread as "decorated with various cunning figures, and on the sides were visible a tsar's town with gates and all." In this fantastic pastry sculpture we apparently have a recollection of the wedding crowns worn by actual tsars' brides during the height of Russian glory in the seventeenth century. At the moment when the attendants redid the tsaritsa's braid to mark her as married, "she received on her head in place of the maiden's wreath a golden crown, set with precious stones and pearls, which depicted the walls of a city."[15] The crown undoubtedly symbolized her new dominions, over which she now reigned as queen, and they remind us that in sixteenth-century descriptions of weddings among the nobility, the bride was often given manorial villages (along with jewelry) as gifts the morning after the consummation of the wedding.[16]

Magic to ensure the success of the marriage union so saturated every act creating the bride's wedding loaf—acts that no men could witness—that even female ethnographers sometimes found the peasant women reluctant to discuss or describe the attendant songs and customs.

With such a loaf as the Frog Princess's, surely the tsar will allow her in—how can he not?

But he has one more test for her.

CHAPTER 12

Trial by Dance

The Frog Princess (4)

After this the king arranged to give a ball, to see which of the brides
could dance the best. All the guests gathered—except for Ivan Tsarevich. He brooded, "Why should I go, with my frog?" And he wept.
But the frog said to him, "Don't cry, Ivan Tsarevich! Go to the ball. I'll
join you there in an hour." The prince cheered up somewhat when he
heard the frog speak. He went off, and the frog threw off her frogskin
and arrayed herself splendidly.

At the palace the elder brothers arrived with their brides, all decked
out. They began to tease Ivan Tsarevich: "What now, brother—you
came without your bride? You could have brought her in a kerchief!
And where did you ever find such a little beauty? You must have
searched through every swamp!" Suddenly there was a great clap of
thunder. . . .

Into the palace courtyard flew a golden carriage pulled by six
steeds. Out of it stepped the most beautiful princess that one could
imagine, such as are found in fairy tales. She took Ivan Tsarevich by
the hand and led him in to the great oak tables that had been laid.
Ivan Tsarevich was overjoyed, and everyone clapped their hands to
see such a beauty.

The guests began to eat, drink, and make merry. When the princess had finished her drink, she poured the dregs into her left sleeve;
when she had eaten her swan-meat, she hid the bones in her right
sleeve. The brides of the elder princes saw her strange acts and did
likewise. It came time to dance. The tsar ordered the brides of the
older princes to dance, but they deferred to the frog princess. She

took hold of Ivan Tsarevich and came forward. How she danced and danced, spun and twirled!

Dance? Making clothes and baking bread: these are necessary, practical skills. But dancing? How does that help to choose a good bride?

We must recall that among Slavic farming communities, women did most of the hard labor in the fields and house. We saw this from Archangel in the far North, where the parents ordered Van'ka to marry a girl to do all the work, down to Bulgaria in the South, where Marinov saw a woman married to a boy just to bring in a worker. And the bride, the householder with the least status and fewest privileges, had to do the worst of it, especially if her mother-in-law didn't like her. No wonder some people referred to a bride as *mlada* "youngster"; and no wonder brides often died young, swelling the ranks of the willies.

But it wasn't just the Slavs. The Greeks, too, expected the bride to do most of the work. This still held true in Greece in 1962, when I met women, both young and middle-aged, who were "resting" at the Meteora nunnery, Roussanou, where I took lodging. "For the nerves," they said—the same phrase used by Greek women run ragged by their mothers-in-law twenty years later.[1] It was also still true in Russia in 1990, when a student I knew, Karen Patterson, stayed with a family near Khar'kov. The father delivered milk in the early morning, then played electronic games and slept the rest of the time, while the wife worked from 4:00 a.m. till nearly midnight—feeding and midwifing the farm animals, cooking all the meals, working all day in the city as a nurse, washing and mending the clothes, and cleaning the house. That was all women's work, which a man wouldn't touch. (Soviet "equality" merely added a man's type of day job to the rest of women's work.) In eighteenth-century Germany, the rather frail writer Jung-Stilling wrote that, when he begged to marry the local pastor's daughter, his own father worried both that she was delicate, not raised to do hard work, and that she was poor, bringing no wealth with her. How could they possibly manage? And later, after they did marry, his big strapping sisters puzzled over why their sister-in-law, a full-grown woman, would always wear out so fast in the fields. Finally they settled on having her do the entire family's sewing instead.[2] As a Swedish dance song (popular here years ago) put it, the typical farm bride "isn't much for pretty, but she's awful good for strong!"

Among the Slavs, certain dances evolved to test whether the bride was physically strong and agile enough to do all that work.

⚜

Traditional dances in the areas Christianized by the Orthodox Church differ radically from those in western Europe. In the West, the rise of medieval notions of courtly love and honoring one's lady led gradually to people dancing as couples: the gentleman with his lady. That lady long stayed at arm's length in high society, although other classes gradually assumed tighter holds, leading to the still-popular northern European "turning dances"—waltz, polka, hambo, etc.—where a tight body clasp is required for the pair to revolve as one.

To the east, however, men and women traditionally danced separately, and in the Balkans most folkdances still maintain this characteristic. The women dance holding hands in one long chain or a circle (figs. 12.1, 12.2b, see also fig. 3.8), the men similarly in another. If two chains link, properly the last man offers the far end of a ritual towel to the lead woman to hold—they do not touch each other.

FIG. 12.1. Small clay sculpture of Minoan women dancing around lyre player. Palaikastro, Crete, ca. 1650 BC. (Compare Macedonian stance, fig. 3.8.)

Russian and Ukrainian folkdances popular today often require couples, but in general this dance form invaded fairly recently from once-Catholic countries farther west—principally Poland, Lithuania, and Scandinavia. Much older types appear in the ubiquitous khorovod (see fig. 3.1) and the so-called contest dance.

Most scholars derive the word *khorovod* from ancient Greek *khorós* "chorus, group dance" and Slavic *vod-* "to lead"—that is, a "led dance" or "follow-the-leader dance," which describes it perfectly.* Russians still love these slow, repetitive, lyrical line dances that sometimes bored American audiences when the Moiseyev Dance Company peppered them liberally throughout their programs. But the khorovod had an important place in social life, uniting its participants in a common ritual. In 1913, Rappoport remarked:

> All rustic feasts in Russia are necessarily accompanied by the *khoro-vod*, a choir formed of the most beautiful young girls and handsomest youths of the village. The girls are dressed in all the colours of the rainbow, red predominating. The youths are more soberly attired in red blouses, full black trousers, blue jerkin, and a black felt hat deco-rated with a peacock feather. The *khorovod* forms into a circle, with girls in the middle, and sings without ceasing until night.[3]

At weddings everyone joined in the chain dances, whether aged three or eighty-three; so easy were they to do that anyone who could walk could participate.

Contest dances (fig. 12.2a), however, belonged to the nimble and high-spirited. Men's dances would dissolve into exhibitions in which each man showed off his flashiest steps, including the wide variety of "squat steps" that Americans equate with Russian dancing (although these are equally characteristic of Ukrainian, Georgian, Armenian, and some Polish danc-ing). Sometimes the men and women faced off in two lines and traded fancy steps—the men striving for bravado, the women for pertness, and both for

---

*The word *khorós* in Greek, not shared by Indo-European languages outside the Balkans, may itself be an ancient borrowing, most likely from an even older, prehistoric Balkan word.

FIG. 12.2. Images of peasants dancing, from Russian popular broadsides (*lubki*). Top: *Plyaski* in which man and woman trade steps, accompanied by balalaika. Bottom: *Khorovod* for girls, accompanied by singing.

agility: "Anything you can do, I can do better!" Contest dances were so basic in Russia that when dramatic ballets became the rage among the upper classes in the nineteenth century, the story had to grind to a halt somewhere before the final curtain so that the principal performers could show what they could do. The ballerina spins through thirty-two *fouettés*, then catches her breath while her prince leaps twenty-four *grands tours jetés*, and so on—back and forth, with roars from the audience after each snippet of dance. The plethora of dances in a Russian ballet outside the storyline often mystifies ballet newcomers, but these "superfluous" numbers merely perpetuate what native Russians expected in a dance event. Adam Olearius, the seventeenth-century German ambassador to the Russian court, left us one of our earliest descriptions of Russian dance, a performance he witnessed in Ladoga:

> At midday . . . while we were at table, two Russians with a lute and a fiddle came to entertain the ambassadors. . . . Observing that we liked their performance, they added some amusing dances and demonstrated various styles of dancing practiced by both women and men. Unlike the Germans, the Russians do not join hands while dancing, but each one dances by himself. Their dances consist chiefly of movements of the hands, feet, shoulders, and hips. The dancers, particularly the women, hold varicolored, embroidered handkerchiefs, which they wave about while dancing although they themselves remain in place almost all the time.[4]

One great exception to the "don't touch" rule, however, was the class of dances intended for bride testing. Such dances have survived to this day in remote parts of Dalmatia, Bosnia, and Croatia. Probably the best known is *Linđo* (or *Lindjo*). In it, the man wrestles the woman through a long, fast series of twirls and high jumps (fig. 12.3), while the feet of both partners pound out a peppy rhythm. Only strength and agility will carry her through.

In other dances of this class, the women travel in a ring, holding hands, while the men circle around them singly. When the man determines whom he will test, he breaks in beside her and dances along, holding her hand and her neighbor's—but all the while pulling down very hard (fig. 12.4). The women's job is to keep dancing. If the girl can't equal his pull, she fails the trial.*

---

*Ankica Petrović, an ethnomusicologist who filmed for TV in the former Yugoslavia, recorded such dances in the Dinaric Alps of Bosnia in the 1980s. She demonstrated on me how the men pull down as they dance—dancing against that pressure is very difficult!

Traces of bride testing seem to lurk also in modern Russian contest-type folkdances, such as *Kamarinskaya*. After the facing lines of men and women finish trading steps, they form couples. But then the man runs his partner through a series of fast, difficult spins and jumps rather like those in the Balkan bride-testing dances, although the matrix is now

FIG. 12.3. Dalmatian dance, *Lindo*, testing potential bride for strength and agility, using fast spins and high jumps. Here, her tucked-up knees must reach his shoulder.

FIG. 12.4. Bosnian bride-testing dance in which man pulls down hard on neighboring women's hands as they dance, to test their strength.

a polka.* The structure is again one of sizing up the girls for a likely candidate, then trying her strength and agility through dancing with her.

In "The Frog Princess," when the tsar demands that the three brides dance, he simply wants to assess their physical strength. Although Afanasiev's nineteenth-century storyteller gives no evidence of knowing about testing *strength* through dance, the fact that the *woman* spins and twirls, while her prince merely partners her, describes this sort of dance exactly.

But our magical Princess has additional tricks up her sleeve. To understand more details of this peculiar scene, we must observe Slavic marriage customs.

In medieval times, according to the records, the first dish at a wedding feast was roast swan.[5] Little wonder: in those days the northern lakes and marshes still teemed with wild geese and swans, a disguise often taken by the willies, spirits of fertility. So when the bride ate swan meat, she analogically fortified herself with some of their very evident fecundity. And just as the village women hoped to absorb vitality from the bride's ritual towels, so the guests hoped to share in the abundance magic of swan meat at the wedding table. The serving of the third roast swan signaled that it was time for the bride and groom to retire to consummate the marriage.[6] As we have said, the frequent eating associated with agrarian holidays, and weddings, too, signaled more than just gorging or freeloading. It united its participants in a common social and magical ritual intended to augment the efficacy of the occasion. (A *com-pan-ion* was originally one you shared *bread with*, from Latin *com-* "with" and *pān-* "bread.") As Vladimir Propp put it,

> all the examples indicate that food at one time was conceived not just as a means of nourishment, but as an act of communion, for the self and the entire household, with those forces and potentials contained in the ingredients of the dishes.[7]

---

*And its close cousin, the *gallóp*. Such dances often alternate repeatedly between "contesting" and "testing" figures, as in *Polyanka*.

Thus, eating grain, eggs, swans, and so forth, on the proper occasions infused one with their respective magical virtues as well as with simple calories. No wonder the bride ate swan meat just before departing for the marriage bed.

In more modern times, when chickens abounded but swans were harder to come by, chickens came to provide the chief meat at nuptial feasts (typically in Russia in a pie called *kurnik*) and also formed the core of several other wedding rituals. For example, as the cart set off to transport the Ukrainian bride and her dowry to the groom's house, the bride's mother laid at the girl's feet a trussed black hen. Maintaining strict silence as she first entered her in-laws' house, the girl carried the hen inside—she must not enter her new home empty-handed—and let it loose as an offering to the resident "house spirit" so it would accept her into the household.[8] Recall that in Romania the călușari dispatched a black chicken as an offering to the willies at the climax of their healing ritual.

Eating egg-laying birds such as chickens and swans as fertility magic—this we have come to understand. But for what magical purpose did the princess stuff the bones of her swan meat up her sleeve? The other two brides must have wondered the same thing as they tried to copy her. The Frog Princess, however, had not finished dancing.

CHAPTER 13

The Magic Sleeve Dance

The Frog Princess (5)

How the princess danced and danced, spun and whirled! What a marvel to behold! She waved her left sleeve and lakes appeared; she waved her right sleeve and white swans appeared swimming on the water. The tsar and his guests marveled. When she finished dancing, it all disappeared.

The other two brides went to dance, but when they waved their left sleeves, they only sprayed the guests, and when they waved their right sleeves, the bones flew out and one hit the tsar in the eye. He was not amused. He shouted, "Enough, enough!" and the brides had to stop dancing.

For the second part of her performance, after she has danced with Prince Ivan, the Frog Princess clearly goes magical. As she waves the sleeve into which she earlier had poured her drink, she conjures up a splendid apparition of sparkling blue lakes, and as she waves the sleeve into which she had tucked swan bones, swans materialize swimming on the enchanted lakes. If not a Dancing Goddess, surely something close to it.

Vestiges of this magic sleeve dance, like the bride-testing ritual, survived into the twentieth century. Furthermore, clear depictions of it occur in a medieval manuscript (see frontispiece; fig. 2.1), as well as on pagan bracelets from the eleventh to thirteenth centuries dug up by archaeologists in Kiev and other parts of the early Rus' empire. To understand what these scenes really mean, we begin with the sleeves and their bracelets.

Kiev, modern capital of Ukraine, began its ascendancy as an East Slav

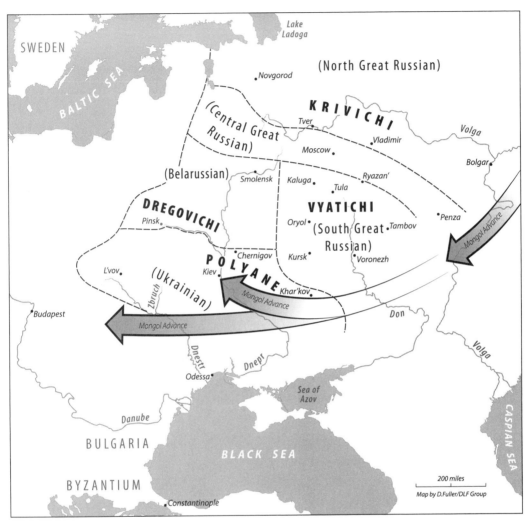

MAP 13: **Historical East Slavs.** Locations of some early East Slavic tribes (Krivichi, Vyatichi, Dregovichi, Polyane), which tend to correspond to modern dialect/culture areas (North Great Russian, Central and South Great Russian, Belarusian, Ukrainian). Warrior-leaders from Scandinavia in northwest and Christianity from Constantinople in southwest had great influence on setting up Kiev and its Rus' empire in this region during 10th through 12th centuries. Then Mongols swept in from the east (arrows), destroying Kiev in 1240 and besieging Budapest in 1241 before returning to Central Asia. (Note Bolgar, in northeast, stronghold of Bulgars who earlier invaded what became Bulgaria.)

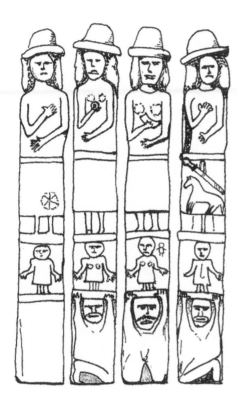

FIG. 13.1. The 4 sides of 10-foot-high stone idol found in Zbruch River, along old Ukrainian/Polish border. Top half: Four heavenly deities under same hat—male with solar disk (Dazhbog?), female holding ring (Lada?), female with horn (Mokosh'?), male with horse and sword (Perun? Svyatovit?). Below them: Four little earthlings (plus child) with arms out, as though performing chain dance. Bottom: Three-faced kneeling deity supporting world from underneath, shown from front and sides. Slavic, 1st millennium AD.

political center in the ninth century. Then, in 980, Prince Vladimir of Novgorod, far to the north, captured the city and made it the capital of his united Rus' empire. He set up statues of the storm god Perun, the vegetation deity Simargl, and four other pagan gods (fig. 13.1) and made his vassals swear allegiance to them. Not content with this, he sent his scouts shopping for a new religion. According to a later chronicle, he first investigated the Muslims but was not thrilled by the notion of circumcision or the laws against eating pork. The prohibition against alcohol proved an even greater barrier, for it went directly against the age-old Indo-European drinking ceremonies that promoted key social bonds among a lord's warriors. One couldn't lightly remove the glue from society. The envoys also complained that the religion contained "no joy." From the Roman Catholics the envoys came home unimpressed: "We saw in the churches many worship services, but nowhere did we see beauty." On the other hand, upon returning from Byzantium, the emissaries so raved of the "heavenly beauty" of Hagia Sophia Cathedral and its rituals that Vladimir officially embraced Christianity from Constantinople in 988, both for himself and for Kievan Rus', and although he immediately had his pagan idols chucked into the river, it took at least another six hundred years to Christianize the general populace.[1]

Over the next two centuries, as princes of different cities waxed strong or lost ground, their armies marched back and forth across the landscape, laying siege to each other's log-built fortresses, carting off the goodies inside, and torching the rest. To reduce the glee of their ravagers, residents developed the habit of burying hoards of their smaller valuables when the fighting got hot—articles of gold, silver, and the like (fig. 13.2). Some of these caches they undoubtedly managed to come back for, but sometimes no one survived to return, and the treasures remained for modern archaeologists and other diggers to find.

Then something much worse happened. In the thirteenth century, hordes of Mongol warriors stormed across the steppes from Asia and invaded the Kievan lands, pillaging, burning, and slaughtering as they came. While Christian priests pronounced that this was God's punishment for sinful living, the citizens tried to defend themselves, organizing their troops and hiding their valuables. But defense there was none. The Mongols smashed down the gates of city after city, fort after fortress, massacring the inhabitants, looting the buildings, and firing the wooden walls. Batu Khan and his men set great Kiev itself aflame in 1240. A huge percentage of the

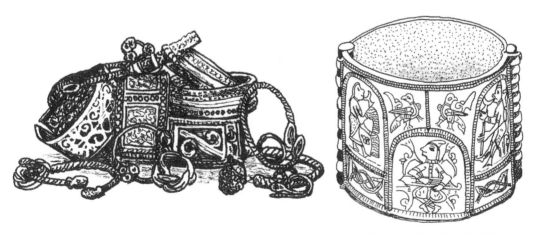

FIG. 13.2. Left: Hoard of 11th-century gold and silver, mostly wedding jewelry, found hidden in basement of Lyubech Castle, overlooking Dnepr River near Chernigov, Ukraine. Right: Hinged wedding bracelet (see appendix), depicting (left to right) woman dancing with extended sleeves, man playing on *gusli*, man with staff or flute; two people hold ceremonial cups. Starïy Ryazan', Russia, ca. 1200.

Slavic population around Kiev either died or fled north into the forests during this time, almost emptying the land of people. Farther and farther west the invaders rode, sacking the cities of Hungary one by one while Europe quaked in terror. Then on Christmas Day in 1241, as suddenly as they had come, the Mongols wheeled and thundered back across the steppes to Mongolia. Messengers had arrived to announce that their ruler, Ogdai Khan, successor and second son of Genghis Khan, had died, and the hordes immediately dropped their siege of Budapest (to the astonishment of the defenders) and rode home across most of Eurasia to select a new leader. Although steppe warriors continued to harry the Russians for centuries thereafter, internal power struggles prevented the Mongols from ever mounting such overwhelming raids again.

Prominent within the treasures so hastily buried between 1000 and 1240 are bracelets of silver and copper. They are thoroughly pagan, apparently mostly wedding jewelry passed down from mother to daughter. The most intricately fashioned consist of two half-cylinders hinged together along one edge, with a clasp along the other, and densely covered with images (see fig. 13.2). Although seldom of exactly matching design, the bracelets usually turn up in pairs, since the women used them to hold up their sleeves, garter-like, at the wrist. Why they needed this help becomes clear from the depictions on the bracelets themselves, for there we see women dancing without their bracelets and discover that the sleeves hung down a foot or two longer than their arms.

Such costumes existed until recently[2]—not in Ukraine, where the Mongols had slaughtered the population, but to the north, where people had not been so hard hit: in Central and South Great Russia, in the territory occupied by an early Slavic tribe called the Vyatichi.* The only recent trace

---

*Some of these tribal names are very old and moved around with little eddies of Slavs as they settled into new territories. *Vyatichi* comes from older forms *Vend- or *Venet-, which (chauvinistically) meant something like "great ones." (Readers of *Beowulf* and *Lord of the Rings* will recognize the Anglo-Saxon cognate *enta* or *Ent*, meaning "giant." The morpheme is also used for the *Wendish*-speaking *Wends* living on the border between Poland and East Germany, and in the name of Good King Wenceslaus (of Christmas carol fame)—*Ventse-slav-s*, a saintly king of Bohemia about AD 900. Equally far-flung, the name *Slav* reappears in *Slovakia* and *Slovenia*, respectively West and South Slavic—that is, Yugo-*slav*—nations; while the ethnonym *Polyane*, the East Slavic tribe trounced by the Mongols, recurs in West Slavic *Poland* and *Poles*; and *Serb*-ian recurs in *Sorb*-ian, another term for *Wend*-ish.

FIG. 13.3. South Great Russian women's traditional dress with ultralong sleeves. Left: Wide-sleeved type, Tambov province. Right: Narrow tubular type, Penza province.

of ultralong sleeves in Ukrainian costume occurs near L'vov (L'viv), in the northwestern corner of Ukraine, apparently just beyond the destructive path of the Mongols.[3] Finds of old cylindrical bracelets, however, occur *both* in the Ukrainian Dnepr valley (the center of Kievan Rus' and the Polyane tribe) and in Central and South Great Russia.* (See map 13.)

As on the bracelets, these extended sleeves may be either broad and floppy or narrow and tubular. They usually attach to the shirt or chemise that forms the costume's undergarment, although early ethnographers mention that women sometimes wore a lightweight smock with ultralong sleeves *over* their clothes in summer.[4] Both peasants and nobility wore such sleeves (figs. 13.3, 13.4). Around Moscow and elsewhere, it grew fashionable to make the sleeves so exaggeratedly long and narrow that it became impossible to put hands through them, so a small slit across the sleeve partway down enabled the hand to emerge there while the rest hung down like a fossil tail (fig. 13.4 right). Ambassador Olearius, in the seventeenth century, describes rich women's sleeves slit even higher:

---

*Hence the ultralong-sleeved costume was known to the Polyane and Vyatichi tribes in Kievan times but not worn among the Dregovichi, who occupied today's Belarus, or the Krivichi, in today's North Great Russia.

FIG. 13.4. Russian women's traditional chemises with ultralong sleeves. Left: Blue silk chemise (with white silk *sarafan* decorated with metallic thread, jeweled *kokoshnik*). Novgorod. Far right: Linen chemise with horizontal slit in each sleeve, below hand, to allow hands to emerge. Moscow area.

> The sleeve is not fully sewn above, so that they may thrust their hands through and allow the sleeves to hang. . . . The sleeves of their blouses are six, eight, or ten ells long, and, if of light cotton, even longer, but narrow; when worn these are drawn into small folds.[5]*

---

*The old "ell" varied greatly depending on the region, from a few inches to four feet. The word itself comes from *ulna*, one of the two long bones running from wrist to elbow. If we estimate Olearius's ell at 9 to 10 inches, an average length for human ulnas, the sleeves were 5 to 8 feet long.

(Because the sleeves were normally pushed or bound up, it is often impossible to tell from depictions whether the individual actually wore ultralong ones.)

Why make a sleeve so long that it needed bracelets to keep it up? That seems an impractical design for a farmwife, especially given how much work we know she had to do.

In fact, the extra length of sleeve had practical aspects: convenient in winter as a mitten and in summer as protection against mosquitoes. Males, too, sometimes wore extended sleeves, and Olearius mentions yet other uses among the menfolk:

> Sometimes when walking, they allow the sleeves to hang free below the hand. Some slaves and rogues carry stones and bludgeons in them, which are difficult to detect. Frequently, especially at night, they attack and murder people with these weapons.[6]

But one of the most important reasons for their existence was ritual. Human hands were thought to block the sacred, whether by touch or through activity; with hands covered, magic could happen.

Even today in rural Slavic weddings, the bride, groom, and other participants must never let their bare hands touch certain key objects or persons. Thus in Bulgaria and elsewhere, the *dever* (groom's brother, acting as best man) leads the bride by means of the ritual towel tucked in her belt, never by taking her hand.[7] In Belarus, the glass with which the ritual toast is drunk cannot be touched: either the hand or the glass must always be wrapped first with a ritual towel or other cloth. At the wedding table the bride and groom may not even *sit* with naked hands—they must cover them with sleeves, tablecloth, or ritual towels.[8] Similarly, when the mistress of the nineteenth-century estate "curled the sheaf" for her serfs at harvest, ritually twisting ears of grain into circles to make their life force infinite (exactly as in "curling the birches" at Semik), "she did not do it with her bare hand, but with a swatch of her dress or her sleeve" covering it so as not to disturb or draw off the grain's powers.[9]

The notion that bare hands interfere with sacred forces occurs elsewhere, too. In Ireland, petitioners approaching the stone *sheela-na-gig* at the shrine and curative well of St. Gobonet (a local female saint at Ballyvourney) must

FIG. 13.5. Morris dancer, Marshfield, Gloucestershire, England. Called "Paper Boy" because body and face are covered with strips of paper for complete disguise.

"touch the figure, not with the bare hand, however, but with a handkerchief."[10] A *sheela-na-gig* is a sculpture of a woman presenting her bared vulva in a most flaunting manner (see fig. 24.1). Her usual location beside a church door, window, or gate suggests the magic involves protection of openings through the power of female fertility.* The association of "transferable" fertility with healing springs so resembles the cult of the willies that one is hardly surprised that, at another holy well with a *sheela-na-gig*, at Castlemagner, County Cork, suppliants attach pieces of linen to the top of the well after drinking the water, hoping for cures from all manner of illness.[11]

The relation between bare skin and sacred forces is actually broader yet. For example, the widespread requirement that sacred players hide their faces with masks—as in Greek drama and the European New Year's

---

*The sheela-na-gig's obscene gesture protects by distracting the spirits (by attracting their gaze) so they fail to carry out their malevolent purposes. Phalli, glittering metal, images of eyes (like the blue eye-beads popular among hippies and others), etc., serve this purpose the world over.

FIG. 13.6. Acolyte with sleeves let down in token passivity/humility as he listens to St. Cyril. Fresco, Church of St. Cyril, Kiev.

masquerades—has to do in part with a requirement that persons perform the sacred rites and dances not as known individuals but as anonymous, nonindividualized representatives of the whole community (fig. 13.5, see figs. 9.2–6).

Another clue about hidden hands: inferiors should not act as independent "hands" but passively await orders. Ambassador Sigismund von Herberstein, visiting Muscovy a century earlier than Olearius, mentions that as the Grand Duke stood listening to the church service, "his hat and kalpak [cap] were borne by one standing before him who had pulled down his sleeves and wrapped them round his fingers. . . ."[12] In still earlier Slavic paintings, men mourning or listening attentively to instruction from a saint or king appear with sleeve-covered hands, as in the frescoes of St. Cyril teaching his acolytes, painted in his eponymous church in Kiev (fig. 13.6). Thus, too, inferiors appear in various miniatures in the Radziwill (Königsberg) Chronicle (named after the powerful Radziwill family of Poland and later the US, into whose possession the manuscript once came).

This particular source, a splendid fifteenth-century manuscript now in St. Petersburg, contains, scattered through its text, more than six hundred colored drawings carefully copied from an older chronicle of 1206, itself partly copied from yet older books. Incontrovertible proof of the antiquity and accuracy of the miniatures came when modern archaeologists unearthed the remains of the Cathedral of the Tithes built by Vladimir in Kiev the year after his conversion to Christianity. The ruins showed that the depiction of this church in the Radziwill Chronicle corresponds exactly to its plan *before* its total destruction by Batu Khan and his Mongols in 1240, not to its rebuilt form.[13]

FIG. 13.7. Funeral of Andrey Bogolyubskiy, surrounded by courtiers mourning with sleeves down. His wife (at right), who helped assassinate him, has let down only one sleeve. After miniature in Radziwill Chronicle, 15th-century copy of 1206 manuscript from Kiev.

Two pages of these miniatures concern us. On one leaf, dead king Andrey Bogolyubskiy lies on his bier surrounded by courtiers weeping into the ultralong sleeves that totally cover their hands. They can do nothing now to help their sovereign; they are ritually passive and perhaps ritually clean—like those receiving instruction from their betters, and like the bride and groom sitting without eating at the wedding table before consummation. Another person there also bewails the dead king—his wife. In a vignette at the top of the page, however, she helps several conspirators kill Andrey, whose severed arm she holds. (Gossip was, she let them into the bedchamber.) With wonderful irony, the painter depicts the queen at the bottom of the page crying for her husband into one lowered sleeve, while the sleeve on her other arm is still braceleted up (fig. 13.7). Code: Those are only crocodile tears, and she isn't as inactive as she pretends to be. Her heart, as it were, is to be found on her sleeve.

These scenes occupy sheet 215. Leaf 6, toward the front of the manuscript, shows peasants celebrating the Rusalii (see frontispiece; fig. 2.1).

FIG. 13.8. Figures from Kievan wedding bracelets (see appendix). Clockwise from mid-upper left: 4 women dancing with extended sleeves; 2 musicians with zither-shaped *gusli*; seated drinker holding flute or staff; 2 bagpipers; 3 male dancers (2 with weapons). Center: Vila.

Gesticulating onlookers watch as two pipers pipe, a drummer swings his drumstick, and a young woman with loosened hair and sleeves dances alongside a half-grown boy. This girl, surrounded by musicians, with her raised arms and long, waving sleeves and hair, corresponds closely to the images on the bracelets. Apparently the type of musician didn't matter, for we see pipes and drums in the manuscript but a flat, oblong, stringed instrument like a simple zither on the bracelets (fig. 13.8). (Archaeologists retrieved a five-stringed gusli of this type from a twelfth-century layer in the Baltic port city of Gdansk, and a thirteenth-century gusli with nine strings in Novgorod.[14] The musical settings signal clearly that the scenes represent dancing, while the characteristic positions of the dancers imply that the central movement involved waving the sleeves—just as in the Frog Princess's magical dance.

So what was the magic?

Again the bracelets tell us—and, with great complaint but little detail, so do the Christian priests trying in vain to wean people of their pagan ways. The priests inform us that the Rusalii festivals at Midsummer, Midwinter, and early spring involved great orgies of dancing and other obscenities—which (if we may read between the lines) had the purpose of promoting fertility:

> Men and women and girls gather together for nighttime diversion and for obscene talk and for demonic songs and for dancing and for jumping and for impious deeds, and there is profanation among the boys and corruption of the girls. [16th century][15]

This sounds, of course, like Russian Semik and English May Day.

Several types of ritual events occurred:

> Some banged the tambourines, others played the flutes, yet others put *skuratï* (leather masks) on their faces and made fun of the people. . . . And the name of those celebrations was Rusalii. [13th century][16] *

---

*Russell Zguta's analysis of the persecuted medieval Russian *skomorokhi* (traveling players) as originally having been fellowships of pagan priests makes them sound remarkably like the Bulgarian bands of rusaltsi (Zguta 1978, 8). See chapter 17.

Whenever Rusalii are celebrated or players perform, or there is a call
to a drinking bout . . . or some gathering for idolatrous tournaments—
stay thou home at such an hour! [13th century][17]

Perhaps most characteristic of these medieval "demonish carnivals" were
"plays spoken by dolls and players, and the dancing of Rusalii."[18] This
sounds like the Balkan Rusalii we explored in chapter 5, with both dancing
and short skits. But closest of all to the women's fertility dance depicted is
the ritual of Enyo's Bride surviving in Bulgarian Thrace at the summer solstice, the time of the summer Rusalii. As the little "bride" flaps the too-long
sleeves of her borrowed bridal chemise like the wings of a bird, she spreads
and also prophesies the fertility of the coming year.

Here we have the key. The long white sleeves of the chemise, as the
Rusalii dancer waves them, resemble the wings of a bird, and most specifically the wings of the white swan whose form the willies typically take.
The girl who dances in this way becomes by analogy one of the swan
maidens, a veritable Dancing Goddess, channeling their cosmic fertility
through her body the way a lightning rod attracts and conducts celestial
electricity down to earth. The magic of this dance, in short, funnels health
and fruitfulness into the community. In older and more thoroughly pagan
times (such as the era of the bracelets), a girl like the Frog Princess who
could successfully perform the dance and reap its magic would constitute
an ideal bride.

⋘

Fertility dances, however, offended the church more than anything save
adultery and murder, and letting *women* perform these dances was worst
of all. One early Orthodox missionary thundered: "A woman dancing is
called Satan's bride and the devil's lover, spouse of the demon"![19] Part of
the problem undoubtedly stemmed from the fact that Rusalii dances, as we
have seen, often worked up to a fevered pitch until the dancers entered a
kind of trance—an altered state often interpreted as possession by spirits
(or, in Christian terms, demons), as with voodoo. Trance involves loss of
rational control, and women especially, according to Christian tradition, sin
through such "temptation by the devil." Translation: Lack of control may
bring about loss of chastity. In western Europe, the churchmen burned at
the stake any women thought to have had truck with the devil; in eastern

Europe, they merely drove women out of ritual dancing, leaving only hints of women's original participation.

The men could still get away with it—their chastity is not deemed important by the church, although the dancers held a different opinion. The men who acted as rusaltsi and călușari set themselves temporarily outside Christianity, swearing not to enter a church or say a Christian prayer *or have sex* during the entire period of the rituals, and even, in some areas, hiding whenever the church bells rang.*

Little girls could get away with it by being young and asexual enough to fly beneath the church's radar. So in Thrace the marriageable girls, who *should* have been the magic sleeve dancers, contrived to carry a tiny girl who waved the magic sleeves for them and predicted the crops, while they did simple *bouenek* steps that you could see on many an occasion—no alarm there.

In eastern Serbia, the job was divided up. Some women (of varying but always childbearing age) fell into trances to commune with the ancestors, while other young women (the kraljitse) and certain young men danced together to retrieve them from the spirits. We see another stage in Bulgaria, where women previously cured by the rusaltsi had to accompany the dancers each year for three years but no longer danced.

Masks provided another way to sidestep the church. Thus, nineteenth-century observers in northern Russia described seeing the white chemise with extended sleeves donned over the person's regular clothes, together with a scary mask, at the Midwinter Rusalii.[20] Who knows who hides beneath that mask?

The Kievan bracelets, which transmit pleas for fertility and prosperity from every device and curlicue on their surfaces (fig. 13.9, see figs. 3.10, 13.2), provide more information. Arches typically divide the space, sometimes detailed to suggest birch trees (see fig. 3.10), whose sacred branches the Russian girls traditionally bent and tied together to form living arcades for the spring and Midsummer festivals. Within these arches the artists have set both male and female dancers (see fig. 13.8–9), the latter with their loosened hair and magic sleeves† and the former with staves or

---

*Bells and other clanging metal were often used to drive off evil spirits.

† As we've seen, proper married women kept their tresses completely covered, while maidens combed and bound theirs into a tidy braid. Only willies and witches—and girls impersonating willies—left their hair loose. (Those dressing as witches in holiday masquerades, from Poland to Macedonia, traditionally deck their heads with mops or tow to look suitably unkempt.)

FIG. 13.9. Kievan bracelet (see appendix) from 12th-century hoard found at Tver' (Kalinin). Arches contain (left to right): woman with conical cup who redirects growth of Simargl creature back into ground, male dancer, spectator with conical cup; hops vine, 2 types of Simargl (vegetation spirit). Lower panels: 3 water symbols (interlaces); 3 hops roots, 2 of which resemble frogs or women in birthing position.

swords, just like the modern rusaltsi, călușari, and kukeri (see figs. 5.1, 5.5, 17.6). There, too, sit the pipers and gusli players accompanying them, and onlookers of both genders. One dancer has an animal mask near her foot (fig. 13.2, in left arch), like the leather masks mentioned by priests as belonging to Rusalii performers (see fig. 17.10). The participants often hold conical cups and chalices in their hands for drinking special brews sacred to the willies.

What filled those cups? Today we associate hops with beer, and the representations of hops vines on the bracelets just below the drinkers suggests the beverage was beer (although the modern rusaltsi/călușari drink a secret brew of magical herbs). Getting intoxicated is, of course, a quick way to see the spirit world. But the Slavs also venerated the hops vine as an important fertility symbol; among other things, they traditionally strew handfuls of its little cones (see fig. 6.3) over the bride at her wedding.[21] One has only to see the buds hanging by the thousands on the long tendrils to understand the association to fecundity. What's more, the upward-seeking tips of the vines can grow as much as nine inches per day in the spring, a splendid symbol of renewed growth. References to hops in western Europe commence only in the eighth and ninth centuries, in monastic and legal records, using a new "Latin" word *humulus*, related to the Slavic term for hops, *khumeli*. Uralo-

Altaic languages from farther east also carry similar words. Who got what from whom? Neither linguists nor botanists nor historians have sorted that out yet for certain, but the Kievan bracelets suggest that the fertility cult of the willies in central Europe may have supplied reasons for mixing hops into beer, with the custom spreading from there as people came to like the taste. This association of hops with the healing spirit maidens may go far back, since for many centuries folk healers have used extracts from hops as medicine for assorted ills.[22]

Hops propagate not through seeds (those copious "fruits" have no seeds) but adventitiously, by sending out subterranean runners as crabgrass does. The bottom panels of some of the bracelets (see figs. 3.10, 13.2) show such runners cloning outward from a central sprout. But the design is often contrived so that it also resembles the splayed legs of a frog and of a woman giving birth (see fig. 13.9): analogy piled on analogy, all pointing to fertility and growth of new life—and to new reasons why our princess bride should be a *Frog* Princess.

Intertwined with the burgeoning vines is another peculiar figure: a four-footed beast whose head might be human, canine, or avian and whose tail sprouts leaves and turns into twisting tendrils. Boris Rybakov identifies this creature as a Simargl (see figs. 17.7–9), a deity borrowed from the nearby Iranians.[23] Simargl made the vegetation grow and was one of the six gods that Vladimir set up for worship in Kiev before turning to Christianity. Others included the storm god Perun, the cattle god Veles (Volos, or Vlas—later transparently worshipped as St. Vlasius), and Mokosh', a female deity often equated with Moist Mother Earth. Hybrid quadrupeds with tails turning to sprouts also appear carved on the wooden window frames of nineteenth-century Russian farmhouses.

The wooden Simargls share these boards with girl-headed birds and mermaids (see fig. 1.1), and all share the purpose of reminding the powers that be to fertilize the crops and women of that farm. Girl-headed birds also appear on other jewelry found in the hoards with the bracelets: large lens-shaped disks of gold (fig. 13.10) carrying bright enamel figures of birds, saints with halos, and girl-faced birds also with halos—you have to look carefully to distinguish Christian from pagan. The bracelets further include signs for life-giving water—a Celtic-looking interlace (see figs. 3.10, 13.2, 13.9)—and the solstice sign, which is an X inscribed in a circle

FIG. 13.10. 12th-century gold pendants (*koltï*) ornamented with colored cloi-sonné enamel, depicting birds and girl-faced birds (willies) with halos. Used as earrings or hung from temple of medieval Kievan woman's headdress.

(see fig. 17.7), related to the Xs found marking solstices on the preliterate calendar vases (see fig. 2.3).

❧

By now we can see why the Kievan silver bracelets were so precious to those who buried them in their hour of despair. Saturated with magico-religious imagery, the costly objects stood for everything that the community desired for the woman in her marriage. Indeed, the success of the woman in produc-ing children functioned as the mainspring of society. How the priests must have bit their lips to see their wealthiest patrons coming in to get married wearing pagan adornment and led by sorcerers chanting spells! To those who lived a secular life, growing the food and propagating the race, fertil-ity was a must, and anything that might secure it could not be abandoned lightly. And so the magic dance of the white wings lived on.

CHAPTER 14

Second Skins

The Frog Princess (6)

During the confusion Ivan Tsarevich availed himself of the chance
to run home. There he managed to find his bride's frogskin, took it,
and threw it into the fire. She too came home, and she searched for it
but realized that it was gone—burnt. She lay down to sleep with Ivan
Tsarevich, but towards daybreak she said to him sadly, "Ivan Tsarevich, what have you done? If only you had been patient a little longer,
I would have been yours forever—but now heaven only knows. Farewell! Search for me beyond the thrice ninth land, in the thrice tenth
kingdom!" She turned into a white swan and flew away through the
window.

Ivan Tsarevich wept bitterly, but there was no help for it. Finally
he prayed to the four directions and went off, following wherever his
eyes turned.

*I*t is well known among the peasants of eastern Europe, and in certain other parts of the world, that the way you catch and keep a spirit
maiden is to steal her second skin—the one she dons to change shape.
This skin is as separate and "alienable" as the clothing it resembles, and as
fertility and the soul were thought to be. Many Eurasian folktales tell us of
this mode of capture, and we have already seen several instances—in particular, the Bulgarian story of Stoyan and Radka in chapter 1.

Like Ivan, Stoyan steals the second skin of the supernatural bride to
make her stay, but when she gets hold of it again (unlike Ivan, Stoyan has not

destroyed it), she flies away. Like the Frog Princess, Radka dances a magical, whirling dance dependent upon a winged chemise; and as she departs each bride tells her distraught husband she is flying far, far away. What's this all about?

⤫

The story of the Animal Maiden Whose Skin Got Stolen occurs as a folktale all the way around the globe—but not worldwide. Rather, it clings most tenaciously to the margins of the Arctic seas, from Siberia to Alaska to Greenland and on across northern Scandinavia back to Siberia, trickling down into the interiors of the northern continents here and there, even to India in attenuated form. A scholar named A. T. Hatto pursued it across this vast territory, and through time as well, finding hundreds of tellings. The oldest he found occurs in a Chinese book of about AD 300, the *Hsüanchung chi* (*Xuanzhong ji*). Hatto summarizes it thus:

> A man once saw seven girls in the fields. He did not know they were really birds. He approached, meaning to take their feather-robes and hide them; but they rushed to their robes, put them on, and flew away, all except one who was too late. He married her, and they had three girls. Learning through her children that her robe was beneath some rice-stalks, she took it and flew away in it. She later returned with feather-robes for her daughters to fly away in.[1]

Most of these elements occur in the Bulgarian tale of Radka, except that the Chinese bird woman takes the children as well. Across cultures, details vary: the woman may or may not take her offspring (which may be of any number and either gender); the husband may or may not eventually find his lost wife; the birds may be white cranes or geese or swans. (Some Turkic and Slavic tales sidestep the choice, calling them swan-geese.) The Lapps tell a version in which a bathing maiden loses her seal skin to a lurking hunter and can return to the freedom of the sea and her seal-people only when she recovers it. The Irish also have seal-maiden stories, familiar to viewers of the film *The Secret of Roan Inish* and to readers of Clarissa Pinkola Estes's *Women Who Run With the Wolves*. One has only to see the hauntingly big eyes of a young seal to imagine a human behind them.

Hatto located a particularly instructive version among the Buryats of

Central Asia, an Altaic group that, like several others possessing this story, derives its mythical ancestry from swans:

> One day three swans alighted beside a lake to swim. After taking off their swan-clothes, they transformed themselves into handsome women. A hunter . . . , who was hiding on the shore, stole one of their dresses and concealed it. When the swan-women had swum for a while, they came out of the water to dress, but the one whose clothes had been taken remained there, naked as she was, while the others flew away. The hunter thereupon took her and married her. In the course of the years the woman bore him eleven sons and six daughters. One day, after a long time, she remembered her old dress and asked her husband where he had hidden it, at which, trusting in the thought that his wife could abandon neither him nor their offspring, he decided to restore her marvelous robe to her. In order to see what she would look like in it, the woman put it on; but as soon as she had done so she flew up into the air through the smoke-hole of the tent.

(So far, this tale runs even more like the Bulgarian story of Radka than the early Chinese version, including flying out where the smoke exits rather than through a door or window. Its continuation, however, while not altering the outcome, shows us something critical about origins.)

> Hovering above her home, she called to those whom she was leaving: "You are earthly beings and remain on earth, but I belong to Heaven and I am going to fly back there!" Then, mounting ever higher, she continued: "Every spring, when the swans fly north, and every autumn when they return, you must perform special ceremonies in my honour!" Thereupon their swan-mother disappeared into the upper air. . . . One of her daughters whose hands were sooty tried to stop her mother from flying away by seizing her feet, so that they got black—and that is why swans have had black feet ever since.[2]

Here at the end we find a bit of a "just so" story, which, although tacked onto the commoner form in which the swan woman simply flies away, nonetheless points us toward paying attention to facts about real swans. And the Buryat swan mother mentions another fact: migration.

Swans, cranes, and geese migrate tremendous distances between the warm zones where they winter and the Arctic where they spend the summer breeding and raising their families. Marshy islands there provide considerable safety from foxes and other predators, not only for the eggs and fledglings but also for the parents. For in order to make the return flight, the adult birds must renew their flight feathers. So they molt, losing their magnificent feather dresses before donning new ones. But now they are as vulnerable as their fledglings: until the feathers grow out, swimming and hiding provide the only escape from predators. Then in the autumn, an overwhelming urge carries them far away south.

People at the southern end of the migration route see the splendid white birds for only part of the year—they do not watch them lose their feathers or produce families. Without modern travel and communication, earlier peoples couldn't know whence the migratory birds came or whither they disappeared. Now, the swan maiden's tale is at heart a story of marriage and childbearing. So although swan girls turn up in tales as far south as India, the key characteristics we have traced are largely lost there, but with little diagnostic details preserved here or there.* Even the Buryats, who live north of Mongolia just east of Lake Baikal, reside too far south to see the mating—though perhaps not so far that they had not heard tell of it from related peoples.

If, then, as Hatto concludes, the Legend of the Swan Maiden originated along the Arctic and sub-Arctic lakeshores, how did the southern Slavs get it? The Bulgarian version is almost exactly like the Buryat one, which in turn closely resembles the circumpolar stories. Yet we have no evidence that the early Indo-European speakers ever lived that close to the Arctic. In fact, all the data suggest that until late Roman times the speakers of Uralic and Altaic (including Finnic and Ugric, Turkic and Mongol: table 14) *always* inhabited the belt to the north of the Indo-Europeans across Eurasia, forming a buffer zone between "us" and those cold Arctic littorals where the swan-geese and dancing cranes breed.

Slavic sources are twofold. The basic story of capturing a bride by stealing her feather robe is likely a very old one, as Hatto suggests,[3] perhaps even Palaeolithic, before agriculture. For the man lurking in the bushes beside

---

*The Indic branch of the Indo-Europeans (see table 6) traveled to India from much farther north in the Bronze Age, some four thousand years ago, proving that the Swan Maiden tale is at least that old.

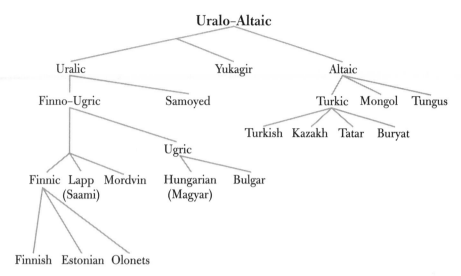

TABLE 14: URALO-ALTAIC LANGUAGE FAMILY
Many branches not shown

the lake is by nature a hunter, and the birds captured are creatures commonly revered as totems in northern hunting societies (several Asian tribes still view hunting swans as taboo[4]).* Furthermore, the notion of a magic skin that transforms a person into an animal, not to mention the habit of flying to another world via the smoke-hole, belongs most particularly to those cultures that practice classic shamanism, cultures found in just the northern areas where this legend is so widespread.

Why storytellers of many lands should continue to recount it for so many millennia need not distress us. As Hatto points out, any wife captured or sold off from elsewhere must watch the free flight of birds and especially their migration with longing. To her, the tale of the swan maiden, who finally flies to rejoin her own kind far beyond the reach of her captors, would become unforgettable.

Nor are the elements of this tale forgotten yet, even in the modern bustle.

---

*Note that southeastern European farmers demanded more of their brides than just fertility. The hunter's bride bears him children, but then she flies away. As Radka says, it's not in her nature to stay. (Even while originally alive, the girls who became willies "copped out" and left, by dying too soon.) The farmer, however, requires a childbearer who will stay and do the work that feeds the family.

In the late 1950s, talent scouts from Moscow arrived in eastern Russia to record three sisters who enjoyed great local popularity. Times were particularly hard for women then, since so many of their men, young and old, had gone off and died in the war. In one of their compositions, the Fyodorova Sisters sing of a girl who sits sewing by the window, lamenting that her beloved has gone away. The girl concludes:

> *I will don a white dress,*
> *Become a little white swan,*
> *And fly away whither*
> *My darling has gone.*

The white garment that transforms and frees a woman still survives in Russian folk poetry.

Why, then, do the closest parallels to the Asian stories occur precisely in Bulgaria?

Although the Bulgarians now speak a South Slavic tongue, they take their name from some Ugric speakers called Bulgars who crossed the Danube en masse into that area in 679, having moved down into the watershed southwest of the Urals to the Volga some three centuries earlier. Upon their heels came Turks and Tatars (themselves a Turkic-speaking tribe). So the fairly pristine, near-Arctic form found in the tale of Stoyan and Radka almost certainly arrived with these northeastern folk at a relatively late date.

Of course, upon hearing the newly imported version of this far-northern tale, the Balkan farmers would have known just where to file it, for they already knew something about spirit maidens in general and bird maidens in particular. Willylike bird maidens go far back in Balkan prehistory, as we'll soon see (Part III). The Uralic hunter's tale would but add a fresh incident to the lore about their mysterious doings. Shape-changing between bird and woman provided the similarity that fostered crossover between the stories, although the Arctic swan maiden is perceived as a bird who takes human shape upon removing her proper skin, whereas the willy is a human soul or spirit who has merely selected the shape of a bird or fish—longstanding emblems of fecundity (fig. 14.1)—as a disguise. The proof of this hypothesis is that willies *dance*, and it is only in the Balkan versions that the swan maiden *dances* as an integral part of the story.

FIG. 14.1. Ladles (Russian *kovshi*) traditionally shaped like long-necked birds (masses of which migrated twice yearly across Eurasia) to promote abundance. Left: Wood, 4th millennium BC, Sarnate, Latvia. Center: Wood, 2nd millennium BC, Gorbunovo bog, Sverdlovsk province, Russia. Right: Silver, 1635, Moscovite workmanship.

But the willy is not a frog, nor the Frog Princess a willy, although the two are so closely associated that (at least in this version of the tale) the Frog Princess, robbed of her frogskin, flies off as a swan exactly like a willy. (In the other two versions collected by Afanasiev, she either flies away in an unspecified form or just disappears.) Furthermore, the hunter eagerly captures his bride, reluctant and shivering on the shore, whereas the Frog Princess must press herself and the fateful token of the arrow on an astounded and reluctant prince. So what *is* the Frog Princess, and what is her relation to the Dancing Goddesses?

Note first that the Frog Princess is treated not as an otherworldly soul forced by capture to maintain human form but as a real girl, and a rather spunky one at that, who *wants* to stay with her husband (unlike Radka) and had somewhere been transformed into a frog. Two of the storytellers don't mention how she acquired this peculiar curse; the third, which gives her name as Vasilisa the Wise (Princess the Wise), flippantly explains that her father transformed her thus for three years because he was irritated that she was smarter than he!

From the three bride tests, we learn that the Frog Princess excels at everything required by the agrarian father-in-law, king of his land and household: she can prepare the food and clothing cleverly, and she is strong.

We also learn that she is breathtakingly beautiful. (In fact, when her name is not given as Vasilisa the Wise, it is said to be Elena the Beautiful, [H]elena being the Greek name of the reputedly most beautiful of all women.)

So she is the perfect bride—or she will be if she is also fertile, for, as we have seen, fecundity is the ultimate goal of the farmer.

Now, fertility is the province of the willies, so the Frog Princess's ability to "channel" them via her magic wing dance, and even to adopt their swan shape, connects her strongly to them. But there is more to it than that—an underlying symbolism that spawns *all* this imagery. In each tale, the man acquires a wife who has a second, highly symbolic shape: frog or bird, or even part fish—a mermaid.

What do frogs, birds, and fish have in common? They lay eggs. And eggs, as we have seen, produce life—hence their use at Easter and other agrarian spring festivals to symbolize resurrection. As a seed is to the plant world, so an egg is to the animal world: the mysterious capsule of life, the miraculous little starter. No wonder the spring feasts consisted of dishes made from eggs and grain. No wonder the Dancing Goddesses took on such forms as birds and fish.

But the frog, another prolific egg-layer, carries this symbolism yet further. The willies, as maidens who died *before* producing children, represent fertility not yet realized. The frog, however, symbolizes the transitional stage *between* maiden and mother: that of pregnancy, when fertility is proven

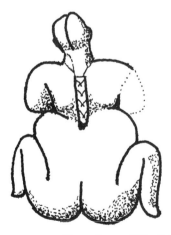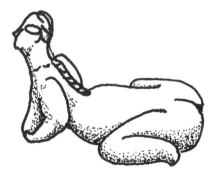

FIG. 14.2. Two views of Neolithic sculpture of frog with woman's head, braid, and breasts—or sculpture of woman on belly, holding her breasts, with legs pulled up like a frog. Early 6th millennium BC, house Q5, Hacılar, Turkey.

and the offspring are on the way but not yet here. For the plump, squatting frog looks like a pregnant woman, legs spread for birthing. We saw this symbolism on the medieval bracelets that depict the sleeve dance (see fig. 13.9), where analogy was piled on analogy—the more the layers, the more effective the magic. But it is far older than that. The early sixth-millennium inhabitants of Hacılar, an early farming village in south-central Turkey (the direction from which the first farming technology of Europe came), left us more than one terracotta figurine that is half woman and half frog or toad (fig. 14.2). The creature squats on its belly with legs drawn up like a frog, raising its head and shoulders on propped elbows. The face and head are human, while the large breasts prove it to be a woman. As with most early figurines, she wears no clothes, but, unlike them, she wears her hair in a single long braid down her back, like unwed Slavic peasant girls. Viewed from the front, the ancient statuette looks human, but from the back (i.e., top), she looks like a frog or toad except for the braid. At the other end of the time scale, twentieth-century women of central Europe still gave frog-shaped votive offerings to the Virgin Mary for protection against barrenness and the dangers of pregnancy.[5]*

Remember the arrows? Who brought them back? The *best* bride is the one who not only passes the practical tests but can prove that the *bridegroom succeeded in fertilizing her*. To put it more crudely, he shot his arrow and she came back a frog.

And so to the final question in this tale: Will the two lovers, now so abruptly parted, be reunited? In fact, in the different tellings, appropriate endings play out in two quite different but equally instructive ways. Although seeming to digress somewhat from our pursuit of Dancing Goddesses, each ending will provide useful internal data for eventually tracking origins of the whole complex (Part III).

---

*Birds, fish, frogs/toads, and snakes constitute most of the egg-layers of Europe. So far we have discussed the first three. Snakes also had a strong relation to fertility and well-being in this agrarian worldview, serving as alternative residences for the spirits of one's dead ancestors, to whom one prayed for help in the struggle to maintain fertility. In parts of northern and central Europe, it is still considered highly unlucky to kill a toad, frog, or snake, and people will go to great lengths to pluck them off the road or out of other inopportune places (Gimbutas 1958, 25–36). Snakes, of course, have ancient and widespread associations with renewed life because they shed their skins—already noted in the third millennium BC in the Sumerian *Epic of Gilgamesh*.

CHAPTER 15

The Hut on Chicken Legs

The Frog Princess (7)

Ivan Tsarevich wandered near and far. He had already traveled long when suddenly he came upon a little hut facing the forest with its back to him. He said, "Little hut, little hut! Stand as of old, as your mother built you—with your back to the forest and facing me!" The hut turned around. He went in. An old woman was sitting there who said, "Foo, foo! Of a Russian bone no sound was heard, no sight was seen— but now one has come all on its own to my very door! Where are you going, Ivan Tsarevich?" "First, old woman, give me food and drink, then ask me questions." The old woman gave him food and drink and laid him down to sleep. Then Ivan Tsarevich said to her, "Granny, I have set out to find Elena the Beautiful!" "Oy, child! How long you have taken! At first she often remembered you, but now she no longer remembers and hasn't come to see me for a long time. Go to my middle sister, she knows more than I."

In the morning Ivan Tsarevich went on his way and came to a little hut and said, "Little hut, little hut! Stand as of old, as your mother built you—with your back to the forest and facing me!" The hut turned around. He went in and saw an old woman sitting there who said, "Foo, foo! Of a Russian bone no sound was heard, no sight was seen—but now one has come all on its own to my very door! Where are you going, Ivan Tsarevich?" "Why, Granny, to find Elena the Beautiful!" "Oy, Ivan Tsarevich," said the old woman, "how long you have taken! She has almost forgotten you and is about to marry another!"

FIG. 15.1. Vasilisa the Beautiful before Baba Yaga's hut with its fence of bones topped by glowing skulls. Illustration by Ivan Bilibin, 1899.

Let's hear it for equality. We've put the bride through three hoops; now let's test the groom. She proved herself worthy of him, but is he worthy of her?

From what we've seen of women's place in more recent Slavic society, one might wonder whether this question was even a concept. Details within the story suggest that the issue, rather, was the young man's worthiness to enter adult society.

The immediate and ostensible reason for the prince's trial is that he destroyed the frogskin. In Afanasiev's longest version of the tale (#269), an old man that Ivan meets along the road even tells him so:

> "Greetings, good youth!" said the little old man. "What are you seeking and whither do you follow your road?" The prince related to him his misfortune. "Ekh, Prince Ivan! Why did you burn the frogskin? It wasn't yours to give or take!"

Then, before giving the prince a magic ball of yarn that, when rolling, will lead him to what he seeks,* the old man tells how the princess's father turned her into a frog, in wrath that she was smarter than he. To transform her thus, the father must have possessed considerable magical prowess.

So the prince has interfered improperly in a deed of magic and perhaps broken an ancient and barely remembered taboo by taking and burning her animal skin. Now he must pay the penalty by losing his prize, the perfect bride. If he is to get her back, he must *work* for her this time. Interestingly, however, *what* he must do to retrieve her differs radically in each of the three versions of "The Frog Princess" that Afanasiev collected—although the tales are essentially the same up to this point. (The simplest and oldest version is apparently the one told above; we'll also consider some variants, which possibly crept in from other stories.)

The bride was tested by her future in-laws. The young man in East

---

*Rolling objects (balls, apples, berries, pearls, etc.) to divine the location of someone or something forms a frequent motif in East Slavic tales and folk songs. (A common first line of songs runs, "Apple, little apple—whither are you rolling?") The human sets the (random) process in motion and the spirits are then supposed to push the rolling object in the direction of its goal.

Slavic folktales, however, typically receives *his* trials either from terrible male monsters or from old women he doesn't know and isn't related to.

Who are these crones? They usually know of the health and where-abouts of his future bride (who visits them also), but they are seldom related to her either. They live in huts beyond civilization—in the woods or on the farthest edge of a village—with or without daughters around but certainly without husbands present. They range from the simple old woman who does what she's asked, through the perilously tricky sort, to the horrifyingly monstrous and perverse old hag. For example, in Afanasiev's tale of "Finist the Bright Falcon" (#235), Finist's sweetheart travels through the dark forest in search of him.

> Suddenly she saw standing in front of her an iron hut on little chicken legs, ceaselessly turning about. The girl said: "Little hut, little hut! Stand with your back to the forest and facing me!" The little hut turned to face her. She went into the hut, and inside lay Bába Yagá ["Hag Woman"—the archetypical Russian witch], stretching from corner to corner, her lips on the platform and her nose touching the ceiling.
>
> "Foo foo foo! Previously, of a Russian soul no sight was seen, no sound was heard, but now a Russian soul comes in the free light of day—just turns up—and flings itself under one's nose! Whither does your road take you, lovely maiden? Are you fleeing something or seeking something?"

Another version of "The Frog Princess" details yet more of the witch's peculiarities, when, after many adventures, Prince Ivan and the rolling ball of yarn finally reach her abode:

> The hut stood on chicken feet and was turning in circles. Said Ivan Tsarevich, "Little hut, little hut! Stand as of old, as your mother built you—facing me and with your back to the sea!" The hut turned around with its back to the sea and its front toward him. The Prince went in and saw that on the stove, on the ninth brick, lay Baba Yaga Bony-Leg; her nose reached into the ceiling, her limbs hung across the threshold, her tits were wound around the hinges, and she was sharpening her teeth.

FIG. 15.2. Top: Baba Yaga flying through the woods on a mortar, rowing with a pestle, sweeping away her tracks with a broom. Bottom: Willies. Illustration by Ivan Bilibin, 1900.

When Vasilisa the Beautiful's wicked stepsisters send her to get a light from Baba Yaga, hoping the witch will kill her (see chapter 8), Vasilisa arrives when no one is home and has ample time to survey the witch's premises—which certainly suit the owner (figs. 15.1, 15.2):

The fence around the hut was made of people's bones, on the fence-posts perched human skulls with eyes; in place of gateposts stood human legs, in place of a bolt—hands, in place of a lock—a mouth with sharp teeth. Vasilisa shuddered with horror and stood as if rooted to the ground. . . . Night came. But the darkness didn't last long: the eyes of each of the skulls on the fence lit up and the whole clearing got bright as midday. Vasilisa shook from fright, but not knowing where to run she stayed where she was.

Soon an awful noise could be heard in the forest: the trees crackled, dry leaves rattled, and out of the woods came Baba Yaga—she was riding in a mortar, driving it on with a pestle, and sweeping away the traces with a hearth-broom. She rode up to the gate, stopped, and snuffling around herself shrieked, "Foo, foo! It smells of Russian spirit!"*

With all those bones, her gate sounds like an entrance to the Land of the Dead!

Nor are the witch's manners dainty—she eats like a pig when she orders Vasilisa to serve her:

> From the skulls on the fence Vasilisa lit a splint and began to pull the food out of the oven and serve it to the hag, but there was enough food cooked for ten people; and from the cellar she brought kvas,† mead, beer, and wine. The old woman ate and drank up everything, leaving for Vasilisa only a little soup, an end of bread, and a bite of pork.

Everything is topsy-turvy, everywhere we find strange perversions and reversals of ordinary life, as in the Other World. Instead of a cottage fence, we see a gruesome palisade of bones and skulls; instead of a pleasant house-wife, we encounter an ugly hag filling the entire hut with her misshapen limbs; instead of a nice granny cooking goodies, we find the witch using ordinary kitchen equipment—mortar, pestle, and broom—to ride about in the woods on nefarious errands. The great indoor oven (see fig. 9.8), normally used to bake meals for the family, serves to roast human flesh for her own gluttonous consumption, as we learn from various tales of lads (or lasses) fallen into her clutches—e.g., #106:

> Yaga Baba [*sic*] dragged the young man home with her, stashed him in the woodbin, fired up the oven herself, and says to her eldest daughter: "Girl! I am going off to Russia; you bake this lad for me for dinner!"

---

* A neatly ambiguous word, actually: *dukh* means both "smell, scent" and "soul, spirit"— concepts linked by another of its meanings, "breath." In many cultures, the next of kin must attempt to catch the dying person's last breath, widely believed to contain the soul. The evidence? Someone with no breath has no life-spirit any more—they stopped/ departed at the same moment.

† Kvas is a sourish beverage fermented from black bread and malt.

"Sure," says the girl. Having heated the oven, she orders the clever youth to come out. He came out. "Lie in the baking-pan!" the girl says. The youth lay down and put one foot against the ceiling and the other on the bench. "Not that way, not that way!" cries the girl. Says he, "Well, how then? Show me!" So the girl lay down in the pan. The youth didn't falter but grabbed an oven-fork and shoved the baking-pan with the witch's daughter straight into the oven and crept back into the woodbin to sit and wait for Yaga Baba. Suddenly Yaga Baba ran in and said, "It's time to gloat and glut on the bones of the lad!" And the youth answered her, "Gloat and glut away on the bones of your own daughter!"

How like the tale of Hansel and Gretel—especially when the clever youth eventually gets the witch herself to demonstrate how to curl up in the baking pan and shoves *her* into the oven to bake.

To find his bride, then, our Prince Ivan must visit in turn three old witches: ancient crones with a reputation for cannibalism who live in weird houses (fig. 15.3) in dark, scary forests, just like their Germanic counterparts. And yet, right from the start we see a significant difference between Russian and Germanic witches. Unlike Germanic ones, Russian witches can be very helpful—scary, yes, but not invari-

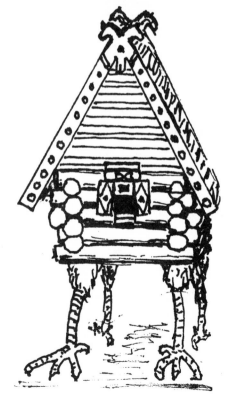

FIG. 15.3. Traditional "hut on chicken legs" of Baba Yaga and other Russian witches. (Compare fig. 8.6.)

ably wicked, often providing the hero or heroine with information and good advice as well as with magical objects, food, and rest. The word often used for such old women is *ved'ma*, usually translated as "witch" or "sorceress" but meaning literally "she who knows." Etymologically it comes from the same Indo-European root **wid-* "know" that gives English *wit, wisdom, witch*, and *wizard*. That is, witches and wizards are people who know things the rest of us don't—hence their great usefulness, but hence also the great power that makes them frightening.[1] And fear generates slander.

People reputed to be witches or wizards still lived in eastern European societies a century ago: real persons, even if we don't believe their "magic" was real. With greater elasticity than in the West, the Eastern Orthodox Church allowed those claiming knowledge acquired by non-Christian means to coexist with the church, seemingly tolerated for the good they might do even if censured for the evil attributed to them. The Catholic Church, on the contrary, cast them out as conniving with the devil, hence evil no matter what. This same difference held for many of the spirits thought to inhabit the countryside: the rivers and wells, lakes and forests, house, barn, and bathhouse. In eastern Europe, such spirits remained ambiguous, not wholly evil.

Thus Russian witches persisted as a force to be reckoned with, an unpredictable force: this one may try to eat you while that one may do you a good turn. When Vasilisa the Beautiful's jealous stepsisters send her to Baba Yaga for a light, the witch threatens the girl by saying, "First [you must] stay and work hard for me, then I'll give you a light; but if you don't, I'll eat you up!" How do you approach such a creature, then, to reap the good and avoid the bad?

In most cases, including those before us, you start by using the right protocol. Humble Vasilisa, with help from the magic mother doll in her pocket, does everything right, and Baba Yaga packs her off home with a light that reduces her wicked relatives to cinders when they look at it. Prince Ivan gives the right answers and the witches send him forth unhurt, armed with useful information.

The ritual character of the interactions between Ivan and his witches becomes clear immediately from the carefully repeated formulaic language. To begin with, our hero must know the ditty for entering the magic hovel where the witch resides: "Little hut, little hut! Stand with your back to the forest [or sea] and facing me!" Thus addressed, the hut duly turns around, away from the wild and toward the civilized, presenting to the caller the side with the entrance. (We'll return to the strange habits of this hut.)

The witch, once encountered, challenges the interloper, usually by remarking on his/her presence and nationality, both of which she has deduced from smell or sound ("Foo, foo! It smells of Russian spirit!"). Western European giants, we note, seem equally hung up on nationality, as in the eerily similar "Fee, fi, fo, fum! I smell the blood of an Englishman!"

The critical moment has arrived. The young traveler, far from home, stands within a stranger's power and must behave exactly right or suffer the consequences. Whereas the young women, like brides, set to work as servants, Prince Ivan, like most young men in these Slavic tales, appeals to the tradition that a host should discharge the sacred duty of feeding and caring for a guest before probing his background. This is the ancient Indo-European, not just Slavic, custom of the "civilized" way to treat a guest, so thoroughly expounded by Homer three millennia earlier in *The Odyssey*. Provide for basic wants first, then talk. Before written laws, the sacredness of the host's relationship to guests was the only security travelers had; knowing and abiding by that sacred trust thus marked a man as a true member of the supportive social group.

At some level, then, the tales expound ideal social behavior—like so many folktales the world around. Future wives must know how to work; future husbands must know the rituals, protocols, and responsibilities of a head of household. If the lad proves to be of "good Russian bone"—that is, if he knows this lore—he passes the test. The crones do not torment him but treat him well and send him on his way with information and encouragement. These episodes resemble the sorts of initiations, documented by anthropologists worldwide, in which adolescents learn about the physical and social aspects of sexuality as well as further details, often secret ones, of what will be expected of them as adults. For these initiations, boys and girls typically are isolated both from each other and from most of society.* Of course the Christian view of sexuality, especially that of the Catholic Church from Thomas Aquinas on, would have discouraged these initiations. Just enough hung on, however, to show outlines through the misty haze of the traditional tales, in which both youths and maidens spend time with old women out in the woods just before marriage, in ways that seem to lead directly *to* marriage.[2]

---

*One may deduce that both boys and girls did indeed go into isolation—such as, for example, the sequestration of daughters in a *terem*, "tower." Perhaps huts-on-legs and towers portray the same half-forgotten pagan initiation sites with descriptions that gradually drifted apart in two different storytelling traditions.

So who were these old women?

In typical peasant communities, women with husbands and children are already overworked, so the only females available to take on extra jobs for society are the young and the old. We've already seen that in eastern Europe the girl's main task, besides making her dowry, was to perform with her age-mates many important agrarian rituals for the welfare of the village and crops. But old women, while not active in most rites other than funerals, served as coaches—repositories of information on how to do things. In short, the lonely old widow served as a keeper of traditional knowledge, a "knower" or *ved'ma*.

It is fear of that knowledge that renders her a scary witch. The American traveler Angelo Rappoport remarked in 1913 on the strength of the peasants' belief in sorcery, commenting that "sometimes the role of wizard is played by an . . . old man, but more often the game is in the hands of wicked, silent old women. The moujik [peasant] treats these people with the deepest respect, but inwardly hates and fears them. Frequent cases of alleged bewitchment give rise to savage scenes."[3]

Some Russian folklorists even see in Baba Yaga an "ancestral helper along the maternal line,"[4] a sort of protectress of the clan, who may be grooming the smartest of the young women to take over her place some day.

But why does every story insist that the witch lives in a house on chicken legs? Where did that come from?

Until quite recently, there *were* little houses in Russia that perched on spindly legs, often standing off at the edge of the woods beside a brook or pond. These were saunalike bathhouses (see fig. 8.6), poised conveniently near both a water supply and the fuel for heating it. Such a bathhouse (fig. 15.4), whether on stilts or not, contained a great, chimneyless stove for heating small stones that were used in turn to heat the water—either by splashing the water onto them to make steam or by dropping the rocks straight into the water buckets. As in any peasant house, benches lined the walls, providing places where one could sit or lie. Usually a higher and wider platform in the corner beside the oven provided an even hotter and more spacious place to stretch out (similar to the stove-corner bed in the house), while a small hole in the ceiling let smoke out. Birch brooms with which to beat one's skin, buckets, and sometimes a supply of aromatic herbs to grind up for scenting the bath completed the usual furnishings.[5]

Baba Yaga would feel at home here: her oven, her broom and grinder,

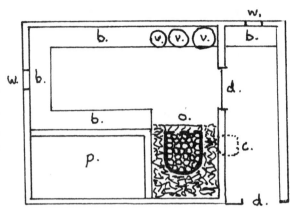

FIG. 15.4. Ground plan of typical Russian bathhouse: *b*, wooden bench; *c*, smoke-hole in roof; *d*, door; *o*, oven full of heated stones; *p*, wooden platform for steam-bathing; *v*, vat for cold or heated water; *w*, window. (Compare oven in fig. 9.8.)

and the platform on which her lip rests are all there. Perhaps poor old widows tended the bathhouse for a pittance when they weren't instructing or testing the young, even treating this shed as home.

But, like Ivan, let's follow the rolling yarn ball farther into Baba Yaga's domain and learn why witches were said to bake people in ovens.

As it happens, a century ago only the populace of North Great Russia and Belarus used bathhouses, whereas the Ukrainians and Bulgarians seldom bathed. The South Great Russians, however, *bathed in their ovens.* After stoking up the giant cooking oven in the house, they would clear out all the coals and ashes, sprinkle in some water to make steam, and climb feet first into the oven to work up a cleansing sweat, leaving at most their noses out so they could breathe.

What would fearful travelers from far away make of seeing some old woman shoving the kids one by one into the oven?

Surely the story came about as a misinterpretation from *observing* old hags "ovening" people and *presuming* that it was in order to eat them. The story would then spread wherever social circumstances invited either the slander or the sensationalism.* Add to this the fact that, like so many

---

*Where the dead are/were rendered inert not by burying but by cutting or boiling the flesh off the bones, outsiders have also regularly misinterpreted this as preparation for eating—cannibalism. Cannibalism is like the phoenix—everyone has heard tell of it but no one has actually seen it. The anthropologist William Arens set out to document ritual cannibalism but could never run to ground *any* unshakable eyewitness accounts. *Everything* proved to be hearsay. In his book *The Man-Eating Myth*, he relates that when Christopher Columbus reached the New World, the Arawaks told him that their enemies to the south, the Car-other peoples, the Slavs bathed their dead just before burial, and only women (mostly elderly) performed this task. Furthermore, the bride took a prenuptial ritual bath just before leaving her natal family forever and becoming as good as dead to them. In a very real sense, then, the bathhouse *was* a gateway to the land of the dead—some who entered there never returned.

The Frog Princess (8)

"Elena lives now with my eldest sister—go there but look sharp! When you approach, they will be aware of it; Elena will turn into a spindle and her dress will become gold. My sister will start to wind up the gold thread. When she has filled the spindle and laid it in a casket and locked the casket, you must find the key, open the casket, break the spindle and throw the top behind you and the bottom in front of you—and she will appear suddenly before you."

Ivan Tsarevich went, came to the third old woman, and entered her hut. She was winding gold thread, finished the spindle and laid it in a casket, locked it, and placed the key somewhere. He took the key, opened the casket, took out the spindle and broke it as he had been told; then he threw the top behind him and the bottom in front. Suddenly Elena the Beautiful appeared and greeted him: "Oy, how late you have come, Ivan Tsarevich! I almost married someone else!"

---

ibs, were people-eaters—and also one-eyed, with dog noses. Columbus was disinclined to believe the tale because he never saw any evidence to support it; furthermore, he knew that the Arawaks thought at first that he and his men were cannibals. But the Spaniards who followed believed it. Slowly, Spanish mouths changed the word *Carib* to *Canib*, and from there to the form *cannibal*, with the meaning of people-eater. In 1503, when a Spanish royal proclamation decreed that the natives of the New World were not to be enslaved unless they were Cannibals, suddenly almost every native group was said (by someone else) to eat people! One could almost derive a rule: if you hate or fear your neighbors, lay on them the grossest slander imaginable—namely, that they eat people, especially defenseless people. The Christians accused the Jews of eating children in the Middle Ages, but in Roman times it was the Christians who were accused of same. It is *all* slander, Arens found. Yet we all insist we "know" there are cannibals, our evidence being . . . well, that someone told us so! Exactly these same processes appear to have engendered the child-eating witches of rural Europe.

The other suitor was due there soon. Elena the Beautiful took a flying carpet from the old woman, sat on it, and they were carried off and flew away like birds. . . . They flew home, everyone rejoiced, and they settled down to live and prosper—to the glory of all the people.

So the missing bride has been off in the woods perfecting her textile skills? (Here she is called Elena instead of Vasilisa.) In several of Afanasiev's tales, stepmothers send girls to the forest hut specifically to spin, sew, or weave (#98, 103). In fact, spinning thread (an act of creation) was viewed in parts of Europe as involving so much magical danger that spinning could be done only at certain times and in certain special places. We've seen that spinning during the Rusalii would anger the willies, and spinning on Friday would anger St. Friday, an honorary willy. Furthermore, plant fibers such as flax and hemp make up into thread much more easily when damp, and the dampest place around was the bathhouse. So the peculiar little house on chicken legs provided a haven for this un-Christianly magical ritual of spinning—another apparently "unclean" female act of creation—just as it did for the "unclean" childbirth for which spinning is so often a metaphor (as with the Fates spinning the thread of destiny for the newborn). Was the crone teaching the maiden the secrets of making cloth out in the woods, along with lessons about baby-making? It might explain why the old hag always seems to know just where the prince's bride has gone off to.

And why must the prince find the spindle in the casket and break it?

First, note that special magic lay in nested objects. In version 2 of the story (#268), the old woman tells him:

> "Take yourself down to the sea, Ivan Tsarevich; there lies a stone, in the stone sits a duck, inside the duck is an egg. Take this egg and bring it to me."

Inside the egg resides the Princess's lost love for him (another alienable possession!). When he finally succeeds in fetching it, with the help of a pike, a bear, a hawk, and a crayfish (each of whom he has spared from death along the way), the crone cooks and feeds the egg to the Frog Princess, who suddenly wants Ivan back. And they live happily ever after.

Second, to break a spell, analogical magic dictates that one break an object associated with the victim.

Third, the imagery of the spindle exactly parallels that of the locks on wedding chests and storerooms. The traditional European hand spindle consists of a shaft stuck into the hole in a spindle whorl (flywheel)—just as the key or arrow-shaped hasp fits into the vulvalike lockplate. The Prince must discard the alien shaft and keep the bottom part with the hole in it, which will magically become the girl. All these analogic actions with box, lock, and spindle constitute ritual "marriage magic"—if the young man does them right, he gets a fertile bride.

The spindle carries further symbolism, however, in carrying the golden thread corresponding to the golden dress of a fertilized bride. A sixteenth-century Russian account of wedding protocol among the upper classes, embedded in a document called *Domostroy* (*Home-Building*), says that gold dresses formed part of the traditional wedding. The morning after the consummation of the marriage in the barn, the groom went off to bathe in the bathhouse while the bride's attendants dressed the bride and led her to the house to wash her and dress her again. The bride's proper outfit for the morning after, we read, consisted of a broad-sleeved white chemise, a head-dress that completely covered her hair, and a special sarafan (gown) made of gold thread.[6] Peasants, of course, could not have afforded dresses of real gold and apparently wore yellow instead, just like the dresses *Domostroy* prescribes for women attending the bride.[7] *Domostroy* also specifies that the bride should wear a yellow virgin's crown for the first day of the wedding.[8] This color tradition was extremely old, for yellow had demonstrably signi-fied women and their fertility in southern Europe for at least four thousand years, occurring in Roman, Greek, and Minoan cultures (as we shall see).

Within Slavic custom, for Elena to be already wearing the gold dress seems to imply that she is already married, even though she is about to marry another suitor. Remember that the prime objective of early agrarian marriage was to produce children, and *early* church writings indicate that the clergy would be happy enough if the couple got officially married at all, never mind the details.[9] From the folk point of view, the Frog Princess began a marriage with Ivan when she moved in to live with him (and the narrator has allowed the couple at least one night together as humans). In his long absence, she may have begun another trial marriage.

When I was six, I used to collect bits of bright-colored glass—red, blue, green, amber—and lay them out in patterns along the dirt pathways in our garden, in hopes that some wizard or fairy would come along and turn them into rubies, sapphires, emeralds, and topaz, just as in my favorite fairy tale. Spinning thread of gold obviously captured the thoughts of earlier generations of women who spent so many hours spinning lesser substances. Every English- and German-speaking child knows of Rumpelstiltskin spinning straw into gold for a beleaguered girl. Back when straw rather than broken glass littered the ground, the feat would have created instant wealth from the commonest of materials. In the Middle Ages, rich princes and churchmen possessed cloth embroidered with or even woven of real gold that had been formed into thread for the purpose. Artisans had developed the technology many centuries earlier, for Roman emperors attired themselves in cloth of gold (despite finding it uncomfortable). So a dress of gold befitted the riches of a bride.

⚮

Finally, restored to her prince's arms, the Frog Princess has to fetch the two of them away from the final danger, the rival suitor, by borrowing a magic carpet from the witch. (This foreign motif has clearly crept into the story from Persia, where people wishing to travel to the spirit world habitually lounged upon their soft, thick carpets with a pipe full of hashish, and off they went to the land of the miraculous. In fact, psychedelic drugs are documented on the Ukrainian steppe around 500 BC and in Russian Turkestan before 2000 BC.)[10]

Anyhow, that's one ending.

In Afanasiev's second version, as we saw, Ivan Tsarevich must obtain the magic egg holding the Frog Princess's love, break the egg (and spell) to release that love, and get her to eat the egg. In the third version, however, the one in which the Frog Princess is named Vasilisa the Wise, Ivan's final destination is not a witch but a wizard, who entails ancient lore of his own. It starts with Ivan Tsarevich following his rolling ball of yarn to another hut on chicken legs, where he encounters a particularly ugly edition of Baba Yaga. She begins to question him, but our hero has learned his catechism well and properly admonishes her that she should feed and bathe him first. "Then you can ask," he adds.

Koshchey the Deathless

The Frog Princess (8 bis)

Baba Yaga fed him, gave him to drink, and steamed him in a bath, and the tsarevich recounted to her that he was searching for his wife, Vasilisa the Wise.

"Ah, I know her!" said Baba Yaga. "She is now with Koshchey the Deathless. It'll be hard to get her back—it's not easy to deal with Koshchey. His death is on the end of a needle, the needle is in an egg, the egg is in a duck, the duck is in a hare, the hare is in a coffer, the coffer stands in a tall oak tree, and Koshchey guards the tree like his own eyes."

The hag indicated the place where this oak grew; Ivan Tsarevich went there but didn't know what to do, how to get the coffer. Suddenly from who knows where a bear ran up and tore the tree up, roots and all; the coffer fell out and broke into smithereens; the hare jumped out of the coffer and took to its heels at full speed; in a wink, another hare was already chasing after it, caught it, clutched it, and tore it to shreds. Out of the hare flew a duck, which soared high, high; she flew but a drake swooped after her, and as he hit her the duck suddenly let fall an egg, and the egg fell into the sea.

Ivan Tsarevich, seeing this irreparable misfortune, burst into tears. Suddenly a pike swam up to the shore holding the egg in its jaws. Ivan took the egg, broke it, got out the needle, and broke off the tip: how Koshchey thrashed about, how he staggered in all directions—and then he fell down dead. Ivan Tsarevich went to the house of Koshchey, fetched Vasilisa the Wise, and returned home. After this they lived together both long and happily.

From Afanasiev's third version of "The Frog Princess" we can see that his second version (given in chapter 15) makes hash of the end of the story but provides key pieces the third storyteller had lost. We need both tales to sort out the message.

When, in the third version, Ivan Tsarevich seeks the egg containing the life of the wizard who holds the prince's wife hostage (a convincing motive), various animal helpers appear simply out of nowhere (unmotivated chaos). When, however, in version 2, Ivan seeks the egg holding the princess's "love" (a rather lame device), he encounters four animals along the road (a careful setup for the final denouement). Each of them—a pike, a bear, a hawk, and a crayfish—he decides to kill for dinner, but he spares them when they beg for life and promise him a future favor in return. So when they arrive in his hour of need to help him get the egg, everything makes sense. The pike helps him reach the requisite stone island enclosing the required egg; the bear smashes the stone open for him; when the duck with the egg inside it pops out, the hawk grabs it; and the crayfish retrieves the egg from the water after it falls in. All neat and tidy. The rather similar animals in version 3—a bear, hares, ducks, and a pike—have similar functions, but the reason for their aid got lost, as did the tight magical structure. In version 2, each animal represents mastery over a vital element (water, land, air), the pike being the top predator among local fish, as the bear and hawk are among land animals and birds.*

What is really new in version 3 is the wizard Koshchey (fig. 16.1).

⚬∽∾⚬

Wherever we find Koshchey in Russian fairy tales, he is evil through and through. He abducts the heroine and never does anything nice for the hero, except to die at the end of the tale. Which he always does, and that in itself is a puzzle, for his full name is Koshchey the Deathless.

Russian tales regale us with another thoroughly evil character who greatly resembles Koshchey in his actions: carrying off maidens to a rich, faraway kingdom (either as brides or with the simple intention of eating

---

*Note the common Russian abracadabra formula "By the pike's command!" Pikes attain large size, have big teeth, and fight hard against fishermen, who in Russia prize their flesh. The pike's polelike shape may have led to its fertility role in stories such as that of "Ivan the Cow's Son" (#136–37), where the queen who eats of the magic pike to cure her barrenness, the scullery maid who licks pike juice off her fingers, and the cow that eats the discarded entrails of the pike all conceive and bear identical boy-children simultaneously.

FIG. 16.1. The wizard Koshchey the Deathless and his soul-egg.

them), battling the hero, and eventually getting killed somehow by the latter. This character is the Zmey, the dreaded Dragon or Savage Serpent. He may have anywhere from one to a dozen heads; he may even occur in fraternal triplicate, the first dragon brother having, say, three heads for the hero to lop off, the second six heads, and the third nine or even twelve—by which time the hero may need the help of a befriended animal to sever the last neck or two with suitable drama and suspense. So the Dragon differs from Koshchey in dining on people, and in perishing by losing his head(s) instead of by losing his egg (Koshchey's traditional way of expiring). On the other hand, enough overlaps exist that running the Dragon to ground will help us solve the riddle of Koshchey.

Russian dragons, like Germanic ones, spend most of their time guarding untold riches, living by preference under the earth or beyond the sea, where they guard not only ancestral treasure but sometimes even the portals to the land of the dead.* Consonant with living down below, dragons have chthonic forms, with scaly, snakelike bodies and heads and perhaps lizardlike short limbs and claws. Unlike snakes and lizards, however, they can fly about and breathe flames. For example, in Afanasiev's tale #155, the king receives a threat from a twelve-headed dragon who says, "If you don't send me your middle daughter, I'll burn down your kingdom with fire and scatter the ashes!" And as the hero stands guard over the girl, like the Greek Perseus over Princess Andromeda, "a savage Zmey flew up to him, breathed fire, and threatened death." The Zmey sometimes takes the form of a whirlwind, scooping up what he likes. The great wealth accumulated by such a Zmey allows him to rule kingdoms and build many-roomed palaces tended by myriad bewitched servants and stolen maidens.

Koshchey the wizard also has magical access to great wealth, flies about (often as a whirlwind, like angry willies as well as like the Zmey), and commands the spirit world. His very name, *Koshchéy*, is generally taken to come from Slavic *kost'* "bone"—that is, "bone-bag, skeleton man," which connects him too with the land of the dead. (Although linguists present another possible etymology, or contaminant—namely, Turkic *koşçi*, "army conscript, slave"[1]—Russian storytellers clearly believed that the name had to do with bones.) To understand Koshchey's nature, however, and to puzzle out why he can both die and be deathless, we must turn to an area of the Slavic world where he has been less thoroughly overhauled by Christianity.

❧

While studying South Slavic folk medicine in the 1920s and 1930s, Phyllis Kemp "found memories of the *zmaj* or dragon-man . . .—men who during sleep become spirits or animals, such as bulls or dragons, and meet at night, or, endowed with supernatural strength, battle with evil spirits, enemies of their own villages. . . ."[2] She summarizes at length a folk epic about the struggle between the Serbs and the Turks, in which the nephew of the Serbian leader turns himself into a six-winged dragon in order to do battle in the sky with the spirit or shade of a Turkish sultan named Murat. The latter

---

* For an analysis of the origins of typical Germanic fire-breathing dragons, see Barber and Barber 2005, chapter 18.

assumes the form of a falcon for the encounter. Before leaving, the nephew instructs his uncle to ask presently of a wise man, "What were our ancient shades?" But as the battle of the spirits rages, a "foolish" man pipes up with the wrong answer: "We have always been grey falcons!"—and the uncle, trying to help his nephew, shoots down the dragon instead of the falcon. As he falls, the dragon man cries out, "What have you done, my good uncle? Catch hold of the falcon under my wings: It is your enemy Murat!"[3]

The falcon is a common image for a heroic young man throughout Slavic poetry—hence the shallow person's reply. But part of the point seems to be that, in *really* olden times, Slavs who knew how to fight successfully in the spirit world turned themselves into dragons, not falcons, to do spirit battle. That is, the Zmey (Zmaj) originally represented a shamanlike controller of spirits, a sort still known in other parts of Eurasia. When, for instance, some kind of meteorite fell in eastern Siberia in June 1908, producing an aerial explosion that flattened trees across two thousand square kilometers and registered on instruments as far away as Britain, the local Tungusic reindeer herders interpreted the event as two ultrapowerful shamans battling it out in midair. Twenty years later, they still refused to approach the accursed/bewitched/devastated part of the forest.[4]

Russians, too, knew of aerial mayhem as related to shamanism. In Afanasiev's tale #129, instead of a dragon demanding a princess, we read of an evil Whirlwind who has carried off the prince's beautiful mother. When the prince tracks them down, Whirlwind seizes the prince and whirls him through all the elements in an attempt to deter him—a very shamanlike way of fighting.

In the Russian tall tale (#312) about Alyosha Popovich (i.e., "Priest's Son"), Alyosha serves Prince Vladimir, Kiev's great Christian prince, by taking on his enemy Tugarin, a fiendish Turkic warrior. But this time, Tugarin Zmeyevich (i.e., "Dragon's Son") turns into a dragon and flies through the air while Alyosha Priest's Son prays from terra firma: "Most Holy Mother of God, order a black cloud! And may God send a torrential rain from the black cloud so it will drench Tugarin's paper wings!" Christian magic now being billed as better than (though not much different from) pagan magic, the black cloud rolls up and delivers its load, Tugarin's paper wings wilt, so he falls to earth and has to meet Alyosha properly (without magic), and Alyosha soon dispatches him.

The final proof that Koshchey represents a shaman resides in the conundrum of why Koshchey the Deathless can die. An old-time shaman who visits the spirit world to do battle for his clients against their enemies (whether human warriors or sickness demons) counts as "deathless" since he alone can enter the world of the dead *and return alive*. Yet he is nonetheless a mortal man, a well-known member of the village who can and will eventually die.

Christian propaganda now kills him off, in fact, at the end of every story as an object lesson—which tells us why shamans and wizards like Koshchey are portrayed so one-sidedly. Christian authorities focused onto such men their total opposition to indulging in non-Christian spirit lore, just as they did onto women "channeling" fertility spirits through dance. The man who battles spirits according to the old ways has become anathema—unmitigatedly evil.

How one kills Koshchey is also no mystery by now, for the notion of keeping a life or soul inside an egg harks back to the ancient image of the egg as life capsule, and we have seen that a spell is broken by analogically breaking something brittle associated with it—here, either the egg itself or a needle inside it. The former method (familiar to balletgoers as the climax of Stravinsky's *Firebird*) may go back to an earlier belief or even voodoolike custom of working analogical "black magic" on another person. The almost comical nesting of one object inside another in multiple succession like a turducken may also descend from an ancient magical ritual for covering or disguising precious "separables" (life, love, a soul, strength, etc.) with magical protective coatings—the more the safer. Samson, by contrast, unwisely kept his strength in his hair where Delilah could get into it. As so often with former rituals after a radical change of religion, all that remains today of this ancient nest magic is a child's game or toy—in this case, the popular nested Russian *matryoshka* doll.

The basic idea is pan-Slavic, however, for the South Slavs tell similar tales, according to Kemp:

> The soul is something infinitely small and precious. a common [Yugoslav] folk-tale describes how a certain dragon-man's strength is kept in a safe place, namely in a pearl, in the nest of a certain dragon. . . . A Bosnian variant says that the pearl was in an egg in a nest of a certain bird on a certain tree and so on. . . .[5]

So typical in Russian folklore is the theme of the precious magic in a nest of coverings that storytellers could produce amusing variations. In Afanasiev's tale #158, when an abducted princess tries to wheedle out of Koshchey where he keeps his death, he tells her that it's in the broom on the doorstep. But her helper, Bulat the Brave, recognizes this instantly as a trick. So it occurs to them to gild and beribbon the broom and lay it on the table. When Koshchey returns and asks why the broom is on the table, she says,

> "How could your death be left lying about on the doorstep? Much better that it lie on the table!"
>
> "Ha ha ha! Silly woman! Your hair is long but your wits are short! So you really think my death is there?"
>
> "Well, where then?"
>
> "My death is hidden in the goat!"

She's catching on and patiently dolls up the goat and gilds its horns while he's gone. Again Koshchey laughs at her upon his return, but the third time—three's the charm for Indo-Europeans—he tells her that on an island in the sea, under an oak, lies a coffer within which is a hare, within which is a duck, within which is the egg that contains his death. This, of course, is the proper answer, and her Prince Ivan sets out immediately with the hero Bulat for the site, where with the usual help they finally obtain the egg. They return with it, kill Koshchey by smashing it on his forehead, and make off with the princess.

❦

So Koshchey embodies a half-forgotten shaman figure, the wise man of an earlier culture, who perhaps helped train and test young men just as the crone in the woods trained and tested young women. (In Eurasia, both men and women could become shamans.) But in Kemp's South Slavs "who during sleep become spirits or animals, such as bulls or dragons, and meet at night, or, endowed with supernatural strength, battle with evil spirits, enemies of their own villages,"[6] we glimpse a yet broader function of this shamanism, one that unites many of the strands of lore we have followed.

Around 1600, in the area of Friuli in northeastern Italy, the Inquisition persecuted numerous peasants—mostly but not entirely women—who claimed they went "four times a year, at night, to battle 'in spirit', armed with bundles of fennel, against male and female witches armed with stalks of sorghum; at stake in these night battles was the fertility of the fields."[7] They called themselves *benandanti* (good-goers) and their opponents (also people who entered the night battles in spirit) *malandanti* (evil-goers). From such stories developed the lore of witchery in western Europe.* So close is this purpose to that of the rusaltsi, călușari, and others who battled the spirits to win health and the fertility of the fields for their villages and battled such troupes from elsewhere for fear of losing their share, that we must suspect a common origin.

Similar trials from other nearby areas document women and men who followed the Good Lady to dance and feast with the spirits and watch the processions of the dead every Thursday night. (Since the "day" began at nightfall, that originally meant a Friday ritual.) Apparently this all forms part of a much older and broader lore of the dead, including dead maidens, that turns up repeatedly in medieval times but with yet deeper roots. To explore the historical connections, it will behoove us to consider next the context of the Dancing Goddesses chronologically, starting with the most recent millennium and working back.

---

*Carlo Ginzburg systematically tackles this whole complex of folklore in his book *Ecstasies: Deciphering the Witches' Sabbath* (1992). Note that ripe fennel and sorghum both carry masses of seeds, appropriate for agricultural battles.

Part Three

Dancing Back through Time

CHAPTER 17

Medieval Traces

You are naught but an onion.
I'm going to peel you now. . . .
—Ibsen, *Peer Gynt*, act 5, scene 5

Christ orders you to refrain . . . [from] dancing, tambourines,
pipes, psalteries [gusli], improper games, Rusaliya. . . .
—St. Cyril of Turov (twelfth century)[1]

By now we have encountered many types of spirits once thought to populate the rural European landscape, yet our inquiries into the Dancing Goddesses keep leading us to the world of the dead: to the all-important dead ancestors as well as to the willies, the dead kin who missed becoming ancestors. Over and over, we have seen willies and ancestors addressed through rituals felt to be so important that repeated massive assaults by the Christian church failed to dislodge them. It took modern communication—via twentieth-century paved roads and eventually TV—to make serious headway.

How far back does this cluster of beliefs and customs go? Where did they come from? And have we any tools to trace them back from the late nineteenth century, when most of the data we've looked at was collected?

In fact, we have two major sources of evidence: material culture (the stuff dug up by archaeologists) and linguistic remains (whether inscriptions, manuscripts, oral literature, or etymologies). Using them, our job becomes one of peeling off the layers of accrued belief one by one, seeing what changed and what didn't, seeing how the onion was built up.

The first layer to remove will be Christianity. We've seen the church continually fighting against a much older "paganism," and after the early fourth century, when Roman emperors began supporting the new religion, this fight gradually became a serious issue. Ironically, from then on, most references to the older beliefs come from the priests and missionaries, as they admonish parishioners *not* to do an abhorred practice—which they then proceed to describe! As one researcher noted, "The more detailed the descriptions of pagan rites, the larger loomed the missionaries' triumphs."[2]

The second layer to investigate and peel away will be the period of Classical Greece and Rome (1000 BC–AD 400: see chapters 18, 19), an era bursting with art and literature, much of which has survived—but from a primarily urban culture. Our task will be to sift through the remains for the remote, bucolic lifeways of farmer and shepherd, people of little interest to either ancient artists or recent museum curators.

Beneath that nestles the Bronze Age (3000–1000 BC: see chapter 20), when civilization first flowered on (southern) European soil. It was also a time of invasions by our own linguistic ancestors, the Indo-Europeans, bringers of their favorite animal, the horse, and a raft of customs and beliefs related to horses. These beliefs had to have differed considerably from those of the crop-growers they moved in on, so off the layer comes, once we know what it brought. With any luck, we may glimpse yet another stratum beneath—that of the first farmers of Europe, Stone Age pioneers struggling to survive in a changing world.

And yes, evidence of "perishable" customs and beliefs *can* survive for millennia. For example, European farm women's traditional dress ("folk costume"—worn even today in some regions) includes in many areas a type of garment awarded to a girl when she reached puberty: the so-called string skirt (fig. 17.1, see figs 3.8, 23.2). Of no use for warmth or modesty, since it consists simply of a belt band or apron with long, heavy fringes hanging from it, the string skirt carried cultural information—indicating to all that the woman was of an age to produce new human beings, a miracle utterly necessary for the survival of the group. This marker occurs in a wide variety of cultures, Indo-European and not, from the Peloponnese in southern Greece to the far northeast, almost to the Urals beyond Mos-

FIG. 17.1. Various string skirts still used post–World War II: Northern Albanian, western Romanian, Mordvin (east of Moscow).

cow.* But representations of women of obviously childbearing age wearing such a garment occur also in ancient times—in Hellenistic Greece ca. 300 BC, Archaic Greece ca. 600 BC, Bronze Age northern Europe ca. 1000 BC, Neolithic Balkans and Ukraine ca. 4000 BC, and Palaeolithic France and Russia ca. 20,000 BC (fig. 17.2, see fig. 3.7). As if that weren't enough, archaeologists have found remains of such skirts on women's bodies in Denmark and Slovakia ca. 1400 BC, and the Tarim Basin of Central Asia (among intruders with roots in eastern Europe) ca. 1800 BC (fig. 17.3). A lengthy reference to it occurs in our earliest preserved European literature, Homer's *Iliad* (14.166–328), around 800 BC. If evidence for the string skirt and its specific cultural use can survive scattered across twenty thousand years, we have some hope of tracing early evidence for the Dancing Goddesses, although we will have to keep returning to the recent ethnographic data to fill out our understanding. The first step is the Middle Ages.

---

*To the extensive catalog in Barber 1999b can be added a small group of blue-eyed Indo-Iranians in Nuristan, the Kalash (called *Kafir* "infidels" by the surrounding Muslims), whose women wear string skirts to mark part of their female cycle (M. Hempstead, pers. comm.). In Ukraine, South Great Russia, and some nearby areas, the *form* of this fertility-marking garment has changed to a square-patterned back-apron, the *panyóva* or *plákhta* (see fig. 17.8). The symbolic fringes may still cling to it and/or transfer to shoulders or headdress (cf. fig. 3.8).

FIG. 17.2. Ancient representations of string skirts. Top: From Hellenistic Greek girl's funerary dish, southern Italy, ca. 330 BC; Archaic Greek statuette, Thisbe, Boiotia, Greece, 550 BC; Bronze Age knife handle (she also carries a flask tied to her back), Itzehoe, Holstein, Germany, 1000 BC. Bottom: Neolithic clay figurines, Crnokalačka Bara, Serbia, and Shipintsi, Ukraine, 4000 BC; Palaeolithic (Gravettian) ivory "Venus" figure, Gagarino, Russia, 20,000 BC (cf. fig. 3.7).

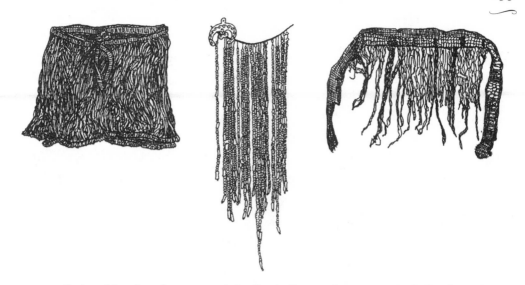

FIG. 17.3. String skirts found on women's bodies in Bronze Age graves. Left: Woolen; Egtved, Denmark, 1371 BC. Center: Faience beads, bronze pendant; Nižná Myšľa, Slovakia, 1600 BC. Right: Woolen; Cemetery 5, Tarim Basin, Central Asia, 1800 BC.

Where to begin looking? Since the cult of the dead has proved so important, let's try funerary monuments.

In Bosnia and Herzegovina, during a prosperous period from the late twelfth to the fifteenth centuries, people buried their dead with increasingly elaborate monuments called *stećci*. Amid the symbols carved on the stones we see rows of people dancing in long lines—sometimes only men, sometimes only women, sometimes both together (fig. 17.4). Until recently, people in this area segregated the dance lines into men versus women. But *mixed* lines, traditionally avoided in most Balkan countries, do occur in certain rites concerning the dead (along with segregated dances).

On Trinity Sunday, one of the old Rusalii dates, Vlach villagers in Duboka, in the Homolje Mountains of eastern Serbia, regularly invited their dead relatives to visit them. In chapter 5 we considered an 1893 account of this ritual. Seventy years later, Marian Wenzel, an American art historian studying the old Bosnian tombs, also observed this Trinity Sunday rite. It began, she said, with householders placing food on the backyard graves of their relatives, inviting them to come for dinner and a chat. Presently they formed a procession from yard to village square, led by a row of women carrying the food and drink, followed by

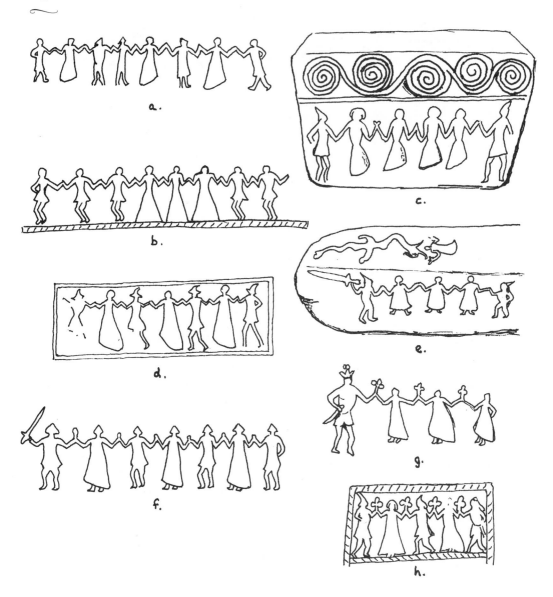

FIG. 17.4. Mixed male and female dancers on medieval Bosnian funerary monuments (*stećci*). Man usually at each end, sometimes brandishing sword (*e–g*), as with ritual dancers from Duboka (see figs. 5.6, 17.5). Sometimes dancers hold bouquets between them (*g, h*): compare Duboka dancers (fig. 17.5) and Archaic Greek funeral dancers (see fig. 19.7). Note peaked caps (*a, c–f, h*), and dragon (upside down) on lid of *e*.

FIG. 17.5. Vlach villagers of Duboka, Serbia, dancing on Trinity Sunday to bring ancestors back (cf. fig. 5.6); bouquets are held between dancers. After sketch by Marian Wenzel.

three virgins and either two or three young men . . . [but] there must be a young man at each end [fig. 17.5]. At least one of the end men carries an uplifted sword, and sometimes both do so. The dancers link hands, and in their linked hands they hold bunches of vegetation, including garlic, herbs, and certain flowers, as well as flasks of wine, eggs, and sometimes lighted candles. . . . On their backs they have . . . small mirrors [to attract spirits] . . . . Following these so-called kings and queens there comes a row of musicians. . . . The whole procession moves with a curious halting gait, involving a forward thrust of the shoulders in time to the music. The impression is of people trying to draw some heavy or reluctant object behind them.[3]

(Compare figs. 17.4, 17.5, 5.6.) In the central square, each family congregates around its own table, while a eulogy for the dead is sung. Then the special group dances anew while being fed from the table, this dance serving as a spirit channel like the sleeve dance. (The "dead" so addressed may include a live person lying beneath the table who has helped pay for the feast, his way of ensuring that the most important rite for his own funeral, the banquet, will have been properly performed!) Although these tables and their ceremonies were private to each family, afterward anyone could join in the communal circle dance, and married women, particularly brides, were obliged to do so—clearly a fertility tradition. A few women fell into trances and were revived by the same teams of *kolo* dancers who had drawn the dead to the feast (just as Gligorić described it in 1893), still headed by a sword-wielding, garlic-and-wormwood-chewing male. The revived women, who delivered news of the welfare of the dead, stated that they had been "with" the vily or "entered by" a vila.[4]*

The parallels between this special line of dancers and the depictions on medieval funerary *stećci* are far too close for accident. Often the carved dancers clutch a trefoil-shaped something in their joined hands, corresponding to the bunches of garlic and other herbs (so familiar from the rusaltsi/căluşari rituals) held this way by the Duboka "kings and queens." Mixed groups are led by a man who might brandish a sword, and some have a man on each end with women—usually three—between them, as in Duboka and among the Romanian *Crăiţe* (see below). Swords protect, of course, and occur frequently on the *stećci*, but their use in contexts of the dead almost certainly parallels the Bulgarian ritual in which, as the wedding party moves down the road, one member continually slashes about with a sword to drive malevolent demons away.[5] Demons are equally unwelcome on the perilous road to and from the nether world.

So the dance rituals serving the dead preserved at Duboka, closely related to the healing dances of the rusaltsi/căluşari, go back at least to the medieval era. But we have a dilemma.

The inscriptions show that the *stećci* were erected by Slavs, whereas the Vlachs in Duboka speak a Romance language, as do the Romanian căluşari. So are these rituals Slavic or Romance? *Rusalii* and *rusalka* are Slavic word formations, yet the leader of the Bulgarian rusaltsi, the vatafin, borrowed his name from *vătaf*, a Romanian title, originally Latin. Then again, the Romanians borrowed *Crăiţe* from the South Slavic name *kraljice* "queens," used by the Slavs for the maidens dancing in teams at Trinity and Pentecost. (The Romanian version refers to women whom the căluşari had healed and

---

* This effectively blurs the modern distinction between trance and possession. It's curious that Gligorić in 1893 didn't mention the first part of the ritual as described by Wenzel—presumably because such feasts for the dead were still so common in Serbia and elsewhere that he found only the trances noteworthy.

who were then obliged to accompany the călușari for three years. Although they didn't actively help in the curing, it was believed they needed to be present for healing to work.)[6] *Kraljica* is the South Slavic feminine form of *kralj*, "king," itself borrowed from the name of the great French (Romance-speaking) king *Carl*—i.e. *Charle*magne—who lived around AD 800. (So this pan-Slavic word cannot predate 800, although the ritual could.)

Back and forth: neither Slavic nor Romance seems prior. What that suggests is that the Slav and Romance speakers possessed much the same pre-Christian belief system and were merely passing around vocabulary for the details. The origins must lie deeper. For now, let's continue with the medieval evidence.

Male dancers wielding swords grace not just the *stećci* but also the twelfth-century cylindrical wedding bracelets from Kiev and surroundings, dancing alongside the gusli players and the girls with ultralong sleeves at Rusalii (see fig. 13.8). We encountered male dancers with swords among both the Romanian călușari and the "police" accompanying the Greek kalogheroi. Some of the male bracelet figures brandish staves, as do the rusaltsi and călușari and English Morris dancers, who also danced for luck and abundance.* Men have danced with swords and staves across much of Europe for millennia— the subject is enormous[7]—but clearly the Rusalii included such dancers in both medieval and modern times (fig. 17.6).

The twelfth-century bracelets tell us, of course, that the women's sleeve dance, imitating and invoking the bird maidens, already existed (see fig. 13.8); the drawing and description of dancing at Rusalii in the Radziwill Chronicle, copied from a pre-1240 chronicle (see fig. 2.1), tell us the same. They also confirm that the tale of the Frog Princess, itself quite innocent of Christian ideology, goes back to that era of the bracelets when girls danced unabashedly, not yet stonewalled by Christian priests.

But pagan imagery saturates the hinged silver bracelets, from intricate symbols to the very arches the dancers populate. In "curling the birches"

---

*When I learned Morris dances as a girl, we sedately tapped our sticks together. When I later saw a side of Morris men in a Shropshire lane, I learned how far off we were, how truly virile the dances—they whaled their cudgels so hard that chips flew.

FIG. 17.6. Bulgarian *kukeri* dancing with ritual hooked sticks (*kljunki*) in circle. Note masks, man dressed as girl. Tutrakan area, ca. 1900.

at Semik, the girls in some parts of Russia tied the tips of neighboring trees together to form living arches, as we saw, then carried out their rituals and picnics in this arcade.[8] On some bracelets, the dancers and musicians occupy arches that sprout with leaves, while the supports may widen at the bottom like tree trunks or sport little dashes resembling birch bark (see fig. 3.10)—living arcades.*

These bowers house not just people but a remarkable bestiary. Birds and hares, both symbols of fertility, comprise the "known" animals, but fantastic hybrids outnumber them. Bird maidens we already know: our dancing willies. Depicted as bird-faced girls, they abound on both the bracelets and the resplendent golden head ornaments, the earrings and strings of ornamented disks that hung from the woman's temples (see fig. 13.10). On a bracelet mold from Kiev, however, we find a pair of birds with the heads of men wearing peaked caps like those on the *stećci* (fig. 17.7). The knotted and interlaced

---

*The arches, especially those not housing dancers, also resemble the architecture occupied by saints on Byzantine and medieval reliquaries—a possible source for the artistic *composition*, albeit not its meaning. The bracelets are entirely pagan. (Compare Rybakov 1968, 53.) Interestingly, the simpler fan-Gothic cathedrals like Denmark's 12th-century Roskilde Cathedral also give the impression of arcades of lofty trees. In fact, early sanctuaries often *were* groves.

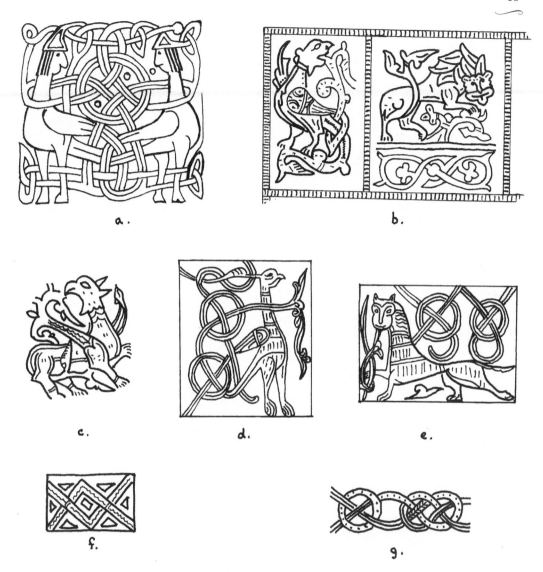

FIG. 17.7. Designs from 12th-century Kievan bracelets. Top: Versions of vegetation deity Simargl: (a) birds with human faces and pointed caps, wings and tails generating interlaced vegetation: (b) bird with dog head, wing and tail generating vegetation; quadruped with lion face, vegetal tail; (c) quadruped with avian head, wings and tail sprouting foliage; (d) bird interlaced with calendrical Xs; (e) quadruped, with calendrical Xs. Bottom (f–g): Filler designs formed of calendrical Xs (doubled for summer solstice; cf. fig. 2.3). More Simargls visible in figs. 13.9, 17.8, 17.9. (From bracelets P, C', C, R, I, F, E, respectively; see appendix.)

FIG. 17.8. Examples of "sown field" motif—lozenge inscribed with X, plus dot inside each sub-lozenge. Top left: Alone. Lower left: On collar of human-headed Simargl (Kievan bracelet C). Center: Woven pattern of nested and repeatedly interlockable "sown fields" on *panyova* (ritual back-apron), Oryol, South Great Russia. Right: "Sown fields" embroidered on *panyova*, using beads for "seeds"; note vestigial "string skirt" at top; from Oryol. (Compare fig. 21.6.)

lines entangling them resemble Celtic and Scandinavian art, but they are equally typical of the jewelry and manuscripts of Kievan Rus'. (These peoples certainly knew each other—in fact, the Kievan empire was jump-started by Scandinavian warrior/traders, who brought with them personal names like Helgi and Helga, which became Oleg and Olga.)[9]

More common are the heads of men, dogs, or felines attached to a quadruped, sometimes winged, whose tail sprouts greenery. (Sometimes the body is biped and birdlike, but then the feet are paws.) This hybrid spirit of vegetal fertility, the Simargl, derives from a Persian winged, clawed, and fanged guardian of the Tree of Life.[10] Simargls on the bracelet from Stariÿ Ryazan' wear collars with the ancient fertility sign still known to Russian embroidresses and weavers as the "sown field" (fig. 17.8): a lozenge with an inscribed X that divides it into four small lozenges, each with a dot in it. Simargls occur as well on one of the two surviving column capitals from the early Christian cathedral of Boris and Gleb near Kiev (fig. 17.9)—one wonders how the priests felt about that! Nineteenth-century farmers still carved leaf-tailed quadrupeds onto the planks decorating their houses, among willies depicted as girl-faced birds and mermaids (see fig. 1.1).

FIG. 17.9. Carved stone capitals representing quadruped vegetation deity Simargl. 11th-century Cathedral of Boris and Gleb near Kiev.

Beneath the arches—usually three to a bracelet half—lie boxes with decorative patterns.* The two most common patterns in them are complex interlaces thought to represent water, and varieties of vinelike foliage that Rybakov dubs "roots and shoots" (see figs. 3.10, 13.2, 13.9, 17.7).[11] Both clearly have to do with things on and under the ground and with the purpose of the Rusalii festivals: inveigling the Dancing Goddesses to supply enough water for the crops to mature. Sometimes the tails of the Simargl critters turn into water scrolls rather than foliage sprouts. In one vegetal pattern we've seen (fig. 13.9), the roots spread out symmetrically like a pair of legs, the shoots like two arms and breasts, while the oval bud at top center resembles a head. The whole looks both like a frog and like a woman in birthing position.

---

* Rybakov (1968, 45–47) maintains that each lower design relates semantically to what's in the panel directly above it, leading him to more detailed interpretations.

Once might be an accident, but it occurs at least twice. Perhaps our Frog Princess wore such ambiguous bracelets.*

The third design typical of these boxes—one that, like foliage, also occurs in the arches—is an X interlaced with a circle that frames and emphasizes it (see fig. 17.7). We encountered this special X in chapter 2, marking the Rusalii festivals on the folk calendars incised on pots. Sometimes this X forms part of the water interlace, sometimes a long tail or wingtip creates an element; occasionally two Xs nestle side by side (circled or not), as if specifying the *summer* Rusalii.

The fully human occupants of the hinged bracelets do not always dance. Several drink from conical cups or footed bowls (see figs. 13.2, 13.9). Is the brew garlic and wormwood to protect them, or something headier like beer or mead that will send them more quickly to see the spirits? Another such bowl floats beside one of the hares (see fig. 3.10), making the former less likely. The presence of musicians in these scenes indicates that the occasion is still the Rusalii. Two men appear to hold bagpipes (see fig. 13.8), an instrument that we associate with the Celts but that was once used widely in Europe and still exists in the central Balkans (see fig. 9.1). Twice the musician plays a psalter or gusli, laying it across his knees to pluck it.

Below the flowing sleeves of a dancer who has stopped to drink floats a mask (see fig. 13.2). Its ears and nose give it a decidedly animal look, very similar to the animal's face on another bracelet (see fig. 17.7b), fitting right in with the toothsome leather masks found in medieval layers of Novgorod and assumed to belong to the class of Russian entertainers called *skomorokhi* (fig. 17.10). These medieval "minstrels" (as the word is sometimes translated) provide another stepping-stone back in time.

> . . . plays spoken by dolls *[kukli]* and players *[skomorokhi]*,
> and the dancing of Rusalii, and all demonish carnivals.
>
> —twelfth-century diatribe[12]

---

*Archaic embroidery motifs depicting birthing women (however stylized) occur on many Russian headdresses and ritual towels (e.g., possibly fig. 11.1, top right, and fig. 11.4, top). See Zharnikova 1986–87; also Barber 1997, fig. 11.

FIG. 17.10. Leather Rusalia masks (*skuratï*) from Novgorod; 13th century. (Compare mask on right to mask by girl's foot in figures 13.2, 13.8.)

The attacks by the church on the skomorokhi and their ilk, starting already in the eleventh century, were so virulent and even incoherent that one senses these men were viewed as priests of a rival religion, the indigenous agrarian belief system. By the sixteenth century, the skomorokhi seem to have become primarily "carnies" and thieves, entertaining the rural populace with music, puppetry, skits, dancing bears, and fortune-telling while parting them from their money and goods. Skomorokhi were often so poor that parishes provided them with hovels to live in.[13] But their pre-Christian predecessors clearly held a more stable position in society. If we ignore the biases and the destitution to which they were driven, and look simply at the contexts in which they functioned, an interesting and familiar profile emerges.

We hear of skomorokhi, a brotherhood of men, taking part in the Russian rituals for dead ancestors, weddings, and seasonal agrarian festivals, especially the spring, summer, and winter Rusalii. They provided music, were experts in sorcery and spells, functioned as healers and entertainers, and often used masks, costumes, and dolls, puppets, or effigies.

But this is essentially the repertoire of the rusalets and călușar brotherhoods—healing people with their music, dances, and spells (remember *Florichika* and also the magic-laden flag in chapter 5), and amusing the villagers with skits and antics, masks and costumes. If a few chickens got stolen, well, these bringers of communal abundance had to eat too: trick or treat! The villagers themselves made "un-Christian" dolls like Caloian and Gherman to stop drought (see fig. 4.2), and fashioned effigies to celebrate Maslenitsa, the Farewell to the Rusalki, and the harvest. Bands of villagers still don animal masks and costumes during the Twelve Days to drive away the demonic armies of the dead—*kallikántzaroi, malandanti*, etc.—and to win abundance for the New Year (see figs. 9.2–6).

The medieval priests complained that although parishioners began the day before Trinity Sunday piously lamenting the dead at their graves, the skomorokhi then would begin to play music, and soon everyone was dancing, clapping, and singing,[14] Christian duties forgotten. But this is just the sequence of events that occurred during Trinity in Serbia's remote Duboka. It sounds as though the same rituals once existed in Russia, too.

At weddings, the priests complained, a skomorokh preceded even the priest and his cross when the marriage party progressed to the church. But we've just seen that in some regions the leader of the procession must continually slash with a sword to protect the bridal pair from demons; and in many areas the first person was the master of ceremonies, the *druzhka* (literally, "other self, friend"), a male relative who avowedly knew how to perform "incantations to ward off the evil eye, the loose woman, the heretic, the slanderer, and so forth from the bridal couple."[15] In short, a sorcerer, however simple.

But we have other traces. Ukrainians sing two types of traditional kolyada songs during the Twelve Days. The long ones, recounting old tales, mention the skomorokhi as coming and entertaining the master of the house and his guests[16]—just as the rusaltsi/căluşari do during that period (healing is done only during the spring Rusalia Week), and just as masked mummers from Greece to England do. In one song from Chernigov, Ukraine, a goat dies and is revived* by someone called a *mikhonosha*—literally a "sack carrier," but specifically the person who collects the gifts of food and money given by the spectators to the mummers during the quête.[17] Remember that the gifts not only repay the mummers for their efforts to *bring* abundance; they also *ensure* abundance through analogical magic with a *display* of abundance. Again the northern skomorokhi turned up in contexts still preserved in the warmer, easier-living South.

The short kolyada songs, on the other hand, are "light, humorous, and even insouciant or bawdy,"[18] typical not only of what we hear that the medieval skomorokhi performed but also of the skits put on by the rusaltsi/căluşari. The long kolyadï, in fact, are entire little dramas in dialogue form,

---

* The goat is closely connected with the grain cult (we encountered another goat play from Belarus in chapter 9), possibly because wheat and other grains have "beards" like goats.

and some were still being acted out as plays in 1915.[19] For that matter, we've mentioned that the multiday wedding rituals, from the Balkans to Archangel, played out as a scripted drama with each part preordained and memorized. And we just saw that these "plays," too, were orchestrated by an incantation specialist, a sort of skomorokh.

What we see, then, is a tradition that used effigies and human maskers essentially interchangeably to carry out the agrarian and mate-finding rituals—that is, remedies for those problems overseen by the Dancing Goddesses in particular and the dead in general. The ancient unity of dolls, effigies, and masked player-dancers even shows up linguistically: the Bulgarian name *kukeri*, for the masked men dancing fertility plays during the Twelve Days (see figs. 9.4, 17.6), comes from Greek *koúkla*, "doll," itself from Latin *cucullus* "hood"—that is, "disguise." The medium didn't seem to matter, as long as some visual and tangible representative of the spirits carried out the rites. Over time, the details of this tradition diverged somewhat across space, just as language and other cultural traditions do.

The Greco-Roman origin of the word *kukeri*, however, suggests that the sources for more of this material may lie in the earlier Classical world, to which we now turn.

CHAPTER 18

Roman Showbiz

e have seen that the willies and their ilk brought *both* good
and evil: rain and drought, fertility and barrenness, cures as
well as the sickness to be cured. The trick was to stay on their
good side—not to offend them, and to get them to dance through the fields,
shedding abundance everywhere. Where people came to focus on a single
goddess of fertility, she usually had a negative side as a death goddess. (In
modern life, we tend to forget the inevitable fact that if you give a creature
life, by that very act you have condemned it to death.)

Similarly, rural farmers viewed those among them who specialized in
knowledge as purveying both the good and the bad. The "knowers" recognized healing herbs as well as poisons, delivered prophecies for both good
times and bad, and had charms both to help and to hurt.

Christianity, as it developed in western Europe, altered this view. The
traditional keepers of these sorts of knowledge came to be understood first
as *deluded* by demons (a sin punishable by penances) and then as *possessed*
by demons—people now hopelessly evil, to be ferreted out and burned at the
stake.* *Wit-ch* and *wiz-ard* (both from the same root as *wis-dom* and *wise*)

---

* See Carlo Ginzburg (1992) for a careful, fascinating assessment of the whole development
of witchery in Europe; Éva Pócs (1989) for data and events simmering at the boundaries
between the area believing in spirits and that believing in witches; and Katherine Morris
(1991) for much insight into the pagan/Christian paradigm shift.

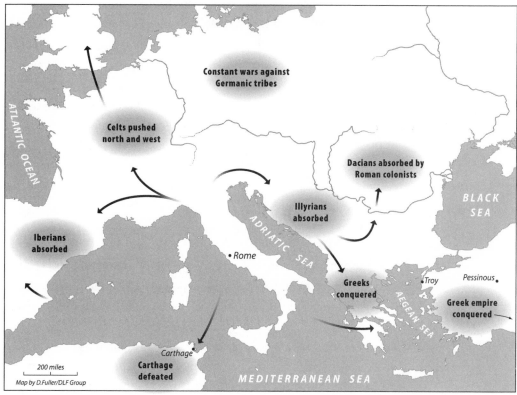

MAP 18: Ancient Romans. Top: Early Italy. Bottom: Spread of Roman Empire

took on new connotations. In other words, those believing in spirits like the Dancing Goddesses treated evil as just one of the consequences of supernatural doings; those believing in witches saw evil as unconditional, coming directly from human malevolence manipulated by Satan. In particular, the church fought paganism—the word is related to *peasant*, "country person"—by treating the peasants' fertility deities not as nonexistent but rather as demons inimical to the One True God. Fertility was not to be celebrated. Women, according to Paul (though not, apparently, Jesus), were basically weak and lustful, and sex was evil. The cult of the Virgin Mary even set up "proper" womanhood as *asexual* (an attitude that developed into the Western medieval notion of courtly love[1]). Christianity, after all, took root primarily as an urban religion amid the disenchanted masses crowded into cities, where overpopulation, not fecundity, was at issue.[2]

In eastern Europe and in distant tracts of the northwest, belief in simple spirits remained. Even in Croatia, in Ireland and Scotland, despite being areas Christianized from Rome, the willies, fairies, and other spirits stayed ambivalent with respect to good and bad, and pagan customs stayed remarkably intact, as we have seen. Much polarization into good vs. evil seems to stem from the church's efforts.[3]

Prior to the rise of Christianity, the cultural powerhouses of the northern Mediterranean were, of course, the Greeks and the Romans, both highly literate at their urban cores. To them we now turn for more evidence of the layers beneath the lore and festivals of the Dancing Goddesses. Some evidence will be archaeological, but much more is linguistic.

Citizens of the Roman Empire loved spectacles of all sorts, from gladiators and bear fights to plays and parades. Obscene farce ranked as a special favorite—one that persisted, to the despair of the church, right up to Shakespeare and beyond.

When Greek colonists had settled in Sicily and southern Italy at the height of Athenian culture, they carried with them their own version of Greek drama, which evolved during the fifth and fourth centuries BC into a special form of "morality" farce called *mimos*, whence our words *mime* and *pantomime*. Now, the people living in west-central Italy, who were developing into the Romans, preferred athletic entertainment; but their neighbors,

FIG. 18.1. Performers disguised as ungainly birds. Left: Classical Greek comic chorister, with cockscomb and wattles, following his flutist. From black-figure vase, ca. 500 BC. Right: Romanian *Brezaia* (wife of Old Man, in New Year's mumming), with miniature plowshare adorned with bell on head.

the Etruscans and Oscans, loved theater as much as the Greeks did. Surrounded, the Romans eventually added theatrical performances to their repertoire. They even borrowed the Etruscan word for an actor, *histrio*, which has come down into English as *histrionic*.[4] From Oscans and Greeks they borrowed the use of comic masks—comic choruses in Athens had long used masks to impersonate chickens, frogs, and other absurd creatures (fig. 18.1).

One of the favorite characters was a comic old woman, sometimes portrayed at New Year festivities as a personification of the Old Year under the name of Anna Perenna (whence our word *perennial*).[5] Certainly March 15, which had served as the Roman New Year until 153 BC, long remained the day on which Anna Perenna was honored. We have met her descendant in the elder woman of death-and-resurrection plays all across Europe. In several stories told about her by the Roman poet Ovid (43 BC–AD 18), she appears as an old woman, but Ovid also relates that Anna was originally the sister of Dido, the queen who committed suicide when the Trojan hero Aeneas left Carthage without her. Anna later fled Carthage to Aeneas's new home in Latium (the area around Rome, whence *Latin*), ran afoul of jealousy from Aeneas's wife, Lavinia, and drowned herself in a river of which she then became the guardian nymph—a willy in every respect.[6] Clearly key parts of the lore we have been tracking were already alive and well in Italy twenty-five hundred years ago.

When New Year was moved to January 1, some of the associated customs moved, too, and began to merge with those of another important holiday, the Saturnalia, December 17. Named after Saturn, god of sowing, the Saturnalia initiated a period of communal relaxation after the fall plowing and sowing.[7] Citizens decked their houses with greenery and lights, as we still do at Christmas (the darkest, least green time of year), and ran around visiting friends and relatives and giving them presents. These gifts, called *strenae* (becoming French *étrennes*), once consisted of green twigs—auspicious for life in the New Year and still potent in the popular French folk song *En passant par la Lorraine*. There a girl has a close encounter with a passing prince. It ends:

> *Il m'a donné pour étrenne*
> *Un bouquet de marjolaine. . .*
> *S'il fleurit, je serai reine,*
> *S'il y meurt, je perds ma peine.*

He gives her as *étrenne* a bouquet of marjoram, saying that if (and only if) his little present "flowers," she'll be queen—that is, mother of a prince. The twigs were originally culled from the grove of Strenia, a little-known Sabine goddess associated with Janus (fig. 18.2), the two-faced god who looked both forward and back in time and space and appropriately lent his name to doorways and the first month of the new year, January. Gradually the presents extended to honey cakes, candles, and metal things, analogically bringing sweetness, light, and material wealth, as well as life. (We continue the cus-

FIG. 18.2. Janus, Roman god of doorways and other boundaries, of which he can view both sides at once.

tom in our annual commercial orgy of Christmas presents but have lost the original significance.)

Hosts, for their part, provided food aplenty (again analogical for abundance in the coming year), and the social system was temporarily turned upside down as slaves dined and played dice with their masters as equals. Each household chose by lot a king of the Saturnalia to lead the torchlight revels and the Feast of Fools, including processions and rude comedies enacted in the streets, with men dressing as women or masquerading as animals.[8] All these reversals of the normal patterns referenced the reversed spirit world.

The masked revelers, plays, and King of Fools (a.k.a. Lord of Misrule) have had a long life, perpetuated in the early Middle Ages by the monks and priests themselves.[9] Some areas of Europe, as we saw, retain them even now as part of the Twelve Days, and elsewhere as part of Carnival (around the older New Year). The Roman term for the first of any month was *kalendae* (from a verb meaning "call, proclaim [a beginning]"), whence the word *calendar*. Where masquerades occur during the Twelve Days, we typically find a form of the term *kalend-* preserved specifically for January 1 and hence for the whole season or for the songs sung then (Russian *kolyada*, Romanian *colind*, etc.). The word clearly spread with the Roman New Year customs throughout Rome's empire—carried first by colonists and later by professional mimes fleeing the Turks who conquered Constantinople.[10] Where masquerades occur at Carnival, however, we often see evidence of the church trying to exercise damage control by persuading people that *all* such wild activities, if done at all, should be confined to Carnival. (This process is still going on today, for example, in Greek Macedonia, where twentieth-century Greek refugees from remote areas brought in a wide variety of local traditions: see chapters 9, 22.)

In Italy, where Christianity took hold early, many Roman traditions attached themselves to Carnival. For example, Roman emperors who won important battles were granted a triumphal procession in which they paraded through Rome in their chariots with their prisoners and spoils of war. When Christianity took over, the "triumphal" parades continued as part of Carnival. Roman soldiers hungry for entertainment had long used carts as stages for playing farces,[11] but now the cars, like modern floats, served as platforms for little scenes depicting Christian virtues such as Temperance and Chastity, as well as threats like Death and the Last Judgment. Sometime after playing cards reached Renaissance Italy in the late 1300s,

FIG. 18.3. Fool (left), Chariot (right): "triumph" (trump) cards from early Taroc-chi (Tarot) deck. Painted ca. 1445 by B. Bembo for Visconti-Sforza family, Flor-ence. "Chariot" shows type of flatbed cart used for "triumphal" processions.

rich families added to the deck a series of twenty-one picture cards called *trionfi* "triumphs; trumps" painted with the typical floats and other char-acters in the Carnival "triumphal" parade (fig. 18.3).* For their new game, called Tarocchi (or Tarot), they also added one wild card, the Fool.

This Fool clearly derives from both the Saturnalian King of Fools and from the stock buffoons borrowed early from the "games" (*ludi*—in this case, rude farces) from the Oscan town of Atella. A particular favorite,

---

*The 21 pictures in the earliest known decks, from about 1445, are: merchant (*bagatto*), pope, emperor, papess, empress, justice, fortitude, temperance, love, chariot, wheel of for-tune, time, traitor (a man hanged by the foot, as customary for that offense), death, devil, tower, star, moon, sun, world, and angel of the Last Judgment. Many of these subjects match the floats in Francesco Pesellino's 15th century Florentine painting of Carnival.

called Maccus, apparently emphasized his absurdity by wearing chicken feathers, a feature retained by the Fool of medieval Carnival, as we see in the early Tarot decks (fig. 18.3, left). Onstage yet later in the *commedia dell'arte*, still sparring with some of his Oscan-derived companions, Maccus (now Macco) sometimes became a glutton, an oafish gulper of noodles. And as noodles and knuckleheads became synonymous, the noodles even adopted Macco's name, becoming *macaroni*.[12] From all this came Yankee Doodle's line, "Stuck a feather in his cap and called it macaroni!"*

Masks of chickens and other ungainly birds like storks continue to this day as favorites during Carnival and the Twelve Days across the former Roman Empire from Romania to Germany (see fig. 18.1). Other antique holdovers include the Fool's multicolored costume and eared cap—originally ass's ears—jingling with bells,[13] which became the jester's garb, and a penchant for making the local authority figures like the priest and doctor take the brunt of what's preposterous and obscene in the satire.[14]

In short, many of the details perpetuated in the rituals of the Twelve Days (now tied to Christmas) and Carnival (now tied to Lent) existed long before Christianity.

⌘

March, the month formerly opening the Roman year, belonged to Mars, the warrior-protector of the city. Legend had it that on March 1 in the seventh century BC a wasp-waisted shield (*ancile*) had fallen into the city of Rome from heaven, stopping a plague—much in the manner of the heaven-sent spear, the Palladium, that had protected Aeneas's Troy. The shield was duly hung up in the temple of Mars as a protective talisman, along with eleven replicas, so no enemy could recognize and steal the original.[15]

Every March, a group or "college" of twelve priests called the *Salii* "Leapers" repeatedly carried the sacred shields and spears in procession around the city, stopping at designated places to dance as they sang. The sacred songs were maintained in a dialect so old that eventually people couldn't under-

---

*Ethnic food items are frequently drafted to refer disparagingly to the members of other cultures or social classes. Historically, bumpkins were referred to in Germany as *Hanswurst* (John Sausage), in France as *Jean Potage* (John Thick Soup), in Hungary as *Paprika Jancsi* (Paprika Johnny), in Greece as *Phasoulis* (Beaner) (see Liungman 1938, 723–24). The reader can undoubtedly supply a multitude of modern derogatory food names for foreigners as well.

stand them (as with the *Rig Veda* in India and the Catholic Mass in Europe), and the dance consisted of circling with majestic leaps while clashing the shields and spears together to the beat of the music. The higher the Salii jumped, the higher the crops would grow, while the noise served to protect the city by driving away evil spirits as humanity crossed the threshold of the New Year. Their music had a three-beat rhythm (*tripudium*), apparently anapestic like the Bulgarian rŭchenitsa: *short-short-long*.[16] To the orator Seneca, the Salii resembled fullers stomping cloth[17]—compare the Bulgarian women we saw dancing the rŭchenitsa to stomp their clay during Rusalia Week.

The Salii wore short multicolored tunics and spiked hats secured with a chin strap:[18] to lose a hat while leaping would be inauspicious. Although the men themselves could be married or single and of any age, they had to have both parents alive, a stipulation encountered elsewhere in Rome and found often in Balkan ritual (e.g., for Enyo's Bride). Unlike other priests, they were chosen not by the Pontifex, the high priest, but by their own officer, the *magister*, whose duties included festival logistics as well as swearing in and instructing newcomers. Another officer, the *praesul*, led the antiphonal dance, while a third, the *vātes*, conducted the songs, keeping the beat and chasing away anyone intruding on their space. The resemblance to the combined jobs of the călușari's vătaf and "mute" is remarkable,[19] and, backed by the Latin term *vātes* from which *vătaf* came, shows that some of these ritual details spread eastward across the Balkans with the Roman Empire.* Points of resemblance in fact abound. For example, sacrifices by the Salii involved a clay pot, while Roman soldiers were partial to using chickens for *their* offerings.[20] (Recall that at the climax of a dance cure for rusalka sickness, the eldest dancer simultaneously smashed a new clay pot and killed the black chicken inside it with a sharp blow from his staff.)

Roman soldiers not only conquered territory for the empire but received farmland in the new regions as their veterans' severance pay. Inscriptions suggest that these settlers brought along such favorite military traditions as the Salii "colleges" and their rituals requiring gymnastic prowess (which would explain why the ribbons on călușari costumes resemble the lappets of

---

*Latin *vātes* meant "(sooth)sayer, prophet," then "master, authority" in ceremonial rites (Lewis and Short 1879/1958; Chambers 1903, 25)—just like the vătaf. By medieval times, Romanian *vătaf* meant simply "overseer," having lost its original specialized meaning outside of these Roman-inherited rituals.

FIG. 18.4. Lion hunter using incurved (figure-8) shield, inlaid on blade of Bronze Age Aegean dagger. Shaft Grave IV, Mycenae, Greece, ca. 1600 BC.

Roman military garb (see fig. 5.1).[21] This Roman origin may even solve the source of the Romanian name *cǎluşari* for what the Slavs call *rusaltsi*.*

On March 14, ten days before hanging up their shields again, the Salii chased out of the city a man dressed in an animal skin—some sort of scapegoat—and pantomimed the forging of metal.[22] (Recall the mimed forging of a plow by kalogheroi in northern Greece and the "beast" mock-killed by Bulgarian kukeri.) Scholars speculate that the Salii rituals themselves therefore go back to the introduction of metalworking in Italy at the end of the Stone Age.[23] But given that the first metals used—namely, copper and gold—were cold-hammered because of their softness, it seems more likely that the occasion was the introduction of iron (which requires extremely hot, expertly controlled furnaces, and often much forgework), not long before the reputed meteorlike arrival of the *ancile*.† The peculiar shape of this shield, common in Late Bronze Age Greece (fig. 18.4) but not elsewhere, along with its Greek name (meaning "incurving," whence our word *ankle*), suggest rather that the rituals came in during the seventh century BC, as Roman sources maintain,[24] with strong input from Greece and per-

---

* As early Rome expanded across its seven hills, another college of Salii was founded, differentiated from the original Salii Palatini, as the Salii Collini. Researchers suggest that *Colli-Salii* became something like *cǎlu-şali*, then *cǎlu-şari* (*l* and *r* often got scrambled in Late Latin), which in turn was folk-etymologized as *cǎl-uş* "horseling, little horse" plus the agent suffix *-ar*, giving "little-horse people." This must have occurred as the athletic bands of Salii among the colonists fused with Balkan notions of Dancing Goddesses and the popular hobbyhorses (as in figs. 5.4, 20.15–17). (See Vulpesco 1927, 189–90.)

† Meteorites, when found, were regularly placed in temples and churches, usually as protective talismans—e.g., the meteorite that fell at Pessinous (in Turkey) and was later taken to Rome and enshrined in 205 BC to protect the city against Hannibal (cf. Cirilli 1913, 13–14; D'Orazio 2007). Meteorites often consist of iron.

haps from the shield dance of the Cretan Kouretes (see chapter 19). Here we see ritual ideas flowing *westward*, long before the Romans spread their empire eastward.

The Romans also celebrated festivals in honor of the dead. In February, the nine-day Parentalia honoring one's ancestors opened with the Lupercalia. For this, men carrying strips of goatskin ran the bounds of the original city of Rome, lashing at the women to make them fertile,[25] much as the Romanian călușari's "mute" swatted women to make them fertile and children to make them healthy.* On May 9, 11, and 13, at the Lemuria, more offerings propitiated the roving dead (*lemures*—whence our animal name *lemur* for a spooky-eyed nocturnal rover). These spirits were so dangerous, despite the black beans thrown to them as a sop at night, that they made the whole month unlucky.[26]

May also saw the *Rosalia* or rose festival, when families strung rose garlands on the tombs and ate a ritual meal beside them after laying out place settings for the dead. It was a minor occasion, of uncertain date, first mentioned in AD 225 and becoming popular only a century later, particularly in Roman North Africa, where harvesting roses for perfume had become big business.[27] Scholars often derive Slavic *Rusalii* from Latin *Rosalia*, but the two festivals share nothing besides propitiating the dead—besides which, we've seen that the Rusalii occur *three* times yearly: in Midwinter, scarcely a time of roses, as well as in spring and summer. The core ideas of the Rusalii came from elsewhere than the Rosalia, although it later attracted details of Roman customs and vocabulary to itself, like iron shavings to a magnet.

Finally the Queen became pregnant and delivered a daughter.
They had a beautiful baptism; as godmothers they gave the

---

*Just before Lent, in a ritual called *Cornii* (from Latin *cornu* "horn"), Romanian boys in animal masks ran about hitting women with a sandal on a stick for fertility (Giurchescu and Bloland 1992, 40)—presumably because Balkan village sandals usually have a horn-shaped toe tip (see fig. 5.2). The symbolism seems clear—certainly hitting for fertility extends across much of eastern Europe.

> little princess all the fairies they could find in the realm (they
> found seven), so that each of them would give her a gift, as was
> the custom at that time, and by this means the princess would
> have all the perfections imaginable.
>
> —Charles Perrault, "Sleeping Beauty" (1697)

We all know the story of Sleeping Beauty: how an uninvited eighth fairy turned up and—insulted (originally) that there was no solid gold table setting laid for *her*—angrily decreed the princess would prick her finger on a spindle and die; and how another fairy, who had hidden, came forward and commuted the sentence to merely sleeping for a century and being awakened by a prince.

Few know, however, that these birth fairies reached us from the Romans.

Our word *fairy* comes, via French *fée*, from Latin *fata*, originally a neuter plural: "things fated to happen." But because feminine singular forms also ended in *-a*, and because the Greek fate goddesses, the *Moîrai*, were female and three in number, the word got reanalyzed as feminine and generated a trio of goddesses with a new plural, *fatae*. Two of the *Moîrai*—*Klōthō* "spinner," and *Láchesis* "allotter"—spun the thread of each person's life, while *Atropos*, "unturnable," snipped the thread at the fated moment of death. The Roman Fates adopted these traits and further merged with the *Parcae*, triplet clones of an indigenous goddess of childbirth, *Parca*, formerly invoked to aid the mother and bless the child with gifts of health, beauty, and the like. (*Parca* comes from Latin *par(ire)* "to bring forth, give birth.")[28]

The La Tène Celts, conquered by the Romans, developed their own related trio, called *Matronae* "Mothers, Matrons, Ancestresses," whose altars archaeologists find by the hundreds in the La Tène area from northern Italy to Spain to Denmark.[29] From this mix came the fairies attending Sleeping Beauty.

Perrault did not invent his tale, although he cleaned it up. Already in the early 1300s, a version appeared in the middle of a lengthy pseudo-Arthurian romance called *Perceforest*. Three goddesses appear at the birth of a girl named Zellandine: the first bestows health, while the second, angered that her place setting lacks a knife, decrees that the girl will later pierce her hand with a distaff and fall asleep till it is pulled out. The third goddess promises rescue. (Jarringly, the rescuer is no Prince Charming: he rapes her as she sleeps. Both the other early versions include this feature, which Perrault kindly eliminated, moving her additional misfortunes to a later chapter seldom printed in English.)

Why the fuss about place settings?

Romans traditionally laid out a knife and maybe a spoon for each ancestor invited to the family feast during festivals honoring the dead—further corroboration of the antiquity of the details in this story.[30]

✎

We can now see why, despite being female spirits who are usually young, beautiful, and likely to dance around, our western "fairies" do not function like eastern European willies: they originated as souls not of *childless* girls but of ancestresses, divine mothers.* The other Roman goddesses encountered in our quest also present anomalies.

Consider the leader of the roving dead. The Irodeasa invoked by the Romanian călușari, like the Croatian *Irudica*,[31] came functionally from Diana and linguistically from the Late Latin *Herodiana* misinterpreted by Christians as the biblical *Herodias*.[32] Classical Roman Diana, herself of uncertain origin, had absorbed many traits from Greek Artemis, with whom she was equated; and myths of Artemis/Diana emphasize her love of going hunting with the nymphs (spirit maidens).[33] But whereas the dead whom the călușari/rusaltsi wished to placate remained girls dead before their time (willies), Diana's nymphs in the West gradually became *all* the roving dead, leading to the notions of the Wild Hunt and Walpurgis Night.

Diana herself seems to have fused also with *Bona Dea*, literally "the Good Goddess," a deity too august to be referred to by a personal name and from whose rites men were strictly excluded. Depicted (like Ceres, goddess of agriculture, and like Fortuna, "Fortune") with a cornucopia full of fruits and grain (fig. 18.5), Bona Dea protected women, their households, and their

---

* The Celtic Wee Folk or Good Neighbors of the British Isles differed less; they had interests in fertility and prosperity and left frequent evidence of their dancing on the grass, much as in the Balkans. The rituals surrounding Irish (St.) Brigid also run parallel to many Balkan customs (cf. chapter 9; Ginzburg 1992, 104, 108–9, 123). Note that the early Celts had lived in central Europe, mining salt and metals and weaving plaid twills, for a millennium or two before migrating to the Atlantic coast about 400 BC (see Barber 1999a, 133–38, with map). An unbiased study of the many Celtic connections could provide many interesting results.

FIG. 18.5. Roman statue of Bona Dea holding horn of plenty (*cornu-copia*).

fertility and helped with the healing arts. Her purview thus resembles that of St. Paraskevi (St. Friday) and the willies. Bona Dea, too, had come to Rome from the Greeks, from those early colonists in southern Italy who brought Greek comedy. The site of her earliest known sanctuary, at Paestum south of Naples, is now known as Santa Venera—another St. Friday.[34]

Faced with Christian persecution, Bona Dea and Diana went underground along with the rural obsession for fertility. But over the next millennium, the Good Goddess continued to resurface under many euphemisms, such as *Bona Socia* (Good Companion), *Abundia* (Abundance), *Richella* (Richness), *Horiente*.[35]* For example, Pierina, a woman of Lombardy, "confessed" in 1384 that every Thursday night (considered the start of Friday!), from age sixteen, she attended the nocturnal meeting of the Lady (H)Oriente—although her inquisitor, recognizing the pattern from older church documents, called it "the game of Diana, whom you call Herodias." After greeting her followers with "Be well, good people (*Bene stetis, bona gens*)," the Lady led her throng

> through the various houses, above all those of the wealthy. There they eat and drink: when the houses are well swept and tidy they rejoice and are pleased and Oriente blesses them. To the members of the soci-

---

*The *Horae* "Hours" were minor goddesses in charge of the hours and passing seasons. *Horiente* thus appears, from the context, to designate a leader—"Lady Season" or the like. Since initial *h* disappeared in many Late Latin dialects, her name was influenced by or reanalyzed as *Oriente* "East."

ety Oriente teaches the virtues of herbs (*virtutes herbarum*), remedies
to cure diseases, how to find things that have been stolen and how to
dissolve spells. But all of this must be kept secret.[36]

Clearly, village women and occasionally men across northern Italy, Croatia,
Switzerland, France, and Germany were quietly learning from each other
how to fall into trances on certain nights and "fly" to the dance feasts of the
goddess, much as the Vlach women of Serbian Duboka learned to fall into
trances and visit the dead on Trinity Sunday.[37] Their purpose was to obtain
abundant crops, healing, and other blessings from the Good Lady and her
army of spirits. It was these night riders, believing they *benefited* their communities, who were first persecuted as witches.

We see that an ancient notion of obtaining fertility from the dead
remained, but the details were wandering off. Furthermore, most of what
matches our Dancing Goddesses in Italy arrived there from Greece. The
Romans, who loved a good spectacle, added a thick layer of showy outer
trappings that have persisted to the present, especially during the Twelve
Days and Carnival. And they spread these customs liberally across their
vast empire. But to uncover the layers underlying *that* in our onion, we must
return to Greece and the Balkans.

CHAPTER 19

Dancing with the Greeks

Leap for full jars,
and leap for fleecy flocks,
and leap for fields of fruit,
and for hives to bring increase!
—Cretan *Hymn of the Koúrētes*

arts of the ancient Greek *Hymn of the Koúrētes* could just as well be a song of the Lazarus maidens, for they too leapt for the flocks, crops, and bees. As with the Lazarki, the annual ritual of the Kouretes apparently marked initiation into young adulthood, at the same time drafting the magical power of new-and-unused sexuality for the well-being of the community. But the Kouretes were male, not female, living and leaping two and three millennia ago in Crete, not Bulgaria, until Christianity obliterated their traditions.

Not only people were to leap, however: fruitfulness was no mere request. The song *commands the god*, Son of Kronos, to leap,* while his votaries sing, play music, and dance for his pleasure.

Exactly as with the Dancing Goddesses, divine movement will create life, and attendant human dancers will lightning-rod it to the community. We've also seen the persistent faith that the higher one leaps (or swings or tosses something), the higher the crops will grow.

Our copy of the hymn dates to AD 200, but its archaic language dates it at

---

*Imperative singular, θόρε. See Harrison 1962, 6–10.

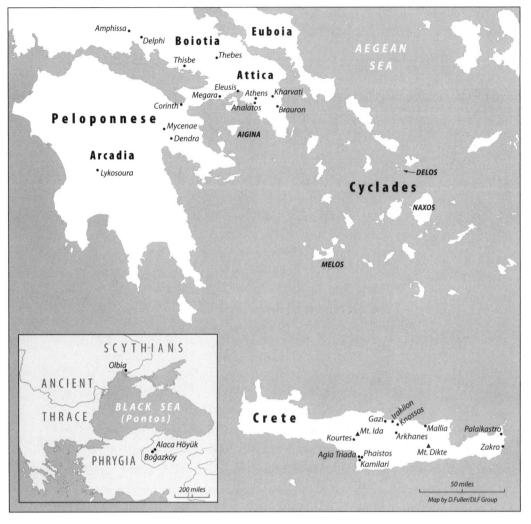

MAP 19: Southern Greece, Cyclades, and Crete.
Inset: Tribes and Sites around Black Sea.

least five hundred years earlier, while the temple of Diktean Zeus at Palaikastro, where it was found, was already thriving in the seventh century BC.[1] Slightly before that, the poet Hesiod, living far across the Aegean in Boiotia, already knew of the Kouretes,* but as mythical beings—hence of an older stratum still.

The Kouretes myth puzzled the Greeks, for to them, Zeus, king of the Olympian gods, was immortal, whereas the Cretans claimed Zeus died!

---

* Fragment 129, quoted by Harrison (1962, 25).

FIG. 19.1. Cretan Kouretes dancing and clashing arms over infant Zeus, to guard him. (Winged object is thunderbolt.) Roman Campana terracotta relief.

It all began when divine Kronos fathered numerous children on the great mother goddess Rhea, but as soon as she bore each child, Kronos swallowed it down. Exasperated, Rhea enlisted help. When birth pangs for the sixth began, she had the company of Kouretes dance about, making so much noise clashing their shields and swords that Kronos could hear neither her cries in labor nor those of the newborn—Zeus himself. Spiriting the babe away, she presented a well-swaddled stone to Kronos, who gulped it down unexamined. Meanwhile, in a cave on Mt. Dikte, the Kouretes continued to raise the infant, covering the sound with their dances whenever he cried (fig. 19.1). But little Zeus had other enemies. The fearsome Titans, a race of giants, lured him from the cave with toys—the list varies, but the toys generally double as divination devices, like mirrors and knucklebones—then tore him to shreds, killing and burying him.

It was this that made the Greeks claim, "All Cretans are liars." Obviously, immortals can't die. Since the story matched the Greeks' version of Zeus's *birth*, however, they either rejected the rest or had someone salvage and resuscitate him. Fully grown, Zeus defeated Kronos and made him disgorge all he had swallowed. First up was the stone, falling to earth at Delphi to become its sacred oracle stone.* Then followed Zeus's five siblings, who became the chief Olympian gods.

---

*See Barber and Barber 2005, chapter 16, for discussion of both the Change of Kingship in Heaven and myths surrounding meteorites. See Rose for sources of each myth.

FIG. 19.2. Young initiate with mostly shaved head, holding sword and tasseled sheath, facing older guardsman (who has more jewelry, fancier loincloth and boots, and long hair). Steatite cup. Minoan, Agia Triada, Crete, ca. 1600 BC.

We have seen enough to sort this out. Crete, invaded by Greeks late in the Bronze Age, still harbored remnants of the earlier non-Greek population during the Iron Age, especially in East Crete, where this hymn was found. The ancient East Cretans mythologized a traditional agrarian spirit who died and was resurrected after being shredded and buried (as we've seen so often), whereas the incoming Greeks, originally herders (see chapter 20), focused on other concepts. We deduce that the Kouretes consisted of a band of youth (Greek *koûroi*) being initiated to adult status and lore, including training at arms. Like the Lazarki, they learned special ritual songs and dances, the performance of which demonstrated this new status to the community. And like the Lazarki, the older probably inducted the younger (fig. 19.2). The loud clashing of arms in the dance perhaps preserves an element of hazing the initiates. The tradition also seems to have jump-started the Salii, the dancing priests we observed in Rome.

Although the Greeks rejected a southern (Cretan) *Zeus* who died, they accepted, if a bit unwillingly, the same story of a dying god from the North, by grafting him into the pantheon as Zeus's son. His name was Dionysos.

❧

Zeus, poets said, lusted after a beautiful princess of Thebes named Semélē and offered to grant her one wish in return for her favors. She accepted, but to his horror she demanded to see him in his full Olympian glory. Sadly he kept his word, knowing she would be incinerated. He rescued his infant son from her body and placed it in his own groin to incubate, while the Thebans marked off as a holy precinct the palace wing where the awesome thunderbolt had struck. When the baby had come to term, he emerged as the god Dionysos, deity of the grapevine and its intoxicating produce.[2]

Classical Greeks of 400 BC treated the worship of Dionysos as recently imported from barbarian Thrace. He wasn't so recent: Dionysos is listed among the gods in Bronze Age Greek tablets, ca. 1200 BC. And Thebes is in south-central Greece, not Thrace. But he was, apparently, Thracian. "Thrace" today is small, encompassing only the little European arm of Turkey, a corner of northeastern Greece, and a strip of southern Bulgaria. But in the fifth century BC, the Greek historian Herodotus (section v.3) referred to the Thracians as the largest group in all Europe, while archaeological research confirms that the Thracian culture extended at times from Thessaly (just north of Thebes) to mid-Ukraine, and from the northern Aegean (including some of the bigger islands) almost to Poland—that is, all of southeastern Europe except for southern Greece and the western half of the Balkan Peninsula.[3] That's huge. Thracians were "barbarians" by the technicality that the chauvinistic Greek word *bárbaros* means "someone who doesn't speak Greek—who says only *bar-bar-bar-*." But their material culture, their command of metalwork and textiles, was exquisite. Nonetheless, they were fiercely independent and never coalesced into a single political group, so they remained largely unknown and unreckoned with.*

Greek reluctance to accept Dionysos (a.k.a. Bacchus) stemmed largely from the vast difference between his rituals and the rest of Greek religion.[4] His chief votaries were women called Maenads ("raving ones") or Bacchants, who went out into the wilds to dance for and with him, intoxicated by wine or other drugs (figs. 19.3, 19.14). Despite their fame, little is known about the actual dances of the Maenads. On Greek vases they appear in stock positions of violent action, throwing their heads back and kicking up their heels, occasionally with an arm flung about a companion. One thinks

---

*So they remained until around 2000, when, after the fall of the Iron Curtain, Bulgarian archaeologists felt safe in revealing that masses of magnificent Thracian material had turned up in Bulgaria over the previous sixty years, only to be hidden away in basements by authorities. Because Soviet propaganda demanded that Slavic culture predominate, it had been unwise to acknowledge any remarkable pre-Slavic materials—anything before about AD 600. See Florov and Florov 2001, 11–14.

Scholars suspect that the Thracians have also kept a low profile because the death-and-resurrection mythology associated with their chief deity, Zalmoxis, allowed them to slip easily into Christianization.

FIG. 19.3. Right: Maenads dancing and playing flutes around Dionysos as pillar draped with robe and mask. Left: Side view of such a pillar. Attic red-figure vases, early 5th century BC.

of traditional gypsy dancing or, stronger, the gyrations of those possessed, as Plutarch describes them[5]—not the usual Balkan line dancing. Interestingly, the Maenads' characteristic cry, rendered by the ancients as *eui!* (εὔι, pronounced *éwi*), is closely echoed by the high-pitched "*yúwi yúwi!*" of girls stamp-dancing today in Dobrudzha, on the Black Sea coast of Bulgaria, heart of ancient Thrace, or spinning the circle in a *drmeš* in Croatia.

Greek culture dictated that worship was a staid and solemn affair, and that "proper" women had to stay at home, leaving the house only for funerals and a very few religious rites. We see their decorous processions on the Parthenon and other Athenian monuments. So for women to rant about the countryside in a superhuman state of intoxication, allegedly rending and eating wild animals raw and mingling with even wilder male devotees called Satyrs and Silens, was obnoxious. (These fellows—see figs. 19.5, 19.14—are distinguishable by their tails and little horns, and sometimes by hooves for feet, traits later transferred to Christian devils.) On the other hand, going against a god was dangerous, as Euripides set forth magnificently in his tragedy *The Bacchae*, and as the women of Amphissa feared.

Residents of Amphissa found, late one night, that a group of Maenads from nearby Delphi (there called *Thyiádes*) had staggered into their marketplace and collapsed, disoriented and exhausted from dancing all night on the steep mountainside where Delphi perches. But the whole area was at war and Amphissa full of enemy soldiers. Fearing that the sacred Thyiades would come to harm, the village women ran to the marketplace and surrounded the sleepers, standing silent guard till they awoke, then fed them and led them safely back to the mountain.[6]

Dionysos was . . . well, tolerated. Yet from his worship in Athens sprang an institution of major importance to both Western culture and certain traditions investigated in this book: Dionysos begat Greek drama and our notions of theater. (The very words are Greek: *drama* is what is *acted*, *theater* is what is *viewed*.)

We know historically that Dionysian drama began with a chorus who danced and sang their way through a story, a myth about Dionysos. (*Chorus*, which English borrowed from Greek, may well have come to Greek from the prior inhabitants. It lives on in all the Balkan languages—and Yiddish—as *horo* or *hora*, a partnerless line- or circle-dance.) The choral dance mimed the words being sung, making them visible, as in traditional hula.[7] At times a leader separated himself out, performing antiphonally to the chorus—he led, they answered. (Balkan dance songs are still sometimes structured thus.) Eventually, up to three "leaders"—actors—represented the characters in the story, while the chorus interacted and commented. By the fifth century BC, the golden age of Athens, the story could be a myth about any god or hero, but the *form* of the drama, as the noted classicist Gilbert Murray has shown, retained the key elements of the original mystical story that the worshippers of Dionysos flocked to hear.[8] Greek tragedies always begin with a prologue setting the scene, followed by a conflict involving the protagonist (another Greek word: "primary contester"), the tragic results of which a messenger relates. The chorus laments this outcome, and finally a resolution occurs.

Just so for Dionysos. He was attacked and killed—in fact, shredded, strewn, and buried like Caloian, Maslenitsa, or a rusalka effigy—greatly lamented, then miraculously resurrected or reborn.[9] It is the same folk drama still enacted today in rural Thrace and elsewhere at the start of the new year. It is the cyclical agrarian Story of Life.

Masks formed a key part of Dionysian rites. Athenian paintings repeatedly show worshippers dancing about a mask of Dionysos hung on a pillar bedecked with a handsome robe and festive garlands (see fig. 19.3). Actors and choristers also all used masks, both to distinguish the characters and to disguise themselves. They performed for the common weal, not for themselves as individuals, so their identities should be effaced. This trait continues strongly in many regions of Europe, where mummers and guisers mask or blacken their faces or wear headgear with so many ribbons or leaves that the face cannot be seen (see fig. 13.5). They also remain silent, or disguise their voices if they must speak a part. As an English woman observing mummers in Cornwall in 1890 put it, "Everyone naturally knows who the actors are, since there are not more than a few hundred persons within several miles; but no one is supposed to know who they are or where they come from, nor must anyone speak to them, nor they to those in the houses they visit."[10] A mummer elsewhere clearly states the reason, maintaining "hit air bad luck to talk with the dumb show folks or guess who they air."[11] The single goal is communal "luck"—abundance—in the coming year.

Clearly, all these features of the surviving agrarian folk rituals already existed in Classical Greece.

The purview of Dionysos included not just grapes and wine, as we tend to think, but *all* vegetation and the creatures that fed on it. As such, Dionysos paralleled the "dying Zeus" of eastern Crete, Great Pan among the remote shepherds of Arcadia, and other male deities who died and revived each year around the Mediterranean in connection with the grain harvest. In fact, the designation *tragedy* for these Dionysian dramas, usually explained as meaning "goat song" (from *trágos* "goat," and *ōïdḗ* "song"), could signify "wheat-harvest song" from a homonymous *trágos* "spelt" (a type of wheat) instead—or as well.[12] Either *trágos* may have received its name from the other, since both wheat and goats have prominent beards, a subject of ancient jesting. And recall the Belarus charade in which "Grandpa" beats to death the "goat," who revives as the singers chant:

> *Where the goat treads,*
> *There the wheat grows. . . .*

It's agrarian analogical magic all the way down.

Tragedy's companion, *comedy*, comes from *kômos*, "drunken revel" (plus "song"), another major part of the proceedings in honor of Dionysos. The Athenians were not alone in performing comedies for such festivals.

FIG. 19.4. Dionysos's *líknon*—winnowing basket that served as his cradle and became Greek equivalent of Roman horn of plenty—filled with fruit plus a phallus. From Roman and Hellenistic reliefs.

The Boiotians, just north of Attica, produced ribald comedies celebrating the Kábeiroi, a mythical race of ithyphallic oldsters who had much the same function as Satyrs.* In fact, the phallus was prominent in Dionysian worship, protruding not only from Kabeiroi, Satyrs, and comic actors in Athens and later Rome but also from a basket or stand carried in procession, much as it still is today in Agia Eleni in Greek Macedonia, when farmers guided by the kalogheros pull a plow three times around the village square to improve fertility at the start of Lent (see fig. 9.7).

The special basket, called a *líknon*, had the shape of a large scoop to aid in winnowing grain, but it doubled as a cradle or harvest basket, hence serving as a prime symbol of Dionysos (fig. 19.4). Presenting examples of "all produce" to an agricultural deity constituted basic agrarian magic for plenty, whether it was a basket (*líknon*) filled with samples of all fruits, a multicupped platter (*kérnos*; see fig. 21.7) bearing different foods in each cup, a porridge of all seeds and grains (panspermia), or a branch hung with all fruits (*eiresíōnē*).[13] Dionysos was called *liknítēs* (he of the basket) as an infant, awakened to his duties by the dancing of the Maenads[14]—and when the modern Thracian "old woman" confronts her phallus-toting kalogheros with a basketed baby she claims is his, *liknítēs* it still is, a demanding creature who grows up rapidly, demands a bride, is killed, mourned, and revived.† The chubby phallus amid the fruit overflowing from Dionysos's

---

* Texts of these plays have not survived, but many representations on pottery have.

† Another parallel: often in Classical rituals two male participants cross-dressed as women,

líknon says it all: fertility for both the animal and the vegetable worlds. The need has never stopped, so why should the tradition?

Dionysos clearly embodies the male principle, but the female is not far to seek—starting with his mother, Semele.

Reclassified as mortal by patriarchal Greeks, apparently via a Theban princess killed by lightning, Semele clearly began as immortal and Thracian. Hints from closely related Phrygian show that her name meant "Earth," as in Mother Earth, cognate with Russian *zemlya* "earth" and Latin *humilis, humus* (borrowed into English for a type of rich soil).[15]* Divine Semele was called up every spring by women, including the Thyiades of Delphi, who danced to awaken Earth and restart the growing (fig. 19.5),[16] just as the Lazarki still do. The infant Dionysos is reborn and needs nurses; but it is Earth who bears *him*, the future bearer of seed.

In addition to channeling as human nurses, the Thyiades invoked the beneficent spirits of the Heroines, who resemble the Heroes in being powerful ancestral dead (whose tombs littered the countryside as shrines), but female: "the collective dead women at their work of fertilization" from their abode down under.[17] Thus the Heroines have the function of willies but without the requirement of virginity.

Semele, Heroines: the story keeps reverting to the earth and crops.

This brings us to the other reason the Athenians didn't quite know what to do with Dionysos: they already had divinities and myths covering agriculture—but these deities were female.

Demeter, one of the three daughters whom Kronos swallowed and disgorged, functioned as Olympian goddess of fruitful plants, especially grain, along with her daughter Persephónē (Persephatta, Proserpina—the form varies), often called simply *Kórē* "Maiden." This agrarian cult focused, like Slavic embroidery, not on Mother and Son but on Maiden and Mother, two stages of womanhood (see figs. 11.1, 11.3). The greatest center of worship lay at Eleusis, some twenty miles north of Athens in the fertile

---

like the two men dressed as "brides" in kalogheros skits. See Harrison 1962, 318–22, for ancient references. (The kernos and panspermia we meet again in chapter 21.)

*Little survives of Thracian itself except proper names; it is clearly Indo-European.

FIG. 19.5. Satyrs opening earth with picks, jumping back as earth goddess (Semele?) arises. Attic red-figure hydria (water vessel), mid-5th century BC.

little Rarian plain. There the Eleusinian Mysteries took place every fall. Although the rites themselves were mysteries revealed only to initiates, we do know the myth.

After Zeus forced Kronos to cough up his five siblings, the three brothers divided the world among themselves. Zeus took kingship of Heaven and those living on Earth's surface; Poseidon ruled the waters, fresh and salty, and the denizens therein; while the eldest brother took the largest kingdom, below ground, which enlarges daily with dead souls. He was therefore called both Hades (from *a-ídēs* "unseen," since underground) and Ploútōn ("wealth," since gold and other wealth come from underground). Zeus married his sister Hera and Poseidon wed a sea nymph, queen of the Nereids, but no goddess wished to live underground. Presently Demeter bore to Zeus a beautiful daughter, Persephone (fig. 19.6), with whom Hades fell in love. Zeus promised the girl to him in marriage, but both knew Demeter would not agree. So one day when Persephone was gathering flowers in a Sicilian meadow, Hades seized her and carried her off to the Underworld.

Frantic, Demeter searched everywhere for her beloved daughter but could find no trace. In her grief, she forgot to tend the plants, and the world began to wither and die. When the Sun, who saw everything, finally told Demeter the truth, she withdrew from the world in anger, ending up in disguise at Eleusis. Famine set in. Finally Zeus compromised—if the girl had

FIG. 19.6. Demeter (with staff and grain), Triptolemos (with plow), and Perse-phone/Kore (with torches). Greek red-figure vase, Eleusis, ca. 500 BC.

not eaten food in her new home, she could return to her mother. But Perse-phone had nibbled a few pomegranate seeds there, so Zeus adjudicated that she would live part of the year below with her spouse and the rest above with her mother. Just so. Her annual descent caused winter, her ascent spring.

Even without the "mystery" details, the arrival of Kore clearly paral-lels the calling-up of Semele. In both, the spring bloom results from female activities, whereas Dionysos presents it as male. But all have Thracian con-nections, since the family that hereditarily conducted the Eleusinian Mys-teries hailed from Thrace. And all had connections with the dead—with the Underworld as the warehouse whence cometh new life: Dionysos died, returned, and died again; people called the dead "Demeter's people";[18] Persephone reigned as the dread Queen of the Dead, gone underground with her fertility still unused, like a willy.

Even if these cults had foreign elements, the notions behind Demeter and Kore existed all over Greece. For example, Pausanias, the second-century AD travel writer, encountered at Lykosoura, in conservative Arcadia, the temple of a goddess referred to as Déspoina "Mistress"—so sacrosanct one couldn't speak her name. Described as the daughter of Demeter and Posei-don, she sat beside Demeter in the huge cult statuary, with Artemis standing near.[19] Like Kore, Despoina ruled agriculture and the dead.

Since people conceived of the cycle of crops as equivalent to death and rebirth, and dancing as bringing life, then dancing at funerals should facilitate the recycling. Indeed, funeral art often depicted dancing. Girls and youths tread stately line dances around the necks of tall jars used as grave markers in the eighth and seventh centuries BC (fig. 19.7). The jar bottom is knocked out so that libations poured into it go directly into the soil, to the souls "down there," while the outside surface shows the deceased laid out on a bier surrounded by mourners and by charioteers who will presumably (judging from the lavish funeral described by Homer) stage races honoring the dead. The dancers, girls and men in equal number, grasp each other by the hand or wrist, often holding upright branches between them (perhaps the magical *eiresione*)—exactly like the thirteenth-century dancers on Bosnian sarcophagi and the twentieth-century dancers of Duboka tugging the souls of their dead relatives to a communal feast in the village square (see figs. 5.6, 17.4, 17.5). When Athenaeus (xiv.629d) describes the dances of Classical Athens as by preference stately and modest, the first two in his list of "simple" ones, *dáktyloi* and *iambiké*, have the names of rhythms still widely used in Balkan dancing: dactylic *long-short-short* (7/8, *kalamatianós*) and iambic *short-long* (5/8, *paidushko*).

These stepping-stones across time demonstrate the strong continuity of the tradition. And the similarities continue. The Athenians also invited their ancestors to dine with them at a spring festival, the Anthestéria, when they served a gruel of all kinds of grains (panspermia) boiled with honey,

FIG. 19.7. Lines of dancers holding branches between them. On neck of funerary urn from Analatos, Attica, ca. 690 BC. Similar urn by same artist shows four women dancing on right and four men on left of lyre player. (Compare figs. 17.4g–h, 17.5.)

a recipe antedating the milling of grain into flour.[20] For protection people chewed garlic and buckthorn; work was taboo. On the third evening, house-holders chased the spirits out, hoping they would take any troublesome ghosts with them and generating a witty way of inviting unwanted human guests to leave: "It's no longer Anthesteria!"[21]

Other goddesses, too, interfaced with the abundance-bringing dead and prob-ably represent yet other substrate cultures. Most persistent was Hekátē, who, like Kore, started out as a goddess causing verdant plant growth. But the cul-turally important plants all sprang from beneath the soil, so, like Kore, Hekate went underground, gradually becoming "queen of the ghosts, and therefore of all sorts of black magic, the blacker the better."[22] Spirits were widely believed to congregate at crossroads and natural clefts: the căluşari treated crossroads thus, and Dostoevsky employed Russian versions of the belief in *Crime and Punishment*. Athenians prayed to Hekate especially at night or at noon, leav-ing meals at crossroads for her and the dead, pouring libations into holes, and setting up triple statues of her so she could view all directions at once.

Hekate's cousin (or sister) Artemis is another such goddess. We think of her as a moon goddess, twin sister to Apollo the Sun, but her lunar connec-tion seems to have derived from her concern with women and their cycles.[23] For Artemis is principally a goddess of burgeoning life (hence death also), roaming the wilds with her attendant nymphs, bow in hand; aiding at the births of humans and animals; and using her arrows to bring sudden pain-less death to women. *Pótnia Thērôn*, people called her: "Mistress of Ani-mals" (fig. 19.8). Her virginal character, like Athena's, was insisted on by the ancients; if any of her devotees slipped up, they could no longer run with her. Modern scholars skeptical of Artemis's virginity will understand it bet-ter in light of the willies: if she does not use her fertility, it maintains its full potency and can be bestowed on others. Little girls dressed as bears danced in Artemis's honor at Brauron in Attica—a rite evidently deemed necessary for proper pubescence, as the saffron color of their dresses indicates. (We learn about saffron yellow as the traditional color for women from Aristo-phanes's comedies—if he wishes to mock a politician as effeminate, he claims the man dresses in yellow, and if a character disguises himself as a woman, he dons yellow robes. The robe Athenian women wove annually for Athena, another virgin goddess, was saffron yellow, too, with purple figures.)[24]

FIG. 19.8. Greek *Pótnia Thērôn* "Mistress of Animals," holding feline and stag. Painted on handle of François Vase by Kleitias, ca. 570 BC. The stunning vase, discovered by Alessandro François in 1844, is in Florence's Museo Archeologico.

Artemis's band of virgin nymphs received worship right along with their mistress; archaeologists find many monuments to them, usually shown in threes. Besides hunting, they spent much time dancing, like willies (fig. 19.9). Sometimes they spun and wove. Homer mentions that on the shore of Ithaca is a lovely cave

> *sacred to the nymphs called Naiads.*
> *Inside are mixing bowls and great jars*
> *of rock; there the bees build honeycombs;*
> *inside too are stone looms, very tall, where nymphs*
> *weave sea-purple cloths, a marvel to see;*
> *and in it is ever-flowing water. (Odyssey xiii.103–9)*

Like willies, nymphs lived around water and liked honey.

Like willies, nymphs played tricks on men, including the naiads who lured handsome young Narcissus to a watery death (recall Marina and Ivan Kurchavïy).

Like willies, some of the female spirits visited madness and destruction on those angering them (particularly for crimes such as murder of kin). In this form they were called *Erinýes* "Furies," or—not to rile them—

FIG. 19.9. Three nymphs dancing in cave, led by Hermes while Pan (perched right) pipes. Hellenistic relief.

Eu-menídes "Good-intentioned Ones," who might be sweet-talked into bestowing their fertility. The term recalls the Bona Dea of southern Italy and the alpine "Good Ladies" who led throngs of spirits in winter as the *benandanti* fought the *malandanti* for the next year's crops.

Like willies, some nymphs also changed shape. Thus, when Zeus fell in love with the Nereid Thetis, daughter of Nereus, the Old Man of the Sea, he learned that her son would be mightier than his father, so he thought better of it and betrothed her to a mortal, Peleus. But first Peleus had to prove himself worthy by catching her. When he clasped her, she changed into one shape after another—a bird, a tree, a tigress, according to Ovid; fire, a lion, a snake, according to others[25]—just like the beloved of the more recent Greek shepherd who piped for the willies' dances (in chapter 1). And, like the shepherd's beloved, ancient Greek nymphs had magical scarves. Homer tells us (*Odyssey* v) that the nymph Ino gave one to Odysseus to keep him afloat during a storm, instructing him to toss it back to her, into the waves, when he reached shore.

FIG. 19.10. *Bereghinya* "Protectress" with raised arms, flanked by birds and animals, embroidered on woman's sleeve. Beneath her is row of geometric "Mothers"—skirted women with arms bent down. Kargopol', North Russia, early 19th century. (Compare figs. 11.1, 11.3.)

Thus, nymphs share most of their traits with willies.

So strong was the cult of Artemis, virgin huntress and Mistress of Animals, that it spread to Rome, being copied in the worship of Diana, and survived to the present in various attenuated forms: as the Irodeasa invoked by the căluşari, as elements of St. Paraskevi and the Virgin Mary, and echoed closely in the Ukrainian and Russian Bereghinya (fig. 19.10, see fig. 11.3).

At the confluence of two streams near where he found Despoina, Pausanias encountered the sanctuary of another Artemis-like goddess called Eurynómē, "Wide-ruling," who from the hips down resembled a fish.[26] On a Boiotian vase of 700 BC (fig. 19.11), we see a divine Mistress of Animals like that: a fish swimming up her apron, a bird on each hand, and lions on either side lapping up the water flowing along her and from her hair.* In stance and attributes, she is virtually indistinguishable from the East Slavic Bereghinya of twenty-six hundred years later; as a water maiden, she is a canonical willy. All this was present in Classical Greek times.

---

*The disembodied bull head and haunch in figure 19.11 are presumably offerings. Pausanias (viii.37.8) mentions that the Arcadians sacrificed to Despoina by lopping off whatever part of a sacrificial animal they happened to grasp. For a winged goddess of 850 BC with birds on her hands, see fig. 20.14.

FIG. 19.11. Female figure wearing extended sleeves, with bird on each hand, fish on skirt, flanked by animals lapping up water (wavy lines) and by dismembered animal parts (offerings?). Boiotian vase, ca. 700 BC. (Compare figs. 11.3, 19.10.)

But another strand of our story already existed too: the ultralong sleeves the Frog Princess used for her magic fertility dance. We traced them back from recent folk costumes to the twelfth-century Kievan bracelets that both depicted the sleeve dance and held up the sleeves. Let us now follow them deeper, first in Greece.

On a ninth-century stele in Athens (fig. 19.12), a woman dances with extended sleeves like those on the

FIG. 19.12. Ninth-century Byzantine stone slab depicting long-haired woman dancing with ultralong sleeves (lower right), accompanied on gusli by Simargl-like hybrid creature.

FIG. 19.13. Attic red-figure vase shaped like knucklebone (astragal). By Sotades, ca. 460 BC. Three sides painted with flying girls (10 in all), some with overfold of dress pulled along arms to resemble wings (right). Fourth side (left) depicts three girls doing line dance out of cave(?), led by male. (Compare fig. 19.9.) (© The Trustees of the British Museum.)

bracelets, while a part-human four-footed creature strums a zither-like gusli, the same instrument that accompanied sleeve dances in Kievan Rus' (see figs. 13.2, 13.8). Because Greeks today think in terms of Classical Greek mythology, they label the hybrid creature a centaur. But in the context of this dance, he is far more likely to be a Simargl (see fig. 17.7), that Iranian-born vegetation deity pictured with the sleeve dancers of Kiev.

Slip back a millennium. At Despoina's temple in Lykosoura, archaeologists found chunks of marble drapery from a second-century BC cult statue of the goddess. Its frieze, unfortunately damaged, depicts dancers wearing animal masks, some with clothes covering their hands.[27]

Now, the usual Classical Greek costume—a rectangle pinned at the shoulders and belted—did not have true sleeves. So how could one lengthen what one doesn't have, to make bird-wing sleeves? A vase of about 460 BC from the island of Aigina, near Athens,* shows one way (fig. 19.13). On three sides of the knucklebone-shaped vessel, girls flutter about, their feet hanging

_____

* It was decorated by the Athenian painter Sotades, though found on Aigina.

FIG. 19.14. Maenads with "wing sleeves" dancing while Satyrs play flutes and lyre. Note woman far left with one sleeve half down. (Bars across lyre player are old repair.) Attic red-figure kylix by Brygos painter, ca. 480 BC.

limp. Several of them have pinned the overfolds of their tunics along the tops of their arms to make pseudosleeves (a trick known from other statues and paintings), then pulled these as far down as possible to make wings. Other girls simply float about. On the fourth side, three women holding hands in a chain follow a man out of a cave(?), but their feet firmly tread the ground. Many a votive sculpture shows Hermes or Pan leading three nymphs in a dance (see fig. 19.9), and caves typically were dedicated to the nymphs—there was even one in Athens. These line dancers could be human—votaries—but those flying are clearly divine—nymphs. The knucklebone shape, presumably chosen to *contain* knucklebones, supports the identification. We saw that girls to this day consult the willies concerning their future marriages and children, and although reflective surfaces like mirrors and water are most common now, the ancient Greeks often performed divinations by throwing knucklebones like dice. (We still say "rolling the bones" for a dice roll.) The use of knucklebones goes far back: one shaped out of solid gold turned up in a grave of 4500 BC at Varna, Bulgaria.[28]

Maenads on quite a few fifth-century BC Athenian vases dance with wing sleeves (fig. 19.14), often watched by Dionysos, a vegetation deity like Simargl. The wings seem fashioned in two ways: some by pinning the tunic into pseudosleeves, as on the Aigina vase, and others by wrapping arms and hands with a sort of poncho worn atop the tunic.*

Whichever, look again now at the Bereghinya-like Mistress of Animals on the 700 BC vase from Boiotia (fig. 19.11), a province where women dressed more like nineteenth-century European peasants than like Classical Athenians. Her hands, too, are covered by long sleeves, which hang well past where her fingers should be.

∝

Not only Greeks knew of the magical ultralong sleeves in the Iron Age. We find them also in the grasslands north of the Black Sea, among the Iranian-speaking Scythians who lived beyond the Thracians. As the Greeks grew prosperous in the seventh and sixth centuries BC, well after the devastating wars that closed the Bronze Age, they began shipping their excess population off to new colonies in southern Italy (where we met them in chapter 18) and along the Black Sea coast. There they encountered nomadic Scythian horsemen who brought quantities of unworked gold to the skilled Greek colonists to make up into handsome ornaments for their costumes and riding gear. (Russian noblemen curried Peter the Great's favor by enlarging the tsar's collection of this goldwork, now in the Hermitage Museum in St. Petersburg, a collection that dazzled museum-goers when sent to the United States in 1975.) One of the richest Scythian burials ever excavated, discovered in 1971 in a kurgan (grave mound) near Ordzhonikidze, Ukraine, included that of a lady—princess, priestess, or both at once—who lay covered in gold (fig. 19.15). She had died in the fourth century BC.

On her head sat a cylindrical gold-covered headdress; three wide gold bracelets encircled her wrists; two hundred fancy gold platelets covered her clothing. Their positions indicate that she wore a sleeved coat or gown and a veil that fell over her shoulders and back. Eleven gold rings crowded her fingers, and evidence suggests her dress was purple.[29] Under one shoulder lay a bronze mirror, near the other a shallow libation dish.

---

* Schöne (1987, 302–3) lists nearly two dozen depictions, mostly red-figure. Lawler (1942) compiled a variety of literary and artistic references to ancient Greek birdlike dances.

FIG. 19.15. Rich burial of Scythian princess found in Ukraine at Ordzhonikidze. Clothes covered with square gold platelets; tall gold diadem or hat; bracelets; bronze mirror at left shoulder; shallow libation dish beyond right shoulder. Accoutrements resemble those of ladies depicted in figure 19.16.

We know ladies of this rank from other Scythian goldwork. Similar gold platelets from a fourth-century BC tomb at Nosaka (Zaporozh'e district, Ukraine) bear the repoussé design of a seated woman holding a mirror and wearing the same type of cylindrical hat and veil as the buried lady. But here (fig. 19.16, left) we can see the complete clothing. Around her shoulders, over the gown, is thrown a coat with *ultralong* sleeves—they hang down much farther than her arm would. Details suggest that this goldwork, like the next find, was prepared by Greek craftsmen in the colonies along the coast.

A gold repoussé covering for the sort of cylindrical headdress these important women wear depicts yet another lady in the same outfit (fig. 19.16, center), her extended coat sleeves dragging on the ground as she holds up a mirror.[30] The mirror and ultralong sleeves in both designs, plus the homage shown her by the surrounding figures, suggest that this personage had a special pipeline to the divine powers, as did the Frog Princess. In fact, the Sakhnovka kurgan, whence came this headdress, lies just southeast of Kiev, capital of Rus' in medieval times when the Frog Princess's tale was set. The other two sites, farther south, also lie close to the Dnepr, the river that became a major Kievan trade route.

As for the three wide bracelets buried on the princess—might she have used them to hold up extended sleeves?

It must be up the river and from the Greek colonies that the *hinged*

FIG. 19.16. 4th-century BC goldwork by Greek craftsmen in colonies along north coast of Black Sea. Left: Design on square gold platelets from rich woman's costume (like that in fig. 19.15), showing seated woman wearing ultralong sleeves and diadem and holding mirror. Kurgan at Nosaka, Zaporozh'e, Ukraine. Center: Central figure from gold diadem (like that in fig. 19.15), wearing ultralong-sleeved coat and tall diadem and holding mirror (for divination). Sakhnovka kurgan, Cherkaska, Ukraine. Right: Gold pendant of woman wearing crescent-shaped tiara, later typical of Russian girls' costume (cf. figs. 3.1, 3.9, 9.8, 12.2). Velikaya Belozerka, Zaporozh'e, Ukraine.

bracelet design eventually came to Kiev, a design that greatly facilitated capturing all that sleeve fabric. Archaeologists have found this structure earliest in Egypt, where many of the thirteen bracelets on the arms of the young pharaoh Tutankhamon (buried about 1350 BC) proved to be both hinged and closed with a pin inserted through tiny tubes. When Alexander the Great conquered Egypt in 332 BC, a mania for Egyptian fashion seems to have hit the Greeks—just as it hit Europeans and Americans when Howard Carter explored Tutankhamon's tomb in 1923—and hinged, sleeve-shaped bracelets spread rapidly east and west.[31] By the late second century BC, two hundred years after the Scythian gold pieces were made, hinged cylindrical gold bracelets were being made in Olbia and other Greek colonies north of the Black Sea, whence they could move easily upriver with other Greek goldwork.*

---

*A fourth-century BC Greek gold pendant found in a Scythian kurgan at Velikaya Belozerka, Ukraine (fig. 19.16 right), represents the head of a Greek woman wearing the

We see, then, that many traits of the recent agrarian rituals go back two and three millennia. Greek and Thracian beliefs and practices, including specific dramatizations, have come through the pipelines of tradition, joined and amplified presently by Roman developments thereof. But the Classical Greeks themselves claimed that their beliefs were ancient.

Maurice Louis points out, on the very first page of his comprehensive history of dance in western Europe, that people generally trace things back to Classical times, then stop, as though the Greeks and Romans

> had to have created everything, upon setting foot on virgin territory. But neither the one nor the other invented anything, for . . . they were only a relay-station in the development of humanity. . . . There existed, before them, on the same territory, other peoples, other humans, who made these [customs] what they were at the moment we learn of them, and which *they* had inherited, just as we have inherited from them. We must then consider the [Greeks and Romans] not as the source of everything, but as links, relatively close to us, in a very long chain and not accord to them an importance greater than to the other links which preceded or followed them in this chain.[32]

Can we follow the chain back still further?

---

distinctive solid tiara that became the hallmark of the Russian girl's costume, known as a *kokoshnik* (see figs. 3.1, 3.9, 9.8, 12.2). Lepage (1971, 8 fig. 13), without traceable references or exact date, gives a sketch of a hinged bracelet "from a tomb in the Cimmerian Bosporus" region. Hinged bracelets continued popular among Byzantine ladies (see any recent work on Byzantine jewelry, e.g., Musche 1988, 75–76) and could have been reintroduced from Byzantium, but local interfacing with the Byzantines began essentially with East Slavic Christianization, whereas the Kievan bracelets, being totally pagan, must have begun earlier.

CHAPTER 20

Back to the Bronze Age

Next [Hephaistos] depicted on [the shield] a dancing-place
Like the one Daidalos once smoothed out
In broad Knossos for fair-tressed Ariadne.
There, bachelors and maidens worthy of many oxen
Danced, holding each other's hands at the wrist.
The girls wore light shifts, and the youths
Fine-spun tunics softly gleaming with olive oil;
The girls wore lovely garlands, the youths carried
Knives—golden ones from silver sword-belts.
Sometimes with their skilled feet they would run around
Effortlessly . . .
Other times they would run at each other in rows.
A great crowd stood about, enjoying the lovely
Dance; and among them a divine singer made music
Playing a lyre; and as the entertainment began,
Two tumblers whirled through their midst.
—Iliad 18.590–606

Homer's great epics sit disquietly on the cusp between the Bronze and Iron Ages. Some of the bard's material clearly belongs to his own era, around 800 BC, whereas other pieces, like descriptions of objects that had not been made or used for centuries, demonstrably came down through oral tradition from the Bronze Age. What of this passage?

Ariadne and her love of dance belong firmly to the "Minoan" Bronze Age (the Cretan civilization archaeologically pegged to roughly 3200–1200

BC). According to legend, Ariadne was the eldest daughter of Minos, king of Crete. Minos had bested the Athenians and condemned them to pay him periodically a tribute of seven each of their finest young men and maidens, to be thrown to the terrible Minotaur—half man, half bull—confined in the Labyrinth. When the Athenian prince Theseus came of age, he insisted on being a member of the "tribute" so he could try to kill the beast and free the Athenians. In Crete, Princess Ariadne fell in love with Theseus and slipped him a sword and ball of string, enabling him to kill the Minotaur and escape with his companions from the Labyrinth.* But though Theseus took her away with him in his ship, he abandoned her on the isle of Naxos. A deserted maiden, Ariadne became a spirit, a canonical willy (nymph, if you prefer), Dionysos's bride, worshipped thereafter as a fertility goddess.

And the dancing? Because—prior to modern film and video—dance evanesced as soon as performed, Homer presumably invented his picture of dancing or described remarkable dances of his own era. But Greek tradition certainly attests to the Cretan love of dancing, from Minoan times to the present. The Classical Greeks, in fact, held Cretan dance skill in such awe that they claimed the Cretans *invented* dance.

Archaeological finds confirm the antiquity of the Cretan obsession and show such continuity of tradition that perhaps Homer's description applied with some accuracy to both eras.

To begin with, Minoan women did dance, on broad floors like Ariadne's, while lively crowds of men and other women watched. Archaeologists have recovered, from Bronze Age levels, both painted depictions of dancers (fig. 20.1) and broad terraces with special walkways, like those in the frescoes, beside the palaces of Knossos, Phaistos, and Arkhanes (fig. 20.2). Convenient bleachers flank them for the spectators.

Labyrinth appears to have meant originally "the *labrys* place" in Minoan, where *labrys* denoted the sort of double-ended axe, made of bronze or even pure gold (hence useless as a tool), found everywhere in Minoan shrines. This central religious symbol must have given its name to the chief Minoan palace, at Knossos: "House of the Double Axe," or Labyrinth. In Theseus's time, Athenian and other Greek kings lived in palaces with two rooms and a porch, plus some side chambers for storage, whereas Knossos had grown to hundreds of interconnecting multipurpose rooms, stacked three and four stories high. To Theseus it would have seemed . . . well, a labyrinth. It was probably not deliberately designed to be confusing. Minoan frescoes and other artifacts, from before 2000 BC onward, frequently show acrobats bull-jumping. We now guess that the young Athenians were to be trained for this deadly entertainment.

FIG. 20.1. Minoan frescoes of dancers. Palace at Knossos, Crete, ca. 1600 BC. Top: Women surrounded by lively crowd, dancing(?) leftward in courtyard with special walkways (cf. fig. 20.2). Bottom: Young woman in red and blue jacket, whirling.

FIG. 20.2. Minoan palace "theatral areas"—courts with raised walkways and bleacherlike arrangements of steps. Top: Knossos; bottom: Phaistos. Early 2nd millennium BC.

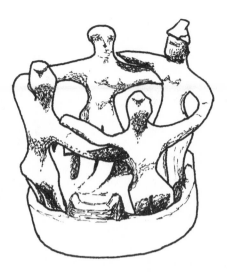

FIG. 20.3. Clay sculpture of Minoan men dancing in circle with shoulder-hold; small "horns of consecration" between them. Kamilari, Crete, ca. 1700 BC.

At Palaikastro, in eastern Crete, diggers unearthed a clay model of three women dancing in a semicircle around a fourth who plays a lyre (see fig. 12.1). The dancers extend their arms in the proud position still seen especially among Macedonian women line-dancing today (see fig. 3.8).* An even earlier clay model from the charnel house at Kamilari shows four men dancing in a closed circle, their hands on their neighbors' shoulders exactly as men still place them throughout the Balkans (fig. 20.3). Coming to life, they could instantly break into a Greek *fast hasápiko*—or Ukrainian *arkan*, or Israeli *hora*; the dances are nearly identical and clearly have a deep European history (see chapter 23). Tradition can preserve dance even where film and video didn't, and these figurines froze interesting information that helps us extend the timetable.

Homer apparently knew Cretan dance habits with some accuracy, for we also find Bronze Age Minoan representations of elegant and skilled tumblers

---

*Lillian Lawler, who wrote extensively on ancient dance but apparently wasn't steeped in Balkan folklore, sees these raised arms as "winglike" (Lawler 1942, 357), but I see them only as a not unusual position for the common *lesnoto* type of line dance (see fig. 3.8). For wings, see below. For the Minoan lyre and much about Bronze Age Aegean music, see Younger 1998. (Younger also makes an interesting case for the famous Minoan Harvester Vase representing a sort of processional dance.)

FIG. 20.4. Minoan tumblers ca. 1700 BC. Left: From sealstone found near Knossos. Right: From gold-covered handle of sword, Mallia (Malia).

(fig. 20.4). We might not call tumbling "dance" (although *Cirque du Soleil* is enlarging our notions), but acrobatic tumbling is another activity not directly related to "useful" work—hence, like tickling and swinging, of the sort associated with the Dancing Goddesses. There is even a Minoan clay model of a girl, pierced to allow her to swing from the uprights found with her (fig. 20.5), like the modern Balkan girls swinging from trees in the spring for taller crops (see fig. 3.6). Atop these pillars perch a pair of doves, associated repeatedly with the chief Minoan goddess and later with the Greek Aphrodite, protectress of love and procreation.

Other Minoan images of dancing exist. From the first palace at Phaistos comes a bowl showing two

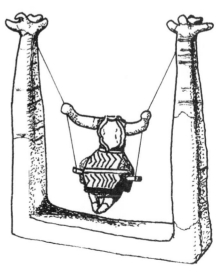

FIG. 20.5. Minoan clay model of woman swinging from pillars topped by doves. Agia Triada, Crete, ca. 1300 BC.

FIG. 20.6. Bowl and "fruitstand" painted all over with women and/or goddesses dancing. Palace at Phaistos, ca. 1700 BC. ("Plate" at lower right reconstructs inside of bowl at lower left; line drawing shows figures inside fruitstand.)

curly-haired females, one arm up and one down, dancing about a triangular figure with a similar head but no arms or legs (fig. 20.6, right). (Her limblessness reminds one of the swaddled mummylike figure that forms a focus of attention on a later painted sarcophagus from nearby Agia Triada.) Similar curly-headed females dance in the center and around the base of a pedestaled "fruitstand" also from Phaistos (fig. 20.6 left), while more figures, bent low, progress clockwise around the rim. But the central figure on the main platter, triangular below and curly-headed above, has arms, and a lily in each hand. Her flowers recall the story of Persephone (Kore), abducted by the lord of the Underworld as she gathered flowers with her girlfriends.[1] The artistic comparisons suggest dances in honor of the dead, while the connection with Persephone adds the expectation of renewed life, which suggests also the Thyiades dancing each spring to awaken dead Semele, mother of Dionysos. In fact, dance floors have been identified not only in the palaces but also beside the great stone charnel houses used for burial in the area around Phaistos at the time of its earliest palace. They are strewn with fragments of small conical cups, apparently used and smashed during funerary or commemorative rites.

❦

Cretan myths lead us to yet more dance and more willies. Legends say that Theseus and his thirteen companions celebrated their escape from the Minotaur and the Labyrinth with a victory dance called the *gerános*, which modern Greeks say they inherited as the *tsakónikos*. The earliest labeled representation we have (570 BC) shows a long line of alternating youths and maidens holding hands and moving to their left (fig. 20.7). Because Greek has a word *gerános* meaning "crane," scholars have long thought of it as the "Crane Dance" and have puzzled over what cranes had to do with it. Lillian Lawler, however, pointed out that the name more plausibly came from another similar-sounding Indo-European root meaning "twist, wind"— that is, the "Winding Dance."[2] Indeed, living tradition insists that the long, winding line of the five-beat tsakonikos mimics the Labyrinth; it contains no crane-like capers. Inscriptions from Apollo's sanctuary on Delos, where the dance was performed regularly, mention supplying the geranos dancers with branches—perhaps carried between participants, as in funerary dances (see figs. 19.7, 17.4, 17.5).

FIG. 20.7. Some of Theseus's companions dancing the *gerános* after the death of the Minotaur. Note handhold, still used throughout the Balkans: dancer actively grasps person in front and is grasped by person behind. François Vase, ca. 570 BC (cf. fig. 19.8).

Theseus's abandoned bride Ariadne is also not the only willylike damsel in Minoan-related myths. Minos, they said, once pursued a maiden named Britómartis, who finally jumped off a cliff into the sea to avoid him. Some fishermen caught her in their nets—whether dead or alive is unclear—and took her across the straits to the isle of Aigina, where she vanished into a grove sacred to Artemis. Like Artemis, she came to be worshipped there as a protectress of females giving birth and nurturing their young. Her purview also included fertility of the seas. The ancient author Solinus tells us *Britómartis* meant "sweet maid" in Cretan, and he adds that it served as a Cretan epithet for Artemis—or probably for a goddess the Greeks viewed as *equivalent* to Artemis. Artemis and Britomartis had similar powers, were both called daughters of Zeus, and shared the title *Díktynna.*[3]

Because of Britomartis's association with nets, *Díktynna* is widely assumed to come from *díktyon* "net," but it may also/instead have to do with a location long associated with female spirits, Mt. Dikte (one of the great limestone vertebrae forming the spine of Crete, or a lesser hill of the same name in eastern Crete). We have already encountered Dikte in the several herbs called *dittany* (from *díktamnon* "of Dikte"), sacred to the willies and their healing arts (see figs. 6.4, 6.5). A temple dedicated to Diktynna still existed in Classical times on the northwest tip of Crete, the nearest jumping-off place (as it were) for a trip to Aigina.[4]

No coincidence, then, that Aigina, second home of Britomartis-Diktynna, is the isle where the Greek knucklebone vase with willylike flying girls was found (see fig. 19.13).

⚭

Not only had the Minoans clearly shipped a spirit maiden to Aigina, they also knew about ultralong sleeves and the wing dance.

A large group of Cretan seals, many datable to around 1625 BC, depict women with typical Minoan flounced skirts and bare bosoms but with the head, beak, and wings of a bird (fig. 20.8). Yet the long "wings" angle out not like a bird's but like human arms sleeved to *look like* wings—as in the costumes of Slavic girls channeling at the Rusalii. What's more, some of the variations in the engravings of bird women make it abundantly clear that procreation is the focus. Scholars have argued whether these creatures represented "real" deities or artistic flights of fancy. But to one familiar with eastern European folklore *and* archaeology, the simplest hypothesis is that these

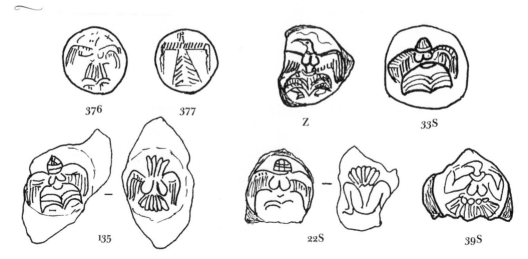

FIG. 20.8. Minoan seals, ca. 1625 BC, depicting women with bird heads and/or wings or wing sleeves. *376, 377*: Steatite seals in Ashmolean Museum, Oxford, provenance unknown. *Z*: Clay sealing from Zakro. *33S, 13S, 22S, 39S*: Sealings from Knossos harbor town. Choice of motifs on second side (*13S, 22S*) confirms theme of female sexuality/fertility.

refer to real women dressed as bird girls and to the selfsame bird-inhabiting spirit maidens who bring moisture and fertility and whose history we have already traced from modern times back to the threshold of the Bronze Age.

Minoan women apparently knew the willies and their sleeve dance, but to perform it they may have donned bird masks as well.*

⚭

Bird-headed figures of women occur elsewhere in the Balkans during the Bronze Age. The Mycenaean Greeks, who colonized the Greek mainland

---

*True sleeves, in 1625 BC, had only just been invented. So women must have drafted them very quickly for this important ritual. Long-sleeved garments did exist in Mycenaean Greece, as we see from the thin gold foil encircling the wrists of Shaft Grave occupants (Barber 1975, 317) and from the sleeved coat of the woman waving good-bye to infantry-men on the Warrior Vase, ca. 1200 BC. Urban Greco-Roman clothing was radically dif-ferent from Minoan and other European dress, being draped rather than sewn, yet certain traditional costume traits continued in Classical times in the periphery. There, in addition to sleeves, we glimpse both string skirts (see fig. 17.2; Barber 1999b) and women's use of saffron yellow (cf. chapters 15, 19; Barber 1992, 316–17). Saffron as a women's herb and color had a strong tradition in Bronze Age Crete and the Cycladic Islands.

FIG. 20.9. Typical Mycenaean clay "idols" found frequently at Late Bronze Age Greek sites. Left to right: Ψ-shaped, with raised arms; Φ-shaped, with lowered arms; Φ-shaped, unusual but not unique in holding baby. (Compare "Maiden" and "Mother" motifs in Russian embroidery, figs. 11.1, 11.3, 19.10.)

during the second millennium BC, produced a long series of little schematic clay figurines of females with pinched-out birdlike faces (fig. 20.9). The two main types resemble in shape two letters of the later Greek alphabet, Ψ (psi) with arms raised, and Φ (phi) with arms curved down as though resting below the breasts. These correspond closely in shape to the traditional Russian embroidery figures known as "Maiden" and "Mother," respectively (see figs. 11.1, 11.3).[5] Occasionally a Φ-idol is shown pregnant or holding a baby.

At least one bird-faced Ψ-figure rides a horse sidesaddle (fig. 20.10, left).[6]* Curiously, from a Mycenaean tomb at Dendra comes a blue-glazed plaque showing another "goddess with upraised arms" riding sidesaddle, but this one has a human face, wears a Minoan flounced skirt and cylindrical hat, and rides a bull (fig. 20.10, right).[7]

---

*Late Minoan clay statues with raised arms occur so frequently that the figure has been nicknamed "GUA" (Goddess with Upraised Arms). But these don't have bird faces and they are often much bigger than the Mycenaean figurines. Some stand inside little clay shrines; occasionally one wears a crown of opium-poppy pods (see fig. 6.2)—evidence of her spirit-world status.

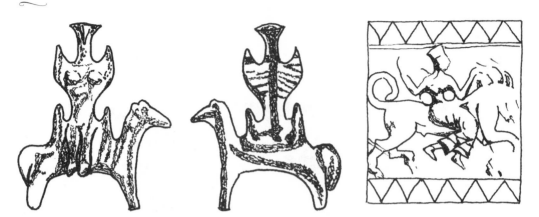

FIG. 20.10. Goddesses with raised arms riding animals. Left: On horseback. Mycenaean clay figurine. Kharvati, Attica, ca. 1200 BC. Note long braid painted down her back. Right: On back of bull. Minoan faience plaque (with attachment holes). Dendra, ca. 1650 BC.

One of the most charming of the bird-faced figurines comes from Dupljaja in the Serbian Banat (fig. 20.11). She rides a three-wheeled cart drawn by ducks (and perhaps once shaded by a decorated parasol), set up so one could roll the whole ensemble like a modern child's pull-toy. Her skirt silhouette and the series of roundels pendant from her girdle resemble those of a large, almost ferocious Φ-statue found nearby at Kličevac (fig. 20.12). Both wear their hair down the back in a peculiar style found on many other central Balkan figurines of this era, and still worn by brides a century ago

FIG. 20.11. Clay figurine of bird-faced goddess on cart drawn by ducks. Late Bronze Age, mid-2nd millennium BC, Dupljaja, Serbia.

FIG. 20.12. Two views of Bronze Age statue of female wearing full-sleeved chemise, sash, deeply fringed apron, and square-patterned overskirt—similar to Ukrainian and South Great Russian traditional dress. Mid-2nd millennium BC, Kličevac, Serbia. Back hairdo resembles style traditional for brides in parts of eastern Europe (see fig. 20.13).

from Attica through Macedonia and Albania (fig. 20.13) to several Ugric (non–Indo-European) peoples near the Urals.

The Dupljaja wagon recalls ancient Germanic and Greek festivals in which celebrants wheeled through the countryside a statue or impersonator of a goddess in charge of fertility, such as Nerthus or Athena.[8] A ninth-century BC urn from Knossos even shows such a goddess on wheels (fig. 20.14). On one face of the urn, two birds perch on her upraised arms, while her wings are lowered and the trees beside her effloresce with curlicues. On the opposite face, her hands are lowered and her wing(s) raised, while birds hang from her hands and perch atop trees whose skimpy foliage hangs downward. Thus, the images seem to portray her in opposing seasons, reminding one of the story of Demeter and Kore.[9]

Reading between the figurines, then, we see repeated references to the fertility of crops and females, plus a tight liaison of all this to birds. These females might not be quite the willies we have come to know, but they are close cousins. The propensity of some of them to ride on horses, bulls, or vehicles, however, needs investigation.

FIG. 20.13. Center: 19th-century traditional Attic bridal attire. Compare hairdo (braids and ornaments) to figure 20.12 and to backs of small Bronze Age figurines shown here. Right: Bird girl from Dupljaja, Serbia (fig. 20.11). Left: Female from cemetery at Cîrna, Romania (mid-2nd millennium BC).

FIG. 20.14. Goddess on wheeled platform, depicted in two phases or seasons; 9th-century BC urn. Teke cemetery, Knossos, Crete.

It was only in the Middle Bronze Age, around 1800 BC, that domestic horses and their handlers entered western Europe and the Mediterranean lands, flooding out from the grassy steppes in the northeast. Before that, people in the Balkan Peninsula had relied chiefly on farming various cereals and legumes, together with such fruits as became domesticated. They also kept some sheep and cattle, originally for meat. From about 3500 BC on, the former also provided wool for clothing, the latter traction power for plowing and transport, while both supplied dairy foods.[10]

But if you have ever struggled to keep crabgrass out of your garden, you will understand the difficulties of clearing enough soil for farming in the Eurasian grasslands without a plow. Far easier to let sheep and cows eat the grass and then to consume the animals—even if the difficulties of managing flocks on foot ensure that the numbers stay small. Eventually, however, when people had not only domesticated wild horses but also learned to harness or bridle them, they could run rings around the slower ruminants and manage vast herds.* More food wealth meant more people, and at intervals, as populations increased, the nomadic herders fanned out east and west across Eurasia. Looking for new pastures, they came in wave after destructive wave (the most recent of which included the infamous Huns and Mongols in the fifth and thirteenth centuries AD).

Archaeological evidence shows that preliminary expansions occurred in the western steppes between 3500 and 2200 BC, overrunning ancient farming communities in Ukraine and Romania (see chapter 21). Various types of evidence indicate that these horsemen were early speakers of the important Indo-European language group (see table 6), and that around 3000 BC some of them entered Anatolia (the geographical term for the Asian part of modern Turkey) via its northwest corner. Thence they filtered south into the interior after founding Troy—that fabled city too fond of horses to reject a treacherous wooden one as the Bronze Age ended.

The next inundation of horsemen, a veritable tsunami, swept into Greece and all the way to the Atlantic around 1800 BC.[11] It carried along not just horses but new rituals and belief systems that puddle here and there, mixing

---

*Recent evidence proves that horses had been domesticated on the steppes during the Neolithic. The old, disputed evidence for bit-wear on the teeth has now been joined by chemical analyses showing that mid-4th-millennium vessels contained mare's milk (Outram et al. 2009). You can't milk a wild mare.

with the indigenous beliefs and customs. This wave included elite drivers of horse chariots, who used their mobility to outmaneuver and overwhelm the local farmers, becoming the ruling class and eventually the rank and file too. Those who took over Greece came to be known as the Mycenaean Greeks, since they built their chief fortress at Mycenae and left inscriptions proving they spoke Greek. Those who conquered Anatolia used remarkably similar architectural principles to build a far bigger Cyclopean-walled capital, Hattušaš (modern Boğazköy), where inscriptions prove they spoke a related language we call Hittite (see table 6).*

༄

It's at this point, with the advent of the horsemen in the Middle Bronze Age, that we can begin to disentangle two main threads that we've been tracing, all balled together, backward from modern times.

We noticed the Mycenaean Ψ-idol from Attica who rides a horse, whereas another young woman with upraised arms, earlier and in the Cretan style, rides a bull (see fig. 20.10). The difference persists in the mythology: Persephone/Kore was abducted from her flowery meadow by Hades driving a

---

*These, along with Hittite's close relative, Luwian, are the earliest recorded languages of the Indo-European or Indo-Hittite family. Writing itself had been invented only about 1,500 years earlier, and these were the first speakers of this language family to move south into the literate area. Early Hittite inscriptions also record some words from the Indic branch—names of deities and terms concerning horses—since apparently they hired their Indic cousins as special experts in horse training.

One enormous pink clay tablet, now at Yale, records in Hittite the ritual of Anniwiyaniš, a female soothsayer, for getting rid of a particular demon (Bawanypeck 2005, 54–57). After some preliminaries involving blue and red yarn, the participants must build a temporary gate, set to each side of it half of every sacrificial item they were told to bring (including bread, liquor, a puppy), run through the gate while shouting, quickly tear down the gate while scooping up all the stuff, and run away down the road, which they then block somehow. (The magic is this: By scaring off the demons while the people pass through a gate that then ceases to exist, they make it impossible for the demons to follow them, thereby losing the demons; noise keeps the demons at bay at the critical moment.) The many parallels here to rites still done, noise and all, during the Twelve Days to prevent demons from following people into the New Year, or to chase demons from the spring crops, demonstrate once again that the roots of these beliefs go back *at least* to the Bronze Age. The special place of metal—bells, jewelry—in the present-day noise-making points again to the Bronze Age as a time when this custom crystallized (but didn't necessarily begin)—a time when the ringing tones of metal, then a new phenomenon, seemed magical.

horse chariot, whereas Europa was abducted on the back of a white bull—Zeus in disguise—to Crete, where she gave name to a continent and birth to Minos and his brothers. The Greeks vilified Minos's queen, Pasipháē, for allegedly having intercourse with a bull, yet their Indic cousins required each queen to fake intercourse with a dying stallion to ensure fertility in the community. (Among another Indo-European group, the Celts, it was the king who had to have intercourse with a horse—a white mare.)[12]

It seems the incoming horse people and the indigenous crop-growers (at least on Crete) had similar "abundance" rituals; it's just that they viewed different large animals as key to the magic. Archaeology shows that the veneration of bulls has an antique history in the lands just north of the Mediterranean, starting around 6000 BC at Neolithic Çatal Höyük in central Anatolia and persisting to this day from Spain to Provence in traditional bullfights and bull-running.

The notion of the horse as special, with a direct pipeline to the spirit world, plays out in two ways in particular: horses could ensure prosperity directly or could divine for mortals what the gods had in store. In the *Iliad*, Achilles's immortal horses, sired by the West Wind, foretell their master's death and weep when his friend Patroklos dies, their manes dragging in the dust.[13] A millennium or more later, Tacitus and Saxo Grammaticus describe northern priests saddling a horse, such as a white stallion, for an invisible rider, leading it past certain obstacles, and extracting divinations from which foot the horse used first.[14]* Neighing also held significance, a belief recorded by Tacitus as well as found in Germany during the last two centuries.[15] One century ago, young Russians still used horses variously to learn details of their future mates.[16] And so on.

The Balkan agrarian tradition, however, looked to the willies—goddesses who danced through the fields and forests—for these same two services. The functional parallels are remarkable.

To access the spirit world through the Dancing Goddesses, one danced; through horses, one rode—in spirit if not in person. Thus, shamans learned

---

*White horses (and gray ones—true white is apparently rather rare) held a special place among Indo-Europeans: Celtic Rhiannon and Epona rode white horses, as did the Slavic gods Svarozhich and Svantovit, while Odin's horse Sleipnir was gray. The oracular horse on the Baltic isle of Rügen was white (Puhvel 1987, 270), as were the Albanian horses used to predict which graves held vampires (P. Barber 2010, 68).

to ride spirit horses to do spirit battle for their clients or to retrieve information from the Other World. Furthermore, in the horse culture one honored the spirit of the deceased by giving him (or her) horses for the next world: graves of the wealthy contain horse skeletons by the dozens, often richly bridled and saddled, surrounding their human.

Like spirit maidens, too, horse spirits could be either beneficent or terrifying.

As the horse people settled and intermarried with the farmers, the two systems clearly mixed. Perhaps people felt they divined different information from the two sources. But in any case one wouldn't want to "diss" a possibly potent spirit by neglecting it, would one? Best to pay court to both traditions.*

One type of horse sacrifice not only survives here and there today among Central Asian nomadic herders but also is archaeologically traceable for seven thousand years. The horse was ritually slain, then slit open to remove the meat and bones for a feast. What remained was a single piece consisting of the head (with skull), hide, and lower end of each leg (with tibia and hoof). This object was then hung over a slanting pole stuck in the ground or on the roof (fig. 20.15), so the horse shape could be seen for a great distance. Both the horse and the pole which represents a divine tree, even a "world tree" (like the Norse Yggdrasil, "Odin's steed"), were perceived as sacred spirit channels, and they persisted, for example, in the protective horseheads carved at the ends of the rooftrees of Russian peasant huts (cf. fig. 15.3).† Sometimes the head, pelt, and attached legs were folded together and deposited in or on a grave, where archaeologists find their remains—thousands of them over the millennia. Known as "head-and-hooves" sacrifices, they occur, after 1800 BC, across Eurasia all the way to Britain.[17]

At Alaca Höyük in central Anatolia, however, excavators of a series of royal tombs from about 2600 BC found a remarkable variant. On the low plank roofs of these gold- and silver-filled graves, they unearthed numerous examples of the head-and-hooves sacrifices of *cattle*, not horses.[18] Horses

---

*This follows a well-attested principle of mythbuilding called "Hedging Your Bets": see Barber and Barber 2005, 62–63.

†Animal heads on gables precede horses, however—e.g., on an Early Neolithic house model from Hungary (Körös culture; Whittle 1985, 51).

FIG. 20.15. Eurasian horse sacrifices. Top: Sacrificial scene on Altaic shaman's drum; Altaic stuffed pelt with head and hooves. Bottom: reconstruction of Old Turkic ritual site, with horse pelt on pole, stone figure, and "world tree" (visitor's horse tethered nearby); reconstruction of 7th-century horse sacrifice over sacred bog, Lejre, near Roskilde, Denmark.

hadn't arrived yet. So, just as in Crete, where horses didn't appear until perhaps 1500 BC, we find a ritual treatment of cattle paralleling that of horses—as though the equine rites were merely the horse breeders' version of a much older, pre-horse performance. Humans had domesticated cattle millennia before horses.

Europeans no longer sacrifice horses, but the excoriated horse figure continues to raise its head among us. In Wales during the Twelve Days of Christmas, a terrific pounding at night on the windows and doors announces a visit of the *Mari Lwyd*, the "Grey Mare," that terrifying appa-

FIG. 20.16. Early Greek representation of centaur as horse's rear half attached to full human body. Proto-Corinthian vase, ca. 680 BC.

rition fashioned from a horse skull (see fig. 9.2). If it gains entry, it chases women and girls in particular. Similar goblins run rampant from England to the Alps and Carpathians.[19]

One is reminded of the noisy, beastly *kallikántzaroi* who traditionally terrorize Greek neighborhoods during the Twelve Days. Indeed, scholars have proposed that the second half of the word, *-kanzaroi*, comes from *kéntauroi* "centaurs"—those rowdy woman-chasers from ancient Greek myth described as half horse, half human.[20] Classical monuments depict centaurs with a human head and torso stuck on a horse's body, but the earliest images (fig. 20.16) show them as a full human with a horse's rear attached—something a person dressing to *represent* a horse demon can manage more easily (see also fig. 13.9, creature second from right).*

Now recall the innumerable "hobbyhorses" accompanying groups of

* In light of this part-human shape and of the horse/bull parallels just mentioned, one wonders if the Minotaur, too, who is always shown with human legs and torso but a bull's head and shoulders, was a mythic conflation of a real bull (as used in bull-jumping) and a person *masked* as the sacred Cretan bull, possibly even for fertility-related New Year events. Recall the Minoan women evidently wearing bird masks, and the variety of animal masks on dancers depicted on the Lykosoura drapery (chapter 19; Jost 1985, pl.45). An animal-masked man also appears on a Minoan seal from Zakro (Gimbutas 1991, fig. 127).

Kalli- is explained as the euphemistic element "good" seen in *kaló-gheros*, etc. Linguists have discarded, however, a proposed etymological equation of *kéntauros* with Indic, Avestan, and Latin words for various demonic apparitions (E. Polomé in Mallory and Adams 1997, 103).

FIG. 20.17. Some western European hobbyhorses. Top: On Corinthian vase, 4th century BC; stick type, from *Biblia Latina*, Venice, 1519. Bottom: Basque *zamalzain*, with "tourney"-type horse body, dancing on wineglass that dancer cannot see, 1930s; British "Padstow Hoss" who traps girls with his body (hoop frame is much wider today), from lost engraving, ca. 1835.

One also wonders—given the frequency with which steppeland horse cadavers were dressed up with felt antlers to look like stags and reindeer—whether some of this fertility magic goes back to the Upper Palaeolithic. It's a short step to the shamanic man fully dressed in an animal pelt with his genitals hanging out prominently behind, found painted in a cave at Trois Frères (Ariège, France) from around 14,000 BC. The presence of antlers has been disputed, but an equally human-legged man prances nearby with a large bull's head covering his own.

male ritual dancers throughout Europe, from the Romanian călușari (see fig. 5.4) to the English Morris dancers. They include the spectacularly agile Basque *zamalzain*, leaping high from the wineglass on which he dances,[21] and the ugly black "Hoss" who yearly traps and blackens girls "for luck" in Padstow, Cornwall (fig. 20.17). ("Luck" of course means fruitfulness, so his attentions are welcomed by brides and avoided by single girls!)[22] The horse revered for channeling abundance, fertility, protection, and information persists in many a masquerade figure in traditional European festivals today.

And just as elsewhere we have seen the ancient fertility rituals, under siege by Christianity, get handed over to the children, so the sacred horse, as a hobbyhorse, trickled down to become the favorite toy of Victorian children—a stick topped with a wooden horsehead, ridden in fantasyland.

CHAPTER 21

Dancing at the Dawn of Agriculture

Привычка свыше нам дана:
замена счастию она.

Habit was given us from on high
In place of happiness.

—Pushkin, *Eugene Onegin*[1]

A seed, properly sown and cared for, will yield a plant that
produces more seeds that can also be sown . . .
so that the cycle is unbroken.[2]

We have tracked many details of the European agrarian rituals,
both calendrical and marital, backward in time. Some features
seem to have evolved in the Middle Ages, through reshaping
of Roman and Etruscan elaborations on earlier Greek practices; and some
of these, we found, already existed in the two cultural streams, pastoralism
and farming, that intermingled in Europe in the Bronze Age. Like other
rituals concerning the dead, those involving the Dancing Goddesses dealt
principally with placation, divination, protection, and fertility.

Concerning fertility, both the restless horse-tamers and the plodding
farmers recognized insemination, gestation, and birth. But the evidence we
have amassed shows that the agrarian culture focused on the female aspects,
reified by dancing spirit maidens, whereas the herding culture focused on

MAP 21: **Spread of Neolithic Farming from Near East into Europe**

the male input, reified by horses and poles. If, now, we peel away the layer of the Indo-European horse breeders to explore the Neolithic and Copper Ages, we should see the ancient agrarian strand in isolation. What traces if any, of Dancing Goddesses?

Yosef Garfinkel, an Israeli specialist in early Near Eastern pottery, kept noticing that whenever he encountered a Neolithic pot or potsherd showing human figures, they always seemed to be dancing. Intrigued, puzzled as to whether that was really so and why it should be, he began to keep records of every Neolithic human representation he could locate in Europe and the Near East, organizing them all into a book called *Dancing at the Dawn of Agriculture* (2003). Potsherds are not for everyone, but the riches of data and of evidence-based analysis in the book make it exceptional.

Garfinkel found that these representations began rather abruptly in the very early agricultural villages of the Near East, in the seventh millennium (fig. 21.1). Sometimes people dance separately. We also discern long lines of dancers holding hands in various ways: identical silhouettes one after another as though seen at night against a bonfire.[3] When I first leafed through his pictures, I wasn't convinced that the former represented dancing, but in the end the weight of his evidence and comparisons (see below) largely won me over. Depictions of dancers continued in the Near East until the rise of city-states and literacy in the Copper Age, when scenes of feasting supplanted them.[4] Why? What common function did dancing and feasting serve for these different clienteles?

As hunter/gatherers settled into agricultural communities, they forfeited a way of life in which if you didn't like your neighbor you could simply move on. As farmers, however, you actively needed your neighbors, and they were permanent. You needed to pool resources for the more demanding aspects of crop-raising; you had to get along. So people now had to find ways to promote community bonding, and one means they hit upon, Garfinkel suggests, was dance.[5]* Dance was certainly not new, but now it held new significance. Eventually, however, dance was shoved to the side in the Bronze Age, when the pressures of life in the first cities caused other means of peacekeep-

---

*Chapter 22 explores the physiological basis of muscular bonding.

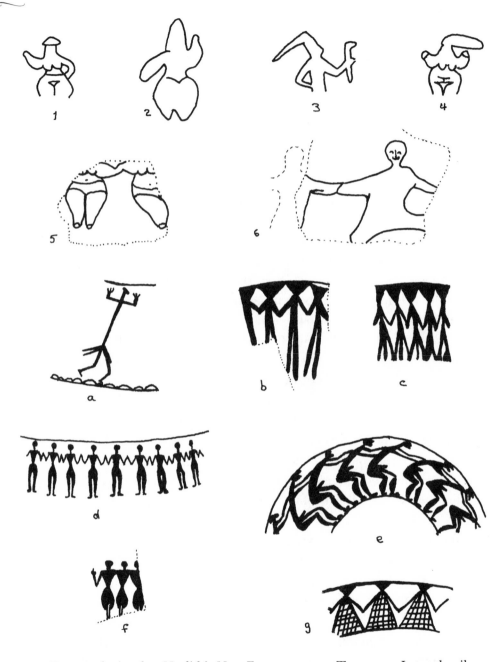

FIG. 21.1. Dancers depicted on Neolithic Near Eastern pottery. Top group: Late 7th millennium, Turkey (1–5, Köşk Höyük; 6, Tepecik). Middle group: 6th millennium—solo and V-hold, northern Iraq (a, Tepe Gawra; b–c, Tell Halaf). Bottom group: 6th to 5th millennia—(d) W-hold (Kazineh, Iran), (e) men's line, crouched (Tall-I Jari, Iran), (f) shoulder-hold (Tepe Sialk, Iran), (g) women's line, V-hold (Tell Halaf, Iraq).

ing to come into existence—things like written laws and social strata topped by elite authority. It then became a king who orchestrated solidarity, providing feasts for his retainers, complete with alcoholic drink, raiment, and lavish entertainment of music and dance.[6]* But these entertainers appear as individual trained professionals, not long lines of equals.

In southeastern Europe, the first area to which Near Eastern agriculture spread, Garfinkel also found depictions of dancers in the Neolithic (fig. 21.2), though sparser and continuing through the Bronze Age (fig. 21.3, see figs. 12.1, 20.1, 20.3, 20.6, 20.8). Why these differences?

First, preclassical Europe never developed the networks of teeming cities that Mesopotamia had. Second-millennium centers such as Mycenae, Athens, and Knossos never held the great populations that Uruk and Ur already contained in 2800 BC.† Writing, too, began later in Europe than in the Near East and remained much more restricted throughout the Bronze Age. What originally made writing necessary was more people trying to live together than could do so with personal contact—a problem with living in cities. If you don't know the people you're doing business with, you'd better get things in writing. (Even if you do know everyone, as property accumulates word of honor may not suffice—and apparently it didn't, for writing first grew out of an increasingly complex rural system of recording *numbers* of things, like sheep taken to pasture by the shepherd. Its beginnings are already discernible in Iraq in 7000 BC.)[7] Europe, however, long remained essentially nonurban and nonliterate.

Second, if Neolithic dance rituals grew out of the difficulties of setting up and maintaining viable farming communities, as Garfinkel and his data suggest, then we need to look more closely at the earliest agrarian villages of southeastern Europe. We can start with the well-established fact that farming entered Europe around 6500 BC with settlers who came across the Aegean Sea from Anatolia and colonized the Greek plain of Thessaly. From there they spread slowly northward into Macedonia and up the Vardar/ Morava River corridor toward the Danube (see Map 21).

---

* Garfinkel (2003, 84) wryly notes that today heads of state are feasted when visiting developed countries but entertained with local folkdances in developing countries. Similarly, the chief use the Chinese find for their "ethnic minorities" is to entertain dignitaries and tourists with colorful costumed folkdances.

† Uruk is calculated to have had some 80,000 inhabitants by 2800 BC (Modelski 1997), a size that Athens began to attain only 2,300 years later.

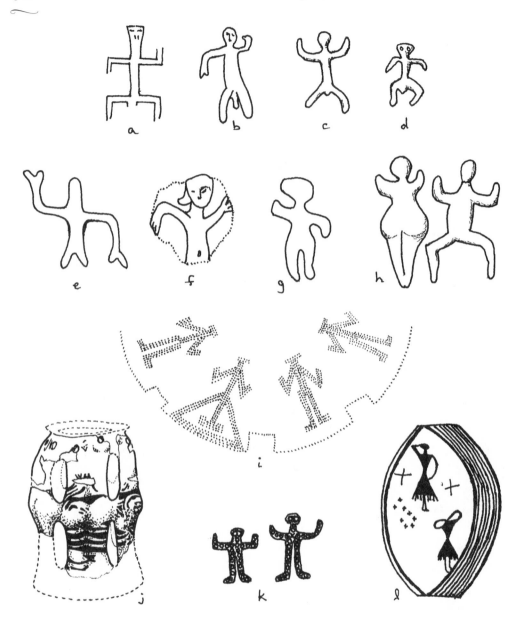

FIG. 21.2. Dancers depicted on Neolithic southeastern European pottery. (a–d) Early to mid-6th millennium, Azmak, Bulgaria. (e–g) Late 6th millennium: (e) Szajol-Felsofold, Hungary; (f) Turdaş, Transylvania; (g) Vinča, Serbia. (h) 5th millennium: Dumeşti, Romania (couple). (i) Mid-5th millennium: Střelice, Moravia (around flask). (j–k) Late 5th millennium: (j) Frumuşica, Romania (vase formed of several body-painted humans in huddle or circle-dance—compare fig. 20.3); (k) Gumelniţa, Romania. (l) Mid-4th millennium: Brinzeni-Tsiganka, Moldova (figures inside repeated oval motif).

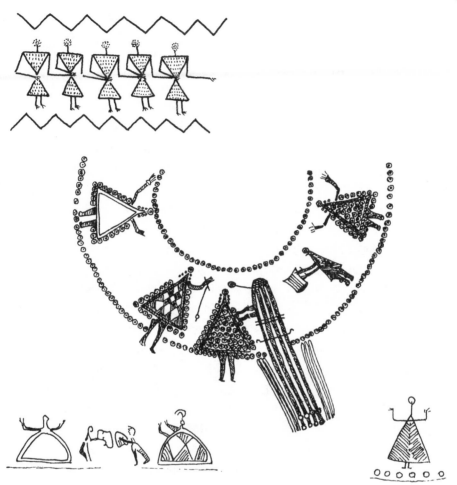

FIG. 21.3. Dancing depicted on other prehistoric European pottery. Top: Line of 5 dancers incised in dish. Neolithic sanctuary, Sassari, Sardinia, ca. 4000 BC. Middle group: Dancers incised on funerary vessels. Hallstatt culture, Sopron, Hungary, 1000–800 BC. (In main scene, 2 women spin and weave while entertained by 2 dancers and lyre player(?), much as at Hungarian working bees until recently. Lower left: Two musicians(?) between 2 dancing women. Lower right: dancer.) Bottom: Bell-shaped clay doll with line dance painted on both sides. Boiotia, Greece, ca. 700 BC.

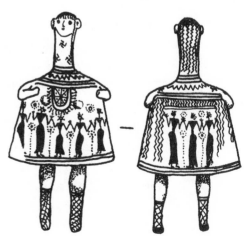

⟨∞⟩

Imagine being one of those colonists, entering a land virtually empty of other people, with some seeds, a few animals and simple stone tools (for this is still the Stone Age), some similarly equipped companions, and practical knowledge of how to build a little house, a fence, a ditch. Where do you park, in this wilderness, where set up your village so it will survive?

These people weren't stupid. A cleverly devised geological survey showed that the early sites neatly straddled different soil types, usually with another eco-zone or two within a five-kilometer radius (an hour's walk)—plus, of course, running water close by. One of the preferred soil types nourished wheat successfully, another type barley and legumes, their three central crops, while a third provided pasture for their sheep and cattle. Swampy ground nearby would harbor good hunting and fishing (a source of food before the crops came in)—but also mosquitoes, and early farmers' bones show some evidence of selection for resistance to malaria.[8]

Excavators of these villages repeat one word in particular like a refrain: boundaries, boundaries, boundaries. A defensive ditch usually marks the edge of the settlement, sometimes with an added palisade, controlling who goes in and out, who belongs and who doesn't, separating Us from Them (whoever They might be). But there were smaller divisions. Houses, a new invention, walled families in and others out—very different from nomadic camp life. For the first time, people had some privacy . . . but when you can't see and don't know what your neighbor is up to, those walls can breed suspicion.[9] Sometimes we find a ditch or a wall right through the middle of a village, apparently separating some prehistoric Hatfields and McCoys—or possibly, when the layouts are very different on the two sides (as at Sesklo, one of the earliest villages in the Balkans), separating, say, farmers from herders.[10] Yet a single boundary encloses them all. One thinks of Auntie Eller in *Oklahoma!* belting out the song, "The farmer and the cowman should be friends!"

Boundaries remained serious matters, dealt with by means of rituals in societies with little or no literacy. In Britain, parishes "beat the bounds" every one to five years, in April, to refresh people's memories of where those important boundaries were. As the older men led the group from one significant tree or stone to the next, boys carrying boughs or willow wands thrashed the markers to help remember their locations.[11] (Sometimes, it is said, the men also thrashed the boys a bit, to make a yet deeper impression.)

In Scandinavia, for millennia criminals and other unwanteds were buried at territorial borders, in no-man's-land, so their ghosts could haunt neither side.[12] We have seen that the rusaltsi, călușari, and Morris bands fought, even to the death, over the agricultural territories into which their magic was to channel abundance. We also saw that on Lazarus Day and Enyo's Day, girls danced the circuit of the village boundaries; and we observed women, naked, with loosened hair, plowing around the village bounds in secret late at night to stop an ongoing plague in its tracks. Many parallels suggest that their nakedness was intended to startle and rout the sickness demons with its potency, while the furrow marked out the magic boundary that the demons now could not cross to do their dirty work.*

Often in this study we have seen the space inside the village limits viewed as belonging to the known, well-regulated, domestic world of the farmers, and the space outside as belonging to the unruly, scary world of everything else, from wild animals to supernatural forces like willies. Once you crossed the boundary, anything could happen, so people wore wormwood, garlic, and other special things in hopes of surviving when they left the safety zone of home. One critical difference distinguishing the village from the outer world was a comforting predictability that derived from what was known and orderly.

This difference between Us and Out There must have seemed particularly stark to those early colonizing farmers, lonely little bands in a vast wilderness. (The population density of Europe, when they arrived, was maybe one person per square mile,[13] as opposed to 135 per square mile today.) Even if the opaque house walls might arouse suspicion among neighbors, you had to stick together: your neighbors were your only source of help.

The strength of this need among primitive farmers, and the reciprocity expected, stand out in the following description of pre–World War I agriculture in Šumadija, the old heartland of Serbia, first farmed in the sixth millennium:

---

*I have often wondered whether the traditional men's stick dances and closely related hilt-and-point sword dances—found from the Balkans to Britain (Alford 1962)—originated partly in marking ritual bounds. Recall the male relative walking ahead of the wedding party while slashing about with a sword to clear the road of unseen demons. Another part, the clashing of the sticks or swords, must represent chasing demons away with noise. Note, too, the oft-encountered magic circle drawn as a boundary between ritual dancers and viewers.

Today you come and hoe or thresh at my place, and tomorrow I'll help you out. . . . A day of threshing must be returned by three days of hoeing, while a day of reaping is returned with two of hoeing.

In former times, people had more oxen, so there was less need for *sprega*, reciprocal loaning of livestock. Then they used the old wooden plow, drawn by three pair of oxen. Today men plow with two pair . . . with the improved plow. Now, if a loan is necessary, two men get together, usually one with oxen and the other with cows. The oxen lead with the cows behind. In former times those who joined in this kind of loan stayed together for ten years, but now often they can't keep together even for a year. Usually they quarrel about whose land will be plowed first.

A *moba* is called for threshing or for hoeing corn. Called to take part are those who cannot do their own threshing alone. It is like a holiday. Bachelors, maidens, and young people come. . . . In former times it began at noon, and then it really was true help. At the *moba* the girls and youths sing harvest songs, and usually a flute-player goes with them and plays constantly. . . . In the evening the head of the household provides supper, after which there is dancing.[14]

And again, for harvesting:

Some individual peasants lease out a horse-drawn reaper, and those with smaller holdings still use the scythe. This latter method . . . represents, however, an improvement over . . . sickles.[15]

[Some] people thought that cutting wheat with a scythe would scatter it. They used to grab a few stalks of wheat and cut them [with a sickle]. It took many people 10 to 15 days to cut the wheat. Their backs used to hurt because they had to bend over double.[16]

Neolithic farmers had *only* sickles, made with sharp slivers of obsidian glued with pitch into an ox's jawbone. Reaping that way was even slower, harder work, and it had to be done quickly once the grain ripened, lest disastrous weather destroy this year's food supply and next year's seed. Everyone had to pitch in.

On the other hand, although sharing labor and resources reduced a particular family's risk, it increased tension and potential conflict because people were often competing for limited resources.[17] With few harvesters and few sickles, whose field would get reaped first?

⟡

Cooperation requires rules of conduct—rules being the source, as we said, of the predictability that made the village a comforting refuge from the wilds. But the early Neolithic European villages show no signs of social classes, so, with no higher-ups setting rules, the group had to self-regulate. For this they developed some remarkable tools, tools that, as one prehistorian put it, "utilize the components of domestic life but provide them with a new emphasis."[18]

Dance was apparently one of these, providing a new emphasis via body movement. For example, most people walk in an even rhythm—in 2/4, as it were—but those accompanying a traditional Bulgarian wedding party may surround it and move forward in 7/8 rhythm (short-short-*long*), a rŭchenitsa. This motion accomplishes two things: its unusualness signals that the occasion and the people are special, not ordinary; and it walls off these highly vulnerable participants from evil spirits by marking a special boundary. As the wedding party, or company of guisers, or Morris "side," moves forward, it may be preceded by musicians, or a ritual herald, or someone clearing unseen spirits from the path with a sword or a broom—not the way you and I go down the street.

We today use primarily textiles to mark ritual people, places, and events: special clothes for bride, groom, and wedding participants; a special black robe for a presiding judge (or clergyman), with a flag (or altar cloth) as ritual backdrop; academic robes with special hoods and hats for school rites of passage; and so on. But cloth had hardly been invented yet in the early Neolithic, its use still limited mainly to belts and straps. It's impossible to *prove* that Neoliths used the rŭchenitsa (or dancing in general) this way, but the inherent necessity of marking ritual as not ordinary and the lack of most other markers that would be possible today make it probable. And don't forget we've seen that this particular rhythm, so unusual to us, existed as a dance in the southern Balkan Peninsula at least twenty-four hundred years ago, in Classical Athens. Far, far less changed between 6000 and 400 BC than between 400 BC and AD 2000.

Folkdance has two other qualities that played into the hands of the early villagers. First, European and Near Eastern folkdance is highly rule-driven—you don't just get out there and wiggle, you do each dance the way the others in the group do it. You coordinate very precisely with their style and movements, or you are ostracized from the dance. And the group regulates the rules from within; there is no dancing master. As Yosef Garfinkel puts it, "the participant in the dance accepts the rules of the community."[19] That very conformity also makes one acceptable to the others, producing a strong social bond.

That doesn't mean there isn't room for some individuality and for varying levels of skill or energy within the code. Thus, in an old-fashioned Serbian or Croatian *kolo*, you must keep the beat and move to right or left (or stay in place) as the particular dance dictates, but you may *dress up* the step in certain places with extra little stamps, kicks, and flurries as long as you maintain the framework. In Greek Macedonia, on the other hand, everyone does the steps of *syrtós* and *kalamatianós* (which differ from each other only in being 4/4 or 7/8) pretty much the way everyone else in mainland Greece does them—but each village has a few dances that only its own villagers do that way. The music (and most of the steps) may be the same in the next village, since one group of musicians services many villages, but you can instantly tell those who belong in this village from those who don't by watching choreographic details. (A century ago, of course, looking at the costume worn would reveal the same information and more—the village, marital status, social and ethnic class, wealth, religion, etc., all at a glance. Again, beyond the mandatory code is room for individuality; and again, textiles took on some of the semantic load.)

On the other hand, dance had the power not just to enfold members but also to exclude outsiders. According to a Romanian account from 1927, if persons not dressed in the manner of the villages—i.e., city dwellers—attempted to join a village dance, the young men would laugh at them and come up and ostentatiously outdance them, making the whole crowd smile, a process "sufficient to discourage even the most resolute."[20]

Second, and stronger still, is an *emotional* bond with one's fellow dancers, forged in the process of rhythmic repetition (see chapter 22). We have seen the strong bonds within various groups we've discussed—among them the Russian girls at Semik, the Bulgarian Lazarki on Lazarus Day, the brotherhoods of rusaltsi, călușari, and Morris dancers. Data from many angles strengthen Garfinkel's hypothesis that early agrarian villagers fixed on dance to promote community.

But apparently the Balkan farmers also found another, equally remarkable tool for promoting community, also tweaked from normal components of domestic life.

When these "tools" come to light during the excavation of eastern European sites of 6500–3000 BC, all work typically skids to a halt as everyone runs to look—to ooh and ah. They are small human figurines, baked from clay like the household pottery and often found in groups (five, a dozen, twenty), nesting together in a pot or houselike bowl, sometimes with little chairs to sit on (fig. 21.4). In most of the cultures, they occur not in graves but in and around the houses.

Their most salient features are their human forms and tiny sizes. Just how small can vary: one pot from Romania contained twelve little ladies that fit nicely in one's grasp, along with eight rather smaller ones and thirteen chairs.[21]* Some sets contain both males and females. The males generally wear a hip belt and shoulder strap, the rest of the skin being smooth and unadorned except for indications of nipples, navel, and penis, while the females are often painted and/or incised all over with linear designs.

One specialist, Douglass Bailey, became so fascinated and even exasperated by the hold of these figurines on human imaginations—speculations about them run rampant in the literature—that he delved into all aspects of the subject, hoping to determine what these little dolls are about. What, he asked, are the powers and consequences of representations of the human body, and what is so special about little three-dimensional ones?[22]

Because they are small, he noted, we tend to pick them up to see them better; and because they are three-dimensional, we cannot see them entirely without turning them over and around. But that very handling brings these

---

*When I was designing an exhibit in Toronto, a gentleman brought into the museum his collection of exact replicas of much older, Palaeolithic "Venus" figurines, sculpted (usually in mammoth ivory) about 20,000 BC. Inviting me to handle them, he mentioned that they nestled surprisingly well into one's hand. So I picked one up. Seeing my puzzlement as I tried to position it in my hand, he did a double take, realizing I'm left-handed. "No, the other hand!" Then it fit quite remarkably. So this trait of deliberately comfortable handling was not new in the Neolithic. (We know from other evidence that humans have been programmed genetically to be right-handed. We lefties are damaged goods of various sorts.)

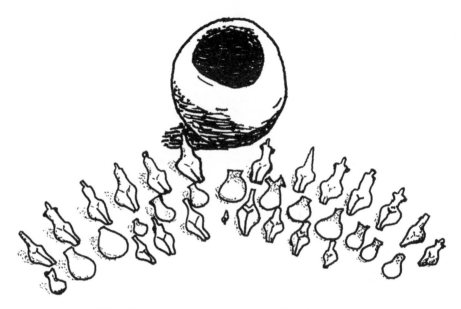

FIG. 21.4. Neolithic clay pot with set of 21 female figurines (one very tiny) and 13 chairs, all of fired clay. Isaiia-Balta Popii, Romania, 4700–4500 BC (pre-Cucuteni III).

little humans into the body zone of touching, an intimacy that changes our attitudes right there.[23]

Furthermore, Lilliputian beings make Gullivers feel not only huge but omniscient and omnipotent—in control, empowered, able to manage at least *that* little world. There's an old joke about how the boss chews out the employee, who goes home and chews out the spouse, who chews out the kid, who turns and chews out the doll. Each controls what he or she can, even if only in fantasy. Little dolls make us feel special—and powerful.

Even more remarkable, Bailey reports, certain psychological experiments have demonstrated that when we handle and interact (playact) with miniature dolls and other three-dimensional objects, our sense of time compresses nearly in proportion to the scale of the miniatures.[24] Thus, people who were asked to judge the passage of 30 minutes while playing with a 1/6-scale "dollhouse" called time, on average, after 5.43 minutes; with a 1/12 model, 2.66 minutes; and with a 1/24 model, 1.49 minutes![25]

In short, miniatures put us in another mental world. There, new things are possible, yet these things relate to our real world. Bailey proposes that the villagers used the little figures somehow to promote the working out of new solutions to the social problems confronting them. But there is more:

> Miniaturism concentrates and distils what is normal . . . then produces a denser expression of a part. . . . At the same time as miniaturism reduces elements and properties it multiplies the weight of the abstracted remainder.[26]

So we must attend to what these simplified little humanoids do show and what they leave to the viewer to imagine or construct.

⤖

First, Bailey points out the striking absence of variation among the figurines of a given cultural area, which he takes to imply a template for social conformity, a "shared conception of what a person was and should look like," where "individual differences are minimized in order to sustain overarching categories."[27] (We saw this same phenomenon with folk dress.)

Often, like the Slavic embroideries of female protective spirits (see figs. 11.1, 11.3, 19.10), the figurines have no faces. This holds true particularly in the Cucuteni/Tripolye culture of Romania and Ukraine (see fig. 21.4). Or sometimes (as with the participants at many calendrical festivals we explored) the face only *seems* to be one, since it is masked (fig. 21.5), often with a prominent bird bill or snout below huge eyes. Such figurines prevail along the west coast of the Black Sea (Hamangia culture) and in Serbia (Vinča culture). We saw that modern (dis)guisers claimed they blackened, masked, or otherwise hid their faces to avoid being recognized by friends and neighbors, since they enacted their rituals not for themselves but for the entire community—hence their own personal identity was irrelevant (see fig. 13.5). Facelessness promotes unity.

Abstract groups of parallel lines, straight and curved, cover the skins of one major class of Cucuteni/Tripolye figures, as on the twenty dolls in the Romanian pot mentioned above. Whether these lines represent body paint is unknown; the full modeling of the legs, etc., indicates that it's not clothing (although the other type, without skin ornament, often wears a sash and/or string skirt, and Vinča figures wear wraparounds).

For those with all-over decorations, special designs cluster on the buttocks, belly, and chest (fig. 21.6).[28] One of the more common motifs is an old

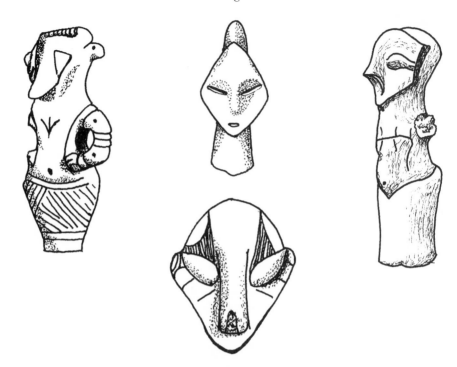

FIG. 21.5. Neolithic masks. Clockwise from left: Clay figurine with typical bird-billed mask; Vinča culture, Ćuprija, Serbia, 5th millennium BC. Removable clay mask on necklike post; Achilleion, north-central Greece, ca. 6000 BC. Clay figurine with clearly marked mask edge; Vinča, Serbia, early 5th millennium. Life-size clay mask with typical bulging almond eyes; Predionica, Kosovo, mid-5th millennium.

friend, the lozenge divided by an X with a dot in each of the four resulting fields, found on Russian and Ukrainian textiles, medieval wedding brace-lets, etc. (see fig. 17.8). Russian peasant women called it the "sown field"[29]—a field (the lozenge) now plowed (the X) and sown (the dots). Did it have a similar meaning six thousand years ago? Wouldn't a claim that it did just be more "feminist pie-in-the-sky"?

I stopped thinking so when I learned that in the Neolithic the four dots were typically made by impressing *actual grains of wheat* into the clay.* So the field is indeed sown, and with wheat! It forms another analogy—we

---

*The plow had not yet been invented, so to turn the soil over more thoroughly, plowless farmers often scrape their shallow furrows in one direction and then again at right angles

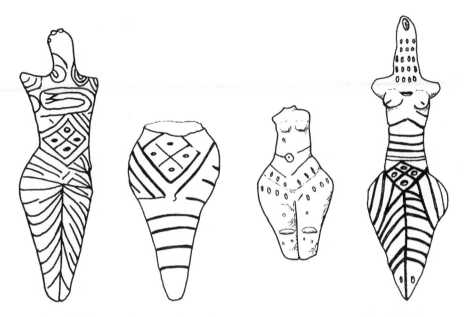

FIG. 21.6. Neolithic female figurines impressed with grains of wheat, often as "dots" in "sown field" motif (see fig. 17.8). Cucuteni/Tripolye culture, mid- to late 5th millennium BC. Left: From Cucuteni, Moldavia, Romania; center two: Luka Vrublevetskaya, Ukraine; right: unattributed.

have seen them so often in European agrarian cultures—between women and crop fields: when both have been "plowed and sown," one can only wait hopefully, patiently, during gestation for the issue. And these are not the only direct and clearly "magical" ties to agriculture in the Cucuteni/ Tripolye figurines. At Luka Vrublevetskaya, Ukraine, the clay used for the figures was found to have been thoroughly mixed with three types of grain, and with flour as well.[30]

∽∾

The ancient Greeks, as we saw, even had a word for this custom of combining several different grains or other produce for magic or for offerings: *panspérmia* or "all-seed." They made special vessels for it, the kernoi, with several little bowls or jars all stuck together so you could put some-

---

to the original furrows. I wonder whether the X, which *we* don't recognize as depicting a plowed field, refers to this primitive sort of cross-plowing.

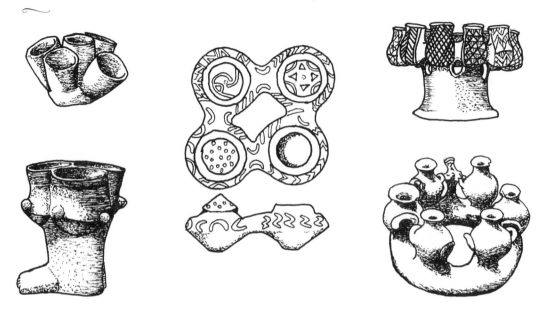

FIG. 21.7. Multicupped vessels (*kérnoi*). Left: Neolithic: Top, from Kamenin, Slovakia; bottom, from Hluboké Mašůvky, Moravia, ca. 4800 BC. Center: Neolithic (ca. 4500 BC), top and side views, Gumelniţa, Romania. Right: Top, Bronze Age (ca. 2200 BC), Melos; bottom, Iron Age (ca. 1000 BC), Kourtes, Crete.

thing different into each one (fig. 21.7). Athenaeus, for example, a Greek writer of about AD 200, describes a kernos carried at the Athenian Kerno-phoria ("kernos-carrying" festival) as including white poppy, barley, pulse, and lentils.[31] Elsewhere he describes a five-mouthed vessel for wine, honey, cheese, meal, and oil.[32] Households also baked all-seed cakes for Dionysos[33] and cooked a special gruel of grain and seeds, called *khýtra*, taking particular care that every type of seed should be present in it. This porridge they offered in the spring specifically to Hermes *Chthonius* ("of the earth"—that is, one who conducted souls to the Underworld) and to the dead themselves. It was never offered to the Olympian gods, we are told, since this was food specifically for the dead.

Well, almost food. As Jane Harrison explains it, the dead

took that "supper," that *panspermia*, with them down to the world below and brought it back in the autumn a *pankarpia* [all-fruit]. . . . It is sown a *panspermia*, it is reaped a *pankarpia*.[34]

Once again we see the now-familiar image of the ancestors underground taking care that the crops sprout and grow, so their descendants will have food. Apparently this is what's behind the Russian, Bulgarian, Greek, etc., Christmas and funerary tradition of eating a porridge (rather like gluey oatmeal mush) of wheat grains boiled with nuts, raisins, seeds, etc., and sweetened with honey.*

But the Classical Greeks didn't invent panspermia.

From the same time period at the opposite end of Europe, archaeologists have retrieved a number of bodies of men sacrificed in the bogs of Denmark. Some were so well preserved that their stomach contents could be analyzed:

> The dead man's last meal, taken perhaps half a day or a day before his sacrifice, . . . consisted of an abundance of just those grains and flower seeds which were to be made to germinate, grow, and ripen [in] the spring landscape. In the three meals which it has so far been possible to analyse [as of 1965] there has been not the slightest trace of summer or autumn fruits . . . ; and it is more plausible to suggest that they were given a special meal of the wild and cultivated plants of the district before being sacrificed . . . than to suggest that they were vegetarians.[35]

What quicker way to send those representative seeds to the divine powers than by special messenger, and what more appropriate pocket for carrying them in than his stomach?

In the Balkans, we don't find bodies preserved, but we do find kernoi by the dozens, from various Bronze Age and even Neolithic cultures, suggesting that the earlier farmers already offered all-seed to the spirits. This fits well with the interpretation that some of the Neolithic figurines—those marked with the "sown field" and those with various seeds and flour in their clay—had to do with seed magic.

Note that the kernoi (as described by Greek authors), like the gruels, cakes, and sacrificed emissaries' stomachs, never contained meat or blood. Animal products—milk and wool—perhaps, but not flesh. Blood sacrifices, preferred by Zeus, Poseidon, and the other gods of Olympus, appear to have come in with the Indo-European Greeks and their pastoral meat-eating tra-

---

* Known, with variants, as *kutia* (East Slavic), *kolivo* (South Slavic), *colivă* (Romanian), *kóllyva* (Modern Greek), etc. (cf. Propp 1987, 27), and as *frumenty* in medieval to modern English.

ditions, whereas the older agrarian culture stuck to milk, honey, and grain, offering them to Demeter and Kore, Dionysos, and other agricultural deities. The tradition continues: milk, honey, and cakes are just what you offer the vily, rusalki, *neráïdes*, etc., to not tangle your flax and to bring back your lost cow—not to mention the milk and cookies we offer Santa.

So where does our argument for the origin of the Dancing Goddesses stand? Imagine that we are the DA's office gathering evidence for a case—here, not for wrongful death but for the rightful birth of the dancing spirit maidens. Who dunnit? Who begat them? Numerous witnesses have given testimony that bird girls and returned spirits of blighted maidens were already present and dancing in the Middle Bronze Age (early second millennium BC), so we need look no later. Earlier? If so, how much? Surely the Palaeoliths are innocent. Since the willies are so closely associated with crops and the rain to grow them, the Palaeolithic people, hunters and gatherers all, are off the hook: no crops, no motive.

The earliest farmers, however, the founders of the Neolithic era, can't dodge suspicion so lightly. The sparsity of evidence from six, eight, ten thousand years back certainly qualifies this as a cold case; but the New Detectives just keep asking, "How else can we get at it? What leads can we follow?"

First, motive. Farming began in the Near East in foothill areas where enough rain fell to propagate hand-sown crops. Eventually people spread south into the vast Mesopotamian valley, where they could divert water from the great rivers to water the crops, thus becoming less dependent upon the vagaries of rainfall. The massive cooperation needed to build and maintain the canals (and defend these lifelines from other water-greedy farmers) clotted more and more people together, eventually creating cities. But those who spread westward across Anatolia and into the Balkans did so quite early and continued to depend on rain, innocent of irrigation. Since suitable weather was not something humans could manufacture, they needed divine help—a strong *motive* for coming up with willies.

Second, circumstantial evidence too peculiar to set aside. For example, the particular crops we hear about in the special care of the willies are cereals and flax. But these were precisely the plants that humans in the Near

East first domesticated: wheat, flax, and barley, apparently in that order. We also documented extreme conservatism in beliefs—for example, in the "sown field" motif and the string skirt, both demonstrably concerned with that fundamental agrarian issue, female fertility.

The prosecution maintains we have located no identifiable representations of Dancing Goddesses in our Neolithic material, and of course there is nothing written, since writing had not yet come into use.

The defense maintains we found trace after trace among the first European farmers of the specific and persistent thought patterns that these spirit maidens embody. We saw strong boundaries laid out between the world of the village (domain of humans) and the wild, dangerous world beyond (domain of the unpredictable spirits): the same attitude we saw constantly attending the willies. We traced back symbols like the "sown field" and symbolic actions like the offering of all-seed, and we noted the Neolithic use of dance as a means of communal bonding—as necessary in those pioneering European villages as in the very first villages of the Near East from which the agricultural way of life spread westward. If the exact notion of a willy did not yet exist in 6000 or even 4000 BC, we have at least charted the cultural river from which she soon emerged to water the struggling farmer's crops by combing her long, wet hair at his behest.

Here we must rest our "historical" case. But we have one more expert witness: dance itself.

Part Four

Gotta Dance!

Keeping Together in Time

Teddy bear, teddy bear, turn around;
Teddy bear, teddy bear, touch the ground!
—traditional song for timing jump rope

Evidence from the brain itself now shows that the phenomenon of dance began sometime in the Palaeolithic, for humans appear to be the only species that developed a brain that will "keep time"—that is, a brain in which an auditory beat elicits synchronized movement.[1] As the great humanist-neurologist Oliver Sacks explains it,

> keeping time . . . depends . . . on interactions between the auditory and the dorsal premotor cortex—and it is only in the human brain that a functional connection between these two cortical areas exists. Crucially, these sensory and motor activations are precisely integrated with each other.[2]

What's more, he points out, studies show that our brains don't just follow the beat. They anticipate it, once they've heard it briefly, lying in wait to pounce on the next round like cat on mouse. And if a beat is mechanically regular (like the *tick-tick-tick-tick* of a clock or metronome), our brains *invent* a periodic rhythm within it (*tick-tock-tick-tock*).[3] Indeed, our brains are so stable in their memory of encountered rhythms that Galileo, by singing tunes, was able to time rolling objects far more accurately than any timepiece then available.[4] And our brains are so hungry for rhythm that deaf people often take great pleasure in dancing when the music has a bass beat heavy enough to feel.

How, and when, did we come to be the only primate to combine sound and motion rhythmically—to dance? Again, some answers lie in our neurons—first, in our unique system of brain connections between sensory (processing the rhythm we perceive from outside) and motor (providing muscular response), as Sacks said; and second, in some peculiar brain cells called "mirror neurons," which help us mimic what we perceive.

Now, apes are so good at aping the *actions* of others that we even took a verb from them. But none of our fellow primates can mimic sounds and synchronize rhythms as we do. (When linguists teach chimps to interact using language, they have to devise a nonvocal medium for the chimps, such as hand motions or plastic symbol-pieces—although Gerald Durrell tells of how much fun both the Fon of Bafut and a caged chimp had in exchanging the bilabial trills known as raspberries.)[5] This ability to imitate sounds, match rhythms, and rehearse them incessantly had to develop before spoken language could come into being; hence the capability for dancing with each other existed before speech emerged.

Note that we have different types of memory. From our "episodic" memory we recall individual events that have happened to us; from our "procedural" memory we pull up exact, well-rehearsed sequences.[6] Somehow the protohuman species found it advantageous to go beyond the other primates in learning to imitate and rehearse sequences in a wide set of modalities, long before language emerged. The brain also developed hardware to integrate many capacities into a single act or sequence (e.g., enunciating a diphthong or reacting rhythmically to an external rhythm). Merlin Donald has dubbed this process "mimetic" culture, pointing out that rhythmic abilities developed in this layer of our brain history, with *Homo erectus*, whereas linguistic abilities came later, with *Homo sapiens* (table 22):[7]

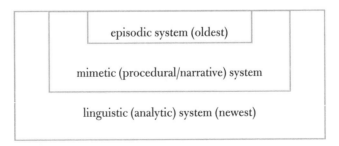

episodic system (oldest)

mimetic (procedural/narrative) system

linguistic (analytic) system (newest)

TABLE 22. Successive, nested development of brain's processors.[8]

How was this new brain function—and rhythm in particular—useful? First, imitating one's family and neighbors creates cultural and social bonds: we are similar, so we stick together and help each other. And timed coordination with others can greatly improve group efforts at defense, food acquisition (like hunting), and removing obstructions. Furthermore, when you have to remember something, you're much more likely to get it right if you've encoded it into more than one sensory mode, such as color, shape, texture, location, sound, rhythm. How many of us have located a book by recalling not its name or author but the fact that it's blue, skinny, and clothbound? The more brain systems one can coordinate the better, and adding rhythmic sound helps. Before writing existed, cultures regularly encoded their clan histories and advice into song because the melody, rhythms, and other concocted regularities (such as alliteration, rhyme, and formulaic tags) helped the official rememberer, the bard, to recall things. One may surmise that before language, some of this cultural information may have found expression in mimetic dance.*

⸎

Remarkable advantages also come from simply matching rhythms with one's fellows, as William McNeill documents in his book *Keeping Together in Time* (1995). Slung into a boot camp so ill equipped (in 1941) that even the sole machine gun for training didn't work, he and the other recruits were kept busy marching. He reports the odd effect:

> Marching aimlessly about on the drill field, swaggering in conformity
> with prescribed military postures, conscious only of keeping in step
> so as to make the next move correctly and in time somehow felt good.

---

*Neuroscientists continue to chase music, rhythm, and dance in the brain, but Oliver Sacks (2008) pulls much information together in highly readable form. Procedural memory, he explains, involves linking portions of the cerebral cortex with primitive subcortical regions like the basal ganglia and cerebellum, while the areas controlling coordination and the timing or succession of movement include the basal ganglia, cerebellum, and hippocampus; the temporal lobes process any auditory information. Williams Syndrome, which produces "almost helpless attraction to music and . . . sometimes overwhelming emotional reactions to it," activates the brain extensively at such times, particularly the amygdala (Sacks 207, 240, 255, with references).

Donald (1991), for his part, has teased out the evolutionary sequence.

. . . A sense of pervasive well-being is what I recall; more specifically, a strange sense of personal enlargement; a sort of swelling out,
becoming bigger than life, thanks to participation in collective ritual.
. . . It was something felt, not talked about. . . . Moving briskly and
keeping in time was enough to make us feel good about ourselves,
satisfied to be moving together, and vaguely pleased with the world
at large.[9]

These effects puzzled him, and later, as a historian, he began to notice and
collect examples of clever military leaders tapping into the power of close-
order drill. It wasn't just the greater efficiency of such troops. There was the
powerful solidarity that he and his buddies came to feel, so that they could
go into battle and die for each other as part of that something "bigger than
life." More broadly, he says,

the emotion it arouses constitutes an indefinitely expansible basis for
social cohesion among any and every group that keeps together in
time, moving big muscles together and chanting, singing, or shouting rhythmically. "Muscular bonding" is the most economical label I
could find for this phenomenon, and I hope the phrase will be understood to mean the euphoric fellow feeling that prolonged and rhythmic muscular movement arouses in nearly all participants in such
exercises.[10]

When Maurice of Orange revived close-order drill in 1590, after a millennium of neglect, it "created such a lively *esprit de corps* among the poverty-
stricken peasant recruits and urban outcasts . . . that other social ties faded
to insignificance among them." His campaigns succeeded so well that soon
all Europe copied him.[11]

We now begin to see the mechanism that could allow dance to function as a powerful and useful cohesive force in Neolithic villages. Muscular
bonding through dance really *can* do what Garfinkel deduced from his Neolithic potsherds. It doesn't have to match our notion of drill, even for military ends. When Balkan guerrilla warriors, the *haiduki* and *klephti*, fled to
the mountains to resist their Turkish conquerors, they forged tight-knit little
fighting bands by using dance to rehearse absolute coordination with each

FIG. 22.1. Men dancing *varí hasápiko* in street. Naousa, Greek Macedonia,
March 2009. (Cf. fig. 20.3.)

other. (These efforts survive today in dances like the *varí hasápiko*, where
information as to which move to make next is signaled silently by a hand
sign, a look, or pressure on one's neighbor's shoulder: fig. 22.1.)*

Oliver Sacks points out from his own set of considerations that rhythmic
work songs "probably arose with the beginnings of agriculture, when till-
ing the soil, hoeing, and threshing all required the synchronized efforts of a
group of people."[12] These, like dance, provided yet more ties.

---

*Novices today who swell the hasapiko dance line, then can't follow the leader, don't
understand that some of the information can't easily be transmitted beyond about four
dancers.

The binding is accomplished by rhythm—not only heard but internalized, identically, in all who are present. Rhythm turns listeners into participants, makes listening active and motoric, and synchronizes the brains and minds (and, since emotion is always intertwined with music, the "hearts") of all who participate.[13]

But the pursuit of dance, and marching, involves more than just muscular and emotional bonding and a cognitive propensity to tap one's feet. As McNeill says, keeping together in time leaves a distinct residue of pleasure: he recalls "a state of generalized emotional exaltation whose warmth was indubitable, without, however, having any definite external meaning or attachment."[14] Let's pick that apart.

Buddhists and certain other practical philosophers view our minds as having two operating systems, sometimes called Big Mind and Little Mind. Big Mind tends to rest in the present, noticing life without attachment, peacefully at one with the world. The past has gone, the future isn't here yet; the only moment that *ever* exists is Now. Little Mind, on the other hand, is our high-powered system for coping with emergencies: stamp out the fire, run from the tsunami, watch out for that tree! Little Mind narrows our focus to the perceived problem, to saving Self—it has also been called Ego Mode. We call on our memories of past experience, we plan our future actions; we notice nothing around us that we don't think pertains. In modern life, we spend most of our time in Little Mind, rushing from one emergency to another.*

McNeill's description of his state of mind during drill seems remarkably close to that of Big Mind, and the paradigm seems to explain a lot about dance. For example, I used to teach class—archaeology, linguistics, cognitive science—and then head to the dance studio at lunchtime to rehearse folkdances with students. As I would start to dance with someone, I'd often say, "Hi! How are you? I haven't seen you for ages!" Then I'd do a double take, and we'd laugh as I realized we had just spent the previous hour in class together. But it wasn't the same Me perceiving the world, and this Me *hadn't* really "seen" this student fully, in the hubbub of class. Many clues now tell me that I, and others too, shift states of consciousness from Little to

_____

*This philosophy sees anxiety as stemming from "too much future" and anger from "too much past," and hurrying as a major gateway to Ego Mode (see below).

Big Mind in starting to dance. (After all, we have those three inherited ways of processing reality, shown in table 22, and can easily switch among them.)[15] "I" have always viewed my body as an inconvenient and rather demanding wheelbarrow that carries my brain around—until I start to dance. Then brain and body merge. Dancing moves us into the Now of motion and rhythm, and, as Galileo found, rhythm resists being hurried.

McNeill also mentions the sense of pleasure. Certain types of sound, such as moaning and other low-pitched vocal sounds, can raise pain thresholds; and mothers know that rhythmic rocking motions soothe as well, possibly by diverting the brain to its habit of anticipating each new beat. This gives an added dimension to both lullabies and rhythmic work songs. The very process of low, rhythmic singing in time with the work combats feelings of pain and fatigue till the labor is finished—so Neolithic farmers may have stumbled on a much-needed pain-reliever by inventing work songs. Chanting or singing while marching falls under the same magic.

Even stronger pleasure in dancing is often compared to runner's high, in which the intense and prolonged motion generates special pain-blocking chemicals (thought now to be endocannabinoids rather than endorphins, since the molecules of the latter seem too big to cross the blood-brain barrier[16]). How many of us dance addicts have danced to live music till we could barely move, too besotted to stop?

Research on music and poetry suggests, further, that our brains go into ecstatic hyperdrive when several cognitive systems get fully synchronized, all firing in unison. Years ago, two authors working on how the brain handles poetic meters referred to the auditory effect of synchrony between poetic meter and brain-processing timing as "stereoscopic."[17] Adding a third mode, such as full muscular response, escalates the effect into even headier multiplexing. I recall us starting to shriek with glee as we danced, quite drunk on rhythm, when we finally "got" a complex 5-against-4 clogging rhythm; or Michael Flatley fairly screaming as he danced Irish complexities, toward the end of *Lord of the Dance*.*

---

*I "caught" the propensity to do this from a Romany girl named Morgiana who folkdanced with us in high school. When the eastern European music and dance became sufficiently exciting, she would just let it rip—and some of us soon found ourselves doing likewise. The tense-throated high-pitched *eeeeeee* in particular startles and embarrasses American folkdancers when they first hear it, but choking it back as it spontaneously erupts can be

More extreme still is trance, to which dance is well known as an avenue. Sometimes the operative force is insistent repetition until the brain shifts into a radically different state of consciousness, as among Central Asian shamans. In other cases, as with the women of Duboka or the Thracian firedancers, we don't yet understand the mechanisms.

Duboka we have repeatedly discussed. Of firedancers, two small groups remain in the Balkans: one in the remote Strandzha Mountains of southeastern Bulgaria, the other a group from there who resettled as refugees in Greek Macedonia in 1924. We possess some informative Bulgarian accounts from before this upheaval, a close study of the Greek group from roughly 1973 to 1986, in addition to many superficial, sensationalist mentions. The Greeks call the ritual *anastenária*, the Bulgarians *nestinári*. At its climax, dancers in a trance move through beds of hot coals barefoot without getting burned. (Rash onlookers trying it without the trance have invariably suffered terrible burns.) The physiology of this trance is still a mystery, but we can learn much from watching the events carefully.

> *Fear not, for I have redeemed you;*
> *I have called you by name, you are mine . . .*
> *When you walk through fire,*
> *you shall not be burned,*
> *and the flame shall not consume you.*
>
> —Isaiah 43:1–3

The firewalking occurs principally at the feast of Saints Constantine and Helena each spring.* In southeastern Bulgaria a century ago, a procession would form early in the day consisting of priests, nestinari, musicians, vari-

---

quite unpleasant physically. I suspect that learning to go into a dance trance proceeds similarly: your brain "catches" it from others. Mirror cells again?

*May 21 in the Julian calendar, June 3 in the Gregorian. The rituals used to occur every day for 8 days (cf. Shivachev 1898–99, 277), but squabbles with the Orthodox Church, disruptive media attention, and other factors have generally reduced it to one day where it survives at all. I can neither verify nor explain the actual firewalking: what concerns us here is its social role.

ous icons and banners of the two saints, and a crowd of onlookers. It progressed from the church or the special chapel of the nestinari to a holy spring (the *ayazma*). After blessing the water, the participants would sprinkle both themselves and the sacrificial bulls tied up nearby. As at funerals, these animals were killed in such a way that their blood soaked into the earth,[18] by the same stroke a rite for the fertility of the earth and an offering to appease the now-bloodless dead, exactly as Homer knew it nearly three millennia earlier (*Odyssey* xi.1–50). In the afternoon, after many cartloads of wood had been hauled to an open space, a bonfire was lit with a flame provided by the head nestinar. The onlookers danced to the rhythm of the musicians while the logs burned down to coals, ready to be spread across an area of many yards. In some of the old Bulgarian descriptions (as in Greek Macedonia today), the nestinari withdrew for a while to ready themselves spiritually, awaiting possession by St. Constantine for the firewalk. The oldest account, from 1866, by an interested visitor named Slaveikov, resembles more closely the spontaneity of the Duboka women in the 1890s. He relates:

> On my journey I arrived in Madzhura just as such a festival was being put on. As we sat at a table near the fire, several people jumped into the coals and began to dance in them. I sat next to my host, . . . his young wife and his mother opposite me. While I was lost in the spectacle of the firedancers, my host tapped me lightly and indicated to me to watch his wife. She was holding her little child, but as I watched her, she suddenly became totally pale and stiff and sweat covered her face. Then she gradually got her color back, and suddenly she threw the child to her mother-in-law, while she cried out, "tu-tu-tu, there he is, tu-tu!" and jumped up, ran into the fire, and began to dance with the others, and then went into the village.[19]

("He" refers to St. Constantine.) The ethnographer Arnaudov, observing events in 1914, states that the firewalkers "turn dark and blue, their muscles tense up, they shake in their whole body, wobble, and appear stunned, as if half dead."[20] *Something* is affecting their blood flow.

Constantine was the emperor who declared the Roman Empire Christian in the early 4th century. Helena, his mother, was a devout Christian reputed to have located the True Cross—the one on which Jesus was crucified.

Marinov adds another event common to this festival: predicting the future while entranced. He describes how each nestinar,

> receiving strength and inspiration, . . . begins to make unusual move-
> ments. . . . The pipe wails and the drum pounds, and the nestinari
> dance. They are "outside" themselves; the expressions on their faces
> show they are in ecstasy. They make their way onto the live coals . . .
> when the ecstasy takes them.
>
> To the nestinar, when he dances in the fire, the doors of the future
> open, and he gives a sign, at which the pipes and drum fall silent and
> then he predicts what will happen. The predicting is for private per-
> sons and for the whole village. . . .
>
> "And the marvel is," conclude Baba Stoya and Baba Dona [Mari-
> nov's informants], "the predictions turned out true, and the feet of the
> nestinari were unharmed. God's work."[21]

The description in 1898 by Shivachev mentions that in one village only a single elderly nestinarka (female nestinar) remained, so everyone depended on her for predictions. Instead of walking on coals, however, she danced in her courtyard with the members of the procession, faster and faster until she became "inspired" by the saints. Entering her small, incense-filled chapel in a trance, she humbly began to divine answers to the questions put to her, such as whether a certain sick person would recover or a particular marriage take place. "At every word," says Shivachev, "she mentions with great rever-ence the saint's name and crosses herself," averring that "she has communi-cation from above for everything that she says or does."[22]

Different witnesses describe the participants as dancing in, walking across, or standing in the coals, and doing so for anywhere from a few sec-onds to an hour or two.[23] We also hear of nestinari sitting alongside, sifting the coals with their hands till the last one is out.[24] Nor does the fire have to be only on St. Constantine's Day: the traditional Midsummer bonfire or even a hearth fire will do, if the trance comes.

Why firewalk? Because the rite was viewed as beneficial—"because the fire burns up all illnesses," and the more who dance on the fire, the greater the fertility will be that year.[25]

In 1924, Greece gave land in Macedonia to a group of Greek-speaking refugees from Bulgarian Thrace after a decade of displacements. They came from Kosti and other destroyed villages nearby that traditionally had carried out both the kalogheros ritual and anastenaria. The Greek government, overwhelmed by refugees at the time, wisely settled the incoming groups *as* groups to the extent possible, so the refugees could maintain their own inner support systems. Keeping up their traditional customs, these villagers found, helped people hold onto their identities. So it is no accident that one village is named Agia Eleni (St. Helena), or that they still hold their rituals of firedancing for Saints Constantine and Helena (despite much friction with the official Greek church, which can't stomach such unusual goings-on, yet is stuck with the icons and two saints as Christian).

The public events are much as in the Bulgarian descriptions: a taboo against work; a procession to the holy well or *agíasma*,* where the leader blesses the water and sprinkles people; sacrifice of a black ram-lamb (as Odysseus did, instead of a bull), causing the blood to fall into a freshly dug hole; lighting the bonfire and spreading the resulting coals; and finally the firedance accompanied by drum and pipes.[26] The dance itself is a

> sacred version of the common "kerchief dance" (μαντιλάτος χορός), which in this context is danced individually. At the konaki and during the firewalk it is danced to a tune with a 2/4 rhythm known as "the tune of the dance" (ό σκοπός τοῦ χοροῦ), while during the processions of the Anastenarides . . . it is danced to a tune with a 7/8 rhythm known as "the tune of the road" (ό σκοπός τοῦ δρόμου).[27]

A sensitive study by the American researcher Loring Danforth, however, *Firewalking and Religious Healing* (1989), adds yet another dimension. Unlike the Bulgarian ethnographers, who arrived at a village, watched its festival, and then left, Danforth lived for a time in Agia Eleni. When he returned to study anastenaria further, people welcomed him back as an old friend and seemed comfortable telling him about their lives and bringing him to their *konaki*, the little shrine building that housed their sacred icons. For it was in the konaki that so much of importance happened.

---

* Greek ἀγί-ασμα, "holy water" (from *hágios* "holy"), borrowed into Bulgarian as *ayazma*.

As Danforth slowly began to realize, a central point of the firewalking was to facilitate psychological healing among people marginalized by society. Most of the firewalkers now are women precisely because Greek society marginalizes women, making them completely subservient to their fathers, husbands, and mothers-in-law. If the mother-in-law doesn't like the bride because, for example, she feels no one is good enough for her son (sons tend to be put on a pedestal), she can make the girl's life hell, both over-working her and working her over. Or it may be her father or husband who oppresses and confines her, till she becomes depressed, then physically sick. (In 1962, village women also took "rest cures" at a remote nunnery for this sort of nervous breakdown (see chapter 12). They referred to it as *tá névra*—"the nerves"—the same expression Danforth encountered.) But if the venerable St. Constantine deigns to enter her body and she becomes visibly able to walk on fire, then her status skyrockets: she has been touched directly by holiness. Her new "power" allows her to hold her head up, regardless of her oppressors, and her physical symptoms decline. As with almost everything in Greece, she must have her husband's or parents' permission—in this case, to apprentice herself to anastenaria and "dance in public." But Danforth points out that if the husband gives permission, then he has aligned himself with his wife, supporting her bid for health through religion, and right there she begins recovery.[28] Clearly Slaveikov's host in 1866 viewed his young wife's propensity to firewalk as worthy of attention rather than interference.*

The anastenarides now become her enthusiastic support group, visiting her, encouraging her, going into little trances from which they give her orders from the saint, such as to attend the meetings at the konaki and correct "ritual faults" (like finding and fixing up a disused family icon—tasks that may cause her family to actively help her recovery). Another ritual fault is working when one should be attending to the saint—exactly like those punished by the willies for working on their sacred days.

In the konaki, old-timers help newcomers (whether male or female) reach

---

* The men who joined were also marginalized—scoffed at, for example, for having had no farmland to inherit, hence having married an only daughter so as to acquire her family's land to till. (Greek women, until almost the present, could not legally control an inheritance; everything required a man.) Since he therefore had to move into *her* village and household, instead of vice versa, his neighbors would ostracize him as a contemptible weakling.

the appropriate state of mind through dancing, encouraging and teaching them to emerge from a "closed" (metaphorically: sick) condition, dancing with them as they "suffer from the saint," handing them a sacred kerchief or icon at judicious moments to help them along, waiting for their "road to open" (as the symbolic phrase goes).[29] Since only men normally are allowed to dance alone, rather than holding hands in a line, this dancing is a new experience for women, one against which they have been culturally conditioned, and they feel very anxious at first. ("When I started to dance, I suffered a great deal . . . as if there were chains on my feet. Then when my husband gave me permission to dance, my feet were untied. I was set free, and I danced.")[30] One has to learn how to "let go" appropriately, and even an old-timer may "suffer" at first while moving toward trance. In both cases, the others

> try to help him dance more easily by dancing directly in front of him, by shaking him in time to the music, or by placing an arm around his shoulder and dancing with him, teaching him in effect how to dance. Gradually he begins to perform what could more properly be called a dance. He stands upright and moves his feet in time to the music in proper dance steps, clapping, bending low at the waist, or waving his arm away from his body in a manner characteristic of the dance of the possessed Anastenarides.[31]

(The same arm motion occurs in the Bulgarian solo rǔchenitsa.) Help continues at the firewalk:

> Yavasis [the leader] stood with Keti, who was dancing hesitantly at the edge of the fire—now toward the fire, now back. Several times he led her away from the fire and guided her around the outside of the bed of coals. Keti was new, and her road wasn't open yet; so Yavasis had to make sure she didn't get confused and go into the fire by mistake. If she did, she might get burned.[32]

When the road opens, however, and

> the power of St. Constantine comes . . . , they experience it as a cool breeze or as an electric shock. They say that when they dance freely and easily they feel light, calm, joyful . . . "flying like a bird."[33]

Their anxiety and sufferings suddenly vanish, just as among the victims of rusalka sickness when the pot shatters and the sufferer leaps up and begins to run and dance. Some of the descriptions of these two healing complexes are remarkably similar, with the big difference that among the anastenarides the sufferers go into the trance, whereas among the rusaltsi/călușari it's the healers who do so.

Where did this firewalking originate? Linguistics can help a bit. Bulgarian *nestinari* (like *ayazma*) was adapted from Greek: the attempt to derive it from Bulgarian *istina* "truth"[34] is a folk etymology. But Greek *anastenária*, explained as coming from *ana-stenaz-* "to sigh" ("because the dancers sigh while dancing"), is itself a typical folk etymology, and records from the twelfth century and earlier prove this. They call it *an-asthenária* "non-sickness, health."[35] Thus, its older name tells us that, just like the rusaltsi and călușari, the practitioners were there to restore people to health. A detailed report by Father Dionisii in 1899 says that the Bulgarian-speaking villages in the Strandzha Mountains that practiced firewalking, such as Madzhura, claimed the custom spread to them from two neighboring Greek-speaking villages, Brodilovo and Kosti (whence the Greek refugees just discussed). The residents of these two villages, the Bulgarian clergyman continues, were "a completely different type from the [Bulgarian] locals: broad heads, ugly faces, strange clothes, and even their dances are heavy and barely moving."[36] Chauvinism aside, everything points to the Slavic-speaking Bulgarians as having gotten it from Greek speakers—yet no trace of it exists in Classical Greece. There's not a hint of firewalking, and furthermore, dance then was accompanied by flutes and plucked strings, not percussion, which the Greeks viewed as foreign.[37] Where did we lose the trail?

The pounding drums that help induce trance suggest the healing practices of Central Asian shamans, pointing in turn to the Huns and Bulgars, the non–Indo-European peoples (largely Turkic) who arrived in the Danube basin from far to the northeast soon after Constantine's conversion to Christianity in 312. The Bulgars eventually settled down, shed their language in favor of Slavic, and swapped their native monotheistic religion for the Christianity pushed on them by their proselytizing (and frightened) Byzantine neighbors. Officially they adopted this religion in the ninth century, but Constantinople, the City of Constantine, center of Greek Orthodoxy, lies just south of Kosti and the Strandzha Mountains. Could it be that a stray eddy of Central Asians adopted both Greek and Christianity a century or more before the Slavs arrived, merging their notions of trance and prediction with Constantine's Christianity and ardently maintaining the mix until the present, in near isolation?*

Whatever the answer, rhythm and dance lie near the heart of this extreme custom, which has long served to keep its people together in time, and in space as well. Dance bonds us.

---

*The Huns swept some of the Bulgars, lodged north of the Sea of Azov, westward with them, marauding central Europe from 377 until Attila's death in 453. Their leader gone, these Bulgars scattered across eastern and southeastern Europe.

Persian fire-worshippers have been suggested as the source of anastenaria, since they view fire as health-giving. But Persians merely jump *over* the fire quickly at New Year's, rather than walking directly into it in a trance. The recurrent biblical metaphor of being assayed and purified by fire, thence becoming untouchable by it (as in the quotation from Isaiah), seems a much stronger starting point for the cult, which only needed coupling with some group that knew how to achieve very deep trances. The two available candidates would seem to be shamanic or Dionysiac trances. Dionysos was considered Thracian, and Kosti was in Thrace, but we have no evidence of Dionysiacs entering fire.

As to the origin of these "ugly, broad-headed" villagers who dressed and danced funny, DNA studies have so far shed no light. One wishes Father Dionisii had actually *described* wherein their clothes were peculiar, since that could reveal so much.

CHAPTER 23

Dancing the Time Warp

The Dancing Goddesses danced in mythical time and space, of course. But what can we reconstruct about the very real dances long performed by their devotees, by the villagers of early Europe? What aspects of the modern "folkdances" of eastern and southeastern Europe can we trace back as antique inheritances?

Granted, dance is as evanescent as spoken language, gone the instant after it is produced. Yet we can reconstruct much about the prehistory of language—language in general as well as specific languages and words. This is possible because languages are arbitrary structured systems serving a purpose.

Although their arbitrariness allows languages to drift and change, their internal structural relations let us reconstruct many (though not all) of those changes. The same is true of *traditional* costume and dance, both of which are arbitrary and structured cultural systems. Like language, costume and dance must function within strict physical, cognitive, and functional constraints, which limit how far these systems can wander. Those limits also make reconstruction easier.

The purpose that constrains language's structure so strongly is two-way communication (although, once created, language can serve other purposes, such as thinking).[1] Dress and dance are also designed to communicate, but without the kicker of reciprocity, so the structures are less confined. The bottom line is that the reconstruction methods developed by linguists are usable to determine some aspects of dance and costume history, though they won't take us so far as in linguistics because the systems are looser.

Within dance, we can apply all this to two physical systems: rhythm and choreography.

Zwei Herzen in dreiviertel Tak. . . .
Two hearts in 3/4 time. . . .
—German waltz lyrics

We have noted repeatedly the occurrence of 7/8 meters in the Balkans, counted in groups of three, both as *short-short-long* and as *long-short-short*. Normal walking is 2/4 (or 4/4)—nothing special about that. But a rhythm in groups of three? Now we're into dance, into nonpractical movement, the realm of the Dancing Goddesses. Another triple time, the waltz, has become nearly synonymous with dancing in the West ever since it swept the European continent in the late eighteenth century, delighting the young with its vigor and close contact, and shocking the old with its . . . um, close contact. ("He puts his hand *where??*") The waltz (from German *walzen* "to roll about") accents the first beat, but other possibilities include the Polish mazurka and kujawiak, which accent the second, and the Swedish hambo, in which the woman lifts on count 2 but the man on 3, producing a lilting seesaw effect.

Then there are 7/8 meters in which one of the three beats is half again as long as the others. Measured out as 3-2-2 (*long-short-short*) we get the kalamatianos, ubiquitous in Greece today and mentioned by the ancient Greek author Athenaeus as one of the stately, modest, and simple dances of Classical Athens.* He called it *dáktyloi*—a dactyl in poetic meter is ¯˘˘ (long-short-short), and linguists peg a Greek metrical "long" as about half again as long as a "short," so, 3-2-2. Counting 7/8 as 2-2-3, we have the rŭchenitsa, used throughout Bulgaria for all manner of ancient rituals, as we've seen, from surrounding the bride with protective magic to stomping the clay for new

---

*Travelers in Greece in the eighteenth and nineteenth centuries jotted down various melodies (now being collected by the Hellenic Music Archives), some of which, by their strained notations, strongly imply that some rhythms were indeed uneven.

bread pans during Rusalia Week, not to mention bringing Vlach women back from the Land of the Dead on Trinity Sunday and helping the firewalkers along their way.*

Odd-footed rhythms—ones that change which foot you start on from measure to measure, as the waltz does—occur across much of Europe: mostly 3/4, plus the Irish 9/8 slip jig. But rhythms with uneven *lengths* of beat seem to occur in Europe only in the Balkan Peninsula, with the tightest cluster of variants in Bulgaria, greater Macedonia, and parts of Serbia and Romania.† (In historical linguistics, the largest numbers of variants occur where the trait is oldest, a principle that probably holds here, too.) When you get north to the arc formed by Italy, Austria, Hungary, Ukraine, Russia, and beyond, they are gone (Map 23). Yet such rhythms occur elsewhere in the world, for example in India.

And it is from central and northern India that the European Gypsies, or Rom (their preferred name), once came, apparently originally a band of warriors and their camp-followers, including musicians, known by the Indian word *Dōm* "untouchable" (whence *Rom*). Leaving northwestern India with their instruments (including a double-reeded woodwind called *surnai*, now the Balkan zurna—see fig. 5.3) and gradually working their way westward via Persia, these Indic-speakers reached Greece in the fourteenth century. But since people thought they had come from Egypt, they received the misleading name of *(E)gypsi-ans*.[2] (The other common European term *tsigan*, German *Zigeuner*, is related to another Greek label, *a-thinggan*-[ἀθίγγαν-] "untouchable.") They sojourned long in the Balkans before spreading across Europe to Ukraine and Russia in the northeast, Ireland in the north-

---

* A restaged version of the Duboka ritual can be seen in the film *Dubočke Rusalje* (1971), posted on YouTube. My thanks to Diana Stojanović for locating this. Yvonne Hunt informs me (pers. com., July 10, 2011) that the anastenarides use both the 3-2-2 and 2-2-3 rhythms. (*Rйchenitsa* and *mandilatos* both mean "handkerchief [dance].")

† Most commonly, in my experience, 5/8 (e.g., *paidushko* "limping" and *rustemul*), 7/8 with 3 beats (just discussed; add Romanian anapestic *geampara*) or 4 beats (e.g., ``‾‾‾``, as in *Eleno Mome*, where the long is double the short: 2-2-1-2), 9/8 (3 shorts and a long beat: length often last as in *Daichovo Horo*, but, for example, second in *Katushe Mome*, ``‾‾``), 11/8 (four shorts with long beat often centered, ``‾‾``, as in *Gankino Horo* or *kopanitsa*); but also 10/8 (e.g., ``‾‾``, as in *Petrunino Horo*), 13/8 (e.g., ``‾‾``, as in *Elenino Horo*), or sometimes rhythms composed of two different "time signatures" alternating, such as 7/8+11/8 (e.g., *Jove Male Mome* or *Sedi Donka*). See Kolar (1974) and Katzarova-Kukudova and Djenev (1976) for more.

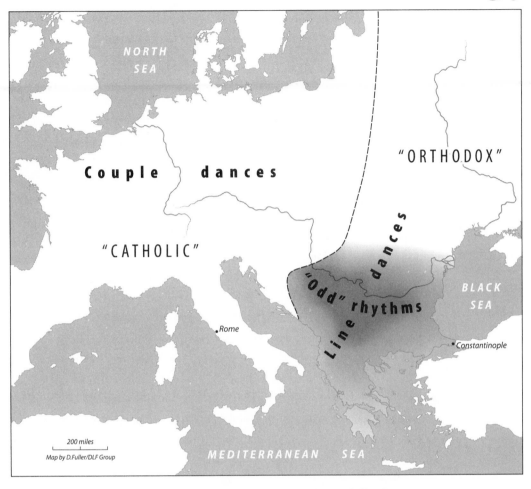

MAP 23: **Distribution of Dance Types in Europe.** North/south line is watershed between areas to west that were Christianized from Rome, which came to have predominantly couple dances, and areas to east that were Christianized from Constantinople, which have almost exclusively line dances. Dances with asymmetrical rhythms (also called *akshak*—additive—or Bulgarian rhythms) occur in the Orthodox south—most strongly in Bulgaria and Macedonia but also in Serbia, Greece, Albania, and Romania.

west, and Spain in the southwest, in all of which areas they continue to live today, often still itinerant and still hiring out to play music for the local people. The locals, of course, want to hear their own tunes, which the Roma learn, blending them with their inherited musical tradition. The complex rhythms they brought from India did not take root in central, northeastern, and northwestern Europe, but in the heart of the Balkans they stuck.*

I have long surmised that it was because Balkan inhabitants already used 7/8 meter and the like that the incoming complicated meters and rhythms of the Gypsies/Roma "made sense" and could naturalize there. Exactly as with belief systems, one doesn't readily adopt a "new" system without already having something similar as a peg to hang it on. The brain, like the body, rejects transplants of material deemed too foreign. Athenaeus's naming of ancient Greek dances in 7/8 and 5/8 meters, however, proves that at least two such musical rhythms existed in the Balkans before the Roma arrived. Songs composed for Classical Greek choral dances actually include many other meters, including trochees (˘˘, literally "running") and anapests (˘˘˘, the now-familiar rŭchenitsa). Aristophanes, in fact, has his comic chorus in *The Acharnians* remark that, after doffing their cloaks, they want to "get at the anapests" to dance.[3] And in a dazzling tour de force for the opening chorus of *The Birds*, presented in 414 BC, Aristophanes gave each type of bird a different—and auditorily appropriate—meter to dance in to. Further support for the antiquity of these dance rhythms comes from the Pontic Greeks, who began colonizing the south coast of the Black Sea centuries before the time of Aristophanes and lived there in increasingly isolated enclaves up to modern times. These Greeks, some of whose dialects preserve features (such as infinitives) that got lost from mainstream Greek a very long time ago,[4] also maintain some of these uneven rhythms.

⌘

Linguists delight in making dialect maps, showing how a language like English varies across the countryside: what people in one region call a *frying pan* may elsewhere be a *skillet* or a *spider* (because it once had spindly legs to straddle a fire). Changes in costume also map across time and space the way linguistic dialects do, and a "costume dialect" map looks much like a linguistic one because both types of "dialect" got there the same way: through gradual change.[5] Rhythm, a fairly tight system, maps the same way—you can show, for example, that the waltz spread across much more of Europe than, say, the

---

*I am not competent to assess the folk music of Spain (southwest). The archaeological record, however, suggests that Iberian Neolithic farmers shared certain ritual and other ideas with the Balkan farmers, so musical connections would be worth exploring.

hambo. (Such maps, whether linguistic, sartorial, or choreographic, are more informative if you stick to periods before mass media homogenized the world.)

It is noteworthy, then, that these odd-footed and uneven rhythms so strange to the rest of Europe cluster within the area of the first European farmers—namely, the east-central Balkan Peninsula. All the languages have changed, yet, like the other belief systems we have tracked throughout this book, this particular notion of rhythm seems to bubble up there persistently from the substrate culture.

Certain choreographic templates also seem to keep surfacing, suggesting that they too are ancient. I will mention a few examples, but much work remains to be done in this field.

We said earlier that if the men in the ancient Minoan model of four male dancers (see fig. 20.3) suddenly came to life, they could break straightway into a *fast hasápiko,* or Ukrainian *arkan,* or Israeli *hora,* dances that are essentially identical. Many Americans know this dance from hours of it at Jewish weddings: step to side, step across, step, kick, step, kick. Some ethnic groups do it to the left, but most move to the right: right foot, left across, right, kick, left, kick. And one can embellish these six counts with many little variations, from quicksteps to backflips.

Observe, now, the structure. It begins with a preamble, as it were, of steps moving to the right; next, a step-kick to the right is mirrored by a step-kick to the left. Then the whole repeats, over and over. This basic template—introit, plus something to one side that is repeated to the other side*—turns up again and again, over a wide area, in any and every rhythm and meter: not just this Ukrainian/Greek/Jewish *hora,* but also (with different introits and/or mirrored steps) Greek *syrtós* (4/4) and *kalamatianós* (dactylic 7/8), pan–South Slavic *lesnoto horo* (dactylic 7/8), basic Serbian *kolo* (4/4), Bulgarian *kopanitsa* (11/8) and "national dance" *Eleno Mome* (4-beat 7/8), and so on. This notion of how to structure a dance, with its simplicity, its ubiquity in the area, and the broad range of variations, implies great antiquity.†

---

* This was first pointed out to me as a principle by Yvonne Hunt (March 2008).

† Another remarkable example of choreographic "dialect shift" with a quite different basic template occurs across southwestern Europe. Dancers on the island of Mallorca perform

That same little Minoan model of men holding their neighbors by the shoulder also indicates that certain handholds characteristic of Balkan folk-dance go way, way back. The V-hold (hands joined and down) and W-hold (joined hands held up with elbows down and bent) are frequent on Garfin-kel's Neolithic Near Eastern potsherds (see fig. 21.1), so they could well have arrived from that region with the early farmers. Dancers joined at the shoulder also occur occasionally in Near Eastern material, but (then as now) people in that area seem disinclined toward the interpersonal distance caused by horizontal arms, whether a shoulder-hold like the Minoan male figures and many current Balkan dances (e.g., *fast hasápiko* and *varí hasápiko*), or a handhold with raised semicircular arms like the Minoan female figures and modern Macedonian women (see figs. 12.1, 3.8). Another characteristic Balkan and Hungarian handhold, known to dancers as a basket-hold, involves crossing arms with one's neighbor to catch the hand of the next person over—attested already in Greek paintings of the mid-first millennium BC (fig. 23.1). (A frequent variant of the crossed handhold, especially in Bulgaria and Serbia, consists of grasping your neighbor's belt near the center front, fig. 23.3: it gives more flexibility, allowing the men leaps and squats and the women a rhythmic wrist flutter.)

As on the Neolithic pots and Minoan models, all these holds serve to link dancers into a chain, whether in a circle or open-ended line. A dialect map of dance formations would show that chain dances with many participants occur all around Europe (from *sardana* to kolo to khorovod to "ring around the rosy"), but couple dances, before the advent of modern mass media, occurred principally in that half of Europe Christianized from Rome (Map 23). The watershed is quite marked, and exceptions are easily traceable. Turning dances like the polka (where you clutch your partner and spin as a unit) entered Russia via Catholic Poland and Lithuania; couple dances

---

what is to all intents the classic Spanish *jota*, but with a great deal more side-swish (as captured so wonderfully by the painter Josep Coll Bardolet), while the Basques perform essentially the same steps and sequences in both 3/4 and 4/4 time (*jota* and *porrusaldu* "leek soup," respectively), styled rather differently for the two rhythms. Moving up into southern France and the Dordogne, one finds *bourrées* (4/4) and even a *bourrée valsée* (3/4), again with essentially the same sequence of steps and two figures but styled yet differently, pounding into the earth rather than leaping skyward. I have not had the opportunity to follow it farther afield. The website connected with this book will attempt to continue such research.

FIG. 23.1. Dancing with crossed handhold. Top: Mural in Greek tomb, Ruvo, southeastern Italy, 4th century BC. Bottom: *Left*, mural in Church of Christ, Nesebŭr, Bulgaria, late 16th century; *right*, sketch of women in Megara, Greece, dancing *Trata* at Easter, 1890s.

in Greece, like the *ballos*, came from Catholic Italy into the islands ruled by Venice. Clearly the chain dances are the older form, since they occur all over Europe, whereas couple dances are spreading from the West like a great ink blot, obscuring but not entirely obliterating the older dance forms.*

Consider choreographically also the bride-testing dances, described in chapter 12, found from Dalmatia and Bosnia to Russia. In Bosnia, the man joins the women's circle beside the girl he wishes to test (see fig. 12.4). But in Russia, for example, the dance begins with facing groups or lines of young women and men who alternate showing off to each other (cf. fig. 12.2). Presently the man selects a woman and tests her strength and agility—a "couple dance" with a specific goal within the cultural mores. Within the current

---

*Maurice Louis (1963, 60–61) describes couple dances in the West as arising around 1400 from circle dances with men and women alternating. Etiquette and choreography caused the man to pay increasing attention to the lady on his right, so the dances gradually became in effect couple dances, as the medieval *carole* became the *bransle* of the Renaissance, and eventually the couples split out of the circle into separate entities. The American square dance, a circle of four couples, is not much beyond this.

FIG. 23.2. Young Vlach girls wearing string skirts, dancing with *călușari* in Serbian Banat.

folkdances (such as *Kamarinskaya* or *Polyanka*, which begin in facing lines), the couples' portion is now conveniently infiltrated by polka-based figures, yet the motivation for these dances is agrarian Neolithic. Indeed, one of the chief functions of traditional European dancing has long been to display each new crop of marriageable girls (fig. 23.2, see figs. 3.2, 12.1–4). We see this clearly in Classical Greece and in rural villages deep into the twentieth century, as well as glimpsing it between those dates and earlier. Girls spent much of their time dancing together—one reason why the willies were believed to dance together all the time.

Beyond the simple and obvious, such as walking, two motions in particular stand out as belonging to early agrarian dance rituals because of their frequency and the important symbolism attached. Jumping we have encountered repeatedly as a local form of analogic magic: the higher you rise, the higher the crops will grow, whether you rise over a fire, while swinging, or in dancing. The other movement consists of slapping the earth to awaken it, so it will start pushing the crops up. In some areas, Greece for example, people bend down and slap the ground with the hand while dancing, for this purpose.[6] In Bulgaria, Macedonia, Romania, and Serbia, it crystallizes as flat-footed slaps in front of oneself (fig. 23.3), different from a stamp or

FIG. 23.3. Bulgarian men dancing with belt-hold, performing characteristic flat-footed slap on ground.

a stomp—occurring, for instance, in *Florichika* and as typical variations in *kopanitsa, Gankino Horo*, and related dances.

Much has been made of circle dances as "sacred"—reverently encircling a sacred object or space, or maintaining an unbroken circle to exclude evil forces from the center or from the participants. Even more has been made of whether the circle rotates clockwise or not. Clockwise is the direction the sun appears to move in the Northern Hemisphere (since the sun's arc is always south of us). So clockwise is sunwise, hence perceived in the farming tradition as health-giving, good. Unfortunately, if you dance clockwise, you move to the left, which, according to the Bible, is the evil side, belonging to the devil. (Even in the twentieth century, some religious communities broke left-handed children's left hands to force them into right-handedness; and *sinister, gauche*, and *maladroit*, all expressing left-handedness, remain terms of abuse.) By the same token, if you dance to the right, the biblical good side, that's counterclockwise—anti-sunwise, widdershins—which the farmer viewed as ill-omened and unhealthful, proper only to the reversed spirit world.[7] This contradiction in interpreting the proper direction for dancing and other ritual movement goes back millennia, but improper or unwanted access to the spirit world is always the issue. Garfinkel, for example, cites evidence from the Mishnah that in Jewish tradition people normally moved and danced to the right unless acknowledging the world of the dead:

> "What aileth thee that thou goest to the left?"
> "Because I am a mourner." (*Middoth* 2.2)[8]

Some have claimed that, because Christianity condones only rightward movement, dances moving to the left are old pagan holdovers, while those moving to the right are Christian.[9] In that case, however, the Hungarians and Croatians, good Catholics all, do many a pagan dance, and so, for that matter, do the Israelis. These matters, however, are not so clear-cut. A single Hungarian dance, for example, may switch back and forth, a Yugoslav *kolo* likewise. Is only half of it pagan? Does starting on the right foot while moving left neutralize the evil? Then what about starting to the right but on the left foot?

Modern lifeways have now cut "folkdances" adrift from their original cultural moorings, making them harder to reconstruct. The Communists, notably intolerant of superstition, weaned folkdancing from religious observance by promoting it among the young people as communal recreation—muscular bonding leading to friendly rivalry among regions. Who had the most show-worthy dances? Which group could win contests with them? The advent of TV and (after the fall of the Iron Curtain) expanded tourism pushed folkdancing even further toward showmanship, elaborating on rather than "preserving" the traditions. (The same thing happened in the United States, years ago, when square dancers had to come up with ever showier figures for their weekly TV exhibitions.) And folkdance teachers—a new breed—have found it far easier to teach a prechoreographed set of figures, culled from what they had seen, than to inculcate the uncodified principles of the ways villagers improvised their variations.

❦

All these reconstructable patterns add to the evidence that people have been "keeping together in time" since the Palaeolithic, that beliefs about the Dancing Goddesses in particular must have begun in the Neolithic with the first farmers of Europe, and that not only fragments of these beliefs but scraps even of the dances themselves have survived to the present. Let us take one more quick look backward in time at this picturesque puzzle—there is always more to see—and set the pieces in place as best we can.

Dancing Divinity

When Hades ("Unseen One," a.k.a. Ploútōn "Wealth") abducted Kore ("Maiden") from a meadow to be his wife in the Underworld, Demeter ("Earth Mother"*) forgot to make the plants grow as she searched frantically for her daughter. In grief and frustration, Demeter finally withdrew from the world, taking refuge—according to Greek myth—with a family at Eleusis, near Athens, and as she pined, refusing all food, the whole earth withered. Finally a woman from the family did a dance so comically obscene that even Demeter giggled. The spell was broken, Demeter began to eat, and life began to return. The world was rescued. The food she accepted, called *kykeōn*, was a gruel of grain boiled in water, flavored with mint.[1] It's no accident that this food resembles the ritual all-seed that we traced back to the Neolithic. And we know mint was recognized already in the Bronze Age, for our word *mint* comes via Greek *míntha* from the Bronze Age Minoan language of Crete. Mint is another of those powerfully—magically—aromatic herbs like thyme and Cretan dittany for which Crete is still known.

There are two versions of who the divine stripteaser was. According to Attic tradition, she was the family's daughter, named Iámbē (apparently

---

*Etymologists generally agree that the name *Dē-mḗtēr* ends with the Indo-European root for "mother" (cognate with English *mother*), but they can't entirely agree on the first portion.

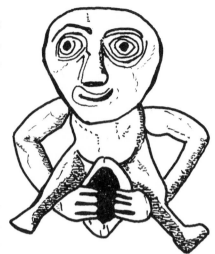

FIG. 24.1. *Sheela-na-gig.* Apotropaic stone carving, on church in Kilpeck, Herefordshire.

related to the iambic rhythm); the Orphic tradition of Thrace presents her as the wife, named Baubó. Baubo eventually came to be portrayed as an *old* woman, one who has already borne children, and turns up still today in the northern Greek Carnival mummeries as Babo, toting her child in a win-nowing basket (cf. fig. 19.4). Her name, from a word for a woman's pudenda,[2] implies that the dancer actually displayed her crotch, just like the old Irish *sheela-na-gig* sculptures that guard gates, doorways, and other places of entry with a blatant gesture thereto (fig. 24.1)* The female body, with its ability to produce life, was as usual viewed as magically potent, and Demeter is restored to her duties by seeing a dancing female flaunting that sexuality.

Baubo is no willy, nor is Iambe, but their dance has the same effect as that of the willies—jump-starting the cycle of reproduction. This wider con-text helps us see yet more clearly the nature of the Dancing Goddesses.

Women, in these agrarian societies, had the central duty of becoming successful mothers, of reproducing and maintaining the chain of life, just as the seedcorn must do for the crops. Only then could they die "perfected" and proceed to the Underworld, just as a warrior had to expire not in his bed but in battle to die fulfilled.[3] This perfection merely restates another

---

*The reader will have noticed many parallels, drawn here and there, to Celtic customs and beliefs. One must remember that the Celts and their direct ancestors (Hallstatt culture) lived in central Europe throughout the Bronze Age, neighbors to the proto-Slavs and vari-ous Iranian peoples, before migrating to the Atlantic coast in historical Roman times. Now that the central European belief system is laid out, someone could make interesting work of tracing the Celtic reflexes.

requirement we've seen many times: the ritually perfect child must have both its parents still living, part of an undamaged family.

Girls who died *before* successful motherhood had, however, failed. They had broken the chain and gotten lost in the transition between girl and woman, daughter and wife, Maiden and Mother, offspring and parent. No wonder everyone labored to surround the bride with all possible magic to guard her from evils during this dangerous transition. The terrible consequence of failure was that lost souls were doomed to wander. They could not rest quietly underground but joined the Restless Dead.*

Enter the Dancing Goddesses, girl souls still carrying the fertility so desperately needed for human families, fields, and flocks to prosper. They were believed to live near, but not quite in, the areas they knew when alive. They lived in limbo, doing what they did in girlhood: dancing in the fields and swinging from the trees, bringing promise of the next round of life.

Perhaps the original defining moment for the lore of the spirit maidens appears, however, in the old Russian form of Semik, stemming from the unavoidable need for girls to become mothers. Childbearing is both painful and dangerous even today; without anesthetics, disinfectants, obstetricians, and surgeons, it was far, far worse.† Euripides had his heroine Medea point out that society absolutely required a woman to marry and thought women had it easy, staying home. But, she concludes,

> *Three times in battle would I rather stand,*
> *than once in childbirth.*[4]

At Semik, as we saw, the girls went off to the greening woods, appeased the willies, and bonded through dance, swearing always to help and support each other. Then, joined by the young men (and liquor), they took the fateful plunge. The whole rite, once paralleled all over Europe by the rituals of May

---

*Well worth reading is Sarah Johnston's perceptive chapter on the ancient Greek problem of "Childless Mothers and Blighted Virgins" in her excellent book *The Restless Dead* (1999). Note, too, that magic was once associated with *everything* that undergoes transformation: seed to plant, maiden to mother, clay to pottery, ore to metal, metal to weapon or tool, fluff to thread, milk to butter, and so on. Magic rituals sought to keep the transformation from going wrong.

† Kristof and WuDunn (2009, 116) provide the remarkable statistic that, "during World War I, more American women died in childbirth than American men died in war."

Day and Midsummer's Eve, was not "just" an immoral orgy, as the later puritanical critics maintained, but rather a pragmatic approach to dicey necessity. Farmers, who depend on fruitfulness to survive, simply have a different set of problems from us city dwellers (including the urbanites who developed the Christian church), who must *curb* our fruitfulness if we are to survive.

⌒∞⌒

Iambe and Baubo are not alone in dancing the ultimate life-bringing dance, the one that saves the world. In Japanese mythology, the bejeweled goddess Amaterasu was born from the left eye of the god Izanagi. She shone so brightly that her father sent her to rule the celestial heights as sun goddess. Her brother Susanoo was sent to rule the waters as the storm god, but he was so obstreperous that he drove her crazy with all his noise. Finally, when he threw a dead horse through the roof of her divine weaving hut, she had had enough and withdrew in a huff to a cave, shutting it with a stone so that no light escaped. With no sunshine, the whole world began to wither. The gods considered what to do. They hung a jeweled mirror in front of the cave and

fetched a rooster. Then the young goddess Uzume began a striptease dance, making the gods laugh loudly at her obscene antics (fig. 24.2). Curious at hearing laughter during so grave an impasse, Amaterasu finally peeked out, releasing a ray of light—upon which the

FIG. 24.2. Uzume, Japanese goddess of mirth and dancing, doing comically obscene dance on upturned tub, to entice angry sun goddess Amaterasu out of cave.

gods made the rooster crow, simulating dawn. Seeing the bright light—her own, reflected in the mirror—and hearing the crowing, Amaterasu thought another sun deity must have appeared, and she emerged to inspect her rival. The gods hastily stretched a magic rope across the cave mouth so she could not reenter it, and the world was rescued.

How happens it that two stories of strip-dancing goddesses saving the vegetal world at opposite ends of Eurasia are so similar? Chance seems a bit far-fetched; the more we learn of trans-Eurasian contacts in the Bronze Age, the less unlikely borrowing seems.[5] A third possibility is that circumstances within early agrarian life led to somewhat similar stories. We don't know—many far-reaching avenues of research remain in dealing with this subject—but these myths add new dimensions to the notion of Dancing Goddesses.

When that remarkable structure we call language colonized our developing brains in the Upper Palaeolithic, we added linguistic ways of representing reality to our mimetic ones.[6] Language is based on sentence structures ("propositions"), which we link together into narratives, story lines. Until we advanced so far technologically that we could develop external memory banks to lean on—first accounting (7000 BC), then writing (3400 BC) and libraries, then reading to oneself (400 BC), then computers—we pretty much stuck to narrative. In fact, most people have always stuck to narrative: learning abstract logic and analysis take a lot of effort and training, and we still aren't very good at them. As Merlin Donald points out, around the dinner table we still swap stories of the day and hammer out a collective oral version of events. Narrative remains our most comfortable mode of thinking and of framing our world.[7]

The nonliterate agrarian cultures of Europe were no different—*rural farmers interpreted and recounted their needs and events as narratives*. A puzzling change in one's health had a story of agents behind it. Weddings unfolded stage by stage as a microcosm mimicking a story of the macrocosm; each bride and groom reenacted the entire narrative of the divine marriage. Every fertilized, nubile girl was the Frog Princess. The yearly cycle of the crops unfurled as a cosmic tale, with divine participants doing their bit at every stage, commemorated in the sequence of festivals that marked off each passing year. Key among the participants were the dead ancestors, laid away underground whence the buried seeds sprouted, and the willies, dead but not ancestral, bringing the growing-power from the rivers and clouds each spring as an overt act. (The power is not there in the winter, so willful agents must have to bring it in the spring.) The trick was to get these spirits to carry it into the sown fields instead of only into the wilds. Nothing just happened; it all belonged to episodes of connected stories, narratives, myths. To see the coherence and logic of their approach, we have to look at the whole system: as long as we just look at little bits, the way urban scholars tend to do, the little pieces seem quite off the wall. In this case, traditional views about the world of spirits and the habits of the dead are as basic to the entire narrative system as logic and hard evidence are to modern science.

Since stories are constructed from actions and actors, and since the world has long been viewed as willful, people have long asked, "Who did it?" rather than, "What might have caused it?" when something happened.[8] It takes an enormous amount of knowledge, stockpiled with the help of writing, to figure out how plants and embryos actually grow. But immediate satisfaction flows from *a story that covers the apparent facts* of the case. If the stories we've investigated seem strange, remember that until Kepler, Galileo, and Copernicus, Europeans thought the sun went around the earth. This narrative covered the apparent facts quite well until the newfangled telescope demonstrated that our facts were inadequate—and even then it took the church four hundred years to absolve Galileo of heresy.

The Dancing Goddesses constitute a narrative view, coherent within itself, of the everyday events and needs of the agricultural life of their communities. It is not the only possible view; it is the one that happened to develop in early agrarian Europe, and it fertilized a rich tradition of dance.

Bracelets from Kiev
with Ritual Motifs

The most thorough sources I know for the eleventh-through-thirteenth-century Kievan bracelets (and their casting molds) are Rybakov 1967 and 1968 (here called R1967/68; some illustrations—mostly drawings—are clearer in the 1967 Russian version, others in the 1968 English translation), Rybakov 1971 (R1971, with many photographs), Rybakov 2001 (R2001), and Darkevich and Mongayt 1967. For ease and compactness of reference, I have assigned the bracelets letters (as in Barber 1999c). Those of interest to this study, and that I can trace, are:

A: Identical pair, gilded silver; ultralong-sleeved dancer and bagpiper, repeated; bird and hare, repeated; froglike vines, interlaces, arches. Provenance unknown; State Historical Museum, Moscow; R1967/68: figs. 10, 15 above; R1971: figs. 159–60. See **figs. 3.10, 13.8**.

B: Silver, niello: ultralong-sleeved female dancer, male dancer with sword and shield, gusli player; Simargls, bird, vines, arches. Kiev; Kiev State Historical Museum; R1967/68: fig. 12; R1971: figs. 42, 149–53. See **fig. 13.8**.

C, C': Nonidentical pair, gilded silver, niello. C: ultralong-sleeved dancer drinking (mask beside foot), gusli player, beverage drinker with staff or pipe; three Simargls, two with sown-field motif on collar; birds, vines, interlaces; arches. C': Simargls, vines, arches. Starïy Ryazan'; Ryazan' Regional Museum; Darkevich and Mongayt 1967 (chief publication, many photos); R1971: figs. 157–58. See **figs. 13.2, 13.8, 17.7**.

D: Casting mold: ultralong-sleeved dancer, bagpiper, beverage drinker; arches. Serensk (hoard), Kaluga province; R1967/68: fig. 11; Nikol'skaya 1981: fig. 48.16. See **fig. 13.8**.

E: Bracelet: Simargls, birds, froglike vines, interlace with X-in-O. Trubetskoy estate, Kiev; R1967/68: fig. 3. See **fig. 17.7.**

F: Bracelet: bird girls, trees of life; vines, interlaces, XX, arches. Rakovskiy estate, Kiev; R1967/68: fig. 8; Váňa 1983:141. See **figs. 13.8, 17.7.**

G: Bracelet: male dancer with spear and hat; birds, arches. Demidovo, near Odessa, Ukraine; R1967/68: fig. 13. See **fig. 13.8.**

H: Silver, niello: male dancer, two beverage drinkers (one bending Simargl to earth); two Simargls, tree of life; froglike vines, interlaces, arches. Tver' (hoard); State Russian Museum, St. Petersburg; R1967/68: fig. 14, 18; R1971: figs. 145–48. See **fig. 13.8, 13.9.**

I: Nonidentical pair, silver, niello: lion with double X-in-O and birds flanking tree of life, repeated; vines with X-in-O, interlaces. Mikhaylovskiy Monastery, Kiev; State Historical Museum, Moscow; Rice 1963: fig. 3; R1967/68: fig. 7L; R1971: fig. 14. See **fig. 17.7.**

J: Silver, niello: bird creatures, interlaces, arches. Kiev (hoard); State Russian Museum, St. Petersburg; R1971: fig. 43.

K: Silver, niello: birds (Simargls?), interlaces. Pechernïy/Vladimir (hoard); State Historical Museum, Moscow; R1971: fig. 15.

L: Gilded silver: bird creatures, interlaces. Pechernïy/Vladimir (hoard); State Historical Museum, Moscow; R1971: fig. 44.

M: Silver, niello: Simargls, birds, vines, interlaces, arches. Terekhov (hoard); State Russian Museum, St. Petersburg, R1967/68: fig. 15 below; R1971: fig. 45; R2001: fig. 129a. See **fig. 3.10.**

N: Gilded silver, niello: two birds pecking tree-of-life interlace growing from two Simargls, hare, lion; vines, interlaces. Provenance unstated; State Russian Museum, St. Petersburg; R1967/68: fig. 16 center R; R1971: figs. 154–56.

O: Hoard of bracelets, at least three hinged: floral (unclear). Lyubech Castle; Rybakov 1965:89. See **fig. 13.2.**

P: Casting mold: peak-hatted Simargls in interlace; avian Simargls in interlace; interlaces cross-shaped. Kiev; R1967/68: fig. 9; R2001: fig. 134a. See **fig. 17.7.**

Q, Q': Nonidentical pair. Q: swordsman, bird girl, Simargl; vines, interlaces, arches. Q': Sawtooth pattern in granulated gold. Provenance unstated; Ukrainian National Museum; *Gold aus Kiew* 1993:315–16.

R, S: Unattributed: birds with tail and wings forming X-in-O. Stylistically similar to Mikhaylovskiy Monastery bracelets (I); R1967/68: figs. 7R, 16 bottom R. See **fig. 17.7.**

Notes

PART I
CHAPTER 1

1. Zelenin 1916, 146.
2. Dobrovol'skiy 1908, 12.
3. Maksimov 1903/1994, 87–88.
4. After Marinov 1914, 204–5, who lists references to variants from several places in Bulgaria and Macedonia. The version in Shturbanova and Ilieva (1994, 86–87) is close to Marinov's; the slightly different one in Nicoloff (1983, 117–18) is in verse, translated charmingly by Henry Bernard in 1904 (#54, 157–59).
5. Lawson 1909/1964, 130–32.
6. Vakarelski 1969, 231–32.
7. Cf. Zelenin 1916, 119.
8. Zelenin 1916, 128.
9. Zelenin 1916, 137–41, 148, 222.
10. Vakarelski, 230–1.
11. Krauss 1890, 71–75; Jurić 2010.
12. Lawson, 143, 132–33.
13. Stratilesco 1906, 186.
14. Zelenin 1916, 155, 158–60; 132; Lawson, 184, 187–89; 179.
15. Zelenin 1916, 163; Lawson, 133, 135.
16. Zelenin 1916, 163–64.
17. Dobrovol'skiy, 13.
18. Dobrovol'skiy, 13.
19. Zelenin 1916, 131, 133.
20. Lawson, 134.
21. Maksimov, 88; cf. Zelenin 1916, 136.
22. Funk and Wagnalls *Standard Dictionary of Folklore* ("iron," 529), Zelenin 1916, 171; Lawson, 140; Puckett 1981, #25668, #26475 (Italian culture), and #25533 (Russian); Ó Danachair (1973) discusses iron amulets in Ireland.
23. Lawson, 140.
24. Zelenin 1916, 168–69; Lawson, 133, 141, 146, 148.
25. Zelenin 1916, 169.
26. Vakarelski, 230.
27. Lawson, 136–37.
28. Zelenin 1916, 128.

29. Zelenin 1916, 135.
30. Gogol, *May Night*, chap. 13 (quoted in Zelenin 1916, 136).
31. Zelenin 1916, 152–53.
32. Zelenin 1916, 161–62; Krauss 1908, 37.
33. Vakarelski, 235.
34. Zelenin 1916, 153, 166.
35. Vakarelski, 231.
36. Dobrovol'skiy, 15–16.
37. Zelenin 1916, 153, 164.
38. Krauss 1890, 102.
39. Zelenin 1916, 132–33.
40. Dobrovol'skiy, 16.
41. Zelenin 1916, 148.

CHAPTER 2

1. Kennan 1870/1903, 345.
2. Brumfield 1981, 13–15, 19–23, 40.
3. Rybakov 1968, 40.
4. Rybakov 1968, 39.
5. Maslova 1978, 131; Rybakov 1981, 508–9 (illustration missing in new edition).
6. Rybakov 1981, 307.
7. Propp 1987, 78.

CHAPTER 3

1. Propp 1963, 60–61.
2. Rappoport 1913, 44; similar to Poltoratzky 1964, 44.
3. Propp 1987, 73–77.
4. Zavoyko, in Propp 1963, 61–62.
5. See Barber and Barber 2005, chapter 6, for "willfulness" throughout mythology.
6. Propp 1987, 43–44; Alexander 1975, 27; Sokolov 1938/1950, 191.
7. Propp 1963, 33.
8. Nicoloff, 68.
9. Propp 1963, 32.
10. Propp 1987, 88–93; Sokolov, 190.

11. Rappoport, 38–39.
12. Barber and Barber, chapter 7.
13. Russ 1983, 42–44; Gallop 1970, 197; Robson 1930, 75–76.
14. Cf. Propp 1987, 138.
15. Vassileva 1982, 24.
16. Vassileva, 16; Aleksieva and Ancheva (1990s), 31.
17. Ilieva and Shturbanova 1997, 311–13.
18. Kazarova 1935, 62.
19. Aleksieva and Ancheva, 28.
20. Lazarouvanè song, details: Aleksieva and Ancheva, 27–29, 36; 33.
21. Vassileva, 18.
22. Kazarova, 68; cf. Aleksieva and Ancheva, 32.
23. Aleksieva and Ancheva, 27.
24. Aleksieva and Ancheva, 32.
25. Cf. Propp 1987, 69.
26. Lawson, 573.
27. Lawson, 575.
28. Cf. Propp 1987, 26.
29. E.g., Haase 1980, 94, with references.
30. Nicoloff, 82–83; Róheim 1926, 366–75.
31. Drazheva 1982, 17–19.
32. Róheim, 375.
33. Ilieva 1977, 5.
34. Drazheva, 14.
35. Barber 1999b, 29–30; Williams 1999, 137–39.
36. Eliade 1951/1964, 205, quoting Harva for data.
37. Full discussion in Barber and Barber, chapter 15.
38. Katzarova-Kukudova and Djenev 1958, 37–38; Nicoloff 75–76.
39. Zelenin 1916, 235.
40. Propp 1987, 147.
41. Selivanov, in Propp 1987, 148.
42. Propp 1987, 149–50, and 1963, 130–31.

43. Poltoratzky, 41.
44. Stubbes 1583, chapter 13.
45. Propp 1987, 149–50.
46. Propp 1987, 150.

CHAPTER 4

1. Afanasiev, tale #148: "Nikita the Tanner."
2. Dömötör and Eperjessy 1967, 401.
3. Stoilov 1900, 293.
4. Derebanov 1897; cf. Ilieva and Shturbanova, 318.
5. Stoilov, 293.
6. Derebanov.
7. Stratilesco, 182.
8. Aleksieva and Ancheva, 15, 19.
9. Dömötör and Eperjessy, 401.
10. Shturbanova and Ilieva, 82–84.
11. Stoilov, 293–94.
12. Eckert 1951, 99.
13. Stratilesco, 17, 183.
14. Stratilesco, 183.
15. Fischer 1908, 15; also Zelenchuk and Popovich 1976, 197.
16. Zelenchuk and Popovich, 197.
17. Fischer, 15.
18. Zelenchuk and Popovich, 196.
19. Haase, 138.
20. Puchner 1982, 107–8.
21. Wace and Thompson 1914, 133; more in Beza 1928, 28–29.
22. Wace and Thompson, 133; Eckert, 99–100.
23. Schneeweis 1934–35, 177.
24. Jordan 1985; Barber and Barber, 171.

CHAPTER 5

1. Marinov 1914, 482.
2. Marinov 1914, 476.
3. Zelenin 1916, 137–41, 148, 222.
4. Marinov 1914, 477.
5. Marinov 1914, 476.
6. Marinov 1914, 477.
7. Marinov 1914, 486.
8. Marinov 1914, 477–86.
9. Marinov 1914, 482.
10. Marinov 1914, 484.
11. Marinov 1914, 485.
12. Marinov 1914, 484–85.
13. Kulišić 1966, XIII.
14. Beza, 42–53.
15. Beza, 47.
16. Beza, 47–48.
17. Beza, 44–45.
18. Beza, 45.
19. Beza, 46.
20. Kligman 1981, 32, 77.
21. Kligman, 2–3.
22. Kligman, 13.
23. Kligman, 27.
24. Kligman, 3, 6–8.
25. Kligman, 10.
26. Kligman, 9.
27. Kligman, 10.
28. Kligman, 19.
29. Kligman, 24.
30. Kligman, 20.
31. Kligman, 20–26.
32. Kligman, 41.
33. Kligman, 32.
34. Kligman, 69.
35. Kligman, 175.
36. Kligman, 74.
37. Kligman, 79.
38. Kligman, 37.
39. Aleksieva and Ancheva, 44.
40. Rappoport, 58–59.
41. Aleksieva and Ancheva, 40–43.
42. Aleksieva and Ancheva, 42; Ilieva and Shturbanova, 315.
43. Kligman, 63–64.
44. Gligorić 1893, 286–87.
45. Gligorić, 304–5.
46. Kuret 1973, 343–44.
47. Kuret, 338–39.

48. Dobrovol'skiy, 14.
49. Ilieva and Shturbanova, 313.

CHAPTER 6

1. Barber 1994, 49.
2. Arnaudov 1917, 5–6.
3. Sarianidi 1994, 388–97.
4. Marinov 1914, 62.
5. Kemp 1935, 234, 232.
6. Rytz and Schwartzenbach 1960, pl. 22.
7. Marinov 1914, 63.
8. Kemp, 95.
9. Arnaudov 1917, 59.
10. Kemp, 94.
11. Turner 1551/1989, 304.
12. Kemp, 52.
13. Wenzel 1967, 374 n.75; Kemp, 90–92.
14. Kemp, 144.
15. John Colarusso, pers. comm. 2/17/09.

CHAPTER 7

1. Nicoloff, 84.
2. Propp 1987, 79.
3. Arnaudov 1917, 70.
4. Propp 1987, 79.
5. Marinov 1914, 489.
6. Marinov 1914, 489.
7. Marinov 1914, 490.
8. Dias 1973, 61.
9. Ralston 1872/1970, 241–42.
10. Ryan 1999, 47.
11. Arnaudov 1917, 70; Marinov 1914, 490–91.
12. Marinov 1914, 491–92.
13. Arnaudov 1917, 71.
14. Propp 1987, 79.
15. Marinov 1914, 492.
16. Marinov 1914, 492–93; Shturbanova and Ilieva, 88.
17. Marinov 1914, 494.

18. Katzarova-Kukudova and Djenev, 43.
19. Marinov 1914, 493–96.
20. Marinov 1914, 496–97.
21. Marinov 1914, 504.
22. Katzarova-Kukudova and Djenev, 44.
23. Marinov 1914, 498.
24. Ushakov 1896, 164.
25. Russ, 68.
26. Giurchescu and Bloland 1992, 40, 25; Haase, 10, 20; Propp 1987, 28, 103–4.
27. Ralston, 240.
28. Ralston, 240; Propp 1987, 103.
29. Propp 1987, 103.
30. Barandiarán 2007, 77.
31. Barandiarán, 110.
32. Propp 1987, 103.
33. Propp 1987, 113.
34. Sheyn, in Propp 1987, 97.
35. Sheyn, in Propp 1987, 97.
36. Propp 1963:80.
37. Propp 1963, 80.
38. Propp 1987, 98 (=1963, 80).
39. Propp 1987, 105–8, 117–18.
40. Ó Duinn 2005, 129–30.

CHAPTER 8

1. Zelenin 1916, 131, 133, 171–72.
2. Zelenin 1916, 163–64; Dobrovol'skiy, 13.
3. Ralston, 141; Zelenin 1916, 171.
4. Lawson, 133–34.
5. Afanasiev, tale #104.
6. Rappoport, 34–35.
7. Barber 1994, 235–39, quoting Seligman.
8. Zerubavel 1985, 6–7.
9. Zerubavel, 8.
10. Zerubavel, 9–11.
11. Zerubavel, 16.

12. Rausing 1995.

13. Delehaye 1921, 134, 236–39.

14. Halkin 1966, 226–28.

15. Halkin, 230.

16. Delehaye 1921, 195.

17. Constantinou 2005, 28.

18. Halkin, 230 n.24.

19. Levin 2006, 134.

20. Halkin, 228 n.16.

21. Haase, 182.

22. Warner 2002, 17.

23. Warner, 19.

24. Warner, 17.

25. Loukatos 1975, 89–90.

26. Haase, 183.

27. Dixon-Kennedy 1998, 214.

28. Zelenin 1916, 233.

29. Haase, 183.

30. Zelenin 1916, 233.

31. Dixon-Kennedy, 214.

32. Haase, 183.

33. Haase, 184.

34. Baranova et al. 2001, 365–66.

35. Warner, 21.

36. Megas, 144–45.

37. Haase, 183–84.

38. Kemp, 99.

39. Baranova et al., 366.

40. Ryan, 50–52.

41. Dixon-Kennedy, 213.

42. Dixon-Kennedy, 214.

CHAPTER 9

1. Megas 1958, 33.

2. Megas, 33.

3. Tille 1899, 108–15.

4. Liungman 1938, 675–76; see also Kutter 1973, 348–50.

5. Megas, 45–46.

6. Russ, 16; Wolfram 1951, 46.

7. Wolfram 1951, 45, quoting Spaur.

8. Wolfram 1951, 29, 44–46.

9. Wolfram 1951, 46.

10. Peate 1943.

11. Ettlinger 1944.

12. Lawson, 191–95.

13. Megas, 35.

14. Pócs 1989, 22–23, 77.

15. Megas, 34.

16. Liungman, 622–23.

17. Kuret, 334, citing also Mircea Eliade.

18. Liungman, 413–18.

19. Liungman, 407–26.

20. Liungman, 693.

21. Tille, 135.

22. Tille, 8–16, 71.

23. Tille, 7, 20, 147.

24. Ó Duinn, 200–201; Tille, 20–26, 58–71, 127.

25. Gaster 1955, 7, 1961, 17.

26. Gaster 1955, 82; Propp 1987, 37; Liungman, 620–22.

27. Gaster 1955, 59–60.

28. Wace 1912–13, 249.

29. Wace 1909, 233, 236–37.

30. Wace 1912–13, 248.

31. Dawkins 1904–5, 72–73.

32. Wace 1909, 243.

33. Liungman, 795, 823.

34. Alford 1937, 16–25.

35. Sheyn in Propp 1987, 130.

36. Sheyn in Propp 1963, 112.

37. Dawkins 1906, 193–97.

38. Newall 1980, 7, 19.

39. Arnaudov 1917, 31.

40. Propp 1963, 49; 1987, 63.

41. Gaster 1955, 63–65; Megas, 38.

42. Ó Duinn, 210.

43. Arnaudov 1917, 16–17.

44. Sanders 1949, 106–7; Megas, 47.

45. Gaster 1955, 57.

46. Gaster 1955, 63; Liungman, 654.

47. Megas, 48; Gaster 1955, 63; Liungman, 410, 426.

48. Propp 1987, 125–27.
49. Gallop, 194–96; Alford 1937, 23, 142.
50. Liungman, 893–924, 1007–9; Pócs, 52, 67 n.19.
51. Giurchescu and Bloland, 38.
52. Ginzburg 1992, esp. 89–92.
53. Gaster 1955, 28–29.
54. Gaster 1955, 37; Russ, 28; MacDermott 1998, 184.
55. Gaster 1955, 47.
56. Liungman, 916.
57. Megas, 37.

PART II
CHAPTER 10

1. Greimas 1992, 173.
2. Balashov et al. 1985, 29.
3. Alexander, 53.
4. Kolpakova 1973, 78.
5. Kelly 1989, figs. 95–96.
6. Mahler 1960, 8.
7. Uspenskiy 1981/1984, 298.
8. Kramer 1963, 140.
9. Ivashneva and Razumovskaia 1981, 35, 41; Ivanova 1987, 53–55; Pushkareva 1990–91, 63.
10. Baron 1967, 164.
11. Curtin 1890/1971, 124–36.
12. Ryall 1989, 38.
13. Pushkareva, 61.
14. Mahler, 12.
15. Ivanova, 9.
16. Ivanova, 61.
17. Cf. Ivashneva and Razumovskaia, 44.

CHAPTER 11

1. Quoted by Ivanova, 13.
2. Ivashneva and Razumovskaia, 34.
3. Sokolov, 207–8.
4. Sokolov, 207–8.
5. Mahler, 293–94.

6. Ivashneva and Razumovskaia, 39.
7. Ivanova, 22–24.
8. Mahler, 304.
9. Mahler, 298.
10. Ivashneva and Razumovskaia, 46.
11. Ivashneva and Razumovskaia, 35, 51.
12. Ivanova, 26.
13. Ivanova, 22 photo.
14. Ivashneva and Razumovskaia, 35.
15. Mahler, 5.
16. Rabinovich 1981, 67–68.

CHAPTER 12

1. Danforth 1989, 29–30, 77–79.
2. Jung-Stilling 1777/1976, 6–7, 21–22.
3. Rappoport, 39.
4. Baron, 48–49.
5. Rabinovich, 56.
6. Rabinovich, 56–57.
7. Propp 1963, 30 (=1987, 43).
8. Zelenin 1927, 309.

CHAPTER 13

1. Froianov et al. 1990–91, 14–15.
2. Zelenin 1927, 206 and pl. II fig. 250; Rybakov 1968, 38; Sosnina, 1984.
3. Krvavych and Stel'mashchuk 1988, 112.
4. Zelenin 1927, 205–6.
5. Baron, 129.
6. Baron, 128.
7. Ivanova, 31 photo.
8. Mahler, 327.
9. Propp 1963, 65 (=1987, 81).
10. Andersen 1977, 25, after Guest.
11. Andersen, 26.
12. Baron, 96.
13. Rybakov 1989, 378–79.
14. Darkevich and Mongayt 1967, 217 and fig. 6.
15. Propp 1963, 131–32 (*Stoglav* Q24).
16. Rybakov 1968, 40.

17. Rybakov 1968, 40 (*Izbornik*).
18. Rybakov 1968, 40.
19. Rybakov 1968, 39.
20. Propp 1987, 134–35.
21. Baron, 168.
22. Gross 1900; Neve 1976; Beck 2005, 183.
23. Rybakov 1968.

CHAPTER 14

1. Hatto 1961, 331.
2. Hatto, 336.
3. Hatto, 350.
4. Brazil 2003, 68.
5. Gimbutas 1982, 176–79.

CHAPTER 15

1. Kravchenko 1987, 189.
2. Kravchenko, 111–12, 121–23, 168–73.
3. Rappoport, 58.
4. Anikin, quoted by Kravchenko, 190.
5. Zelenin 1927, 253–56.
6. Rabinovich, 60.
7. Rabinovich, 69.
8. Rabinovich, 69.
9. Pushkareva, 61.
10. Rudenko 1970, 285; Barber 1991, 17–18, 26–28; 1999a, 162–63.

CHAPTER 16

1. Vasmer 1950–58/1964–73, *sv.* Кощей.
2. Kemp, 6.
3. Kemp, 15–16, with reference.
4. Suslov, in Menges, 4–6.
5. Kemp, 16.
6. Kemp, 6.
7. Ginzburg, 10.

PART III
CHAPTER 17

1. Rybakov 1967, 96–97.
2. Rybakov 1968, 34.

3. Wenzel 1967, 370.
4. Wenzel 1967, 370–74.
5. Ivanova, 51; Genchev 1988, 86.
6. Kligman, 64.
7. See, e.g., Wolfram 1932; Alford 1962; Corrsin 1997.
8. Propp 1987, 75; Rybakov 1968, 53.
9. Chadwick 1946, 157–59.
10. Rybakov 1968, 35.
11. Rybakov 1968, 45–46.
12. Rybakov 1968, 40.
13. Zguta 1978, 15, 48–49.
14. Zguta, 10.
15. Zguta, 14.
16. Zguta, 11.
17. Zguta, 11–12.
18. Zguta, 11.
19. Zguta, 12.

CHAPTER 18

1. K. Morris 1991, 6.
2. Chambers 1903, 94.
3. Pócs, 24.
4. Chambers 1903, 2, 6.
5. Liungman, 1125–26.
6. Ovid, *Fasti* iii. 543–656.
7. Chambers 1903, 237.
8. Chambers 1903, 236–38; Salzman 1990, 75, 80–81.
9. Chambers 1903, 328, 384; Liungman, 739, 1017, 1126–28.
10. Chambers 1903, 329; Liungman, 910.
11. Liungman, 721.
12. Chambers 1903, 6; Liungman, 722–25.
13. Chambers 1903, 384–85; Liungman, 717–21.
14. Chambers 1903, 42–43.
15. Cirilli 1913, 147, 15; Staples 1998, 150.
16. Corssan, in Cirilli, 98.

17. Cirilli, 27, 102, 97–98.
18. Cirilli, 82–88; Liungman, 738.
19. Cirilli, 56–57, 69–70.
20. Vulpesco 1927, 204–5.
21. Vulpesco; Larson (pers. comm.).
22. Cirilli, 128, 133–34.
23. Cirilli, 143–44.
24. Cirilli, 22–25, 96.
25. Frazer 1931, 390; Salzman, 241.
26. Ovid, *Fasti* v. 429–44; Frazer 1931, 424–25; Perowne 1969, 82.
27. Beard et al. 1998, 73–77; Salzman, 97–98, 129.
28. Rose 1959, 24.
29. Rose, 24; Liungman, 586–93; Dumézil 1970, 392, 500.
30. Ginzburg, 105; Burchard of Worms, quoted by Liungman, 593.
31. Pócs, 14.
32. Ginzburg, 104.
33. Liungman 582–83.
34. Brouwer 1989; Staples; Johannowsky et al. 1983.
35. Liungman, 627.
36. Ginzburg, 93.
37. Ginzburg, 93–97.

CHAPTER 19

1. Harrison 1962, 3–7.
2. Apollodorus iii. 4.3.
3. Hoddinott 1981, 11–13.
4. Cf. Harrison 1962, 48.
5. Plutarch, *Moralia: Isis and Osiris* xxxv/364e–f.
6. *Moralia* 249e.
7. Athenaeus xiv.628d–e.
8. Murray, in Harrison 1962, 341–63.
9. *Moralia: Isis and Osiris* xxxv/364e–365b.
10. Florence Grove, quoted by Chambers 1903, 211n.
11. M. Campbell 1938, 10, in Brody 1969, 25.

12. Harrison 1922, 415–16, 420–21.
13. Harrison 1962, 318–22, 502–3; 1922, 548.
14. Cf. Harrison 1922, 518–23, 528–31.
15. Harrison 1922, 403–4; Rose, 149.
16. Harrison 1922, 416–17.
17. Harrison 1922, 417.
18. Harrison 1922, 275.
19. Pausanias viii.37; Rose, 67.
20. Burkert 1985, 240.
21. Harrison 1922, 36–63.
22. Rose, 123.
23. Rose, 113.
24. Barber 1992.
25. Ovid, *Metamorphoses* xi.243–45; Rose, 26.
26. Pausanias viii.41.4–6.
27. Jost 1985, pl. 45.
28. Anthony 2010, fig. 9-5.
29. Trippett 1974, 22.
30. Klochko 1992; Barber 1999c.
31. Barber 1999c.
32. Louis 1963, 11.

CHAPTER 20

1. Burkert 1985, 42.
2. Lawler 1946, 124–25.
3. Solinus ii.8; Rose, 117, 131; Roscher 1884–1937, 822–28.
4. Strabo x.4.13.
5. Durasov and Jakovleva 1990, 30.
6. Levi 1951, pl. 4.
7. Levi, 119 fig. 4; Persson 1931, fig. 43, pl. 25.
8. Tacitus, *Germania* 40; Davidson 1981, 94–95; Herodotus i.60.
9. Burkert 1988.
10. Barber 1991, 20–30.
11. Kristiansen and Larsson 2005.
12. Puhvel 1987, 271, 273; Alford 1978, 13–15.
13. *Iliad* 16.149–51; 17.426–40; 19.404–20.

14. Saxo, xiv; Tacitus, *Germania* 10.
15. Alford 1978, 118.
16. Ryan, 109.
17. Piggott 1962; Mair 2007.
18. Koşay 1951, pl. 191.
19. Alford 1978, xxi, 4–7, 12, 63, 128, 138–39 and passim.
20. Dumézil 1929, 26, 37.
21. Alford 1937, 145–46 (197 for "White Mare"); Gallop, 198–99.
22. Alford 1939, 231.

CHAPTER 21

1. Chap. 2 verse 31, after Chateaubriand.
2. Bradley 2005, 168.
3. Garfinkel, 56–57.
4. Garfinkel, 81–83.
5. Garfinkel, 75–79.
6. Garfinkel, 82–84.
7. Schmandt-Besserat 1992.
8. Barker 1975.
9. Garfinkel, 76–77.
10. Bailey 2005, 174–75.
11. Spence 1947, 87.
12. P. Barber 2010, 55, 139.
13. McClellan and Dorn 2006, 6–12.
14. Halpern and Halpern 1972, 52–53.
15. Halpern and Halpern, 55.
16. Halpern and Halpern, 65.
17. Bailey 2005, 5.
18. Bradley, 119.
19. Garfinkel, 80.
20. Vulpesco, 233 n. 1.
21. Bailey 2010, 113 and fig. 5–2.
22. Bailey 2005, 24.
23. Bailey 2005, 38–39; cf. Hall 1959, Fast 1970.
24. Bailey 2005, 36–37.
25. Bailey 2005, 37, quoting Delong.
26. Bailey 2005, 32–33.
27. Bailey 2005, 199–200, 142.
28. Bailey 2005, 93, 95.

29. Rybakov 1981, 182; Durasov and Yakovleva, 30 and passim.
30. Anthony, 43.
31. Harrison 1962, 293.
32. Athenaeus xi.496; Harrison 1962, 319.
33. Brumfield 1981, 149.
34. Harrison 1962, 292.
35. Glob 1965/2004, 163.

PART IV
CHAPTER 22

1. Sacks 2008, 240, citing Patel.
2. Sacks, 241, citing Chen.
3. Sacks, 243.
4. Sacks, 240 n. 1.
5. Durrell 1960, 152–53.
6. Sacks, 207.
7. Donald 1991, 186.
8. Donald, 269–75.
9. McNeill 1995, 2.
10. McNeill, 2–3.
11. McNeill, 3.
12. Sacks, 246.
13. Sacks, 244–45.
14. McNeill, 2.
15. Donald, 368–71.
16. Reynolds 2011, citing Matthew Hill.
17. Turner and Pöppel 1983, 301.
18. Hunt 1996, 58, citing Kakouri.
19. Quoted by Arnaudov 1917, 50–51.
20. Arnaudov 1917, 54.
21. Marinov 1994, 630–31.
22. Shivachev 1898–99, 278.
23. Arnaudov 1917, 55.
24. Danforth 1989, 19, 25; Arnaudov 1917, 55.
25. Arnaudov 1917, 56.
26. Description summarized chiefly from Danforth 1989.
27. Danforth 1979, 143n.
28. Danforth 1979, 149 and note; 1989, 112–18, 124.

29. Danforth 1989, 124–25.
30. Danforth 1989, 124.
31. Danforth 1979, 158.
32. Danforth 1989, 19.
33. Danforth 1979, 159.
34. Shivachev in Arnaudov 1924, 30.
35. Puchner 1981, 53 #14.
36. Arnaudov 1924, 34–35.
37. Burkert 1985, 102.

CHAPTER 23

1. Barber and Peters 1992, 308.
2. Manush 1986–87, 21, 24.
3. *Acharnians* l. 627: noted by Lawler 1964, 67–68 n. 8.
4. "Pontic Greek," *Wikipedia* (online), for examples and excellent bibliography.

5. Barber 1975; 1999c.
6. Hunt, 22.
7. Barber and Barber, chapter 15.
8. Garfinkel, 46; similarly for Bulgaria: Shturbanova and Ilieva, 82–84.
9. See also Wolfram 1951, 31–33.

EPILOGUE

1. Rose, 92, 100 n. 59; *Homeric Hymm to Demeter* ll. 202–10.
2. Guthrie 1952, 135.
3. Johnston 1999, 176.
4. *Medea*, ll. 250–51.
5. Barber 1999a, chapter 10.
6. Donald, 259 and passim.
7. Donald, 257.
8. Frankfort and Frankfort 1946; Barber and Barber.

Bibliography

ABBREVIATIONS

AJA   *American Journal of Archaeology*
JEFDSS *Journal of the English Folk Dance and Song Society*
JIES   *Journal of Indo-European Studies*
SA&A   *Soviet Anthropology and Archeology*

For Russian, as in the text, *y* represents *ŭ* (etc.) and *ï* represents *ы*.

Afanas(i)ev, Aleksandr. 1855–64. *Народные Русские Сказки*. Reprint 1957, V. Propp, ed. Moscow: ГИХЛ. (Abridged translation: N. Guterman. 1973. *Russian Fairy Tales*. New York: Pantheon.)

Aleksieva, Ekaterina, and Dinna Ancheva. n.d. (1990s) *Ancient Magic in Bulgarian Folklore*. Sofia: Kalimana.

Alexander, Alex. 1975. *Russian Folklore*. Belmont, MA: Nordland.

Alford, Violet. 1937. *Pyrenean Festivals*. London: Chatto and Windus.

———. 1939. "Some Hobby Horses of Great Britain," *JEFDSS* 3.4:221–40.

———. 1962. *Sword Dance and Drama*. London: Merlin Press.

———. 1978. *The Hobby Horse and other Animal Masks*. London: Merlin Press.

Alford, Violet, and Rodney Gallop. 1935. *The Traditional Dance*. London: Methuen.

Andersen, Jørgen. 1977. *The Witch on the Wall*. London: George Allen & Unwin.

Anonymous. 1900. "Пеперунга" (Peperunga), *Вести* (newspaper), 28 March, reprinted in Vasileva et al.: 295(#54b).

Anthony, David, ed. 2010. *The Lost World of Old Europe*. Princeton, NJ: Princeton University Press.

Arens, William. 1979. *The Man-Eating Myth*. Oxford: Oxford University Press.

Arias, P., and Max Hirmer. 1961. *A History of 1000 Years of Greek Vase Painting*. New York: Abrams.

Arnaudov, Mikhail. 1917. *Die bulgarischen Festbräuche*. Leipzig: Parlapanoff.

———. 1924. *Студии върху българскитъ обреди и легенди*. Sofia: Khudozhnik.

———. 1969. *Очерци по българския Фолклор*. Sofia: Bulgarski Pisatel.

Ayres, James. 1977. *British Folk Art*. London: Barrie and Jenkins.

Bailey, Douglass. 2005. *Prehistoric Figurines*. London: Routledge.

———. 2010. "The Figurines of Old Europe," in Anthony 2010:112–27.

Balashov, D., Yu. Marchenko, and N. Kalmïkova. 1985. *Русская Свадьба*. Moscow: Sovremennik.

Barandiarán, José Miguel de. 2007. *Basque Prehistory and Ethnography*. F. Fornoff, L. White, and C. Evans-Corrales trans. Reno, NV: Center for Basque Studies.

Baranova, O., T. Zimina, E. Madlevskaya, A. Ostrovskiy, N. Sosnina, V. Kholodnaya, and I. Shangina. 2001. *Русский Праздник*. St. Petersburg: Iskusstvo-SPB.

Barber, Elizabeth Wayland. 1975. "The Proto-Indo-European Notion of Cloth and Clothing," *JIES* 3:294–320.

———. 1979. "Diachronic Syntax and the Principle of Dynamic Stability," *Hawaii Working Papers in Linguistics* 11:89–108.

———. 1991. *Prehistoric Textiles*. Princeton, NJ: Princeton University Press.

———. 1992. "The Peplos of Athena," in J. Neils, ed., *Goddess and Polis* (Princeton, NJ: Princeton University Press) 103–17.

———. 1994. *Women's Work—The First 20,000 Years*. New York: W. W. Norton.

———. 1997. "On the Origins of the *vily/rusalki*," in M. Dexter and E. Polomé, eds., *Varia on the Indo-European Past* (*JIES* monograph 19): 6–47.

———. 1999a. *The Mummies of Ürümchi*. New York: W. W. Norton.

———. 1999b. "On the Antiquity of East European Bridal Dress," in Welters 1999: 13–31.

———. 1999c. "The Curious Tale of the Ultra-Long Sleeve," in Welters 1999:111–34.

Barber, Elizabeth, and Ann Peters. 1992. "Ontogeny and Phylogeny: What Child Language and Archaeology Have to Say to Each Other," in J. Hawkins and M. Gell-Mann, eds., *The Evolution of Human Languages* (Redwood City, CA: Addison-Wesley) 305–52.

Barber, Elizabeth, and Paul T. Barber. 2005. *When They Severed Earth from Sky: How the Human Mind Shapes Myth*. Princeton, NJ: Princeton University Press.

Barber, Paul. 2010. *Vampires, Burial, and Death* (2nd ed.). New Haven, CT: Yale University Press.

Barchilon, Jacques, and Peter Flinders. 1981. *Charles Perrault*. Boston: G. K. Hall.

Barker, Graeme. 1975. "Early Neolithic Land Use in Yugoslavia," *Proceedings of the Prehistoric Society* 41:85–104.

Baron, S., trans./ed. 1967. *The Travels of Olearius in Seventeenth-Century Russia*. Stanford, CA: Stanford University Press.

Bawanypeck, Daliah. 2005. *Die Rituale der Auguren*. Heidelberg: Winter.

Beard, Mary, John North, and Simon Price. 1998. *Religions of Rome*, vol. 2. Cambridge: Cambridge University Press.

Beazley, J. 1958. "A Hydria by the Kleophrades Painter," *Antike Kunst* 1:6–8, pl.2–6.

Beck, Hans. 2005. "Caffeine, Alcohol, and Sweeteners," in G. Prance and M. Nesbett, eds., *The Cultural History of Plants* (New York: Routledge) 173–90.

Bernard, Henry. 1904. *The Shade of the Balkans*. London: Nutt.

Bešlagić, Šefik. 1982. *Stećci—Kultura i Umjetnost*. Sarajevo: Veselin Masleša.

Beza, Marcu. 1928. *Paganism in Roumanian Folklore*. New York: Dutton.

Blome, Peter. 1982. *Die figürliche Bildwelt Kretas*. Mainz: Von Zabern.

Bocharov, G. 1984. *Художественный металл Древней Руси*. Moscow: Nauka.

Boguslavskaya, I. 1984. *Русское Народное Искусство*. Leningrad: Khudozhnik.

Bosanquet, R., and R. Dawkins. 1923. *The Unpublished Objects from the Palaikastro Excavations*, Suppl. 1. *Annual of the British School at Athens* (London).

Bradley, Richard. 2005. *Domestic Life in Prehistoric Europe*. London: Routledge.

Brazil, Mark. 2003. "Swan Culture," *Journal of Rakuno Gakuen University* 28: 65–83.

Brody, Alan. 1969. *The English Mummers and Their Plays*. Philadelphia: University of Pennsylvania Press.

Brouwer, H. 1989. *Bona Dea*. Leiden: Brill.

Brumfield, Allaire. 1981. *The Attic Festivals of Demeter and Their Relationship to the Agricultural Year*. Salem, NH: Ayer.

Burkert, Walter. 1977/1985. *Greek Religion*. J. Raffan trans. Cambridge: Harvard University Press.

———. 1988. "*Katagógia-Anagógia* and the Goddess of Knossos," in Hägg, Marinatos, and Nordquist 1988: 81–88.

Campbell, Marie. 1938. "Survivals of Old Folk Drama in the Kentucky Mountains," *Journal of American Folklore* 51:10–24.

Cawte, E. 1978. *Ritual Animal Disguise*. London: D. S. Brewer.

Cawte, E., Alex Helm, and N. Peacock. 1967. *English Ritual Drama: A Geographical Index*. London: Folk Lore Society.

Chadwick, Nora. 1946. *The Beginnings of Russian History: An Enquiry into Sources*. Cambridge: Cambridge University Press.

Chambers, E. K. 1903. *The Mediaeval Stage*. Oxford: Clarendon Press.

———. 1933. *The English Folk-Play*. Oxford: Oxford University Press.

Cirilli, René. 1913. *Les Prêtres danseurs de Rome*. Paris: Geuthner.

Constantinou, Stavroula. 2005. *Female Corporeal Performances*. Uppsala: Uppsala University.

Cook, Robert. 1960. *Greek Painted Pottery*. London: Methuen.

Corrsin, Stephen. 1997. *Sword Dancing in Europe: A History*. Enfield Lock, UK: Hisarlik Press.

Curtin, Jeremiah. 1890/1971. *Myths and Folk-Tales of the Russians, Western Slavs, and Magyars.* New York: Blom.

Danforth, Loring. 1979. "The Role of Dance in the Ritual Therapy of the Anastenaria," *Byzantine and Modern Greek Studies* 5:141–63.

———. 1989. *Firewalking and Religious Healing.* Princeton, NJ: Princeton University Press.

Darkevich, V., and A. Mongayt. 1967. "Старорязанский клад 1966 года," *Советская Археология* 1967.2:211–23.

Davidson, H. R. Ellis. 1981. *Gods and Myths of the Viking Age.* New York: Bell.

Davis, Ellen. 1987. "The Knossos Miniature Frescoes and the Function of the Central Courts," in Hägg and Marinatos 1987:157–61.

Dawkins, R. 1904–5. "A Visit to Skyros: The Carnival," *Annual of the British School at Athens* (London) 11:72–74.

———. 1906. "The Modern Carnival in Thrace and the Cult of Dionysus," *Journal of Hellenic Studies* 26:191–206.

Delehaye, Hippolyte. 1921. *Les Passions des Martyrs et les genres littéraires.* Brussels: Société des Bollandistes.

———. 1927. *Sanctus: Essai sur le culte des saints dans l'antiquité.* Brussels: Société des Bollandistes.

———. 1998. *The Legends of the Saints.* D. Atwater trans. Dublin: 4 Courts Press.

Demakopoulou, Kaiti. 1996. *Ο Θησαυρός των Αηδονιών.* Athens: Politismou.

Derebanov, Yak. 1897. "Ойлулето," *Новини* 8.12 (newspaper), 15 November 1897, reprinted in Vasileva et al. 1999: 272(#38).

Dias, Jorge. 1973. "Heilige Bäder und Heilbäder," in Escher et al.: 60–62.

Dixon-Kennedy, Mike. 1998. *Encyclopedia of Russian and Slavic Myth and Legend.* Santa Barbara, CA: ACC-Clio.

Dobrovol'skiy, V. 1908. "Нечнстая снла въ народныхъ верованіяхъ (по данным Смоленской губ.)" *Живая Старина* 17:3–16.

Dömötör, T., and E. Eperjessy. 1967. "Dodola and other Slavonic folk-customs in County Baranya (Hungary)," *Acta ethnographica Academiae Scientiarum Hungaricae* 16:399–408.

Donald, Merlin. 1991. *Origins of the Modern Mind.* Cambridge, MA: Harvard University Press.

D'Orazio, Massimo. 2007. "Meteorite records in the ancient Greek and Latin literature," in Luigi Piccardi and W. B. Masse, eds., *Myth and Geology* (London: Geological Society), 213–25.

Drazheva, Raina. 1982. *Gergyovden.* Sofia: Publishing House.

Dubočke Rusalje [film]. 1971. youtube.com/watch?v=ct949VnvqOs.

Dumézil, Georges. 1929. *Le Problème des Centaures.* Paris: Geuthner.

———. 1970. *Archaic Roman Religion.* Chicago: University of Chicago Press.

Dummett, Michael. 1985. "Tracing the Tarot," *MFR* 1985.8. 6 pages.

Durasov, G, and G. Yakovleva. 1990. *Russian Embroidery: Traditional Motifs.* Moscow: Sovetskaya Rossiya.

Durrell, Gerald. 1960. *A Zoo in My Luggage*. New York: Viking.

Echtermeyer, Theodor. 1962. *Deutsche Gedichte*. Benno von Wiese, ed. Düsseldorf: A. Bagel Verlag.

Eckert, Georg. 1951. "Das Regenmädchen," *Jahrbuch des Linden-Museums Stuttgart* n.F. 1:98–101.

Eliade, Mircea. 1951/1964. *Shamanism*. W. Trask trans. Princeton, NJ: Princeton University Press.

Escher, W., T. Gantner, and H. Trümpy, eds. 1973. *Festchrift für Robert Wildhaber*. Basel: Krebs.

Ettlinger, Ellen. 1944. "The Occasion and Purpose of the 'Mari Lwyd' Ceremony," *Man* 44:89–93.

Fabritskiy, B., and I. Shmelyov. 1974. *Сокровища Древней Руси: Treasures of Mediaeval Russia*. Moscow: Progress.

Fast, Julius. 1970. *Body Language*. New York: Evans.

Fischer, Emil. 1908. "Paparudă und Scaloian," *Globus* 93:13–16.

Flint, Valerie. 1991. *The Rise of Magic in Early Medieval Europe*. Princeton, NJ: Princeton University Press.

Florov, Irena, and Nicholas Florov. 2001. *The 3000-Year-Old Hat*. Vancouver: Gold Vine.

Folk Art in Rumania. 1955. Bucharest: Rumanian Institute for Cultural Relations with Foreign Countries.

Frankfort, Henri, and H. A. Frankfort. 1946. *Before Philosophy*. Chicago: University of Chicago Press.

Frazer, James. 1922. *The Golden Bough* (1 vol., abridged ed.). New York: Macmillan.

———. 1931. *Ovid's Fasti*. London: Heinemann (Loeb).

Froianov, I., A. Dvornichenko, and Iu. Krivosheev. 1990–91. "The Introduction of Christianity in Russia and the Pagan Traditions," *SA&A* 29.3:12–24.

Funk and Wagnalls Standard Dictionary of Folklore, Mythology, and Legend. 1972. Maria Leach, ed. New York: Funk and Wagnalls.

Furmánek, Václav, and Karol Pieta. 1985. *Počiatky odievania na Slovensku*. Bratislava: Tatran.

Gallop, Rodney. 1970. *A Book of the Basques*. Reno, NV: University of Nevada Press.

Garfinkel, Yosef. 2003. *Dancing at the Dawn of Agriculture*. Austin: University of Texas Press.

Gaster, Theodore. 1955. *New Year*. New York: Abelard-Schuman.

———. 1961 (2nd ed.). *Thespis*. New York: Anchor/Doubleday.

Genchev, Stoyan. 1988. *The Wedding: Bulgarian Folk Feasts and Customs*. Sofia: Septemvri.

Gimbutas, Marija. 1958. *Ancient Symbolism in Lithuanian Folk Art*. Philadelphia: American Folklore Society.

———. 1971. *The Slavs*. New York: Praeger.

———. 1982. *The Goddesses and Gods of Old Europe*. Berkeley: University of California Press.

——. 1989. *The Language of the Goddess*. New York: Harper.

——. 1991. *The Civilization of the Goddess*. New York: Harper.

——. 1999. *The Living Goddesses*. Berkeley: University of California Press.

Ginzburg, Carlo. 1992. *Ecstasies: Deciphering the Witches' Sabbath*. R. Rosenthal trans. New York: Penguin.

Giurchescu, Anca, and Sunni Bloland. 1992. *Romanian Traditional Dance*. Bucharest: Express.

Gligorić, D. 1893 "Русаље," *Босанска Вила* 19 (15/9/1893) 286-87 and 20 (30/9/1893) 304-5.

Glob, P. V. 1965/2004. *The Bog People*. New York: New York Review of Books.

Gold aus Kiew. 1993. Vienna: Kunsthistorisches Museum Wien.

Goodison, Lucy, and Christine Morris. 1998. "Beyond the 'Great Mother,'" in Goodison and Morris, eds., *Ancient Goddesses: The Myths and Evidence* (Madison: University of Wisconsin Press), 113-32.

Greimas, Algirdas. 1992. *Of Gods and Men*. M. Newman trans. Bloomington: Indiana University Press.

Gross, Emanuel. 1900. *Hops*. London: Scott, Greenwood.

Guthrie, W. K. C. 1952. *Orpheus and Greek Religion*. Princeton, NJ: Princeton University Press.

Haase, Felix. 1980. *Volksglaube und Brauchtum der Ostslaven*. Hildesheim Olms.

Hägg, Robin, and Nanno Marinatos, eds. 1987. *The Function of the Minoan Palace*. Stockholm: Åström.

Hägg, Robin, N. Marinatos, and G. Nordquist, eds. 1988. *Early Greek Cult Practice*. Stockholm: Åström.

Haider, Friedrich. 1968. *Tiroler Volksbrauch im Jahreslauf*. Innsbruck: Tirolia.

Halkin, François. 1966. "La Passion de Sainte Parascève par Jean d'Eubée," in P. Wirth, *Polychronion* (Heidelberg: Winter), 226-37.

Hall, Edward. 1959. *The Silent Language*. Garden City, NY: Doubleday.

Halpern, Joel, and Barbara Kerewsky Halpern. 1972. *A Serbian Village in Historical Perspective*. New York: Holt, Rinehart, Winston.

Harrison, Jane. 1908/1922. *Prolegomena to the Study of Greek Religion*. (3rd ed.) Cambridge: Cambridge University Press.

——. 1912/1962. *Epilegomena to the Study of Greek Religion; and Themis*. New York: University Books.

Hartwig, Paul. 1893. *Die griechischen Meisterschalen*. . . . Berlin: Spemann.

Hatto, A. 1961. "The Swan Maiden: A Folk-Tale of North Eurasian Origin," *Bulletin of the School of Oriental and African Studies, University of London* 24:326-52.

Herberstein, Sigmund von. 1966. *Description of Moscow and Muscovy, 1557*. B. Picard ed., J. Grundy trans. London: J. M. Dent.

Higgins, Reynold. 1967. *Minoan and Mycenaean Art*. London: Thames and Hudson.

Hoddinott, R. 1981. *The Thracians*. London: Thames and Hudson.

Hoernes, M. 1898. *Urgeschichte der bildenden Kunst in Europa.* Holzhausen: Vienna.

Hogarth, D. 1902. "The Zakro Sealings," *Journal of Hellenic Studies* 22:76–93.

Holweck, Frederick. 1924/1969. *Biographical Dictionary of the Saints.* Detroit: Gale Research.

Hood, Sinclair. 1971. *The Minoans.* London: Thames and Hudson.

Hunt, Yvonne. 1996. *Traditional Dance in Greek Culture.* Athens: Centre for Asia Minor Studies.

Ilieva, Anna. 1977. *Bulgarian Dance Folklore.* T. Roncevic trans. Pittsburgh: Dutifa-Tamburitza.

Ilieva, Anna, and Anna Shturbanova. 1997. "Some Zoomorphic Images in Bulgarian Women's Ritual Dances. . . ." in Joan Marler, ed., *From the Realm of the Ancestors* (Manchester, CT: Knowledge, Ideas, and Trends), 309–21.

Ivanova, R. 1987. *Traditional Bulgarian Wedding.* Sofia: Svyat.

Ivashneva, L., and E. Razumovskaia. 1981. "The Usviat Wedding Ritual in Its Contemporary Form," *SA&A* 20:25–54.

Janković, Ljubica and Danica. 1953. *Narodne Igre* VII. Belgrade: Jugoshtampa.

Johannowsky, Werner, John Pedley, and Mario Torelli. 1983. "Excavations at Paestum 1982," *AJA* 87:293–303.

Johnston, Sarah Isles. 1999. *The Restless Dead: Encounters between the Living and the Dead in Ancient Greece.* Berkeley: University of California Press.

Jordan, David. 1985. "A Survey of Greek Defixiones," *Greek, Roman, and Byzantine Studies* 26:151–97.

Jost, Madeleine. 1985. *Sanctuaires et cultes d'Arcadie.* Paris: J. Vrin.

Jung-Stilling, J. 1777/1976. *Lebensgeschichte.* Darmstadt: Wissenschaftliche Buchgesellschaft.

Jurić, Dorian. 2010. "A Call for a Functional Differentiation of the South Slavic *Vila*," *JIES* 38:172–202.

Katzarova, R. 1935. "Lazarnica," *JEFDSS* 2:62–71.

Katzarova-Kukudova, Raina, and Kiril Djenev. 1958. *Bulgarian Folk Dances.* Sofia: Science & Art State Publishing House.

Kelly, Mary. 1989. *Goddess Embroideries of Eastern Europe.* Winona, MN: Northland.

Kemp, P. 1935. *Healing Ritual: Studies in the Technique and Tradition of the Southern Slavs.* London: Faber and Faber.

Kenna, V. 1960. *Cretan Seals.* Oxford: Clarendon Press.

Kennan, George. 1870/1903. *Tent Life in Siberia.* New York: Putnam & Son.

Kligman, Gail. 1981. *Căluș.* Chicago: University of Chicago Press.

Klochko, L. 1992. "Плечовый одяг скифьянок," *Археология* 3:95–106.

Kluge, Friedrich. 1975. *Etymologisches Wörterbuch der deutschen Sprache.* Berlin: de Gruyter.

Kolar, Walter. 1974. *Introduction to Meter and Rhythm in Balkan Folk Music.* Pittsburgh: Duquesne University Tamburitzans.

Kolpakova, N. 1973. *Лирика русской Свадьбы*. Leningrad: Nauka.

Koşay, Hamit. 1951. *Les Fouilles d'Alaca Höyük, 1937–39*. Ankara: Türk Tarih Kurumu.

Kramer, Samuel Noah. 1963. *The Sumerians*. Chicago: University of Chicago Press.

Krauss, Friedrich S. 1890. *Volksglaube und religiöser Brauch der Südslaven*. Münster i. Westf.: Aschendorf.

———. 1908. *Slavische Vorschungen*. Leipzig: W. Heims.

Kravchenko, Maria. 1987. *The World of the Russian Fairy Tale*. Berne/New York: Peter Lang.

Kristiansen, Kristian, and Thomas Larsson. 2005. *The Rise of Bronze Age Society*. Cambridge: Cambridge University Press.

Kristof, Nicholas, and Sheryl WuDunn. 2009. *Half the Sky*. New York: Knopf.

Krvavïch, Dmitriÿ, and Halïna Stel'mashchuk. 1988. *Українский народний одяг XVII–XIX ст. акварелях*. Kiev: Naukova Dumka.

Kulišić, Špiro. 1966. *Traditions and Folklore in Yugoslavia*. Belgrade: Jugoslavija.

Kuret, Niko. 1973. "Frauenbunde und maskierte Frauen," in Escher et al.: 334–47.

Kutter, Wilhelm. 1973. "Maskenzeiten und Larventypen in Südwestdeutschland," in Escher et al.: 348–71.

Lawler, Lillian. 1942. "The Dance of the Holy Birds," *Classical Journal* 37:351–61.

———. 1946. "The Geranos Dance," *American Journal of Philology* 77:112-30.

———. 1951. "The Dance in Ancient Crete," in Mylonas 1951:23–51.

———. 1964. *The Dance of the Ancient Greek Theatre*. Iowa City: University of Iowa Press.

Lawson, John. 1909/1964. *Modern Greek Folklore and Ancient Greek Religion*. New Hyde Park, NY: University Books.

Lehtinen, Ildiko. 1979. *Naisten Korut*. Helsinki: Museovirasto.

Lepage, Claude. 1971. "Les Bracelets de luxe romains et byzantins. . . ," *Cahiers archéologiques* 21:1–25.

Levi, Doro. 1951. "La Dea Micenea a Cavallo," in Mylonas 1951: 108–25.

———. 1976. *Festòs e la civiltà minoica*. Rome: Edizioni dell'Ateneo.

Levin, Eve. 2006. "The Christian Sources of the Cult of St. Paraskeva," in J. Hinka and A. Zayarnyuk, *Letters from Heaven* (Toronto: University of Toronto Press), 126–46.

Lewis, Charlton, and Charles Short. 1879/1958. *A Latin Dictionary*. Oxford: Clarendon Press.

Lissarrague, François. 1999. *Vases grecs*. Paris: Hazan.

Liungman, Waldemar. 1938. *Traditionswanderungen Euphrat-Rhein*. Helsinki: Suomalainen Tiedeakatemia.

Louis, Maurice. 1963. *Le Folklore et la danse*. Paris: Maisonneuve et Larose.

Loukatos, Dimitrios. 1975. "'Αργίαι καὶ 'άγιοι τιμωροί" 'Επετηρίς, 'Ακαδημία 'Αθηνῶν Λαογράφικον 'Αρχεῖον 20–21.

MacDermott, Mercia. 1998. *Bulgarian Folk Customs.* London: Jessica Kingsley.

Mahler, Elsa. 1960. *Die russischen dörflichen Hochzeitsbräuche.* Berlin: Harrassowitz.

Mair, Victor. 2007. "Horse Sacrifices and Sacred Groves," *Eurasian Studies* 6:22–53.

Maksimov, Sergey. 1903/1994. *Нечистая, Неведомая и Крестная Сила.* St. Petersburg: Poliset (1994 version in modern spelling of 1903 original).

Mallory, James, and Donald Adams. 1997. *Encyclopedia of Indo-European Culture.* London/Chicago: Fitzroy Dearborn.

Maluckov, Mirjana. 1973. *Narodna Nošnja Rumuna u Jugoslovenskom Banatu.* Novi Sad, Serbia: Voivodina Museum.

Manush, Leksa. 1986–87. "The Problem of the Folk Music of the Gypsies," *SA&A* 25.3:17–34.

Marinatos, Nanno. 1987. "Public Festivals in the West Courts of the Palaces," in Hägg and Marinatos 1987:135–43.

Marinatos, Spyridon, and Max Hirmer. 1960. *Crete and Mycenae.* New York: Abrams.

Marinov, Dimitŭr. 1907. *Известие на Етнографические Музей въ София* (=*Жива-Старина*, vol. 1). Sofia: Bulgarian Academy of Science.

———. 1914. *Народна Вяра и Религиозни Народни Обичаи* (=*Жива-Старина*, vol. 8). Sofia: Bulgarian Academy of Science.

———. 1994. *Народна Вяра и Религиозни Народни Обичаи.* Sofia: Bulgarian Academy of Science (1994 version in modern spelling of 1914 original; pages do not correspond).

Maslova, G. 1978. *Орнамент Русской Народной Вышивки.* Moscow: Nauka.

McClellan, James, and Harold Dorn. 2006. *Science and Technology in World History.* Baltimore: John Hopkins University Press.

McNeill, William. 1995. *Keeping Together in Time.* Cambridge: Harvard University Press.

Megas, George. 1958. *Greek Calendar Customs.* Athens: Prime Minister's Office.

Mellaart, James. 1961. "Excavations at Hacılar," *Anatolian Studies* 11:39–75.

Menges, Karl: 1983. *Materialien zum Schamanismus der Ewenki-Tungusen . . . von I. M. Suslov 1926/28.* Wiesbaden: Harrassowitz.

Modelski, George. 1997. "Cities of the Ancient World: An Inventory," on homepage of *Evolutionary World Politics.*

Morris, Katherine. 1991. *Sorceress or Witch?* Lanham, MD: University Press of America.

Morris, Sarah. 1992. "Prehistoric Iconography and Historical Sources," in Robert Laffineur and Janice Crowley, eds., *ΕΙΚΩΝ* (Liège: Université de Liège), 205–12 and pl. 48–51.

Moser, Henri. 1885. *À travers l'Asie centrale.* Paris: Plon, Nourrit et Cie.

Müller-Karpe, Hermann. 1968. *Handbuch der Vorgeschichte: II. Jungsteinzeit.* Munich: C. H. Beck.

———. 1974. *Handbuch der Vorgeschichte: III. Kupferzeit.* Munich: C. H. Beck.

———. 1980. *Handbuch der Vorgeschichte: IV. Bronzezeit.* Munich: C. H. Beck.

Munksgaard, Elisabeth. 1974. *Oldtidsdragter.* Copenhagen: Nationalmuseet.

Musche, Brigitte. 1988. *Vorderasiatischer Schmuck.* Leiden: Brill.

Mylonas, George, ed. 1951. *Studies Presented to David Moore Robinson,* v.1. St. Louis: Washington University Press.

Neve, R. 1976. "Hops," in Norman Simmonds, *Evolution of Crop Plants* (New York: Longman), 208–10.

Newall, Venetia. 1980. "Throwing the Hood at Haxey: A Lincolnshire Twelfth-Night Custom," *Folk Life* 18:7–23.

Nicoloff, Assen. 1983. *Bulgarian Folklore.* Cleveland: self-published.

Nikol'skaya, T. 1981. *Земля Вятичей.* Moscow: Nauka.

Ó Danachair, Caoimhin. 1973. "The Nine Irons," in Escher et al.: 471–76.

Ó Duinn, Sean. 2005. *Rites of Brigid: Goddess and Saint.* Blackrock, Ireland: Columba Press.

Olearius. See Baron.

Oprescu, G. 1929. *Peasant Art in Rumania.* London: The Studio.

Outram, Alan, N. Stear, R. Bendrey, S. Olsen, A. Kasparov, V. Zaibert, N. Thorpe, and R. Evershed. 3/6/2009. "The earliest horse harnessing and milking," *Science* 323:1332–35.

Peate, Iorwerth. 1943. "Mari Lwyd: A Suggested Explanation," *Man* 43:53–58.

Perowne, Stewart. 1969. *Roman Mythology.* London: Hamlyn.

Perrault, Charles. 1697. *Histories ou Contes de temps passé.* Paris.

Persson, Axel. 1931. *The Royal Tombs at Dendra near Midea.* Lund, Sweden: Gleerups.

Petrović, J. 1930. "Votivna kolitsa iz Dupljaje," *Starinar* 5:21–29.

Piggott, Stuart. 1962. "Heads and Hoofs," *Antiquity* 36:110–18.

Pócs, Éva. 1989. *Fairies and Witches at the Boundary of Southeastern and Central Europe.* Helsinki: Suomalainen Tiedeakatemia.

Poltoratzky, Marianna. 1964. *Russian Folklore.* New York: Rausen.

Pop, Mihai, and Constantin Eretescu. 1967. "Die Masken in rumänischen Brauchtum," *Schweizerisches Archiv für Volkskunde* 63:162–76.

Popov, Rachko. 1989. *Butterfly and Gherman.* Sofia: Septemvri.

Prach, Ivan. 1790. *Собраніе Народныхъ Рускихь Песенъ* [n.p.].

Propp, Vladimir. 1963. *Русские Аграрные Праздники.* Leningrad: Leningrad University.

———. 1987. *Les Fêtes agraires russes.* Lise Gruel-Apert trans. Paris: Maisonneuve et Larose. (Translation of Propp 1963.)

Puchner, Walter. 1981. "Beiträge zum thrakischen Feuerlauf (Anastenaria/Nestinari) und zur thrakischen Karnivalsszene Kalogeros/Kuker/Köpek-Bey)," *Zeitschrift für Balkanologie* 17:47–75.

———. 1982. "Zur Typologie des balkanischen Regenmädchens," *Schweizerisches Archiv für Volkskunde* 78:98–125.

Puckett, Newbell. 1981. *Popular Beliefs and Superstitions.* Ed. W. Hand, A. Casetta, and S. Thiederman. Boston: G. K. Hall.

Puhvel, Jaan. 1987. *Comparative Mythology.* Baltimore: Johns Hopkins University Press.

Puntev, Penko, M. Čerkezova, Ž. Stamenova, and V. Kovačeva. 1980. *Bulgarian Folk Art.* Sofia: Septemvri.

Pushkareva, N. 1990–91. "The Woman in the Ancient Russian Family (Tenth to Fifteenth Centuries," *SA&A* 29.3:57–73.

Rabinovich, M. 1981. "The Wedding in the Sixteenth-Century Russian City [Part 2]," *SA&A* 20:55–72.

Rajchevski, Stojan, and Valerija Fol. 1993. *Кукерът.* Sofia: Universitet.

Ralston, W. 1872/1970. *The Songs of the Russian People.* New York: Haskell House (1970 reprint of 1872 original).

Rappoport, A. S. 1913. *Home Life in Russia.* New York: Macmillan.

Rausing, Gad. 1995. "The Days of the Week and Dark Age Politics," *Fornvännen* 90:229-39.

Reynolds, G. 2011. "Phys Ed: What Really Causes Runner's High?" *Well* (blog), *New York Times,* February 20, http://well.blogs.nytimes.com/2011/02/16/phys-ed-what-really-causes-runners-high/.

Rïbakov: see Rybakov.

Rice, Tamara Talbot. 1963. *Concise History of Russian Art.* New York: Praeger.

Robinson, Naeda, and Maria Canavarro. 2009. *Macedonian Village Dress Going, Going, Gone.* Bitola, Macedonia: International Music and Arts Foundation, Vaduz.

Robson, Edgar. 1930. *A Guide to French Fêtes.* London: Methuen.

Rodd, Rennell. 1892/1968. *Customs and Lore of Modern Greece.* Chicago: Argonaut (reprint).

Róheim, Geza. 1926. "Hungarian Calendar Customs," *Journal of the Royal Anthropological Institute of Great Britain and Ireland* 56:361–84.

Roscher, Wilhelm. 1884–1937. *Ausführliches Lexikon der griechischen und römischen Mythologie.* Leipzig: Teubner.

Rose, H. J. 1959. *Handbook of Greek Mythology.* New York: Dutton.

Ruckert, Anne. 1976. *Frühe Keramik Böotiens.* Bern: Franke.

Rudenko, Sergei. 1970. *Frozen Tombs of Siberia.* M. Thompson trans./ed. Berkeley: University of California Press.

Russ, Jennifer. 1983. *German Festivals and Customs.* London: O. Wolff.

Ryall, Rhiannon. 1989. *West Country Wicca.* Custer, WA: Phoenix Publishing.

Ryan, W. 1999. *The Bathhouse at Midnight.* University Park: Pennsylvania State University.

Rybakov [Rïbakov], Boris. 1965. *Early Centuries of Russian History.* Moscow: Progress.

——. 1967. "Русалии и бог Симаргл-Переплут," *Советская Археология* 1967.2:91–116.

———. 1968. "The Rusalii and the god Simargl-Pereplut," *SA&A* 6.4:34–59 (translation of Rybakov 1967).

———. 1971. *Русское Прикладное Искусство X–XII Веков*. Leningrad: Aurora.

———. 1981. *Язычество древних Славян*. Moscow: Nauka.

———. 1987. *Язычество древней Руси*. Moscow: Nauka.

———. 1989. *Kievan Rus*. S. Sosyinsky trans. Moscow: Progress.

———. 2001. *Язычество древней Руси* (2nd ed.). Moscow: Sofia.

———. 2002. *Язычество древних Славян*. (2nd ed.). Moscow: Sofia.

Rytz, W., and H. Schwartzenbach. 1960. *Flowers in Color*. H. Edlin trans./ed. New York: Viking.

Sacks, Oliver. 2008. *Musicophilia*. New York: Knopf.

Sakellarakis, John. 1982. *Heraklion Museum*. Athens: Ekdotike Athenon.

Salzman, Michele. 1990. *On Roman Time*. Berkeley: University of California Press.

Sanders, Irwin. 1949. *Balkan Village*. Lexington: University of Kentucky Press.

Sarianidi, Viktor. 1994. "Temples of Bronze Age Margiana," *Antiquity* 68:388–418.

Schmandt-Besserat, Denise. 1992. *How Writing Came About*. Austin: University of Texas Press.

Schneeweis, Edmund. 1934–35. "Fremde Beeinflussungen in Brauchtum der Serbokroaten," *Revue des Études balkaniques* 1:172–79.

Schöne, Angelika. 1987. *Der Thiasos*. Göteborg: Åström.

Sharpe, Cecil. 1911–13. *The Sword Dances of Northern England* (3 vols.). London: Novello & Co.

Sharpe, Cecil, and Herbert MacIlwaine. 1907–13. *The Morris Book* (5 vols.). London: Novello & Co.

Shivachev, S. 1898–99/1999. "Нистинаре," *Светлина* 1898–99, reprinted in Vasileva et al., vol. 2, 277–85.

Shturbanova, Anna, and Anna Ilieva. 1994. "The Dance and the Nether World," in *Studies in Bulgarian Folklore* (Sofia: Bulgarian Academy of Sciences), 78–93.

Snodgrass, Anthony. 1998. *Homer and the Artists*. Cambridge: Cambridge University Press.

Sokolov, Yu. 1938/1950. *Russian Folklore*. New York: Macmillan.

Sosnina, Natal'ya. 1984. *Русский народный костюм*. Leningrad: Khudozhnik.

Spence, Lewis. 1947. *Myth and Ritual in Dance, Game and Rhyme*. London: Watts.

Staples, Ariadne. 1998. *From Good Goddess to Vestal Virgins*. London: Routledge.

Stasov, V. 1872/1976. *Russian Peasant Design Motifs*. New York: Dover.

Stoilov, Khristo. 1900. "The 'Doudoula' Ritual in the Village of Leshko, Gorna Djoumaya Region," *Вести* (newspaper), 14 January 1900; reprinted in Vasileva et al. 1999: 292–94(#53).

Stratilesco, Tereza. 1906. *From Carpathian to Pindus*. London: T. Fisher Unwin.

Stubbes, Phillip. 1583. *The Anatomie of Abuses.*

Tarasov, L. 1965. "Палеолитическая стоянка Гагарино," *Материалы и исследования по археологии СССР* 131:111–40.

Taruskin, Richard. 1991. "Slava!" *Opera News* (January 19), 18–21.

Tiddy, R. 1923. *The Mummers' Play.* Oxford: Oxford University Press.

Tille, Alexander. 1899. *Yule and Christmas.* London: Nutt.

Toporkov, A. 1987. "Pottery-making: Mythology and Craft," *SA&A* 26.1:71–81.

Trippett, Frank. 1974. *The First Horsemen.* New York: Time-Life Books.

Turner, Frederick, and Ernst Pöppel. 1983. "The Neural Lyre: Poetic Meter, the Brain, and Time," *Poetry* 142:277–309.

Turner, William. 1551/1989. *A New Herball.* G. Chapman and M. Tweddle, eds. Manchester, UK: Carcanet.

Ushakov, D. 1896. "Матеріалы по народнымъ вѣрованіямъ Великоруссовъ," *Этнографическое Обозрѣніе* 8 #2:146–204.

Uspenskij, B. 1981/1984. "On the Origin of Russian Obscenities" (R. Cleminson trans.), in Ju. Lotman and B. Uspenskij, *The Semiotics of Russian Culture* (Ann Arbor: University of Michigan Press, 1984), 295–99.

Vakarelski, Christo. 1969. *Bulgarische Volkskunde.* Berlin: Walter de Gruyter.

Váňa, Zdeněk. 1983. *World of the Ancient Slavs.* Detroit: Wayne State University Press.

Vasileva [Vassileva], Margarita. 1982. *Lazarouvane: Bulgarian Folk Customs and Rituals.* Sofia: Septemvri.

Vasileva, Margarita, Y. Zareva, V. Nicolova, D. Vasileva, and L. Dimitrova, comps. 1999. *Из Българския Следосвобожденски Печат 1878–1900 (From the Bulgarian Post-Liberation Press 1878–1900).* Sofia: Prof. Marin Drinov Academic Publishing House.

Vasmer, Max. 1950–58/1964–73. *Этимологический Словарь Русского Языка.* O. Trubachev trans. Moscow: Progress.

Vassileva: see Vasileva.

Vulpesco, Michel. 1927. *Les Coutumes Roumaines Périodiques.* Paris: Émile Larose.

Wace, A. J. B. 1909. "North Greek Festivals and the Worship of Dionysos," *Annual of the British School at Athens* (London) 16:232–53.

———. 1912–13. "Mumming Plays in the Southern Balkans," *Annual of the British School at Athens* (London) 19:248–65.

Wace, A., and M. Thompson. 1914. *Nomads of the Balkans.* London: Methuen.

Wallace, Robert. 1967. *The Rise of Russia.* New York: Time-Life Books.

Warner, Elizabeth. 2002. *Russian Myths.* London: British Museum.

Welters, Linda. 1988. *Women's Traditional Costume in Attica, Greece.* Nafplion, Greece: Peloponnesian Folklore Foundation.

Welters, Linda, ed. 1999. *Folk Dress in Europe and Anatolia.* Oxford: Berg.

Wenzel, Marian. 1962. "Graveside Feasts and Dances in Yugoslavia," *Folklore* 73.1: 1–12.

———. 1965. *Ornamental Motifs on Tombstones from Medieval Bosnia*. Sarajevo: Veselin Masleša.

———. 1967. "The Dioscuri in the Balkans," *Slavic Review* 26:363–81.

Whittle, Alisdair. 1985. *Neolithic Europe: A Survey*. Cambridge: Cambridge University Press.

Williams, Patricia. 1999. "Protection from Harm: The Shawl and Cap in Czech and Slovak Wedding . . . ," in Welters 1999:135–54.

Wolfram, Richard. 1932. "Sword Dances and Secret Societies," *JEFDSS* 1:34–41.

———. 1951. *Die Volkstänze in Österreich und verwandte Tänze in Europa*. Salzburg: Otto Müller.

Wolters, Paul. 1892. "Βοιωτικαὶ ἀρχαιοτητές," Ἐφημερὶς ἀρχαιολογική 212–39, pl.10.

Younger, John. 1998. *Music in the Aegean Bronze Age*. Jonsered, Sweden: Åström.

Zelenchuk, V., and Yu. Popovich. 1976. "Антропоморфные образы в обрядах плодородия у восточнороманских народов (XIX–начало XX в.)" in *Балканские исследования: Проблемы истории и культуры* (Moscow: Nauka), 195–201.

Zelenin, D. 1916. *Очерки Русской Мифологіи*. Petrograd: Orlov.

———. 1927. *Russische (Ostslavische) Volkskunde*. Berlin/Leipzig: Walter de Gruyter.

Zerubavel, Eviatar. 1985. *The Seven Day Circle*. New York: Free Press.

Zguta, Russell. 1978. *Russian Minstrels: A History of the Skomorokhi*. Philadelphia: University of Pennsylvania Press.

Zharnikova, S. 1986–87. "Some Archaic Motifs in the Embroidery of Sol'vychegodsk *Kokoshniks* . . . ," *SA&A* 25.3:3–16.

Zvrantsev, Mikhayl. 1968. *Нижегородская Резьба*. Moscow: Iskusstvo.

Illustration and Credit List

Figures 3.2, 3.6, 5.3, 6.1, 6.3–4, 7.1, 8.1, 8.3–4, 9.3–7, 9.9, 10.1, 12.3–4, 13.5, 16.1, 18.2–3, 18.5, 19.9, 20.13, 22.1, 23.2–3, 24.2 by Ann Peters; all other drawings and photos by author unless otherwise indicated.

Geographical Maps. A: Eurasia. B: Eastern Europe. C: South-Central Europe. D: Western Europe.

PART I

1.1. Wood carvings of willies. After Zvrantsev 1968, fig. 63; Wallace 1967, 49; Boguslavskaya 1984, fig. 28; Zvrantsev, fig. 76.

2.1. Woman with extended sleeves dancing at Rusalii. After Radziwill Chronicle, leaf 6; Library, Russian Academy of Sciences, St. Petersburg.

2.2. Embroidered calendars. After Maslova 1978, fig. 70.

2.3. Calendar bowls. After Rybakov 2002, fig. 88; Rybakov 1987, figs. 30–31.

3.1. Russian *khorovod*. Painting by Konstantin Makovsky, whereabouts unknown; Rappoport 1913, opp. 40.

3.2. *Lazarki*. After Vasileva 1982, 40.

3.3. Easter eggs, bread. After *Folk Art in Rumania* 1955, final plate; Puntev et al. 1980, 241 #24.

3.4. St. George's Day loaf; wedding loaf. After Drazheva 1982, fig. 10; Genchev 1988, 58.

3.5. Minoan bowl with shepherd and flock. Iraklion Museum #2903; Bosanquet and Dawkins 1923, pl. 7.

3.6. Bulgarian swinging. After Drazheva 1982: cover, fig. 14.

3.7. Venus of Lespugue. Musée de l'Homme, Paris.

3.8. Macedonian dance (S. Sheffield, A. Soriano, C. Brown).

3.9. Russian *lubok*: divination. After Taruskin 1991, 18–19.

3.10. Kievan bracelets A, M. See appendix for sources.

4.1. Peperuda. After Popov 1989, 9.

4.2. Caloian/Gherman. After Beza 1928, opp. 30.

5.1. Călușari. Staged performance, Constanța, Romania, May 1997.

5.2. Balkan sandals. Author's collection.

5.3. Bulgarian musicians. Nigrita, Greek Macedonia, March 2008.

5.4. Romanian hobbyhorse. After Beza 1928, 45.

5.5. "Mute" călușar. Photo by Radu Rautu, courtesy of Gail Kligman: Kligman 1981, fig. 13.

5.6. Dance lineup, Duboka, Serbia.

6.1. Wormwood.

6.2. Minoan poppy goddess. Iraklion Museum #9305.

6.3. Hops.

6.4. Fraxinella/dittany.

6.5. Cretan dittany.

7.1. Jumping bonfire. After Megas 1958, pl. XXI.

7.2. Corn dollies. Museum of English Rural Life, after Ayres 1977, 9; after Puntev et al. 1980, 244 #30.

8.1. Bosnian shepherdesses. After videos by Ankica Petrović.

8.2. Spinning. Kalambáka, Greece, July 1962.

8.3. St. Paraskeva. After 17th-century icon, Halïch, Ukraine.

8.4. Shrine of Agia Paraskevi, near Nigrita, Greece, March 2008.

8.5. Votive clothing. Shrine of Agia Paraskevi, March 2008; Banat, Serbia, after Kemp 1935, opp. 48.

8.6. Russian bathhouse. Kostroma Museum. After Fabritskiy and Shmelyov 1974, pl. 22.

8.7. Russian shirts. Author's collection.

8.8. Medieval Russian amulets. After Rybakov 1971: figs. 132–41.

9.1. Romanian *buhai*, bagpipe. After Vulpesco 1927, 110; Stratilesco 1906, 345 fig. 8.

9.2. *Mari lwyd, Schnappvieh*. National Museum of Wales, after Alford 1939, 223; Peate 1943, 54; after Alford 1978, pl. III; after Haider 1968, 97.

9.3. Greek Bride and Beast. Vamvakophyto, Greece, March 2008.

9.4. Bulgarian *kukeri*. After Rajchevski and Fol 1993.

9.5. *Baboúgheros* kissing. Anthi, Greece, March 2008.

9.6. *Baboúgheroi* dancing. Phlambouro, Greece, March 2008.

9.7. *Kalógheroi*. Agia Eleni, Greece, March 2008.

9.8. Russian *lubok*: divination. After Propp 1987, opp. 81.

9.9. Bells on *baboúgheroi*. Phlambouro, Greece, March 2008.

PART II

10.1. Frog claims prince's arrow. After Russian lacquer box.

11.1. "Maidens" and "Mothers." After Stasov 1872/1976, #36; Boguslavskaya 1984, fig. 198; Durasov and Yakovleva 1990, 73 #12; Boguslavskaya, figs. 64–65; Durasov and Yakovleva, 49 #107; Rybakov 1981, 341.

11.2. "Protective rose" embroideries. Author's collection.

11.3. *Bereghinya* (Protectress). After Durasov and Yakovleva 1990, 132 #159, 59 #17.

11.4. Ritual towels. Author's collection.

12.1. Minoan women dancing. Iraklion Museum #2634. Photo by John Younger.

12.2. Russian peasants dancing. After Baranova et al. 2001, 12, 603.

12.3. Dalmatian bride testing. After photo of Linđo Dance Ensemble, Dubrovnik.

12.4. Bosnian bride-testing dance. After videos by Ankica Petrović.

Map 13. Kievan Rus'; Mongol invasion; Russian dialect areas.

13.1. Zbruch idol. After Rybakov 2001, figs. 50–51; Váňa 1983, 87; Wallace 1967, 15.

13.2. Medieval bracelets, Lyubech Castle; bracelet C (see appendix for details). After Rybakov 1965, 89; Rybakov 1971, fig. 157.

13.3. South Great Russian ultralong-sleeved dresses. After Sosnina 1984, 10; Rybakov 1968, fig. 4.

13.4. Russian ultralong-sleeved dresses. State Historical Museum, St. Petersburg. Photos by Clara Gresham.

13.5. Marshfield Morris dancer. After photo by R. Winstone; Brody 1969, fig. 1.

13.6. Acolyte. Fresco, Church of St. Cyril, Kiev.

13.7. Andrey Bogolyubskiy's funeral. After Radziwill Chronicle, leaf 215; Library, Russian Academy of Sciences, St. Petersburg.

13.8. Kievan bracelet figures. From C, A, D, B; B, C; C; D, A; H, B, G; F. See appendix for sources.

13.9. Kievan bracelet H (see appendix for details). After Rybakov 1967/68, fig. 14.

13.10. Gold *koltï*. After Rybakov 1971, fig. 153, Kiev State History Museum; after Bocharov 1984, 53.

14.1. Bird-shaped ladles. After Gimbutas 1991, fig. 4–32.3; Rice 1963, figs. 61–62.

14.2. Neolithic frog/woman. After Mellaart 1961, fig. 20.

15.1–2. Drawings by Ivan Bilibin for tale *Vasilisa the Beautiful.*

15.3. Hut on chicken legs. After sketch by Ivan Bilibin, 1899.

15.4. Ground plan of Russian bathhouse. After Zelenin 1927, fig. 196.

16.1. Koshchey the Deathless. In style of Russian lacquer boxes.

PART III

17.1. Recent string skirts. Author's collection; after Oprescu 1929, frontispiece; Lehtinen 1979, pl. 142.

17.2. Ancient representations of string skirts. Dish at Art Institute of Chicago, K. Adler Memorial Fund 1984.10; Louvre figurine S1643; Munksgaard 1974, fig. 50a; Gimbutas 1982, pls. 21, 13; Tarasov 1965, fig. 14.

17.3. Preserved Bronze Age string skirts. After Munksgaard 1974, fig. 44; Furmánek and Pieta 1985, pl. 25; Barber 1999a, fig. 5.7.

17.4. Dancers on Bosnian *stećci*. After Wenzel 1965, pls. LXVII.7, LXXIII.7, XCVI.5, 16, 3, 18, XCV.16, XCVI.6.

17.5. Vlach dancers, Duboka, Serbia. After Wenzel 1967, fig. 3d.

17.6. Bulgarian *kukeri*. Marinov 1907, opp. 22.

17.7. Simargls, calendrical signs. From Kievan bracelets P, C'; C, R, I; F, E. (See appendix for sources.)

17.8. "Sown field" motif. After Darkevich and Mongayt 1967, fig. 2; Rybakov 1981, 47.

17.9. Simargls on stone capital. Kiev park, September 1979.

17.10. Medieval Russian masks. After Rybakov 1971, fig. 142.

Map 18. Early Italy; Roman Empire.

18.1. Greek, Romanian performers disguised as birds. After Liungman 1938, fig. 81; sketch by Vulpesco 1927, 30.

18.2. Janus. Roman Republican coin, 225–212 BC.

18.3. Early Tarot "Fool," "Chariot." Pierpont Morgan Library, New York; after Dummett 1985.

18.4. Mycenaean figure-8 shield. National Museum, Athens.

18.5. Bona Dea.

Map 19. Ancient Greece, Crete.

19.1. Koúrētes dancing. Campana collection; after Harrison 1912/1962, fig. 3.

19.2. Chieftain Cup, Agia Triada. Iraklion Museum #341; after S. Morris 1992, pl. 48c.

19.3. Dionysos as pillar; Maenads. Kylix by Hieron, Berlin; krater, Louvre. After Harrison 1908/1922, figs. 130–31.

19.4. Dionysos's *líknon*. Roman Campana terra-cotta; Hellenistic relief, Munich Glyptothek #601; after Harrison 1908/1922, fig. 146–47.

19.5. Satyrs freeing Earth Mother. After Harrison 1912/1962, fig. 126.

19.6. Demeter, Triptolemos, and Persephone/Kore. After Harrison 1908/1922, 273.

19.7. Archaic Greek dancers, piper. Louvre #CA2985. After Arias and Hirmer 1961, pl. II.

19.8. *Pótnia Thērôn*. François Vase, Florence; after Arias and Hirmer 1961, pl. 46.

19.9. Dancing nymphs. Kunsthistorisches Museum, Vienna; after Harrison 1908/1922, fig. 74.

19.10. Russian embroidery: *Bereghinya*. After Durasov and Yakovleva 1990, 47.

19.11. Greek goddess with birds, animals, 700 BC. Wolters 1892, pl. 10.

19.12. Ultralong-sleeved dancer; Byzantine. Epigraphic Museum, Athens; after Darkevich and Mongayt 1967, fig. 9.4.

19.13. Knucklebone-shaped Attic vase; Aigina. © The Trustees of the British Museum; #1860, 1201.2; vase E804.

19.14. Maenads with wing sleeves. Cabinet des Médailles (Paris) #576; Hartwig 1893, pl. 32.

19.15. Scythian princess. After Trippett 1974, 23; *Gold aus Kiew* 1993, 198.

19.16. Scythian gold platelets, pendant. After Klochko 1992, fig. 2; Klochko 1992, fig. 1; *Gold aus Kiew* 1993, #40.

20.1. Minoan frescoes: women dancing; girl. After Marinatos 1987, 142; Marinatos and Hirmer 1960, pl. 69.

20.2. Minoan "theatral" areas.

20.3. Minoan men dancing. Iraklion Museum #15073.

20.4. Minoan acrobats. Seal: Ashmolean Museum, Oxford, after Hood 1971, pl. 98. Hilt: Iraklion Museum #636; after Marinatos and Hirmer 1960, pl. 38.

20.5. Minoan swing. Iraklion Museum #3039; after Hood 1971, fig. 121.

20.6. Minoan dancers on pottery. Iraklion Museum #10576, 10583. Drawing after Levi 1976, pl. LXVI; Goodison and Morris 1998, fig. 54a.

20.7. *Gerános* dance. François Vase, Florence; after Lissarrague 1999, fig. 11.

20.8. Minoan seals: bird women. After Kenna 1960, #376–77, 13S, 22S, 33S, 39S; Hogarth 1902, fig. 8.20 (Zakro).

20.9. Mycenaean Ψ- and Φ-shaped "idols." After Higgins 1967, figs. 149, 151; Demakopoulou 1996, fig. 11.

20.10. Aegean goddesses riding. After Levi 1951, pl. 4, 119 fig. 4.

20.11. Bird-faced goddess on wagon. After Petrović 1930, pl. IX.

20.12. Bronze Age cult(?) statue, Kličevac. After Hoernes 1898, pl. 4.

20.13. Attic bride; Bronze Age figurines with similar hairdos. After Welters 1988, pl. 1; Müller-Karpe 1980, pl. 326.11, 326.6.

20.14. Seasonal goddess on wheels. After Burkert 1988, figs. 1–2.

20.15. Eurasian horse sacrifice. After Mair 2007, figs. 5, 3, 2, 1.

20.16. Archaic Greek centaur. Boston Museum of Fine Arts #9512; after Cook 1960, pl. 9B, and Snodgrass 1998, fig. 30.

20.17. Hobbyhorses. Musée archéologique, Béziers, after Louis 1963, 194; Canterbury Cathedral Library, after Alford 1978, pl. II; Alford 1937, 145; Cawte 1978, 211.

Map 21. Spread of agriculture from Near East to southeastern Europe.

21.1. Dancers on Neolithic Near Eastern pottery. After Garfinkel 2003: top group (1–6): figs. 7.7b, c, d, f, a, g; middle group (a–c): figs. 8.3e, 8.9b, c; bottom group (d–g): figs. 9.5a, 9.29c, 9.15c, 9.34a.

21.2. Dancers on Neolithic southeastern European pottery. Top group (a–h): after Garfinkel 2003: figs. 10.18c, a, 10.13e, 10.14b, 10.4a, 10.18g, e, 10.3a. Middle (i): after Gimbutas 1989, fig. 490. Bottom row (j–l): Bailey 2005, fig. 5.2; Garfinkel 2003, fig. 10.2b; Gimbutas 1989, fig. 378.2.

21.3. Dancers on other prehistoric European pottery. Top: after Gimbutas 1991, fig. 5–15.2. Middle: Barber 1991, figs. 2.15, 13.3 (Naturhistorisches Museum, Vienna); Gimbutas 1991, fig. 7–116. Bottom: Ruckert 1976, 29, Te4 (Louvre).

21.4. Set of 34 Neolithic figurines. After Bailey 2010, fig. 5–2.

21.5. Neolithic masks. After Gimbutas 1982, fig. 121; Gimbutas 1991, figs. 7–50, 3–19, pl. 11.

Index

Entries in *italics* refer to *maps*, by map number rather than by page. Entries in **bold-face** are **figures**; **bold italics** indicate ***tables***. Greek and Russian words listed in their common English respelling have not been given accents.

7/2013